State and Institution Building in Ukraine

Edited by

*Taras Kuzio, Robert S. Kravchuk,
and Paul D'Anieri*

St. Martin's Press
New York

ISBN 0-312-21458-8

Library of Congress Cataloging-in-Publication Data
State and institution building in Ukraine/edited by, Taras Kuzio,
Robert S. Kravchuk and Paul D'Anieri.
    p.   cm.
Includes bibliographical references and index.
ISBN 0-312-21458-8 (cloth)
1. Ukraine—Politics and government—1991– 2. Post-communism—
Ukraine. I. Kuzio, Taras.II. Kravchuk, Robert S., 1955-
III. D'Anieri, Paul J., 1965-
JN6635.S7   1999
320.9477'09'049—dc21   98–54118
                                                                          CIP

Design by Letra Libre, Inc.
First Published: September 1999
10 9 8 7 6 5 4 3 2 1

Contents

Transliteration Note

The editors have followed the standard Ukrainian-to-English transliteration schema approved by the Ministry of Justice, Government of Ukraine. Every effort has been made to ensure consistency of its application throughout the text.

CHAPTER 1

Stateness and Institutions in Ukraine: A Theoretical and Comparative Introduction

Taras Kuzio

This volume focuses upon the role of the state as the keystone institution in Ukraine's post-Soviet transition. It argues that the state (and nation) should be brought back into the scholarly analysis of post-communist transitions. Indeed, the presumption is that post-socialist transitions cannot be understood properly in the absence of analysis of the key political and administrative institutions that serve to concentrate, channel, fragment, check, and enable the exercise of power. This introduction lays the groundwork for the study of various aspects of the state and institution building processes underway in post-communist states such as Ukraine. Our aim is to introduce the subject, to demonstrate the relevance of institutional analysis, and to highlight the many areas that remain open to scholarly investigation.

A. The Failure of "Transitology"

The Missing Link

Transitology has until recently ignored questions of "stateness." As Juan Linz and Alfred Stepan point out, this now has to change and therefore, "stateness problems must increasingly be a central concern of policy activists and theorists alike."[1] Transitology and democratic theory (with the exception of Robert Dahl)[2] had previously largely ignored both questions of stateness and nationhood, taking these factors for granted. Consequently, the triadic relationship of the modern state, nation, and democracy remains undertheorized. Yet the presence of a sovereign state that rules the territory and population has the capacity to raise and collect taxes, implement policies, and institutionalize a judicial system is a prerequisite for democracy. Adam Przeworski points out that without an effective state, "there can be no democracy and no markets."[3]

Immediately after the disintegration of the former USSR,[4] the obvious absence of consolidated states and nations inevitably led to the prioritization of these factors. This "almost pushed matters of democratic crafting off the normative and institutional agenda of politics."[5] The overwhelming majority of the "transitology" literature published during the 1990s thus adopted three dubious assumptions. First, that transition in the former USSR is identical to that in Central and Eastern Europe (and, by implication, the earlier transitions in Southern Europe and Latin America). Second, therefore as mirrors of previous transitions, post-Soviet countries face only two transitions: one, from totalitarianism to democracy; and two, from a command-administrative to a market economy. Finally, the third dubious assumption was that the former USSR did not differ to any great degree politically from its outer empire.

Despite abundant evidence to the contrary, these assumptions remain influential among Western policymakers, academics, and governments. Consequently, they should be subjected to a more exacting scrutiny. First, is transition in the former USSR fundamentally different from that in Central and Eastern Europe? Only transition in Central and Eastern Europe resembles that of Southern Europe or Latin America, all of which confronted only the twin transitions of democratization and marketization. Latin America and Southern, Central, and Eastern Europe all inherited states and nations from previous authoritarian regimes. These regimes never completely eradicated civil society or the private sector; religion was not unduly controlled; citizens could travel more freely; a middle class (of sorts) existed, while a semi-independent press was tolerated.

In the former USSR none of these conditions existed. Post-Soviet transitions are *both* post-totalitarian (not authoritarian) *and* post-imperial. Exceptions of course exist. Portugal lost an empire and gained a national identity. Slovakia, Macedonia, and some other Central and Eastern European countries are also undertaking certain aspects of state and nation building. Nevertheless, the scope of the post-totalitarian and post-imperial transition facing countries like Ukraine is not reflected either in earlier or concurrent transitions outside the former USSR.

Second, the Soviet successor states not only must undertake political-economic transitions but also build new states and nations. This triple or even quadruple transition presents unprecedented complications for the overall transition process. Alexander Motyl believes that the simultaneity of this quadruple transition, "was historically unprecedented in its magnitude."[6]

Third, the former USSR was vastly different from either its outer empire, Southern Europe or Latin America. It was both a totalitarian regime and, until the Gorbachev era, an empire. True, totalitarianism gave way to authoritarianism late in Gorbachev's rule. This occurred in Ukraine only after 1989, and, of course, 3 years of authoritarian rule were entirely eclipsed by 67 years of totalitarianism. Totalitarian rule had never taken hold in Southern Europe or Latin America, while in Central and Eastern Europe it had lasted only from the late 1940s to the mid-1950s. The former USSR itself was also an empire, with 15 constituent republics, each possessing far less autonomy than the 50 states that comprise the United States. Latin America freed itself from Spanish and Portuguese imperial rule in the nineteenth century. By contrast, Spain and Portugal were the imperial centers of their respective empires—neither was the colony that Ukraine was under the Soviet regime.

The Third Wave of Decolonization

State and nation building were raised as important objectives to be pursued by all of the non-Russian successor states to the former USSR. Russia, as the former imperial metropolis, was the only exception, preferring to introduce economic and political reform first.[7] Under President Leonid Kravchuk (1991–1994) Ukraine and Russia therefore adopted vastly different policy agendas.[8]

Despite the striking similarities between transitions in post-colonial countries in Africa, Asia, and Eurasia,[9] scholars in Ukrainian studies have yet to apply post-colonial theory to Ukraine. Their transitions are "imperial" with elites grappling to overcome their weak institutional inheritances.[10]

All post-colonial countries, from Zimbabwe to Ukraine, define the former imperial power as the "Other" that denied them their rights to genuine self-governance and was arrogant and often racist, defining the colonized peoples as "inferior" in significant ways. The newly independent state sees regaining self-esteem as a central policy objective. In the early stages of state building, national culture and nationalism are usually the domain of elites who rule over parochial masses divided by religious, regional, and clan loyalties.[11] Who controls the state and who belongs to the nation are two questions central to the political life of all post-colonial societies. In this vein, ongoing struggles over the resources of the state as a "gigantic dairy cow" can be viewed as a key "preoccupation of the various elite factions in a bureaucracy and their ethnic clients."[12]

All post-colonial societies attempt to rejuvenate themselves by confronting "Otherness" through a renewal of self-respect, which involves overcoming perhaps deeply rooted inferiority complexes. Emerson pointed out that "The search for a solid and acceptable base of their own is of immense importance for peoples whose religions and ways of life have been openly disparaged as backward, superstitious, and corrupt."[13] Such attitudes were as much foisted upon Africans as they were upon Ukrainians.

In addition, the drive to national cohesion also serves to overcome the lack of internal unity, "which earlier played so large a role in rendering them unable to resist the imperial pressure of consolidating nations."[14] The drive to national consolidation inevitably comes into conflict with both older communities (which possess only local identities) and cosmopolitans. The role of the state is crucial in promoting development of institutions and national unity within plural societies (the norm) through public education, communications, a single language, law, and the public administration as well as a consolidated polity and economy.

The Previous Regime Factor

The path of democratization and democratic consolidation is largely conditioned by the previous regime type and the character of stateness. The previous regime type shapes the number and difficulty of challenges that newly independent states have to face. In Latin America and Southern Europe, for example, stateness was not an inherited problem.[15] If a tradition of political parties exists (Central Europe, Western Ukraine, Latin America, and the Baltic states), democratization tends to be easier to achieve.[16]

Another inherited problem is ethnic heterogeneity, because multinational societies will find democratic consolidation to be a more difficult and protracted process.[17] Latin America, Southern, Central, or Eastern Europe, with a few exceptions (such as Spain, Slovakia, Bosnia, and Romania), did not face this challenge. In the former USSR, Ukraine, Estonia, Latvia, Moldova, and Kazakhstan inherited large Russian populations whose national identity was usually more "Soviet" than that of the republic they had been sent to.

Multiethnic coalitions are based on anti-colonial platforms that usually disintegrate after independence has been achieved. State and nation building requires that certain choices be made concerning specifically who is/are the titular nation(s) and who are the national minorities. It seems that states can never be completely fair when they decide which language or languages should be the state or official ones. In some cases, such as in Moldova, Azerbaijan, and Georgia, these decisions have led to internecine violence and even civil war.[18] In others, such as Ukraine, Latvia, and Estonia, resolution of these questions did not lead to ethnic strife, although between 1992 and 1995 the Crimea flirted with violence.[19]

Nationalism, Mobilization, and Modernization

In post-communist and post-colonial states, the economic bases for development of a genuine civil society are generally lacking. The economic infrastructure to support development of a middle class—the foundation of modern civil society—does not yet exist in post-Soviet countries. Therefore, "political mobilization of the population is only possible along nationalist or fundamental lines."[20] As I point out in this volume, all societies are composed of both civic and ethnic elements. Yet in post-colonial and post-communist societies the civic element is still weak, and hence the ethnic can often appear dominant. The Polish political leader Adam Michnik described nationalism as the "last stage of communism." The foundational elements of liberal democracy—civil society, the rule of law, a democratic political culture, and civic organizations—will need to grow over the medium-to-long terms. Democratic consolidation will be impossible without development of mechanisms of citizen mobilization and increasing institutionalization of political parties.[21]

Nationalism in Russia is exclusive, reactionary, and conservative. National sentiment in Ukraine, by contrast, "is an instrumental force pushing for change and reform rather than for maintaining traditional orientations."[22] To illustrate the Ukrainian case, two ideological polarities dominated the December 1991 referendum on independence:

1. nationalism as against the imperial center; and,
2. liberalism as against the totalitarian regime.[23]

The Ukrainian state was therefore born in January 1992 having a built-in raison d'être tied to its quadruple transition. Ukrainian elites, regardless of their regional origins or linguistic preferences, would, if reformist, promote the "liberating seeking nationalism" described by the nineteenth century Italian Mazzini. In Asia and Africa on earlier occasions, and in the former USSR today, nationalism was and is equated with the drive to modernity and a breach with the past. This nationalism resembles that of early Western Europe and North America in that it was and is, "forward looking and not a reactionary force, a spur to revolution and not a bulwark of the status quo."[24]

Ernest Gellner writes that the rise of nationalism was an unavoidable consequence of modernity, which helped to consolidate civil society by transferring loyalties to the state-nation. State-nations are created by elites during the process of modernization and dramatic social change.[25] Modernization and state and nation building have gone—and will continue to go—hand in hand.[26] Liah Greenfeld provides an apt metaphor:

> Democracy was thus born with the sense of nationality, the two are inherently linked, and neither can be fully understood apart from this connection. Nationalism was the form in which democracy appeared in the world, contained in the idea of the nation as a butterfly in a cocoon.[27]

Defining the Political Community

State and nation building are conceptually separate processes that have historically occurred at different periods. In Western Europe and North America, state building largely *preceded* nation building, a phenomenon most would associate with the nineteenth and twentieth centuries. Agreement on "stateness" is necessary prior to the crafting of democratic institutions because democracies logically need territorial-social "units." Robert Dahl, one of the few theorists who has linked these questions, has written, "If the unit itself is not considered proper or rightful, if its scope or domain is not justifiable—then it cannot be made rightful simply by democratic procedures."[28] This means that the territorial-social unit simply must achieve some measure of internal consistency as a basic precondition for democratic consolidation.

Dankwart Rustow also addresses the dyadic relationship among state, nation, and democracy, arguing that it is important for the vast majority of citizens to "have no doubt or mental reservations as to which political community they belong to."[29] The boundaries of the state and the composition of the population must be defined, particularly vis-à-vis peripheral communities whose inclusion in the community assists in the process of democratic consolidation.[30] In Western Europe, state and nation building in the early modern era defined the political communities within which marketization and democratization could take place. Post-Soviet states such as

Ukraine have little choice but to undertake all four transitions simultaneously, a path Rustow would warn against.[31] Democratic consolidation, Rustow asserts, requires a "prior sense of community, preferably a sense of community quietly taken for granted that is above mere opinion and mere agreement."[32] Indeed, membership in such a community is viewed as a "taken-for-granted" understanding upon which democratic political development must stand.

The greater the proportion of the population that is unclear about or disinterested in being part of the community upon which the state is founded, the more difficult it will be to consolidate democracy. Further, the greater the linguistic, ethnic, religious, and cultural heterogeneity of the population, the more complex the process of democratization will be. Democracies are not impossible in multicultural settings, but they do require greater attention to problem areas and sensitivity to the needs and aspirations of minority groups to achieve a desired measure of self-expression. In former Soviet states where violence has been used in attempts at quelling separatism, the overall process of democratization has suffered.

Newly independent states in the throes of state and nation building seek to legitimize their independence and sovereignty over their territory by stressing the *primordial* nature of their ethnic group. Andrew Wilson remains concerned that this use of primordialism, historical myth, and legend associated with only one ethnic group (that is, Ukrainophone Ukrainians) will exacerbate ethnic and linguistic divisions.[33] We, the editors, on the other hand, believe these fears are unfounded and exaggerated.[34] The introduction and revival of national historiography, the promulgation of new myths and legends as well as the claim to primordial right over contested territory is taking place without a backlash on the order of magnitude feared by Wilson.[35]

The process of defining a political community has to address a number of critical questions. Public debate surrounding these questions consumes tremendous amounts of energy in the early years of independence, distracting the regime from equally critical and necessary issues of political and economic reform. The state must simultaneously create a new administrative apparatus, legitimize its boundaries through international law and primordial claims of first settlement, and inculcate a common national identity. The new state has to decide upon the extent to which power will be centralized or devolved to territorial regions. Przeworski points out that during transition, "when the center is weak vis-à-vis culturally distinct regions, demands for autonomy are likely to develop."[36] Crimean separatism only constituted a threat to a weak Ukrainian state in the first half of the 1990s, a state which had been made all the more weak by economic mismanagement and hyperinflation. In this case, increasing cohesion and governmental capacity building at the center was accompanied by reduced demands for autonomy from the periphery.

The formation of a common national identity necessitates a cultural differentiation from foreign "Others," as well as defining the cultural core of the newly emerging nation. As Kuzio points out in chapter 8 of this volume, the choice was always to define Ukraine as either Ukrainian, the view of democratic groups and nationalists, or as Eastern Slavic (Russian-Ukrainian [*Rus'kij*]), the view of the ideological left. Modern states have traditionally promoted national languages, a national education system, military service, tariffs and customs controls while increasing domestic homogeneity and external heterogeneity.[37]

An effective state is a precondition for the realization of the benefits and responsibilities of citizenship. The transition to a unified political community will be accompanied by debate over the set of mutual obligations that governs the relationship between the state and citizen. New states and democracies must simultaneously address the civil, political, and social requirements of citizenship. Is the rule of law implemented irregularly throughout all the state's territory, or does an ineffective state coexist with regionalism and clannish kleptocracy? (See chapter 3 by Paul Kubicek.) Is the state maintaining or expanding its level of social services and education (in Southern Europe democratization was accompanied by the state's expansion as the provider of these services). Cuts in social and educational expenditures, such as those demanded by international financial institutions in Ukraine in the 1990s, threaten the integrity of the state.[38] Effective states require legislative institutions to promote the public good, administrators to execute the law, and an effective judiciary to ensure equality of all citizens before that law. The state inherited by Ukraine was therefore not too large, as some have claimed, but too intrusive.[39]

The political community in Ukraine is still only at the early stages of development, a process made all the more difficult by the ongoing socioeconomic crisis.[40] In this volume Kuzio (chapter 8) discusses the debates among Ukrainian and Western scholars about how to define the political community. This issue appears to have been largely resolved by the June 1996 Constitution, which defined Ukrainians as the titular core nationality and therefore Ukrainian as the state language and the language of communication. The constitution also defined Russians as one of many national minorities, although not providing any preferences for the Russian language. In chapter 10, Oliver Vorndran provides an analysis of the constitutional process in Ukraine, and particularly the ethnolinguistic dimension.

The overwhelming majority of states are multinational and multicultural in their social composition. A central problem common to all post-Soviet republics is the tightrope they have had to walk between creating a common identity and the kind of *fraternité* characteristic of the French Revolution, which is indispensable to the proper functioning of a state, democratic institutions, and protection of polyethnic rights. Social unity is predicated upon shared values and a shared identity that is the result of a complex of factors: history, political culture, language, and religion. Social cohesion is especially important in multiethnic states. As Will Kymlicka, an advocate of polyethnic rights, observes, "multinational states cannot survive unless the various national groups have an allegiance to the larger political community they cohabit."[41]

Liberals and nationalists are both concerned with minority rights. Liberals worry that they might inhibit development of a shared identity, while nationalists see minorities as a threatening "third column." In this regard, the newly emerging state is caught between a hammer and an anvil. If polyethnic rights are provided, social unity and internal consolidation might be thwarted. On the other hand, if they are denied, the resulting social and political upheaval may threaten the entire state building and democratizing processes. Violence can break out, as it did in Georgia between 1992 and 1994.

Therefore, in any study of state and institution building, due attention must be provided to the question of nation building. Through trial and deliberation, states must tread carefully between forging social unity while granting polyethnic rights to defined national minorities. "Identifying the bases of social unity in multinational states," writes Kymlicka, "is one of the most pressing tasks facing liberals today."[42] This very issue is of continuing importance in post-Soviet Ukraine.

B. Bringing the State Back In

States and Democracies

As expressed succinctly by Skocpol et al., modern political theorizing failed to take adequate account of the state as political institution. Likewise, respecting the circumstances and challenges facing republics of the former Soviet Union, neoliberal prescriptions underestimate the role of the state and institutions in both the public and private domains. Yet, as Adam Przeworski rightly argues, sustainable democracy requires that the state guarantee territorial integrity, physical security, conditions for the "effective exercise of citizenship," the mobilization of public savings, and coordination of resource allocation. If state institutions are to be capable of performing these tasks, he adds, "they must be reorganized, rather than simply reduced."[43] This is the essence of what Leila Fritschak has termed the "paradox of the reforming state." A "viable state," Przeworski concludes, is necessary to encompass the democratic institutions that enable democracy and citizenship to be exercised.

Democratization is threatened not only by the power of an already intrusive state apparatus but also—paradoxically—by a weak state and underdeveloped institutions. The political development of Ukraine cannot be divorced from the creation of viable "national-states," in the sense that Charles Tilly uses that term.[44] Democracies and market economies require national-states within which to function effectively.

A modern market economy cannot be built outside of the framework provided by a state, its institutions, and its laws. Motyl has been a strong advocate of post-Soviet countries such as Ukraine adopting nation and state building *before* launching into democratization and marketization.[45] He argues that a strong national identity, as in western Ukraine or Poland, facilitates marketization by raising the tolerance threshold of the population. Therefore, immediately after achieving independence it is perfectly understandable, in Motyl's eyes, for these states to prioritize state building ahead of political and economic reform because the state, institutions, and elites are predicates of democracy and market economics.

Institutions

Ukraine inherited from the former Soviet state only 13,000 government administrators.[46] Perhaps this was a sufficient number to run a Soviet colony, but it is certainly far too few to staff the institutions of a modern, independent state of 52 million souls. The United Kingdom, for example, a country with roughly the same population as Ukraine, has nearly half a million administrators.[47] President Kuchma has complained that Ukraine's lack of capable officials hampers its political and economic reform programs.[48] In his earlier tenure as prime minister he complained that he was unable to release even inefficient and corrupt administrators because by law they had to be offered other posts. In addition, the administrators inherited from the *ancien regime* are likely to be disoriented, reeling from an "ideological defeat." "Uncertainty is what they [apparatchiks] abhor ideologically, psychologically, and politically," writes Przeworski.[49]

It is clear that the crafting of democratic institutions will not occur quickly or without conflict. During the early stages of the transition we may expect there to be *continuismo:* a regime that combines elements of the *an-*

cien regime with the new. This is particularly to be expected in the case of ne-gotiated transitions, such as Ukraine's, where the counterelites and former ruling elites block out extremists on both sides. Przeworski warns that during this uncertain transition "Conflicts over institutions are likely to be protracted. The actors bargaining over the institutions are unlikely to 'get it right' the first time; it often takes several attempts before a stable framework emerges."[50]

Conflicts within Ukraine over the direction and content of state and nation building (who constitutes the political community, titular nation, and national minorities), the nature of the democratic regime (presidentialism versus parliamentarism), and the economic system (the proportional division between the state and private sectors) remain ongoing questions. These issues were at their most intense during the Kravchuk and early Kuchma periods, prior to the adoption of the constitution in June 1996. (See chapter 2 by Charles Wise and Volodymyr Pigenko.)[51]

Elites

Elites are an essential factor in the state and institution building process. The transition from the *ancien regime* is inevitably opposed by the traditional elites (whether tribal or communist) who remain in conflict with the modernizing and pro-Western elites.[52] During liberalization the former elites may be divided into soft- and hard-liners, with the former usually defecting to ally themselves with moderate nationalists. In transformations and transplacements, those who committed crimes may be left to draw their pensions; meaning, to go into retirement (only in replacements are they ordinarily punished).

Almost all smooth transitions are negotiated affairs between moderate elements in the *ancien regime* and in the opposition. Radicals from both camps are excluded from the initial transition, as they were in Ukraine through the banning of the Communist Party between August 1991 and October 1993. However, compromise between moderate forces in both camps may lack any "consistency of purpose and coherence of outcome."[53] The alliance of moderates may be able to guarantee a smooth transition from the *ancien regime* to the new state, but it cannot provide for clear and coherent policies in other critical areas (for example, privatization, industrial restructuring, trade liberalization).

Soft-liners who have successfully defected to the nationalist cause, such as Ukraine's Leonid Kravchuk, have been able to both shape the economic system and the underlying ideology of the emerging state.[54] This ideology had to face down the hard-liners by pursuing what Huntington terms a "backward legitimization": looking to historical myths, symbols, and legends to legitimize the notion that independence was *always* the goal of Ukrainians.[55] In this regard, Taras Shevchenko's role is akin to that of Butler and Yeats in the "Irish Renaissance" of the early twentieth century, insofar as the mythological foundation for the birth of Ukrainian national consciousness was laid.

Post-colonial countries are also disadvantaged by the retreat of the colonial power, which leaves an "administrative void" (See chapter 6 by Bohdan Krawchenko).[56] President Kuchma complained that in contrast to Russia, Ukraine started from scratch with no bankers, diplomats, or economists, because "All the finest specialists, as usual, had gone to Moscow."[57] This left Ukraine with a dearth of administrative talent at its most critical period. Yegor Gaidar, former Russian prime minister and leader of the Russia's Choice party, admitted that one factor in Ukrainian economic reforms lagging behind those of Russia was a lack of cadres:

> In general, however, your [Ukraine's] situation with personnel is worse than ours. It is clear that personnel was literally vacuumed by Moscow under the conditions of Soviet super centralization.[58]

The absence of efficient cadres to manage the transition usually is ignored by scholars, who are apt to compare progress in reform in Russia and Ukraine.[59] Yet, as Gaidar has put it, Russia entered the post-Soviet era with a distinct advantage over Ukraine. It has become clear that a "competent central bureaucracy" is required to manage economic reform.[60]

During the early stages of state building, it seems that rulers must compromise over the loyalty and effectiveness of their bureaucracy. Loyalty may emerge only in the medium-to-long terms, as greater numbers of citizens develop a stake in the survival of the regime. As state building progresses, local elites are increasingly integrated into the machinery of the state through penetration, standardization, participation, and redistribution.[61]

The development of a state administration is also closely connected to the nation building process. After all, young people are increasingly attracted to such critical areas as the diplomatic service *not* by the poor salaries and long hours but, as Foreign Minister Borys Tarasiuk maintains, "out of an awareness of their duty to the nation."[62] Ukrainian leaders often point to a major difference between Ukraine and Russia being the lower level of patriotism found in the former among state officials whose loyalty is therefore first and foremost to themselves and their clan.[63] This is probably a contributing factor to the corruption and lack of responsibility toward a state for which they harbor no patriotic feelings. (See chapter 9 by Roman Zyla.)

State Building

In Western Europe the initial phase of state building is generally seen to have taken place from the High Middle Ages to 1789. This phase of political, economic, and cultural unification first occurred at the elite level. The second phase is defined by Charles Tilly as one in which the masses are increasingly drawn into the system through the communications media, education, interpenetration of the periphery by the center, and a growing identification with the state. (See chapter 7 by Robert S. Kravchuk). This process of state and nation building was never smooth as it inevitably came into conflict with traditional loyalties to the Church, regions, or peripheral ethnic and linguistic groups. "Successful state-makers had to absorb, check, or destroy most of their immediate rivals," Tilly argues.[64] He sees the third phase as one in which the masses are brought into active participation in the political system. This is followed by a final phase, in which the state apparatus is expanded to include provisions for social welfare and progressive taxation.

These four phases of state building common to Western Europe and North America are unlikely to be repeated elsewhere. Countries on these continents had the luxury of pursuing a gradual process of state building, nation building, marketization, and democratization occurring over several hundred years. In the post-colonial and post-communist world, these four processes often occur simultaneously, which has "left [precious] little time to reach even temporary institutional solutions to one set of challenges before they were forced to cope with the next set."[65] Simultaneous transitions are the rule in the former Soviet Union, with all of the problems and challenges that this presents.

The penetration and integration of state building was followed by nation building, which inculcated loyalty, commitment, and acquiescence of the subject population within a bounded territory.[66] State building provided for the emergence of specialized personnel, control over consolidated territory, loyalty, and durability, permanent institutions with a centralized and autonomous state that held the monopoly of violence over a given population.[67]

State building was also synonymous with center formation and periphery incorporation. The center was—and remains—the key to state building because consensus building flows outwards across Ukraine from Kyiv through the mass media (that is, in the transfer and refinement of moral beliefs, images, values, symbols, history, language, and territory) and its institutional structures. It is from the center that the institutions and transmission of a common culture flow.[68] The capital city therefore holds the key. It is the "nuclear area" or "primate city" that dominates the hinterland[69] and is inhabited by the state and nation building elites and therefore bears the "earmark of intense nationalism."[70] Here Ukraine, with its ancient capital city, has a clear advantage over Belarus, which long ago lost its primate city (Vilnius/Vilna) to Lithuania.

State and nation building are synonymous because the former attempts to impose a common culture emanating from the center.[71] Political and international relations theory often assumes states to be highly homogenous in scope, where orders issued from the center have a similar effect throughout the territory.[72] State and nation building, Tilly reminds us, were synonymous with the simultaneous processes of internal homogenization and external heterogenization. It is far more difficult to implement policies in multiethnic and multicultural societies, which hold potential either to stagnate or explode.[73] Hence Gianfranco Poggi associates the state with "a commitment to a distinct, unified and unifying set of interests and purposes."[74]

Through a process of penetration, integration, participation, identity formation, legitimization, and distribution, the state comes into existence for the twin purposes of extraction and control.[75] The state is defined by its ability to exert coercive control, defend its sovereignty and territory, centralize its institutions, inculcate a sense of common identity (without which a civil society is impossible), provide for citizenship, legitimize itself through democratic institutions, and impose the rule of law.[76] Developing and integrating these processes are constituent parts of the transition to modernity for feudal, post-colonial, or post-communist states.[77]

Ukraine inherited only a quasi-state from the former USSR. It "crossed the Rubicon" only in mid-1996 when it adopted its post-Soviet constitution. The adoption of a new constitution is a milestone in the creation of all states. (See chapter 10 by Oliver Vorndran.) The Ukrainian case was no exception, with the Ukrainian elites believing that their country crossed the "point of no return" in June 1996.[78] Despite the severity of the socioeconomic crisis, opinion polls in support of independence have never dipped below 54 to 65 percent.[79] Ethnic issues were absent from the March 1998 parliamentary elections,[80] in which even Crimean election blocs only agitated in defense of Russian speakers and pan eastern Slavism and not separatism. In reality, as chapter 11 by Kuzio and Meyer points out, separatism in Ukraine was a problem in the Crimea only between 1992–1995 and never was a real issue in Eastern Ukraine.

Many Western and Russian scholars did predict that Kuchma would turn out to be a "Ukrainian Lukashenka," turning the country away from reform, statehood, and "Europe," toward Eurasia and eventual reintegration with Russia.[81] Yet this view was premised on the mistaken view that the quadruple transition is compatible with Eurasian integration. Both President Kuchma and former speaker and head of the Socialist Party Oleksandr Moroz have repeatedly linked the continued progress toward a market economy and democratic consolidation with the July 1990 declaration of sovereignty and the December 1991 referendum on independence.[82]

In other words, the four aspects of Ukraine's post-Soviet transition are closely bound together and inevitably influence its foreign policy orientations toward "Europe" or Eurasia. Ukraine's desire to "return to Europe" is conditioned upon the success of its quadruple transition (see chapters 4 and 5 by Paul D'Anieri and Sherman Garnett). A very different process appears to be at work in Ukraine than in Belarus. Kuchma clearly is no Lukashenka. The Russian scholar Alexei Arbatov observed that "Kuchma has in fact turned out to be more consistent and rigid on this issue than his predecessor, Leonid Kravchuk, who was more vulnerable in relation to Crimea and eastern Ukraine."[83]

Although there is unlikely to be a return to the former USSR or even the "Belarusian option," the Ukrainian state faces four challenges: (1) The undertheorized difficulties outlined earlier of the simultaneous quadruple transition; (2) The fact that one of the largest political parties and parliamentary factions (the Communists) is hostile to the existence of the independent state;[84] (3) The Russian elites who find it difficult to reconcile themselves to the permanence of the independent Ukrainian state; and (4) The conflict between political and economic reform, which is wrapped up in the choice between parliamentarism and presidentialism.

In the Commonwealth of Independent States (CIS), political reform has largely been relegated to the back burner by emasculating parliaments while radical economic reform has been pursued by an authoritarian executive (See chapter 2 by Wise and Pigenko.) In Ukraine this was President Kuchma's favorite option, but he failed to secure the adoption of a Russian-style presidential constitution. Political reform has therefore progressed faster in Ukraine than in Russia while economic reform has lagged. In addition, the Ukrainian executive (in the form of the Presidential Administration) has also been an important agent promoting state and nation building. Through an "ideology of state-building," the national idea, myths, and legends, the state has been promoted much in a manner similar to previous projects in the West.[85]

The debate among scholars about the virtues of presidentialism versus parliamentarianism is as yet unresolved. Clearly there are valid arguments on both sides. As argued earlier in this Introduction, post-Soviet societies lack the economic bases for the development of a civil society. Therefore, economic reform may be logically predisposed to come before democratization. At the same time, parliamentarianism is more closely in tune with Ukrainian political culture, is a bulwark against authoritarianism,[86] and a central aspect of state and institution building. The development of parliamentarianism is closely tied to the establishment of other state institutions such as local self-government, the state administration, Constitutional Court, Higher Arbitration Council, Institute of Law Making, Accounting Chamber, and Plenipotentiary of Human Rights. The parliaments of 1990 –1994 and 1994–1998 adopted an astonishing 402 laws with 1,625 resolutions, and 402 laws with 1,134 resolutions respectively.[87] In the multicultural environment of post-Soviet Ukraine, the Rada "is performing the role of absorber of social tension and its unique stabilizer." It is thanks to this, Moroz argues, that Ukraine is evolving peacefully by avoiding the twin pitfalls of authoritarianism and social upheaval.[88] Moroz sees Parliament as a reflection of Ukrainian society in that "It hosts various stances, viewpoints, and the entire political spectrum of society."[89] Of course, he and his left-wing allies are also utilizing Parliament to slow and moderate the economic and political movement away from the Soviet command-administrative, totalitarian system (which has placed them in direct conflict with the executive) while being themselves divided over their attitudes toward statehood.

Meanwhile, building administrative capacity is a key concern for the government. One in five of the presidential or government assignments are either fulfilled late or not at all. Of the 105 instructions issued in 1996, only 63 were implemented.[90] The year 1998 was the first in which Ukraine began to control its tax revenues after each Ukrainian was issued a tax identity code.[91] Until the appointment in 1997 of Ievhen Kushnariov as head of the Presidential Administration, its presence was not felt outside Kyiv.[92] Clearly, then, state and institution building still had some way to go in Ukraine despite the grossly exaggerated claim by President Kuchma in 1996 that state building had been "completed."

C. Conclusions

This Introduction and the volume that follows argue three points. Firstly, that "transitology" has focused upon Latin America and Southern and Central Europe, where questions of "stateness" were largely not an issue. In Ukraine and the other post-Soviet states "transitology" has to broaden its theoretical and empirical reach to effectively "bring the state back in." Secondly, the quadruple transition faced by Ukraine is undertheorized. These four transitions took place slowly over centuries or decades in Western Europe and North America while in Ukraine these often-contradictory transitions are occurring simultaneously. Finally, states do not exist without ethnic bases composed of one or more titular nations and state languages. Again, when we talk about bringing the state back in, we cannot afford to ignore national factors.

State building in Ukraine will continue to steer a middle course between two extremes.[93] The first is that commonly associated with creating an exclusive, ethnic state which would absolutize independence, particularly vis-à-vis Russia. This possibility is remote, since ethnic nationalism has a weak base in Ukraine, as reflected in the 1994 and 1998 parliamentary elections. In the modern world and at a time of globalization any attempt at absolutizing independence would be catastrophic. The opposite extreme would be where state building (and reform) is sacrificed in the "Belarusian option." This is also highly unlikely since, as we argue in this Introduction, state building is tightly bound up in the entire process of economic and political reform.

Notes

1. J. J. Linz and A. Stepan, *Problems of Democratic Transition and Consolidation: Southern Europe, South America and Post-Communist Europe* (Baltimore: John Hopkins University Press, 1996), p. 366.

2. R. Dahl has pointed out in many of his works that prior agreement is required for democratic consolidation. He has also pointed to the inheritance of ethnic heterogeneity impacting upon democratization.

3. Adam Przeworski, *Sustainable Democracy* (Cambridge: Cambridge University Press, 1995), p.11.

4. This was recognized by some authors. See Karen Dawisha, *Post-Communism's Troubled Steps Toward Democracy: An Aggregate Analysis of Progress in the 27 New States* (College Park, MD: Center for the Study of Post-Communism, 1997) and Barnett R. Rubin, and Jack Snyder (eds.), *Post-Soviet Political Order. Conflict and State Building* (London: Routledge, 1998).

5. Op cit., J. J. Linz and A. Stepan, *Problems of Democratic Transition and Consolidation,* p. 387.

6. A. J. Motyl, "The Non-Russian States," *Freedom Review,* vol. 28, no. 1 (January-February 1997), p. 53. To arrive at this conclusion, Motyl has ignored the

decolonization process after World War II, where all four aspects were also initially present. Eventually, though, democratization and at times marketization were dropped in many of these Western former colonies.

7. Richard Sakwa pointed out that "The sentiments of Massimo d'Azeglio at the inaugural session of the Italian National Assembly, 'We have made Italy, now we have to make Italians,'" were echoed in Ukraine and other post-Soviet states but not in Russia." See his "Democratic Change in Russia and Ukraine," *Democratization,* vol. 1, no. 1 (Spring 1994), p. 44.

8. See Philippe Schmitter's review of the J. J. Linz and A. Stepan volume in *Journal of Democracy,* vol. 8, no. 2 (April 1997), pp. 168–173.

9. Writing about the former Western colonies, Gabriel A. Almond and Sidney Verba argued that "Few Western statesmen have ever been called upon to cope with such a range of issues and choices all at once." Quoted from *The Civic Culture: Political Attitudes and Democracy in Five Nations* (Princeton: Princeton University Press, 1963), p. 504.

10. Mette Skak, *From Empire to Anarchy: Postcommunist Foreign Policy and International Relations* (London: Hurst, 1996), p. 69.

11. Rupert Emerson, *From Empire to Nation* (Cambridge, MA: Harvard University Press, 1967), pp. 382 and 150.

12. Andreas Wimmer, "Who owns the state? Understanding ethnic conflict in post-colonial societies," *Nations and Nationalism,* vol. 3, part 4 (December 1997), p. 644.

13. Op cit., R. Emerson, p. 152.

14. Ibid., R. Emerson, p. 380.

15. Gerardo L. Munck, "Bringing Postcommunist Societies into Democratization Studies," *Slavic Review,* vol. 56, no. 3 (Fall 1997), p. 545.

16. Op cit., G. O'Donnell, P. C. Schmitter, and L. Whitehead, p. 61.

17. Ibid., p. 548 and Rupert Emerson, *From Empire to Nation* (Cambridge, MA: Harvard University Press, 1967), p. 222.

18. J. J. Linz and A. Stepan argued that independence for most former Soviet states "meant deepening, codifying, and realizing the collective rights of their 'titular' nationality." Op cit., J. J. Linz and A. Stepan, *Problems of Democratic Transition and Consolidation,* p. 389.

19. See chapter 3, "The Crimea Returns to Ukraine," in T. Kuzio, *Ukraine under Kuchma: Political Reform, Economic Transformation and Security Policy in Independent Ukraine* (London: Macmillan, 1997), pp. 67–89 and chapter 4, "Federalism, regionalism and the myth of separatism" in T. Kuzio, *Ukraine: State and Nation Building* (London: Routledge, 1998), pp. 69–99.

20. Jadwiga Stankis, a Polish sociologist, as quoted from Claus Offe, "Capitalism by Democratic Design? Democratic Theory Facing the Triple Transition in East Central Europe," *Social Research,* vol. 58, no. 4 (Winter 1991), p. 876.

21. Jose Casanova, "Ethno-linguistic and religious pluralism and democratic construction in Ukraine" in op cit., J. Barnett and T. Snyder, p. 84.

22. Arthur H. Miller, Vicki L. Hesli, and William M. Reisinger, "Comparing Citizen and Elite Belief Systems in Post-Soviet Russia and Ukraine," *Public Opinion Quarterly,* vol. 59, no. 1 (Spring 1995), p. 29.

23. Vasyl' Kremen', Dmytro Tabachnyk and Vasyl' Tkachenko, *Ukraiina: Al'ternatyvy Postupu: Krytyka Istorychnoho Dosvidu* (n.p.: ARC-UKRAINE, 1996), p. 581. See also Bohdan Krawchenko, "Economic Reform, Democracy and National Movements in the USSR," *Regional Politics and Policy,* vol. 1, no. 2 (Summer 1991), pp. 182–190. Krawchenko pointed out that the drive to reform was coterminous with the national movement.

24. Op cit., R. Emerson, pp. 203 and 206.

25. Jan N. Pieterse, "Deconstructing/reconstructing ethnicity," *Nations and Nationalism,* vol. 3, part 3 (November 1997), p. 25.

26. Adam Przeworski, *Sustainable Democracy* (Cambridge: Cambridge University Press, 1995) p. 4; W. Kymlicka, "The Sources of Nationalism," in Robert McKim and Jeff McMahan (eds.), *The Morality of Nationalism* (New York: Oxford University Press, 1997), p. 57; John Plamentaz, "Two Types of Nationalism" in Eugene Kamenka (ed.), *Nationalism: The nature and evolution of an idea* (Canberra: Australian National University Press, 1974), pp. 34–35 and James Tully, "The Crisis of Identification: The Case of Canada," *Political Studies,* vol. 42, Special Issue (1994), pp. 82–83.

27. L. Greenfeld, *Nationalism: Five Roads to Modernity* (Cambridge, MA: Harvard University Press, 1992), p. 10. See also Edward Mansfield and J. Snyder, "Democracy and War," *Foreign Affairs,* vol. 74, no. 3 (May-June 1995), pp. 79–97.

28. R. Dahl, *Democracy and Its Critics* (New Haven: Yale University Press, 1989), p. 207.

29. D. Rustow, "Transitions to Democracy: Towards a Dynamic Model," *Comparative Politics,* vol. 2, no. 3 (April 1970), p. 350.

30. Susan J. Henders, "Cantonisation: historical paths to territorial autonomy for regional cultural communities," *Nations and Nationalism,* vol. 3, part 4 (December 1997), pp. 530–531.

31. Ibid., p. 360.

32. Ibid., p. 363.

33. See A. Wilson, "The Donbas between Ukraine and Russia: The Use of History in Political Disputes," *Journal of Contemporary History,* vol. 30, no. 2 (April 1995), pp. 265–289; and A. Wilson, "Myths of National History in Belarus and Ukraine" in Geoffrey Hosking and George Schopflin (eds.), *Myths of Nationhood* (London: Hurst, 1997), pp. 182–197.

34. Op cit., chapter 9, "History, myths and symbols," in T. Kuzio, *Ukraine: State and Nation Building,* pp. 198–229. See also Robert S. Kravchuk and Victor Chudowsky, "The Political Geography of Ukraine's 1994 Presidential and Parliamentary Elections," paper presented at the 1996 Annual Meeting of the New England Slavic Association, College of the Holy Cross, Worcester, Massachusetts, April 19–20, 1996.

35. See T. Kuzio, "Borders, Symbolism and Nation-State Building: Ukraine and Russia," *Geopolitics and International Boundaries,* vol. 2, no. 2 (Autumn 1997), pp. 36–56.

36. Op cit, A. Przeworski, *Sustainable Democracy,* p. 32.

37. Craig Calhain, "Nationalism and Ethnicity" in Judith Blake and John Hagan (eds.), *Annual Review of Sociology,* vol. 19 (1993), pp. 211–239.

38. Ibid., pp. 37–38.

39. G. O'Donnell, "On the State, Democracy and Some Conceptual Problems: A Latin American View with Glances at Some Post-Communist Countries," *World Development,* vol. 21, no. 8 (August 1993), p. 1358.

40. Op cit, chapter 3, "Forging a political community" in T. Kuzio, *Ukraine: State and Nation Building,* pp. 43–68.

41. W. Kymlicka, *Multicultural Citizenship* (Oxford: Clarenden Press, 1996), p. 13.

42. Ibid., p.9.

43. Op cit., A. Przeworski, *Sustainable Democracy,* p. 12.

44. We use "national-states" rather than "nation-states" following Charles Tilly's advice that very few European states are "nation-states" in the sense of commanding strong linguistic, religious, and symbolic identities and homogeneity. Tilly believes that only Ireland and Sweden can be defined in such a manner. We would add Poland, Slovenia, and the Czech Republic. See Tilly's *Coercion, Capital and European States, AD 990 – 1992* (Oxford: Blackwell, 1992). Other authors prefer to use "state-nations" rather than "nation-states" where loyalty is more to the territory, citizenship, and constitution. See op cit., J. J. Linz and A. Stepan, *Problems of Democratic Transition and Consolidation.*

45. A. J. Motyl, "The Conceptual President: Leonid Kravchuk and the Politics of Surrealism" in Timothy J. Colton and Robert C. Tucker (eds.), *Patterns in Post-Soviet Leadership* (Boulder, Co: Westview Press, 1995), p. 114, and "The Non-Russian States," *Freedom Review,* vol. 28, no. 1 (January-February 1997), pp. 50–60.

46. Op cit, V. Kremen', D. Tabachnyk and V. Tkachenko, p. 496.

47. See Marc Nordberg, "State and Institution Building in Ukraine" in T. Kuzio (ed.), *Contemporary Ukraine: Dynamics of Post-Soviet Transformation* (Armonk, NY: M. E. Sharpe, 1998), pp. 41–56.

48. *The Guardian,* 18 May and *The Times,* May 21, 1993.

49. A. Przeworski, "Some Problems in the Study of the Transition to Democracy" in Guillermo O'Donnell, Philippe C. Schmitter, and Laurence Whitehead (eds.), *Transitions from Authoritarian Rule: Prospects for Democracy* (Baltimore: Johns Hopkins University Press, 1986), p. 59.

50. Op cit., A. Przeworski, *Sustainable Democracy,* p. 49. President Kuchma admitted that, "We are still very young. This is the time of the first steps. They are never easy and simple for a child, and are even less so for a country. There are therefore unresolved problems and, unfortunately, mistakes and miscalculations" (*Radio Ukraine world service,* January 1, 1997).

51. See op cit., chapter 4, "Political Reform and an End to the Soviet System" in T. Kuzio, *Ukraine under Kuchma,* pp. 90–136; C. R. Wise and T. L. Brown, "Laying the Foundation for Institutionalization of Democratic Parliaments in the Newly Independent States: The Case of Ukraine," *The Journal of Legislative Studies,* vol. 2, no. 3 (Autumn 1996), pp. 216–244; and C. R. Wise and T. L. Brown, "The Consolidation of Democracy in Ukraine," *Democratization,* vol. 5, no. 1 (Spring 1998), pp. 116–137.

52. Op cit, R. Emerson, p. 208.

53. Donald Horowitz, "Democracy in Divided Societies," *Journal of Democracy,* vol. 4, no. 1 (October 1993), p. 36.

54. Gwyme Oosterbaan, "Clan Based Politics in Ukraine and the Implications for Democratization" in John S. Micgiel (ed.), *Perspectives on Political and Economic Transitions After Communism* (New York: Columbia University Press, 1997), p. 221.

55. Samuel P. Huntington, *The Third Wave: Democratization in the Late Twentieth Century* (Norman: University of Oklahoma Press, 1993), p. 138.

56. Op cit, M. Skak, p. 26.

57. *Segodnya,* June 5, 1998.

58. *Kievskiye vedomosti,* July 1, 1998.

59. Volodymyr Horbulin, Secretary of the Ukrainian Security and Defense Council, believed that Ukraine could not be compared to the West which has been developing state institutions for "decades." In contrast, Ukraine began this "from scratch" in 1992 with few economic, trade, or banking experts (*Uriadoviy Kur'er,* March 15, 1997).

60. Leslie E. Armijo, Thomas J. Biersteker, and Abraham F. Lowenthal, "The Problems of Simultaneous Transitions," *Journal of Democracy,* vol. 5, no. 4 (October 1994), p. 172.

61. C. Tilly, "Reflections on the History of European State-Making" in C. Tilly (ed.), *The Formation of National States in Western Europe* (Princeton: Princeton University Press, 1975), p. 63.

62. *Uriadoviy Kur'er,* May 14, 1998. See also the discussion of the reasons behind the influx of young people into the diplomatic service by former Foreign Minister Hennadiy Udovenko (*Uriadoviy Kur'er,* August 10, 1996).

63. See the comments by President Kuchma in *Kievskiye Novosti,* June 20, and *Uriadoviy Kur'er,* November 13, 1997.

64. Op cit, C. Tilly in C. Tilly (ed.), p. 77.

65. Stein Rokkan, "Dimensions of State Formation and Nation Building: A Possible Paradigm for Research on Variations Within Europe" in op cit, C. Tilly (ed.), pp. 572–574.

66. G. A. Almond, *Comparative Politics: A Developmental Approach* (Boston: Little, Brown, 1966), p. 35.

67. Op cit., C. Tilly, pp. 70–71.

68. Edward Shils, *Center and Periphery: Essays in Macrosociology* (Chicago: The University of Chicago Press, 1975), pp. 78–79, 87–88, and 177.

69. Karl W. Deutsch, *Nationalism and Social Communication* (Cambridge, MA: The MIT Press, 1966), p. 39.

70. Mark Jefferson, "The Law of the Primate City," *Geographical Review,* vol. 29 (1939), p. 229.

71. Op cit, E. Shils, pp. 38–39.

72. Op cit., G. O'Donnell, "On the State, Democratization and Some Conceptual Problems," p. 1358.

73. Op cit, C. Tilly in C. Tilly (ed.), pp. 78–79.

74. G. Poggi, *The State: Its Nature, Development and Prospects* (Stanford: Stanford University Press, 1990), p. 19.

75. Op cit., C. Tilly in C. Tilly (ed.), p. 611.

76. Op cit., G. Poggi, pp. 21–29.

77. See Karen Barkey and Sunita Parikh, "Comparative Perspectives on the State," *Annual Review of Sociology,* vol. 17 (1991), pp. 523–549.

78. See the comments by President L. Kuchma on the fifth anniversary of the referendum on independence (*Radio Ukraine World Service,* December 1, 1996), in an interview in *Zerkalo Nedeli* (December 25, 1996), in his annual address to the Rada (*Holos Ukrayiny,* March 25, 1997), to the Ukrainian diaspora (*Interfax,* June 24, and *ITAR-TASS,* June 27, 1997), to the second World Forum of Ukrainians (*Uriadoviy Kur'er,* August 23 1997), to the newly elected Rada (*Radio Ukraine world service,* May 12, 1998), then Speaker Oleksandr Moroz in an interview (*Trud,* November 29, 1997)and to the Rada (*Holos Ukrayiny,* April 15, 1998) and Vasyl' Kremen', then head of the directorate on Humanitarian Affairs in the Presidential Administration (*Uriadoviy Kur'er,* June 21 and *Ukrayina moloda,* July 3, 1997) and Roman Bezsmertnyi, the president's representative in the Rada (*Ukraiina moloda,* September 9, 1997). The same views were outlined by Serhiy Pirozhkov in "Suverenna Ukraiina: Postup u XXI Stolittia," *Narodna Armiya,* July 26, 1996 and V. H. Kremen' et al., *Sotsial'no-Politychna Sytuatsiya v Ukrayini: Postup P'iaty Rokiv* (Kyiv: NSDC and NISS, 1996), p. 10. A major survey of Ukrainian elites found that they were confident that statehood had been consolidated. See P. Terrence Hopmann, Stephen D. Shenfield, and D. Arel, *Integration and Disintegration in the Former Soviet Union: Implications for Regionalism and Global Security* (Providence, RI: Thomas J. Watson, Jr. Institute for International Relations, 1997), p. 46.

79. Valerii Khmelko, a leading sociologist of the International Institute of Sociology, Kyiv Mohyla Academy on the program "Shim Dniv" (*Ukrainian Television—2,* March 22, 1998).

80. The then-newly appointed Foreign Minister Borys Tarasiuk believed that this was a sign that "the society is mature and united" (*Uriadoviy Kur'er,* April 18, 1998).

81. This is most discernible in Andrew Wilson, *Ukrainian Nationalism in the 1990s: A minority faith* (Cambridge: Cambridge University Press, 1997).

82. See the speech by Kuchma to the Council of Regions (*Uriadoviy Kur'er,* March 14, 1997).

83. A. Arbatov, "Russian foreign policy thinking in transition" in Vladimir Baranovsky (ed.), *Russia and Europe: The Emerging Security Agenda* (Oxford: Oxford University Press, 1997), p. 149.

84. See the views of Horbulin in *Uriadoviy Kur'er,* December 25, 1997, and with former President Leonid Kravchuk in *Nezavisimost,* March 17, 1998. Although the left as a whole are usually defined as anti-statehood, this is not the case in our view. The Socialist and Peasant Parties of Ukraine, linked together in the Left-Center parliamentary faction, are pro-statehood. See Moroz's speech reprinted in *Sil'ski Visti* and *Holos Ukrayiny* (January 15 and 16, 1998).

85. See the comments by Valerii Matviyenko, the former political adviser to Kravchuk, in *Kyivski vidomosti* (July 24, 1997).

86. Former Speaker Moroz in *Sil'ski Visti* (May 7, 1998).

87. Quoted from Moroz's speech to the Rada (*Holos Ukrayiny,* April 15, 1998).

88. Moroz to the Rada (*Golos Ukrainy,* July 2, 1997).

89. Moroz as quoted from *Holos Ukrayiny,* December 12, 1997.

90. *Uriadoviy Kur'er,* February 18, 1997.

91. *Eastern Economist,* May 25, 1998.

92. *Demokratychna Ukrayina,* June 7, 1997.

93. President Kuchma warned against this in his speech on the fifth anniversary of independence (*Uriadoviy Kur'er,* August 29, 1996). Sherman Garnett agrees that Ukraine will stick to this middle course. See his *Keystone in the Arch: Ukraine in the Emerging Security Environment of Central and Eastern Europe* (Washington, DC: Carnegie Endowment for International Peace, 1997), pp. 23–24.

CHAPTER 2

The Separation of Powers Puzzle in Ukraine: Sorting Out Responsibilities and Relationships between President, Parliament, and the Prime Minister

Charles R. Wise and Volodymyr Pigenko

Introduction

Although Ukraine is often relegated by the international community as lagging behind in the reform process relative to other democratizing nations like Hungary, Czech Republic, or Poland, a closer look at Ukrainian political dynamics hardly reveals a lack of significant processes on the level of institution building.

On the other hand, one would also find a high level of political tension and confrontations both within and among national political institutions. These tensions reflect an ongoing struggle over the future of the country, the type of political system it is going to have and the proper role of legislative and executive branches of power in the reform processes.

The issue of the separation of powers between the executive and legislative branches has been among the most significant on the agenda of Ukrainian politics since the institution of the office of the president in 1991. After the second presidential elections in 1994, the role of the president in the reform process has become a critical point of legislative-executive relations, which to a large extent reflects the decisive and often controversial acts of the second Ukrainian president Leonid Kuchma.[1]

Rapid, sometimes chaotic, and often unpredictable dynamics of interaction between these two institutions pose an important question—what kind of system of separation of powers is Ukraine developing? Is it likely to lead to a workable system of government and thus contribute to the eventual consolidation of democracy? Or is the system developing in such a way that it brings even more chaos into other existing inefficient governmental institutions? What is the value of the institutional arrangements that seem constantly to provoke conflicts between the branches of power?

It may have been expected that Ukraine's national political branches would be engaged in some serious institutional politics, given not only that the players were trying to construct a wholly new national government in a new state with little experience in self-government but also that they were trying to do so while also adopting fundamental policies and new laws required to respond to entirely new economic, political, social, and international situations and demands. Conflict would be all the more normal given no prior experience with any division of power system. These factors would in themselves lead one to expect considerable conflict as actors in both executive and legislative branches seek to pick up key reins of governmental power. However, the conflict was considerably exacerbated by both the economic crisis and the scramble by the respective branches to get sufficient control in order to respond to a populace reeling from the economic deterioration, and also the ideological chasm that divided and still divides the communists and the reformers over the future direction of the country. All three dimensions—institutional, economic, and ideological—have influenced the conflict between the branches of government and have also influenced the evolution of the separation of powers system in Ukraine.

Our analysis begins with an overview of the propositions generated by the comparative scholarship on the characteristics of institutional design that have been demonstrated either to contribute to the establishment of stable democratic governments or to create governmental inefficiency and political instability. It then briefly examines the context within which Ukraine's separation of powers system developed. Following this is an enumeration and discussion of the specific powers of the institutional actors as they evolved, accompanied by an analysis of the political dynamics that have affected the nature of the separation of powers system as it has developed to this point. The analysis focuses in turn on three time periods from independence to the adoption of the temporary constitutional law ("Law on

Power"), from the temporary constitutional law to the adoption of the constitution, and then under the new constitution.

The State of the Scholarship:
What Systems Work and Why?

Creation of new democratic institutions is now occupying a prominent place in the burgeoning field of transition politics. The attention has often focused on the relationship between the regime type and the prospects for successful democratic consolidation.[2] At the macro level of regime choice, the scholarly community is now divided into proponents of the parliamentary system of government and advocates of presidentialism.

Linz, for example, opposes presidential systems in favor of parliamentary systems, because he asserts that the latter minimize legislative-executive conflicts, promote consensus building, prevent deadlock, and enhance a more flexible institutional environment.[3] On the other hand, Horowitz argues that it is in fact quite possible for presidentialism to maintain a strong party system and represent the interests of minorities through the system of separation of powers.[4]

The questions implied by this debate are these: Is Ukraine moving into deadlock, as Linz would predict, Or is it moving into a workable system of checks and balances, as Horowitz would predict. Proponents of both approaches identify the institutional framework of legislative-executive interaction as a central variable influencing the prospects of building a stable democracy. However, to the extent that both conceptual frameworks are concerned with the *ideal types* of the regimes, that is, pure presidential versus parliamentary systems of government, their applicability is limited. The empirical reality of the post-communist world is the greatest challenge to the current typologies simply because all of the post-Soviet countries have instituted mixed presidential systems with different institutional arrangements concerning the powers of presidents and legislatures over the government, the type of electoral systems, and impeachment provisions.[5]

In their comparative study of the institutional characteristics of mixed regimes, Shugart and Carey explicitly deny the uniformity of the presidential regimes as being the same on every dimension and especially in their relationship with the legislature, types of electoral system, and the effects they produce on the stability of political systems.[6] Shugart and Carey point to the specific arrangements of the powers of *appointment and dismissal* of the cabinet or what they call the "appointment game" as being key.[7] According to the typology developed by Shugart and Carey based upon the power of appointment of the cabinet, the Ukrainian political system very closely approximates the premier-presidential type. However, at various stages the relative powers of national institutions have deviated in significant ways, and thus the factors influencing their variation or continuity must be addressed.

The constitution provides the starting place for identifying some of the factors that need to be addressed. McGregor argues that in Eastern and Central Europe, with little experience with democracy and few traditions of civic culture, a firm anchor is required to provide bearings for the new democracies, and constitutions play a significant role in providing this anchor by determining what is legal behavior and what is not and by granting legitimacy to political systems and actors. Even so, the constitutions are not determinative but rather serve to channel behavior.[8] Constitutions may be an entry point, but they are not the entire venue for the analysis. Analysts must take care not to fall into the fallacies of the "old institutionalism" and must guard against assuming that the choice of specific institutions largely determines the actual distribution of political power. Instead, the formal constitutional framework is to be treated as the terrain on which the different institutions and their incumbents struggle to define their influence.[9] Thus, in the analysis presented here, we begin by charting the constitutional terrain and move to an examination of the political dynamics that have defined the legislative-executive relationship in Ukraine.

Whereas the prior regime invoked a hierarchy of power, the hybrid separation of powers system created in Ukraine introduced three major political actors—president, prime minister, and parliament and much later added an arbiter: the Constitutional Court. Thus, in order to understand the development of the policy making power in Ukraine, it is initially necessary to analyze the evolution of the relationships between the parliament, president, and the prime minister. It is this triad that has really constituted the separation of powers system in the initial stages of regime formation.[10]

In Ukraine we have an opportunity to witness the institutionalization of the relationships between president and the parliament, president and prime minister, and prime minister and the parliament as parts of a bigger puzzle of the development of separation of powers from its beginning in 1990–91. In order to do this, it is necessary to examine both the structural features of the national government as they were framed by policy decisions represented in constitutions and laws, but also to analyze the political dynamics and the interactions among the political actors occupying various positions within the triad. However, both structural features and political dynamics were conditioned by the context of Ukrainian statehood at the point of independence, and thus it is necessary to understand certain contextual features before proceeding.

The Context of Development of the Separation of Powers:
Ukraine at Independence

At the time of independence, the Ukrainian parliament was a highly under-developed institution. The composition of the Verkhovna Rada and its in-stitutional structure were a little more than a "parliament of the Soviet type."[11] The initiation of the representative institution in independent Ukraine was unlike the experience of several Central and Eastern European countries in which parliaments were created from the ground up as a result of popular uprisings that swept out the old regimes, and created the legisla-tures as a result of negotiations between the representatives of major nascent political groups in the country.[12] Ukraine started with the legislative institu-tion that had been created under the Soviet regime at the point of indepen-dence.

The process that has provided for a fundamentally new role of the Verk-hovna Rada as a legislative institution has had both external and internal roots.[13] Following the Declaration of Independence on August 24, 1991, the process of building new institutions began *within* the existing government structures.[14] These provided extremely favorable conditions for the rank and file of the old regime to protect their power positions. In fact, as one Ukrain-ian analyst observes, the independence was a painless and even organic tran-sition from a totalitarian communist *nomenklatura* to a neo-totalitarian post-communist one.[15]

The Republic Parliament elected in 1990 was dominated by the com-munist candidates due to their control of media, government institutions, and electoral commissions, but with the Democratic bloc winning close to 25 percent of the seats. This development stands in direct contrast to the revolutions that have taken place in East-Central Europe. In Poland and the Czech Republic as well as the Baltic states, the first governments that came to power were elected on anti-Communist platforms,[16] and represented a clear break with the *ancien regime* and the former communist *nomenklatura*. In Ukraine, development of new political institutions has taken place within the structures inherited from the Soviet system, and this hangover continues to exert significant influence due to the continued presence of cadres of the old regime. As such, the process of institution building has no other alter-native but to be *evolutionary* rather than *revolutionary*.[17] The communists occupied 373 out of 450 seats in the first parliament that continued to func-tion after Ukraine became independent and lasted until 1994. The center of the opposition was *Rukh* (Popular Movement) known before the events of 1990 for its efforts to democratize the Ukrainian political system. Although not being a party in a strict sense, this organization was able to provide an important forum for democratic and nationalistic forces. Political demands formulated within *Rukh* to a large extent set the agenda for the parliamentary debates that led to the Declaration of Sovereignty in 1990. Nonetheless, *Rukh*'s base was localized in Ukraine's western region, and its development was slowed by indecision over whether to remain as an umbrella movement or to become a formal political party. The first formal parties appeared in western Ukraine, including the Ukrainian National Party (UNP), Ukrainian Christian Democratic Party (UCDP), and Ukrainian People's Democratic Party (UNDP). These parties adopted radical nationalistic stands and advocated the end of communist rule and complete independence of Ukraine.[18] Beyond these demands, the type of political and economic future they envisioned was unclear. Hardly any of them had been able to attract enough followers as to claim national representation and constitute a *mass* party. Even in 1992, the total membership of all opposition parties hardly exceeded 40,000 members.[19]

Despite the fact that the Communists were an exception for their discipline and internal accountability, none of the parties at the time were *parliamentary* parties in a proper sense—there had been a clear lack of constituency accountability on the one hand, and a lack of responsibility on the part of government on the other.

With the Communist Party in disrepute as a result of the attempted coup (and banned by law), the communist deputies renounced all party affiliation and declared themselves independents. They continued to caucus as a group, however. Party affiliation was not recognized as an organizing principle in the parliament, with the presidium consisting of the parliamentary leaders and the chairs of the committees. Deputies could form factions, but deputies were not required to join one. During this period, new factions formed continually, and members shifted freely among them, some more than once. The main divide was largely between ex-communists and reformers.

Not surprisingly, parliamentary deliberations were largely confined to philosophical debates between the opposing blocs with little sense of purposeful participation in government. As such, political parties appear to have had little influence in the initial period of the development of new institutional arrangements and might be better understood as proto-parties scattered along the Left-Right ideological continuum.[20] As such they were in a poor position to challenge or direct bureaucracy.

After the first round of free elections in 1994, it became evident that both the emergence of new factions within the parliament and the fragmentation of the old ones appeared to reflect the *intensity and the direction* of reform efforts, which in turn largely depended on the changes that had taken place in the legislative-executive equilibrium after Kuchma had been elected president.

It became clear to members that the absence of any recognition of factions in the organization and operation of parliament had hindered the legislative process, and so the structure was changed to recognize factions more formally by placing faction heads on the Presidium (which set the agenda), by providing office space for them, and by providing caucus time for faction meetings before major plenary votes. Nonetheless, factions had no sanctions with which to control and sanction members, and deviation from faction decisions in voting by deputies was quite common.

Active parties led by a strong leadership capable of forming non-ideological coalitions have yet to be formed.[21] During the course of the first parliament after independence, the factions came to take on more importance in organizing coalitions to pass major bills and in the negotiations over the interim constitution (the Law on Power) and over the final constitution. Nonetheless, they still fell short of constituting the major organizing axis for the parliament. As a result, forming coalitions with any stability among party groups to formulate a policy program or to take on the president was exceedingly problematic, and parties were not in a position to be the driving force behind institutional development.

Political Institutions:
Constitutional Process and Separation of Powers

Ukraine was the last post-Soviet country to adopt a new constitution. For six years of transition, the old Soviet constitution of 1978 supplemented by 15 separate laws and hundreds of numerous amendments had provided the legal basis for the development of new institutions and the functioning of existing ones, as well as the relationships between them.[22] Although these numerous amendments sometimes generated as much confusion as they provided guidance, their role in designing the new institutional framework for governance should not be underestimated.

The institution of the office of the president was itself a result of a political struggle between the communists and national democrats which democratic forces won. The presidency was established as a symbol of Ukrainian statehood. Communists, whose governing ideology was based on collective decision making (for example, the Politburo), finally accepted the move to create the office of the president after initially arguing against it.

In December of 1991, Ukraine elected its first president, Leonid Kravchuk, the former speaker of the parliament, who received 61.6 percent of the total votes. From that time on, the central challenge of the constitutional process has been to "ensure either that there is harmony between branches or else that, when the branches differ, there are institutional mechanisms for reaching compromise in order to avert inter-branch crisis."[23]

For communists, Kravchuk was nothing more than "the first among equals" and his background as the communist party *apparatchik* seemed to prove that the collective style of leadership would be preserved. Nonetheless, his election as the first Ukrainian president in December of 1991 introduced a new institution in the existing power structure. Now the parliament and the government were supplemented by a directly elected chief executive granted significant powers over the government structure as well as a significant role in law making.

On the national level, the powers of the branches were defined as following:

a. President—the head of state and chief executive;
b. Verkhovna Rada—supreme legislative branch with wide oversight functions;
c. The cabinet of ministers—the highest executive body, subordinated to the president and responsible to the Verkhovna Rada.

To begin the analysis, we have arrayed the legislative-executive powers in Table 2.1.

Institutional Powers—At Independence

Key factors conditioning legislative-executive relations and the degree of conflict between them are constitutional provisions for survivability of the president and the parliament. The greater separation of survivability (the ability of one branch to cause the dismissal of the other without precipitating its own dismissal), the greater the likelihood of inter-branch attacks.[24] As can be seen from cell C-1, the president was not authorized to dismiss parliament. In addition, cell B-1, which outlines the procedure of impeachment of the president, shows that the president could be voted out of office by two-thirds of the parliament, but the process had to be initiated by the Constitutional Court, which was not in place. Thus there was little basis for one branch to attack the other with the hope of causing its dismissal.

Another factor, and one that most directly affects the triangular relationship between president, parliament, and prime minister, is cabinet accountability, or the provisions for appointment and dismissal of the cabinet. As can be seen from cell E-1, the president appointed the prime minister, and ministers of defense, foreign affairs, and interior, but his selections were subject to a confirmation vote by parliament. The president could appoint other ministers without confirmation. However, parliament could remove the prime minister or individual ministers by means of a no-confidence motion (G-1). In addition, the chairman could suspend actions of the cabinet of ministers. Thus, overall there is no direct line of authority to the cabinet. The prime minister was in a particularly weak position, in that he did not form the government and parliament could remove individual positions, and the Chairman could even suspend cabinet actions (G-1). There was thus great potential for the ministries to be subjected to the directives of multiple masters, and there was also the risk of potential confusion over who was responsible for the direction of the government's program. Great potential for a struggle over control of the cabinet and the activities of government also existed.

Another key factor in legislative-executive relations is the degree of involvement of the president in lawmaking. As can be seen from cell K-1, the president did not have a veto over legislation. He did have the right of legislative initiative, but so did many others, including the cabinet of ministers. Both the president and the prime minister had decree authority. However, in that the prime minister could be removed by a no-confidence motion and the president could not, the president may have had more temptation to use his. The absence of a presidential legislative veto combined with presidential decree authority provides an incentive toward the use of decrees when the president is frustrated in the legislative process. However, as shown in cell L-1, with the parliament possessing power to override the president's and the prime minister's decrees, the president would still have to gauge the likelihood of parliamentary disapproval prior to issuing a decree. Overall, the prime minister was in the weakest lawmaking position. In addition, the president risked having parliament legislating over his head as the normal state of affairs.

Another factor conditioning relations is the degree of parliamentary involvement in administration. As can be seen from cells P-1 and P-2, parliament had no power to request the testimony of government officials to use in its oversight role. An individual deputy could request information, but there was no procedure specified, or any sanction for agency refusal to comply (R-1). The president was responsible for submitting the budget for parliamentary approval, and once approved, he was responsible for submitting reports on budget implementation (I-1). Nonetheless, there was no procedure specified for the submission of such reports. The prime minister was required to submit programs to the parliament for review, but once again the

Table 2.1   Development of Legislative-Executive Powers in Ukraine (1991–1996)

- Declaration of Sovereignty (1990) has established the principle of the division of powers.
- According to the Declaration of Independence (1991), only parliament can claim direct
- In essence, there have been two constitutional processes at work between 1991 and 1996. adoption of amendments to the existing constitution. For the period of 1991–1995, the separation of powers.[1]

Time/Powers	*Institution of the Office of Presidency (1991)* *1*
A. General Status	1991: President is the chief executive 1992: President is the head of state and the head of the executive branch; Verkhovna Rada is the sole legislative body[2]
B. Impeachment or Removal of the President by the Parliament	The president may be removed in the event of violation of the constitution and the laws of Ukraine. Procedure must be initiated by the Constitutional Court [*Constitutional Court not in place and not in the law*]. Decisions on removal must be adopted by a constitutional majority (no less than two-thirds of the parliament). Parliament can declare referendum on termination of powers of the president upon popular initiative.
C. Dissolution of Parliament by the President	Absent
D. Presidential Term Limits: Concurrent or Non-concurrent Elections	Two separate laws on elections. Sequence is not specified.
E. Powers of Appointment and Dismissal	President appoints prime minister and several other cabinet members with the approval of VR.[3] President is required to submit proposal for the dismissal of prime minister for VR confirmation.
F. Confirmation of Prime Minister and the Cabinet Members by the Parliament	President appoints prime minister with the approval of simple majority of VR.
G. Vote of No Confidence and Suspension of Government's Actions	VR has a power to pass a vote of no confidence in the prime minister, individual members, or the cabinet as a whole, which

legitimacy from the people.

First is the work of the constitutional commission on the new constitution, and second, the amendments to the old constitution are considered as the basis outlining the system of

Constitutional Agreement (1995) 2	*Constitution (1996)* 3
President is the head of state and the head of the executive branch. The Verkhovna Rada is the sole legislative body.	President is the head of state. The Verkhovna Rada is the sole legislative body.
The right of Verkhovna Rada to remove (impeach) the president was excluded until the adoption of the constitution.	President may be removed VR (impeached) in the event of commission of state treason or another crime in violation of the constitution or the laws of Ukraine. Impeachment must be initiated by a constitutional majority of the VR. Decision of removal must be adopted by no less than three-fourths of the constitutional composition of the Verkhovna Rada.
President cannot dissolve the legislature during the interim period.	President has power to terminate the activity of the current parliamentary body in the case of the parliament failing to convene for a session within thirty days. In this case, president has the power to call for parliamentary elections.
Not specified.	President is elected for 5 years. VR has authority to designate elections of the president.
Parliamentary power of approval is removed. President unilaterally appoints prime minister and the cabinet. Nominees to handful of other key positions must be approved by the VR.[4] President can dismiss the members of cabinet without VR approval.	President appoints the prime minister and other members of the cabinet. President can dissolve cabinet without parliamentary approval.
President independently forms the government and appoints a prime minister without VR confirmation.	President appoints prime minister and several other specified officials with the approval of simple majority of VR.[5]
The VR has a power to pass a limited vote of no confidence in the government as a whole or in an individual minister. If the	VR has a power to pass a vote of no confidence in government as a whole as well as the Procurator General of Ukraine, which results

(continues)

Table 2.1   *(continued)*

Time/Powers	Institution of the Office of Presidency (1991) *1*
	results in their dismissal. Chairman of VR can suspend actions of cabinet ministers, where, in his opinion, they lack conformity with the constitution and other legislation.
H. Government Programs Implementation	Prime minister must submit programs to the Supreme Soviet for review [procedure is not specified].
I. Parliamentary Approval of the Government's Budget	President is responsible for submitting budget for VR approval.
J. Budget Implementation	President submits reports on budget implementation to VR [procedure is not specified].
K. Presidential Veto	Absent for legislative acts of VR. President has a right to annul the acts of the Cabinet of Ministers.
L. Presidential Decree Authority	1991: President has an authority to issue decrees on economic reforms that are not regulated by the laws of Ukraine. 1992: *VR* suspends the right of the president to adopt decrees with the force of law.
M. Prime Minister Decree Authority	Prime minister exercises the right of decree delegated by VR. Decrees have a force of law. Can suspend particular legislative acts.
N. Right of Legislative Initial	People's deputies, presidium of the VR, president, Constitutional Court, Cabinet of Ministers, Supreme Court, the General Procurator, Supreme Rada of the Autonomous Republic of Crimea, Academy of Science.
O. Powers to Call National Referendum	Parliament makes decisions regarding conducting all-Ukrainian referenda.

parliament accepts the program of the government, it cannot pass a vote of no confidence for a period of one year.

in their dismissal. Vote of no confidence must be initiated by no less than one-third of constitutional composition of VR and adopted by the constitutional majority. Vote of no confidence cannot be considered more than once during a single regular session. If the parliament accepts the program of the government, it cannot pass a vote of no-confidence for a period of one year.

The VR exercises control over the implementation of government reform programs [procedure not specified].

Prime minister is responsible for reporting on the status of government programs to VR.

President is responsible for submitting budget for VR approval.

Prime minister is responsible for submitting the state budget for approval of VR.

President submits reports on budget implementation to VR [procedure is not specified].

Cabinet is required to submit regular reports on the implementation of the budget to VR. Accounting Chamber is established to oversee implementation.

President has a power of veto and may return any legislation for reconsideration of the VR (Veto must take place within 15 days of the passage of the law). The VR must reconsider returned legislation.

President has a power of veto and may return any legislation for reconsideration of VR. Veto must take place within 15 days of the passage of the law. VR must reconsider returned legislation.

President has authority to issue decrees in economic sphere and other areas where there are no corresponding legislative acts. Decrees have the force of law until the adoption of corresponding legislation by VR.

President has a power of decree. In the transitional period, the president has a power of issuing decrees on economic issues where there is no corresponding legislative acts (three year limit). Decree becomes a law within 30 days if VR does not adopt corresponding legislation.

No legal decree authority; has power to issue binding resolutions and ordinances.

No legal decree authority; has a power to issue resolutions and ordinances which must registered according to the law.

People's deputies, standing commissions of the VR President, Cabinet, Supreme Court, Highest Arbitration Court.

President of Ukraine, People's Deputies, Cabinet, and the National Bank.

President has a right to call national referenda on constitution. Draft must be agreed upon by the parliament. VR has a right to initiate

Both the president and the parliament have a constitutional power to call national referenda. VR powers to call referenda are

(continues)

Table 2.1 *(continued)*

Time/Powers	Institution of the Office of Presidency (1991) [1]
P. Power of Parliament to Request the Testimony of Government Officials	Absent
R. Power to Request Information	The deputy request can be directed to any government official [procedure not specified].
S. Judicial Review of Prime Minister, President, and Parliament	None
T. Highest Legal Authority (For Interpretation of the Law)	Consitutional Court absent Verkhovna Rada
U. Execution of Presidential Authority in Cases of Removal or Death	Delegated to the chairman of the VR until the presidential elections.

[1]This table is compiled on the basis of analysis of the amendments to the Constitution of Ukraine,
[2]Verkhovna Rada (VR) is the parliament of Ukraine. Until 1994, it was the Supreme Soviet of Ukraine.
[3]The president must submit for parliamentary approval the candidates for ministers of defense, foreign
[4]The VR approves appointments of the Chairman of the Supreme Court, the Chairman of the Highest
[5]The officials whose confirmation is required by the Verkhovna Rada include the following cabinet members:
    the Chairman of the State Committee on Television and Radio Broadcasting.

procedure was unspecified (H-1). With the president having the responsibility for submitting the budget and the prime minister the government's program, leadership over administration was essentially split along with the accountability for it. With almost nonexistent oversight tools, the incentive for the president and prime minister to share information with the parliament was weak.

Another factor conditioning relationships is the provision for dispute resolution among the actors. As can be seen from cell T-1, provision for an independent arbiter in the form of judicial review did not exist. Instead, the highest legal authority for interpretation of the law was the parliament itself. This obviously slanted the situation toward the parliament in the event of an overt dispute over some action, and such an arrangement could not induce confidence in the executive that a legislative-executive dispute could be adjudicated fairly.

| Constitutional Agreement (1995) | Constitution (1996) |
2	3
referendum either itself or upon the petition of at least 3 million voters.	limited to the issue of changing the borders of the state. The president has the power to initiate referendum on changes to constitution. Must be approved by constitutional majority. President has a right to announce referendum upon request of the people.
Absent	Government Day is instituted as a regular procedure.
Not specified	The deputy request can be directed to any government official.
None [Constitutional Court absent].	The power of Constitutional Court is functioning.
Not specified	Constitutional Court is the sole organ of constitutional jurisdiction in Ukrain [functioning].
Not specified	Delegated to the prime minister until the presidential elections.

Constitutional Agreement, and the Constitution of Ukraine adopted in 1996.

affairs, and interior.
Arbitration Court, Chairman of the National Bank, and the Procurator General.
the Chairman of the Antimonopoly Committee, the Chairman of the State Property Fund of Ukraine, and

Political Dynamics I—From Independence to the Law on Power

As McGregor has argued, there are quite a few factors that determine *how* the formal presidential powers will be used.[25] The specific status of the president is a function of the constitutional powers assigned to the office, the personal power on which he can draw, and personality traits that make a president an active or a passive player.[26]

As we have demonstrated, the constitutional framework made it difficult for the president to prevail in the normal legislative process and difficult for the parliament to oversee the administrative process. It also made it difficult for either the president or parliament to remove or dismiss the other. The incentives seemed to run in the direction of having the president keep his head down in terms of high profile policymaking in favor of administrative maneuvering. In addition, the prime minister appeared to be in a weak position in either policymaking or administrative spheres with no direct line of accountability for the cabinet.

Survivability was not really an issue for the two branches during Kravchuk's term as president. Kravchuk, having served previously as a secretary of the Communist Party of Ukraine responsible for ideology and propaganda and then chairman of the parliament, was of the *nomenklatura* and had no disposition to challenge the ruling elite in industry or parliament. He was most of all a wily political tactician. Kravchuk chose to focus on state building for which he drew support from liberal and nationalist forces, while at the same time he permitted continued credits and subsidies to state industries pleasing the *nomenklatura,* even while it drove the country into hyperinflation and impoverished the populace.

Thus the communists were not far from the truth assuming that the president would not be a threat. Kravchuk, the first Ukrainian president, did very little to strengthen his office or even to use his constitutional power to issue decrees in the economic sphere. He refused to take responsibility for economy until the last year of his presidency and focused his attention on nation-state building and symbolic acts, thus limiting the possibilities of conflicts that would inevitably arise due to the unclear division of powers.[27]

Although students of Ukrainian politics cannot agree what exactly has been the role of the first Ukrainian president, his extraordinary abilities in political maneuvering are rarely disputed.[28] On the other hand, the statement he made in 1990 before he became president indicates his assessment of the possible consequences of assuming the direct responsibility for government: "We need to find a person who can be held responsible, some visible figure, then we will be free, because there will be an executive power to decide and to take responsibility. The market will be unpopular, why should we take a responsibility knowing that we will not be able to deliver."[29] In essence, Kravchuk eschewed lawmaking, an area in which he was unlikely to prevail even if he was so disposed.

With respect to cabinet accountability, as cells E-1, F-1, and G-1 demonstrate, the division of powers between the president and the Verkhovna Rada over the prime minister and the cabinet as a whole in the period of 1991 to 1995 was unclear and even contradictory. As we will show, this deficiency of the system of separation of powers has provided a venue for a prolonged conflict between the executive and the legislature.

In essence, the dual responsibility of prime minister to the Verkhovna Rada and the president created a situation characterized by two interrelated tendencies. First, Prime Minister Fokin, who was appointed by Kravchuk and approved by the Verkhovna Rada without difficulty, found himself and the cabinet being constantly pulled in different directions by contradictory orders from the president and parliament. Second, by the same logic the cabinet became a power center in itself, playing on the uncertainty of the situation in general and the differences between the president and the parliament in particular.[30]

Kravchuk, quickly losing the support of the reform-oriented minority in the parliament, focused his efforts at creating a support base among the center-left, center, and center-right-oriented deputies. In 1992, he even appealed to the national democrats to use *Rukh* as a base for a political coalition that would unite all pro-reform forces. Although some of the democratic and nationalistic deputies within the parliament responded favorably to the call of the president, the radical wing of the national-democratic forces led by Viacheslav Chernovil announced its direct opposition to the government. This time, a more organized and focused opposition achieved its goal. The vote of no confidence in the government resulted in the dismissal of Prime Minister Vitold Fokin and resignation of the cabinet in the fall of 1992.

The new prime minister, Leonid Kuchma, was given extraordinary powers by the Rada for six months: full control over government policy and legislation over economic matters. However, he could not control the composition of the cabinet, which largely consisted of Fokin cabinet holdovers with the addition of only two advocates of structural reform. The left-dominated parliament could grant emergency powers to such a cabinet with a clear conscience.[31] In addition, most real economic structural reform, such as privatization, still required legislation, which was beyond the prime minister's control. At the end of the six months, little was changed, and the Rada blamed the cabinet for unsatisfactory measures to stabilize the economy and refused to extend the extraordinary powers. Kuchma had received little support from the president for the attempted reforms and decided to resign. Even before Kuchma's resignation, President Kravchuk started a campaign for concentrating all executive power under his control. The six-month period of extraordinary authority granted to the cabinet had shown to the president that he could be blocked from influencing the management of the national economy by direct arrangements between the parliament and the cabinet. Therefore, Kravchuk openly announced that only the directly elected chief executive should have control over the national government and not the prime minister. Kravchuk's attempt to establish control over the executive brought him very limited success: he preserved his powers to issue decrees with the power of law and weakened Kuchma, who already was seen as a serious competitor in the next presidential elections. In this regard, Kravchuk's choice of the new prime minister was not accidental. Yukhim

Zviahils'kiy, the former mayor of Donets'k, did not show great political ambitions and was easier to control.

As Potichniy has observed, the tug of war between the executive and legislative branches of power made the cabinet of ministers an exceedingly weak institution suspended between the presidency and the parliament without real contact with the local structure of power. "The temporary right to issue decrees that was granted to the Cabinet, but without any real means to implement them proved to be nothing more than 'revisionism' without teeth."[32]

The next Ukrainian president, Kuchma, elected in the summer of 1994, began his term with a committed effort to bring the government under his full control. In this respect, the differences between Premier Kuchma and President Kuchma are negligible, despite the political rhetoric of the election campaign.

The most oft-quoted change to take place after the new president assumed office was his economic program. However, this program underwent considerable change within the first six months after it had been announced. As time went by, the initially ambitious program was slowed down and compromised on various occasions. It is possible to argue therefore that a much more significant change has taken place in the political and institutional realm. More specifically, as the passage of the "Law on Power" demonstrates, the institutional balance of power has been affected the most. Bringing the government under control of the president and establishing a clear system of separation of powers has been and continues to be the issue on which Kuchma has demonstrated utmost persistence and determination in his relationship with the legislature. In this respect, Kuchma's behavior has not only been systematically different from Kravchuk's relationship with the parliament but also different from his own approach to the economic reforms over which he often compromised.

In the summer of 1994, the newly elected president issued decrees that placed both the national government and local councils directly under his control. Kuchma also established the Council of Regions in the fall of 1994 to serve as his advisory body. Finally, the new president made it clear that he expected the parliament to pass a new constitution within a short period of time, which in his opinion was absolutely necessary in order to continue the reforms.

However, unable to push his reform proposals through the Verkhovna Rada, Kuchma turned the presidency into a law making institution. He often attempted to achieve his goals by issuing decrees. In addition, he pushed legislation allowing him more power. The first serious interbranch conflict took place over the draft law "On State Power and Local Self-

Government" submitted by the president for the Verkhovna Rada's consideration. This legislative initiative outlined Kuchma's vision of the separation of powers. The draft clearly favored a strong president with legislative powers and control over the national and subnational governments, whereas the powers of the legislature were limited to law making activity without any means to influence or oversee directly the government's actions and program implementation.

It was not that the parliament had enjoyed a strong hand with respect to the bureaucracy either. With regard to parliamentary involvement in administration, as cells P-1 and P-2 indicate, the Verkhovna Rada had no institutional oversight mechanisms prior to 1995. Not surprisingly, it found itself constantly struggling to obtain information necessary for legislation from the cabinet and individual ministries. The cabinet was thus put into a position of information-broker, and this situation certainly provided for the possibility to manipulate or delay information about government activities and implementation of the laws.

The inability of both legislative and executive branches of power to create a coherent reform strategy resulted in the situation in which individual ministries were left alone to struggle for their survival—finding new resources and markets in a rapidly deteriorating national economy and severing links with the former Soviet Republics. On the one hand, the cabinet complained about the contradictory orders received from the parliament and the president, while on the other both branches of power complained about their orders being ignored by bureaucracy.[33]

The Law on Power initiated by President Kuchma had one central goal: to establish his control over policymaking and implementation by changing the system of separation of powers. Under the existing system as it evolved since 1991, the Ukrainian parliament had enjoyed the power of approval of the government appointments and could vote out of office not only the whole cabinet but individual ministers as well. As cells E-2 and F-2 of Table 2.1 demonstrate, the most significant changes introduced in the Law on Power directly addressed the issue of control over the cabinet. These changes in the system of separation of powers were intended to terminate the Verkhovna Rada's powers of approval of the government as a whole and the power to affect the appointments of individual members of the cabinet. As cell G-2 demonstrates, it also intended to limit the power of the parliament to express a vote of no confidence.

The left majority in parliament strongly resisted the president's Law on Power initiative but was hampered by a lack of public support. The president, using his relatively high popularity, announced that he would call a referendum if the parliament did not proceed to adopt the Law on Power. Kuchma seemed to have occupied a no-lose situation: if the parliament adopted the Law on Power, his position would be greatly strengthened, and if it failed to do so, the president would have had a legitimate reason to call a national referendum, since the parliament would have demonstrated that it was incapable of producing legislation on critical issues.

The parliamentary left, knowing all too well that it would lose in the case of a national referenda, yielded. It voted on the Law on Power in June 1995 to preserve its position in the national legislature and simply to avoid extinction from the political scene.[34] The implementation of the Law on Power required constitutional amendments, suspension of 60 out of 170 articles of the 1978 constitution, and at least two additional laws to bring it into force. However, even at that stage it was clear that the adoption of this legislation ended the Soviet power in Ukraine.[35] Legislative-executive relations in Ukraine moved to a new stage.

As the conflict over the passage of the Law on Power developed and reached its height in 1995, it became evident that the existing system of separation of powers was not capable of providing an institutional solution to the differences in positions of the left majority in the parliament and the president. Specifically, the deadlock over the appointments to the Constitutional Court precluded the emergence of that institution, and thus left no mechanism for conflict resolution. According to the amendments to the old Soviet constitution, only the Verkhovna Rada had the power to interpret the provisions of the constitution as they applied to the specific issues of the separation of powers between the branches. It had become almost impossible to resolve the numerous deadlocks that appeared prior to the passage of the Law on Power, precisely for the reason that there was no independent authority to interpret the confusing and overlapping legal provisions.

Not surprisingly, the president and the parliament differed in their understanding of the constitutional provisions, and both accused each other of unconstitutional actions. In this respect, it must be pointed out that the absence of a Constitutional Court could have also served as a limit to the scope of interbranch struggle. According to the existing mechanisms of separation of powers, neither the president nor the parliament could easily initiate the procedure of dismissal of the other branch. As cell O-2 demonstrates, the president had no legal power to dismiss the legislature except through a popular referendum, to which he later resorted. On the other hand, the Verkhovna Rada could not by itself initiate the dismissal of the president because this power belonged exclusively to the Constitutional Court (B-1).

Institutional Powers—
From the Law on Power to the Constitution

The Law on Power shifted some of the key institutional factors and retained others. With respect to survivability, neither the president nor the parliament could cause the removal of the other during this period, decreasing the potential for attacks. With respect to cabinet accountability, the president could now independently appoint a prime minister and form a government without parliamentary approval, strengthening his hand vis-à-vis the cabinet and further weakening the prime minister. The parliament's power of ministerial removal was reduced in that if the parliament accepted the program of the government, it could not vote a motion of "no confidence" for one year. In addition, the president could dismiss members of the cabinet without parliamentary approval. These provisions strengthened the president's hand over the cabinet and established more of a direct line of cabinet accountability to the president.

With regard to lawmaking, the president retained his right of legislative initiative, but more importantly gained the right of legislative veto, which required a two-thirds parliamentary majority to override. In addition, the president had the authority to issue decrees in the economic sphere and other areas, but parliament could override them if they were "anti-constitutional." Significantly, the president gained the right to call a national referendum on the constitution.

The cabinet's independent policy authority was also greatly weakened—the right of the cabinet (and the prime minister) to issue decrees with the force of law was permanently removed. Thus the president's lawmaking hand was substantially strengthened, and the prime minister's decreased, although the prime minister still submitted the government's program for parliamentary approval. This was not accompanied by a concomitant strengthening of the parliament's role in administration, however. The principle of Soviet power so much valued by the left was dealt a fatal blow, and the president moved on to build a vertical intergovernmental executive structure with the assistance of the Council of Regions created in 1994. Further, the parliament was not specified as the highest legal authority and gained no further leverage in the budget process.

Overall, the Law on Power established a clearer control over the national government by introducing a disequilibrium in favor of the president. Shugart and Carey argue that a system of separation of powers that gives one branch more direct control over the composition of the Cabinet is more likely to be stable than the systems in which none of the branches of power can fully control the appointments to the cabinet. However, this argument takes into consideration neither the volatility of the economic and political context nor the desire of a ruling branch to escape responsibility for societal crisis. As will be demonstrated below, the control of the cabinet was by no means decisively decided and cabinet accountability continued to be problematic.

Political Dynamics II—
From the Law on Power to the Constitution

Perhaps the most important outcome of the Law on Power for the future was that it set up the framework for interactions over the structure of power and preserved the system of separation of powers at the time when the interbranch conflict was dangerously high. The president and parliament consistently clashed over the direction of economic and administrative reform. A survey of the Verkhovna Rada deputies conducted by the Parliamentary Development Project for Ukraine (PDP) in February of 1998 demonstrates the extent to which the situation in legislative-executive relations in the preconstitutional period was perceived as dangerous to the parliament as an institution. In fact, 73.4 percent of the parliamentary deputies interviewed believed that the level of conflict between the branches at that time had been threatening to the future of democratic governance in Ukraine.

The passage of the Law on Power had set the stage for the constitutional struggle, but it did not predetermine the outcome. Thus this legislation institutionalized uncertainty over the future but did not create permanent winners and losers. As Przeworski argues, such "institutionalized uncertainty" is an important component of political institutionalization during the process of democratic transition.[36] The shape and form of the new Ukrainian constitution remained an open political question to be decided within the institutional context of executive-legislative relations.

The survivability issues between the president and parliament were off the table for the period in which the Law on Power was in force. This amendment to the existing system of separation of powers, even if temporary, provided important stability for both institutions and enabled the political factions within the Verkhovna Rada to continue to debate the specific provisions of the new constitution.

According to the Constitutional Agreement as a part of the Law on Power, the new constitution was to be adopted within a period of one year. Notwithstanding the positive effects of the relative stability brought by the

Law on Power, it was clear that time was working against the Verkhovna Rada in that only passage of the new constitution could ensure its future as an institution with real powers in the structure of the national government. At the time immediately following the passage of the Law on Power, such an outcome was by no means certain.

With regard to cabinet accountability, the dual executive structure continued to be a source of difficulty. First, the Law on Power had not outlined any implementation mechanisms available to the president so that he could use these powers effectively. The dual executive structure remained intact, making the coordination between the governmental units far more difficult than predicted, especially on the intergovernmental level. Kuchma was not able to obtain full control over the subnational governments, especially in the regions where the local and regional governments were dominated by the former communists and supporters of the left.

When appointing Yevhen Marchuk as prime minister, Kuchma appeared to have decided to allow the prime minister to run the economy without his direct interference. Since the president could now appoint a like-minded personality without having to go through parliamentary approval, this seemed to be a most likely solution. However, following exactly the same route as his predecessor, Kuchma eventually realized the potential danger of having a powerful and popular prime minister. Marchuk was able to navigate a reformist budget through the parliament and made a major effort to reorganize the national executive structure by bringing individual ministries under the control of the cabinet. At this point, Kuchma reversed his tactic and began to play the blame game, claiming that the cabinet had contravened his policy decisions.[37] Kuchma started firing the ministers and finally dismissed Marchuk in May of 1996, blaming him for his inability to implement the presidential reform program.

As the choice of the next prime minister demonstrated, Kuchma has continued on the path of his predecessor and instead of appointing a nationally known politician, he selected Pavlo Lazarenko of Dnipropetrovs'k who came from the same regional clan as Kuchma. Lazarenko lasted a little longer than a year and was dismissed on charges similar to the ones brought against Marchuk: the failure to implement reform while using state resources to build personal political power. If Marchuk's dismissal was somewhat unexpected, Lazarenko's was known and contemplated well in advance, also due to his alleged machinations and personal enrichment while in office. Thus, two prime ministers learned that in the dual executive structure, the power of the other executive—the president—is really the one that counts.

With respect to parliament's participation in administration, the Verk-hovna Rada undertook a major effort in attempting to strengthen itself as an institution. Soon after the passage of the Law on Power, the parliamentary leadership and all the factions realized the dangers of having no means of control over the ministers. Therefore, beginning in 1995 and through the next year, much legislative time was devoted to a bill aimed at creating an "Accounting Chamber"—an agency that would be directly responsible to the legislative branch and equipped with extraordinary powers of oversight of the government programs and ministerial budgets. The proposed powers of this agency became the focus of much interbranch wrangling between the president and the parliament and focused not only on the legislation, but also on the provision in the constitution that sought to empower it.

With respect to lawmaking, of singular importance was the president's involvement in the developing and passage of the fundamental law of Ukraine: the new constitution. He was greatly aided in his role as constitution maker in having the power to call a public referendum on the constitution. According to the special provision of the Law on Power, a Constitutional Commission was convened to draft a new constitution. The commission was composed of representatives from both branches of government and was chaired by the speaker of parliament and the president. In the spring of 1996, the initial draft was submitted to the parliament for review.

The Commission's draft was rejected by the communists as unacceptable, and so they prepared their own draft—one that did not include provision for a president—and insisted that their draft be the basis for parliamentary consideration. The parliamentary leadership appointed an "Agreement Commission" to reconcile the rival options, but the Communists refused to participate and instead engaged in delaying tactics. President Kuchma announced that since there was no real progress toward a new constitution, he would call a public referendum on his own draft constitution—one that gave the president more power than any of the other drafts. Realizing that with parliament's low public popularity, such a referendum threatened the majority's very existence, the socialist-peasant faction led by Rada Chairman Moroz joined democrats in supporting the Agreement Commission's draft and was able in the end to even draw in a majority of the communists to vote for it after a 24-hour-long parliamentary session of June 27–28, 1996.

The president's ability to appeal to the public by the means of calling a referendum meant that he could go over parliament's head. This ultimately proved decisive.

Institutional Powers under the New Constitution of 1996

The new constitution further altered the institutional factors conditioning relationships among the president, prime minister, and parliament. With respect to survivability, provision was now made for impeachment of the president by the parliament, but it requires adoption by no less than three-quarters of the constitutional composition of the parliament. Concomitantly, the president can dissolve the parliament, but only in the case when the Parliament fails to convene for a session within thirty days. Thus it is very difficult for one branch to bring about the removal of the other.

With respect to cabinet accountability, the president appoints the prime minister and a few specified cabinet officials, but these appointments now require parliamentary confirmation. Of particular note is the requirement of confirmation for the chairman of the State Property Fund. As events unfolded, the parliament would refuse to confirm the president's choice for chairman with the left citing displeasure with the president's privatization program as the reason. Other cabinet ministers could be appointed without parliamentary approval. The provision allowing the president to dismiss the cabinet without parliamentary approval was also retained. However, the parliament could vote a motion of no confidence to remove the cabinet with a vote of over one-half of the constitutional majority required, but only once per session.

The President's lawmaking provisions did not change very much from those included under the Law on Power. One change was a provision that the president can issue decrees on economic issues not otherwise regulated by law, as long as he simultaneously submits a draft law on the same subject. The decree becomes law within 30 days if the parliament does not adopt corresponding legislation or has not rejected the submitted draft law by a majority of its constitutional composition. This decree power is to last for three years after the constitution enters into force.

With regard to the parliament's role in administration, the constitution included some new provisions designed to strengthen parliament's hand. One provision instituted Government Day, which allows the parliament to summon ministers and other executive branch officials to appear before the plenary to answer questions. Another provision created a Control Chamber responsible to the parliament whose powers were to be specified in subsequent legislation. The Control Chamber in particular posed a significant challenge to executive branch authority and legislation concerning its powers set up a classic interbranch confrontation. Still another provision established a parliamentary ombudsman for human rights.

Perhaps the biggest change portending an alteration of interbranch dynamics in the future was the provision for Judicial Review. The Constitution established the Constitutional Court as the sole organ of constitutional jurisdiction in Ukraine with review powers over acts of the prime minister, president, and parliament with regard to their conformity to the constitution. It provided that one-third of the justices of the court would be appointed by the president, one-third by parliament, and one-third by the judiciary.

Political Dynamics III—
Under the New Constitution of 1996

At this point, it is still too early to determine the effect of the constitution on legislative-executive relationships in Ukraine. It is clear however, that the presidential-parliamentary dyad is the key relationship. The prime minister and the cabinet occupy a secondary, if ambiguous, position. Cabinet accountability is still unclear, but the president has somewhat more control in that he controls the appointments and can dismiss the cabinet without parliament's approval. In terms of lawmaking, the president's economic reform legislation has been largely stymied by the left opposition in parliament. The March 1998 parliamentary elections resulted in a parliament with a larger left contingent that the previous one, but with some new players such as the Green Party. Because of the mixed electoral system by which half of the parliament was elected on party slates, it is clear that parties will play a stronger leadership role in the parliament than they have in the past. The new deputies decided to amend the parliament's rules mandating that deputy factions be formed out of political parties that had topped the 4 percent barrier in elections and also that deputies join one of these factions. This will undoubtedly affect not only the relationships within the parliament but also the relationships with both the president and the prime minister. In the past, the president had benefited in his battles with the parliament from the lack of organization and cohesion among factions; this may change under the new rules.

It must be emphasized that the adoption of the constitution in the summer of 1996 could hardly provide an immediate solution to all the political problems of the relationship between the Verkhovna Rada and the president; neither could it have been expected to produce a direct change in the situation overheated by the three years of constant conflicts and occasional stalemates. For example, 56 percent of the deputies surveyed by the PDP in 1997 continue to believe that the system of separation of powers as outlined in the constitution is not capable of providing a foundation for democratic governance, and only 31 percent believe that the constitution represents a fundamental agreement between the political forces. The survey responses also appear to indicate that the intensity of conflict in the post-constitutional period has hardly changed: 38.6 percent of the respondents think that it continues to be very high.[38]

Nevertheless, an important change in the political dynamics can be found in the deputies' evaluation of the threat that the post-constitutional legislative-executive conflicts pose for the future of democratic governance in Ukraine. Only 56 percent of the survey respondents think that the level of conflict continues to be threatening democratic institutions in the post-constitution period, as opposed to 74 percent who believe that this had been the case prior to the adoption of the constitution. Also, 15 percent of the respondents now believe that the current level of institutional conflict is actually supportive of democratic government institutions. Only 2 percent believe that this had been the case prior to the adoption of the constitution.[39] This significant change in the attitudes of the Ukrainian parliamentarians can be at least partially attributed to the positive influence of the framework established by the constitution. As McGregor observes, the most important effects of a constitutional framework are indirect and can hardly be seen in day-to-day politics, especially before the rules have a chance to become institutionalized over time.[40]

Important implications can be also drawn from the survey data on the deputies' attitudes toward the compliance of both branches of power with the constitutional provisions. Only 13.8 percent believe that both institutions are following the constitution, whereas 46 percent of the deputies think that neither the president nor the parliament is following the constitution. The pessimism of the deputies toward the ability of the constitutional framework to last might be a result of opportunistic behavior of both branches of government and not a reflection of dissatisfaction with the constitution itself. Even the most well crafted rules do not eliminate conflict, and interinstitutional trust can hardly develop overnight.[41]

On the other hand, compliance with the constitution emerges as an issue of great significance for both institutions and the future of the system of separation of powers in Ukraine. In this regard, the establishment of the Constitutional Court as a mechanism of interbranch conflict resolutions is of major significance. Serving as a check and enforcer of the constitutionality of actions of both institutions, a successful and impartial Constitutional Court could definitely contribute to increasing the legitimacy of the constitution itself.

Even a very short history of the court's existence provides grounds for optimism. On several occasions, the Constitutional Court has defended the interests of one branch of power against another. Thus it upheld the authority of the parliament after the president issued an executive order placing the National Guard exclusively under his control. This order contradicted the Law on National Guard and a petition from 45 deputies to the Constitutional Court followed immediately. In response, Kuchma quickly initiated amendments to his executive order that gave the parliament and the president joint control of the National Guard.[42]

In the second case, following the appeal from the president, the Constitutional Court has twice reached decisions reducing the powers of the Accounting Chamber, an oversight agency of the Verkhovna Rada, thus defending the powers of the executive branch. The court struck down the articles in the law that gave the chamber control over sources of budget revenues and wide-ranging powers to investigate public and private financial institutions. Following the court's decisions, both the executive and legislative branches have adjusted their behavior. If this continues, legislative-executive disputes over powers may be characterized more routinely as legal disputes than as cataclysmic political battles at the brink.

Conclusion

Ukraine's separation of powers system has evolved from one that was heavily legislatively centered to one that is somewhat more presidentially centered but one that is also more balanced between president and parliament. The system will be even more balanced when the president's decree authority over economic matters expires after three years. It is a system in which the survivability of the president and the parliament is largely assured. It is very difficult for either to remove the other, and thus attacks on the other branch per se should diminish. Cabinet accountability continues to be ambiguous, and the prime minister appears to be the odd man out. He is more beholden to the president but has the responsibility to sell his program to the parliament. Not being the leader of a ruling party coalition in Parliament, he has little political reserve on which to draw in times of severe political turmoil or deadlock over policy. The prime minister seems destined to occupy the position of fall guy, with short terms for incumbents in the office likely to be the rule.

Lawmaking is very much a shared responsibility of parliament and the president. Without a commanding majority, even the dominant left bloc cannot legislate over the head of a president who does not share the parliamentary bloc's views. However, the parliament is not beholden to the president either and must be persuaded that his legislative course is the correct one.

Two new factors likely to affect these interbranch relationships are the activity of the Constitutional Court and the organization and operation of parties within the parliament. The court has already made some key decisions that indicate that it will be a most active player in addressing the disputes over power involving the other two branches. If it plays the role of a balancing wheel and avoids taking sides, its activity may add to the chances for a normalization of interbranch relations. The organization of the parliament is likely to be more heavily influenced by party groups with roots in the electorate than ever before. The ability of the parliament to speak with a strong voice will depend on the skill of deputies and especially their leaders to engage in coalition formation and maintenance activities with which Ukrainian parliamentarians have had little experience in the past.

As we have seen, from the declaration of independence to the passage of the new constitution, the development of the system of governance has been heavily influenced by political conflict between forces of the left, which have dominated parliament, and a reform-minded president supported by forces of the right, which have constituted a minority in parliament. Policy deadlock has often been the experience, but the division was not sufficiently severe to prevent a constitutional accord. From here, it is unlikely that either the president or the left bloc will gain much from trying to pursue continued constitutional brinkmanship. Instead, disputes will be centered on policy and on economic policy in particular. To accomplish any movement, each branch needs the other. If one party or the other insists on its own course, there is nothing in the current system to prevent policy deadlock. In the event of such deadlock, both sides are sure to appeal to the voters on grounds that the lack of action was the other branch's fault.

Notes

1. Kataryna Wolchick, "Presidentialism in Ukraine: A Mid-Term Review of the Second Presidency," *Democratization,* vol. 4, no. 3 (Autumn 1997), p. 154.
2. Matthew Shugart and John Carey, *Presidents and Assemblies* (New York: Cambridge University Press, 1992).
3. Juan Linz, "The Perils of Presidentialism" in Larry Diamond and Marc F. Plattner (eds.), *The Global Resurgence of Democracy* (Baltimore: The John Hopkins University Press, 1996), p. 124.
4. See Donald Horowitz, *A Democratic South Africa? Constitutional Engineering in a Divided Society* (Berkeley: University of California Press, 1991).

54   •   Charles R. Wise and Volodymyr Pigenko

5. Matthew Shugart, "Executive-Legislative Relations in Post-Communist Europe," *Transitions,* December 13, 1996.
6. Shugart and Carey, *Presidents and Assemblies.*
7. Ibid., p. 107
8. James P. McGregor, "Constitutional Factors in Politics in Post-Communist Central and Eastern Europe," *Communist and Post-Communist Studies,* vol. 29, no. 2 (1996), pp. 151, 157.
9. Thomas A. Baylis, "Presidents Versus Prime Ministers: Shaping Executive Authority in Eastern Europe," *World Politics,* vol. 48, no. 1 (April 1996), p. 300.
10. The analysis here is confined to the legislative and executive branches, in that the Constitutional Court did not convene until February 1998.
11. Volodymyr Litvin, *Politychny: Portret Ukrayiny* (Kyiv: Arbis, 1995), p. 205.
12. Thomas Remington, "Introduction: Parliamentary Elections and the Transition from Communism" in Thomas Remington (ed.), *Parliaments in Transition* (Boulder: Westview Press, 1994), p. 16.
13. Taras Kuzio, *Ukraine Under Kuchma* (New York: St. Martin's Press, 1997), p. 1.
14. Yuri Shemshuchenko, "Problemy Realizatsii Konstitutsii Ukrainy" in Yuri Shemshuchenko (ed.), *Pravova Derzhava* (Kyiv: Institut Derzhavy i Prava NAN Ukrainy, 1997), p. 4.
15. Volodymyr Polokhalo, "The Neo-Totalitarian Transformation of Post-Communist Power in Ukraine," *Political Thought,* no. 3 (Spring 1994), p. 134.
16. Thomas Remington, pp. 1–2.
17. Kuzio, *Ukraine Under Kuchma,* p. 3.
18. Peter J. Potichnyi, *The Multi-Party System in Ukraine* (Koln: Budesinstitut fur ostwissenschlafte und internationale studien, 1992).
19. Taras Kuzio and Andrew Wilson, *Ukraine: Perestroika to Independence,* (New York: St. Martin's Press, 1994), p. 150.
20. Volodymyr Litvin, "Pro Suchasni Ukrains'ki partii, ikhnikh prykhyl'nykiv ta lideriv," *Politolohichni Chytannia,* no. 1, 1992, p. 67
21. Shugart and Carey, pp. 173–175.
22. Working Group Parliament—Government—Local Government, "How to Adopt New Constitution for Ukraine," *Vysnik,* no. 3, (September 12, 1995), p. 5.
23. Shugart and Carey, p. 204.
24. Matthew Shugart, "Executive-Legislative Relations in Post-Communist Europe," *Transitions,* Dec. 13, 1996, p. 7.
25. James McGregor, "The Presidency in East Central Europe," *Politics,* vol. 3, no. 2 (January 14, 1994), pp. 23–25.
26. James McGregor, "The Presidency in East Central Europe," p. 23.
27. Litvin, pp. 250–255.
28. For a discussion of this point, see Alexander Motyl, "The Conceptual President: Leonid Kravchuk and Politics of Surrealism," in Timothy Colton and

Robert Tucker (eds.), *Patterns in Post-Soviet Leadership* (Boulder: Westview Press, 1995), pp. 103–22.

29. Litvin, p. 255.

30. Charles R. Wise and Trevor Brown, "The Separation of Powers in Ukraine," unpublished manuscript, 1998, p.17.

31. Ilya Prizel, "Ukraine between Proto-Democracy and 'Soft Authoritarianism'" in Karen Dawisha and Bruce Parrott, (eds.), *Democratic Changes and Authoritarian Reactions in Russia, Ukraine, Belarus, and Moldova* (New York: Cambridge University Press, 1997), p. 346.

32. Peter Potichnyi, p. 19.

33. Charles Wise and Trevor Brown, "Democratization and the Separation of Powers in Ukraine: The Role of the Parliament in the Passage of the New Ukrainian Constitution," Paper presented at the Midwest American Political Science Association Annual Meeting, Chicago, Illinois, April 1997, p. 14.

34. C. Wise and T. Brown, "The Separation of Powers in Ukraine," p. 19.

35. T. Kuzio, *Ukraine Under Kuchma*, p. 101.

36. For a detailed discussion of this point, see Adam Przeworski, *Capitalism and Social Democracy* (New York: Cambridge University Press, 1986).

37. C. Wise and T. Brown, "The Separation of Powers in Ukraine," p. 22.

38. The mean of the degree of conflict prior and after the adoption of the constitution has dropped only by 3 degrees on the scale of 100 for the sample of 109 parliament members.

39. This change is statistically significant at the .001 level, R =.341

40. James P. McGregor, "Constitutional Factors in Politics in Post-communist Central and Eastern Europe," *Communist and Post-Communist Studies,* vol. 29, no. 2 (1996), p. 158.

41. James March and Johan Olsen, *Rediscovering Institutions* (New York: Free Press, 1989), pp. 155–165.

42. Charles Wise and Trevor Brown, "The Constitutional Court of Ukraine," Paper presented at the Midwest American Political Science Association Annual Meeting, Chicago, Illinois, April 1998, p. 27.

CHAPTER 3

Ukrainian Interest Groups, Corporatism, and Economic Reform

Paul Kubicek

As the Soviet empire began to disintegrate, Ukrainian civil society, long suppressed by Soviet authorities, began to reassert itself. This was most clearly manifest in the national-democratic movement *Rukh*, which spearheaded the drive for Ukrainian sovereignty and eventual independence. When independence was gained and overwhelmingly approved by Ukrainian citizens in the December 1, 1991 referendum, there was hope that popular mobilization would continue and play a fundamental role in pushing forward democratization and dismantling the Soviet economic system.

This wish proved to be rather naive. The national-democratic movement, with its primary goal of independence achieved, refused to challenge the communists-turned-nationalists in the "Party of Power." Instead, it formed a *marriage de convenance* with the latter, which was seen as the guarantor of Ukrainian statehood. Democratic ideals were at best relegated to a subordinate position. Some even held them in disdain, preferring imposition of "state thinking" (*derzhavnyts'ky myshlennia*) that would provide a "spiritual cement" for society.[1] Obviously, such deference to the state only strengthened the hands of the state elite, which used its power in ways not always conducive to democracy. The late *Rukh* leader V'yacheslav Chornovil later lamented this development, claiming at *Rukh*'s Fourth Congress that, "Our biggest mistake was to surrender our ideals of independence and democracy to other hands, which have always been indifferent or hostile to these ideals."[2] The compromises and weakening of the national-democratic movement are described in detail elsewhere and will not be the focus of my attention.[3] Nonetheless, this case shows that simple faith in the "triumph of civil society" was misplaced.

Less dramatic perhaps, but no less important, have been the cases in which civil society never really got off the ground at all. This has been the case among organized economic interest groups representing labor, business, and agricultural interests. David Ost, writing about the Polish case, found a "gaping hole" where these organizations should exist,[4] and Ukraine, which did not have anything to equal the Solidarity movement, is in an even less developed position with respect to these groups. True, they are by membership the largest organizations in civil society, dwarfing all political parties and social movements. However, most have had minimal impact on Ukrainian politics. All major organizations were formerly controlled by the Communist Party, and they have yet to establish themselves as a truly independent voice. On questions of economic reform, instead of pushing ahead with new proposals, most have tried to preserve as many elements of the old system as possible. Their primary "contribution" to date has been to serve as an adjunct of the "Party of Power" and to provide a power base of sorts for elements of the *nomenklatura*.

How can one best conceptualize this sort of system? Clearly, it is not one based upon a vibrant civil society of competing, independent groups. In other words, it is not pluralism, the system of interest intermediation in many Western democracies. In addition, given the "leading role" of the formerly communist-controlled groups, it is not exactly a liberal corporatist arrangement like those found in Scandinavian states. One could more accurately call this a version of state corporatism, a system that in effect limits the voice and influence of interest organizations. Their freedom to maneuver and their role in the policymaking process have both been highly circumscribed. The effect, especially from 1992 to 1994, was to stifle movement toward serious economic reform.

More recently, economic reform has been introduced in Ukraine, but largely "from above" by President Leonid Kuchma, elected in July 1994. Many of these interest organizations now feel themselves under assault and have made efforts to preserve their position. While there is now a differentiation of sorts occurring between pro- and anti-reform groups, the fact remains that most of these organizations themselves remain bit players, and that political and economic life in Ukraine is dominated by members of an oligarchic, bureaucratic-technical elite. Civil society, a phrase commonly used in the initial state building years, has largely vanished from the political discourse.

This chapter will outline the elements of the still-evolving Ukrainian corporatist system and what effect this has had on questions of economic reform. In sum, it suggests that less has changed in Ukraine than one might initially think, and in some crucial areas Ukraine has made little progress toward liberalization and democratization.

Corporatism: Definitions, Typologies, Rationale

Corporatism has a long history in political science and has been applied to a variety of ideologies and political systems. As a system of interest intermediation, it contrasts with pluralism. Whereas pluralism is predicated upon multiple, independent, competitive, non-hierarchical groups free from state interference, corporatist systems are based upon singular, non-competitive, hierarchically ordered interest associations recognized by the state, which enjoy a representational monopoly in return for observing certain controls on their behavior.[5] Corporatism has also been used to describe a particular mode of political participation among these limited interest associations. The key feature here is institutionalized participation by organizations in policy making and implementation. The classic corporatist formula is tripartite bodies (state, business, labor) charged with determining a host of socioeconomic policies. In this vein, corporatism can be seen as a form of social partnership between interest groups and the state.[6]

Of course, not all corporatist arrangements are the same, and the key differences lie in their development and the nature and degree of constraints on associations' activities. The most common differentiation is between "societal" or "liberal" corporatism and "state" corporatism.[7]

Societal corporatism describes a system in which groups enjoy some autonomy from the state and in which they voluntarily form to preserve social peace. It is not imposed from above but evolves from below, usually to press for establishment and support of a social welfare state. It is the basis for the much-heralded "Swedish" model and exists to varying degrees throughout Northern Europe and Austria. Some have suggested its utility for post-communist states well-advanced along the path toward reform.[8]

State corporatism, in contrast, depends on the heavy hand of the state, which creates, guides, and structures social life. Associational independence is severely curtailed, and "bargaining" heavily favors the state. Groups themselves may be little more than appendages of the state, and order is imposed from the top to prevent spontaneous action from below. This system was commonly associated with now-defunct authoritarian regimes in southern Europe and Latin America. Given the legacy state-directed rule and the self-described "Latinamericanization"[9] of Ukrainian society—meaning economic and social chaos—one might find fertile ground for this type of system in post-Soviet Ukraine.

Why might corporatism make sense—analytically, empirically, even normatively—to assess the structure and role of interest groups in Ukraine? Part of the answer, as suggested above, derives from the communist experience itself. Interest associations during the Soviet era met many of the requirements of state corporatism (non-competitive, officially sanctioned, constraints on activities, etc.), and many of these groups, which have witnessed minimal reform, continue to exercise a dominant, if not exclusive, role in interest representation. Meanwhile, independent groups that might be able to challenge these Soviet-era creations have had immense difficulties in establishing themselves. This is due to a number of obstacles: problems of collective action, limited resources, an uncertain economy, widespread apathy and lack of political efficacy, and intervention from state authorities. In short, Ukraine did not inherit a *tabula rasa,* and political actors must build from the remains of the old system. Completely dismantling all structures—including links between the state and interest associations—would be costly for both sides. Therefore, in large measure, Ukraine may suffer from "residual corporatism," as elements of the old system are preserved. One might argue, however, that this will be only temporary, as these groups will evolve over time, assume a more independent role, and be subjected to internal divisions and new challengers.

This system, however, need not simply wither away. Political actors—both within the state and within the groups themselves—may promote it as a means of preserving their own positions. Corporatist arrangements may also be attractive due to their promise to limit and channel interest group activity and preserve social peace. In particular, social partnership compacts among economic actors may provide order in a very dynamic environment and a means to promote controlled change while avoiding social explosion. These concerns may become magnified as new classes, cleavages, and tensions emerge in post-Soviet societies, and it becomes imperative to perpetuate the idea (or illusion) of a harmony of interests.

One finds support for these notions among many Ukrainian writers and political figures. One Ukrainian historian suggested the need for a "corporative society" (*korporatyvne suspil'stvo*) that will allow people to recover gradually from communism and provide a means for the elite to consolidate society around itself.[10] An economist noted that privatization will succeed only if it is accompanied by close cooperation among the state, business, and labor on the basis of social partnership.[11] As for pluralism, this was seen by one Ukrainian legislator as proof that society is not structured. The solution, in his view, is state sponsorship or structuring of groups so that all voices can be heard.[12] Some labor union officials essentially agreed, maintaining that only through unified groups can unions have real power. One labor official suggested that, "the union organism is similar to a cloth, and little rips in it soon mean that there is no fabric at all."[13] Another added that labor unity is necessary to prevent individual unions from "pulling the blanket over themselves," meaning that they would manage to obtain special benefits and stay comfortable while others are left to freeze.[14]

Of course, corporatist arrangements may not live up to this promise, and an important question from a political economy perspective would be in whose interest do these institutions actually work. Naturally, some goals will be stressed more than others, and given the relative power of state structures over nascent civil society in Ukraine, one would not be surprised to see a general authoritarian and conservative leaning in state-interest group relations. "Safe" groups may therefore be given special rights, and those that would challenge the status quo are shut out of the political process.

Economic Interest Groups in Ukraine

Let us now turn to the major economic interest associations in Ukraine. These organizations represent labor, business, and agricultural interests. We are concerned not only with how they do or do not correspond to the corporatist "model," but also what effect, if any, they have on the important questions of economic reform.

Trade Unions

The largest organization of any kind in Ukraine today is the Federation of Ukrainian Trade Unions (FPU), an umbrella organization of 42 branch and 27 regional unions and the successor to the republic-level, communist-dominated trade union organization. As of 1994, it claimed over 20,000,000 members—approximately 40 percent of the entire population and 97 percent of the unionized workforce. In most industries, it exercises a monopoly on worker representation. While union membership is by law voluntary, the FPU continues to hold onto members by habit, inertia, and economic coercion, since those who leave the union can lose important benefits (distributed via the FPU monopoly) and even their jobs.

Despite the fact that the FPU confederation is nominally independent, it remained linked with the state structure and conservative political forces. Its initial chairman, Oleksandr Stoian, was previously Kravchuk's adviser on social and labor questions, and many conceded that Stoian's appointment to the FPU depended upon Kravchuk's patronage. In return, during Kravchuk's tenure in office, the FPU was remarkably quiescent and criticism of the government very muted, despite deteriorating conditions for workers and the government's repeated breaking of promises made to workers. Many claim that the FPU is still best understood as an "official" or "state" union, an organization little more than the labor relations branch of the government. Notably, the FPU enjoys special privileges (formal discussions and consultations with the government, legislative prerogatives, de facto control over social insurance funds) not granted to other unions. In addition, enterprise managers are still allowed to be union members, and in many cases they have themselves elected to be the union chair at the enterprise. FPU officials see little wrong with this, as these officials are also "workers," but critics point out that the old Soviet troika of party, management, and union leaders has not been broken, and rank-and-file members, if given a leadership role at all, are merely "*shesterki*," the lowest playing card.[15] Yaroslav Kendzior, the leader of the L'viv branch of the FPU and a dissident within the FPU ranks, lamented that the FPU is "the most conservative social organization at the current moment," one that has essentially abandoned its role of fighting for worker rights.[16] It is small wonder, then, that FPU unions are not trusted, a fact that itself belies the claim that membership is purely voluntary.[17]

FPU officials relish their near-monopoly role and believe that competition among unions would be detrimental to the movement. Volodymyr Zlenko of the Auto and Agricultural Machine-Building Union argued that "separate unions, each having recognition in a single branch, are small and this opens them up to manipulation from certain circles and sometimes their opinion will be simply ignored."[18] Ivan Zvinnyk, chairman of the Union of Aviation Workers, argued that the FPU colossus would have much more influence than a small, independent union would have, and that certain questions (interbranch collective agreements) can be decided only by the FPU. Indeed, when assuming the leadership of the FPU in 1993, Oleksandr Stoian declared that the FPU would take it upon itself to represent *all* unions in negotiations with the government and individual enterprises, thereby pushing would-be competitors aside.[19] In Stoian's view, the FPU should act as a corporatist "peak association." Decentralization of and defections from the FPU structures are strongly frowned upon. FPU officials speak of the need to re-establish democratic centralism, and the one defector to date, the Union of the Academy of Sciences, was put under severe financial pressure to return to the FPU fold.[20]

While the FPU has a virtual monopoly on representation, there are independent or, in FPU parlance, "alternative" unions. Many of these emerged in 1989 together with the national-democratic movement, and they aspired to be important actors in Ukrainian civil society. Most, however, remain very small, politically and economically marginalized. Their total membership is roughly 600,000, making them Lilliputians compared to the FPU. In addition, most of these members are in two unions of workers and owners of small firms in the non-state sector, which refused to join the FPU because of the latter's hostility to entrepreneurs and economic reform in general. These "unions" do push for their own special interests, although they could be more accurately viewed as organizations of owners.

The most important and most truly "independent" of all unions in Ukraine are those of the coal miners (the NPGU, with 65,000 members), railway machinists (10,000), and air-traffic controllers (1,000). These unions finally won government recognition after a strike in September 1992 that brought much of Ukrainian transport to a halt. These unions have been critical of what they see as FPU kowtowing to the government, and they generally have a more combative attitude toward management. There are also smaller, more local "independent" unions, such as textile workers in Donets'k and longshoreman in Illichevsk.

In general, these unions have had a difficult time both attracting members and gaining recognition as a legitimate form of organization from political authorities and management. Some of their problems have "objective" causes: collective action dilemmas, lack of resources and experience, apathy and disillusionment, and poor economic conditions. More troubling have been the numerous reported incidents of interference and intimidation in these unions' work: threats of job loss, denial of promotion, loss of social welfare provisions, even physical violence. These actions have been committed, according to the allegations, by FPU officials working with management, neither of which have any interest in seeing the emergence of independent unions.[21] Gregory Nedviha, a member of parliament and activist with the independent rail union, put it very succinctly:

> Imagine that you are the director of a state enterprise. Are you interested in the development of a free trade union? Of course not. It only means trouble

for you. It will not be subjugated to you and it will have its own independent voice. You would prefer to work with the loyal state trade union, with which you have always had good relations and which you can rely upon to execute your orders.

Despite a number of common problems, it has been very difficult to establish a united front among the various independent unions. Some splits have been regional (for example, coal miners in western Ukraine accusing their Donbas comrades of being too pro-Russian), others based upon personalities or access to resources. The most serious split has occurred in Donets'k, where the local independent miners' union has broken with the national body and allied itself with the Donets'k strike committee, which is both father and sworn enemy of the NPGU, accused by many of being a wolf in sheep's clothing, an arm of the management. In 1995, one report opined that lack of unity and the rise of personal ambition had done more than government or FPU action to weaken the free trade union movement.[22] In June 1995, Oleksandr Mril, the much-maligned head of the NPGU, resigned as head of the umbrella organization Free Trade Unions of Ukraine (VPU) due to disagreements with the chairs of the constituent unions. A later conference attempted to resolve a number of outstanding issues, but one report, commenting on the conference, noted that internal quarrels among the various unions (on questions such as leadership, funds, programs on social insurance, and collective bargaining) had sapped 90 percent of the constructive potential away from the movement, and that all the unions had managed to do was perform a "senseless dance" around a host on trivial issues.[23] In short, as we shall see below, the independent union movement, barely off the ground, has lost its momentum and has become a marginal political force.

Business and Entrepreneurial Associations

By far the most important business association in Ukraine is the Ukrainian Union of Industrialists and Entrepreneurs (USPP). According to its 1994 data, this organization unites over 14,000 economic actors, employing over 4.5 million people. Over half the members come from the state sector, and the organization represents about 80 percent of Ukraine's state industrial enterprises. Formally founded in 1990, the USSP emerged from directors' networks of the Soviet era, and it enjoys extensive links with various government ministries. Many of its leaders even wear two hats—one as leader of an interest group, the other as state or government official—and so it may be more accurate to think of the USPP more as an arm of the administration than as an "independent" group. Its most prominent figure was Kuchma, who was its president from 1993 to 1994 and who used the USPP as a base for his successful presidential campaign. Kuchma's election in turn bolstered many of the links between the USPP and the state administration.

According to its own statutes, the USPP's goal is to "carry out the radical economic reforms necessary to promote the formation of a market economy as quickly as possible." Several groups of entrepreneurs are therefore affiliated with the USPP as a means to influence government policy. The USPP has pushed for a variety of measures, including trade liberalization, currency reform, and laws conducive for foreign investment, which all clearly fall under the rubric of reform.

Nonetheless, many continue to see the USPP as a haven for the more conservative "red directors" of the industrial complex, who are more interested in subsidies for their own enterprises than free markets. The general director for the Union of Small Entrepreneurs, itself a USSP affiliate, conceded that the state directors, by virtue of their enormous resources, have "ninety per cent of the weight in the organization."[24] Much of the USPP's agenda is oriented toward obtaining credits, lower taxes, and special export rights for state enterprises. Volodymyr Lanovyi, formerly head of a rival organization and chairman of the State Property Fund, argued that the state directors of the USPP were fundamentally anti-reform and were attempting to tilt the playing field even further in their favor and thereby stifle the emergence of a nascent Ukrainian private sector.[25] Most revealing was a comment by Ludmila Yakhovleva, one of the USPP's vice-presidents, that "yesterday's director is tomorrow's most natural entrepreneur." "Reform" therefore seems to include what is commonly derided as "*nomenklatura* privatization," which does little more than consolidate the political and economic position of a new oligarchy.

The USPP is not the only industrial-entrepreneurial organization rooted in the old system. There is also the Ukrainian National Assembly of Entrepreneurs and the All-Ukrainian Association of Entrepreneurs (VOP). Both of these exist, however, within the USPP's umbrella, although officials from VOP, headed by Valery Babych, himself a 1994 presidential candidate and Kravchuk protégé, claim that their relations with the USPP are more conflictual than cooperative. Both of these groups have *nomenklatura* roots, and Oleksandr Shnychko, general director of VOP, even claimed that there simply was no alternative to "*nomenklatura* privatization" since workers and citizens lacked the requisite knowledge to be managers or even stockholders.

Organizations from the non-state sector also exist, although many, such as the Union of Small Entrepreneurs, the Union of Cooperatives, the Union of Renters, and the Ukrainian League of Entrepreneurs with Foreign Capital, are all in the USPP structure. Some of these groups, however, appear to be little more than an *apparatchik,* a secretary, and a fax machine. One official from the nominally "independent" Union of Independent Entrepreneurs conceded that all such groups, including his, were "created from the top down, and all structures remain tied to and dependent upon the state."[26] Despite the multiple organizations, then, it is hard to say that there is true pluralism in this sector, and the USPP functions as a corporatist-style umbrella organization. The position of these smaller groups is that this arrangement is the only means through which they can have a voice. Otherwise, they would be ignored, cast aside as nobodies.[27]

Apparently this was the fate of the most "independent" entrepreneurs' organization, the All-Ukrainian Association of Private Owners and Entrepreneurs, headed by Lanovyi. Through 1994, it did not cooperate with the USPP, which it viewed as a "pro-state organ." This organization, together with the Center for Market Reforms, did submit reform proposals to the government, but these went nowhere. In the words of the center's co-director, "It's no use offering rubies to pigs when they're content to play in the mud."

Agricultural Associations

As in the above cases, the main players among Ukrainian agricultural associations are guardians of the old system. The leading organization is the All-Ukrainian Committee of Collective Agriculture Enterprises (*Kolkhoz* Council). This organization was founded in 1969 to protect the interests of collective farms, and since the collapse of the USSR it has done little more than add the prefix "All-Ukrainian" to its name. In the words of Ivan Yemets, the assistant chairman, "Our functions have not changed at all. Our task is to defend the interests of the *kolkhozy.*" In practice, according to one of his phrases reminiscent of the 1930s, this means battling against those individuals and objective forces that are creating "unfavorable conditions" in the countryside.

The main issues for the *Kolkhoz* Council are obtaining funds and benefits from the state, especially equipment and low interest credits or "advances" for collective farms. Reform via land privatization is decidedly *not* on the agenda. Collective farms should be preserved as collective farms. Konstantin Husarov of the Ministry of Agriculture conceded that the *Kolkhoz* Council, insofar as it represents the *directors* of collective farms, has a "natural corporate interest in preserving the old system," since privatization, by definition, undermines their position.

The council claims that it is the only representative organ of the more than 9,000 collective and state agricultural enterprises in Ukraine. Competition, although legally allowed, is, at least for Yemets, both unnatural and unnecessary. He declared, "We think it would be right if there was only one social organization which would defend the interests of collective farms, farmers, and state farms."

Determining the real membership of the council is a rather tricky proposition. The council claims all agricultural collective enterprises as its members. However, no membership dues are collected, meaning that membership attributes seem rather loose. "Membership" is not compulsory; it is simply assumed. Moreover, it is clear that the farm directors maintain and run the organization. Since these directors can be regarded as state functionaries, the council—even more so than the FPU—is an organization of the economic administration in the garb of a social organization.

Indeed, one could say that a "special relationship" exists between the ministry and the *Kolkhoz* Council. For example, Yemets attends all of the ministry's scheduled sessions (other organizations are invited when the ministry thinks the discussion will be relevant to them), and Oleksandr Borovik, the chairman of the *Kolkhoz* Council, regularly accompanies the minister to make recommendations to the president. Thus despite the fact that the constitution states that "All civic organizations are equal before the law," it seems that the *Kolkhoz* Council, by virtue of its power and/or political affinities, is more equal than other groups that do not receive such special treatment.

One could perhaps best classify the relationship between the *Kolkhoz* Council and the state as corporatist in content if not in form. By this I mean that even though some formal requirements of corporatism may be lacking, the outcome is basically the same: an alliance between state structures and a co-opted/coerced/cajoled/compliant leadership of social organizations, which is usually designed to defend the status quo and control demands from below.

The *Kolkhoz* Council, however, while perhaps the most privileged of the Ukrainian agricultural associations, is not the only one. Another organization is the Agrarian Union. It was founded in 1990 under the aegis of the Party Central Committee and is designed, in the words of its chairman, Ivan Mozgovoi, to "defend the interests of all agricultural workers—collective and state farms, farmers, workers in processing, individual owners—regardless of form of property." However, this organization also seems directed to the interests of collective farms, as the Agrarian Union has been very slow in assisting farmers. Mozgovoi claimed in 1994 that only 48 farmers are members of his organization (out of a total claimed membership of 1.5 million), and he is passionately opposed to the idea of selling land, which he declares would be the same "as if we sold our mother and our people." According to him, those who debate the merits of private or collective ownership have "clouded vision." The task, he claims, is to unify the agricultural sector.

The tasks of the Agrarian Union closely resemble those of the *Kolkhoz* Council: problems of equipment, prices, subsidies, and credits. In a sense, it is a redundant organization, which would seem to violate the "singular" and "representational monopoly" requirements of corporatism. However, officials within the Ministry of Agriculture (and the *Kolkhoz* Council) dismissed the Agrarian Union as basically a non-functioning organization that has lost its sponsorship from above. Concrete achievements of the Agrarian Union exist more on paper than in the countryside itself.[28]

The only other national agricultural association is the Ukrainian Association of Farmers (AFU). In 1994 it claimed a membership of 15,000, which is about half of the total number of farmers in Ukraine. Its goal is to secure good conditions (equipment, land, credits) for farmers and work for genuine land privatization. Its natural opponent is the *Kolkhoz* Council. While the AFU does lack a competitor (there is only one farmers' organization), membership is clearly voluntary and much of the impetus for its creation has come from below.

Representatives of the AFU claim that they are entirely self-governing and have not experienced state intervention in their internal affairs. Its leader, Mykola Shkarban, a former member of parliament, did concede that there are certain informal restrictions placed upon the organization's activity:

> I can express my opinion on TV, the radio, in the press. I can lobby parliament to change the law. But if I press too hard, I will be tossed aside, ignored . . . One could say that we have restricted freedom.

The biggest problems for the AFU, however, are the many barriers that prevent the emergence of private farmers in Ukraine. Many of the problems have objective causes: lack of equipment and lack of money. However, the laws themselves often work against would-be farmers. One major difficulty is that decisions about land distribution to farmers are granted, to local councils, which are controlled by the directors of *kolkhozy* and/or their allies. Thus, by virtue of their "second hat," the *kolkhoz* directors de facto fulfill a corporatist role by implementing the state's land "reform" program. This is a bit like having the fox guard the hen house. The local leaders have every incentive to thwart the emergence of farmers, and because of the weakness of the state, no one can compel them to obey the law. In the localities, "the director of the *kolkhoz* is a combination President, Verkhovna Rada, and Prime Minister. The final word is with him, not the law."[29]

Laws to protect farmers exist, but they are little more than pieces of paper that the local directors simply ridicule. Harassment campaigns are organized against farmers, and one locality even wanted to declare itself a 'no farmer zone.' Shkarban declared that the legal impediments to farmers are essentially a plot by the "leading stratum" against the development of farmers.[30]

Interest Groups and Reform in the Initial Post-Soviet Years

During the first three years of independence, Ukrainian leaders stubbornly avoided many basic and essential economic reforms. The consequences—hyperinflation, a dramatic drop in output and GDP, declining living standards, growing social alienation—were evident for all to see. Interest associations arguably contributed to this stagnation, as conservative groups found favor with the government while pro-reform organizations were largely shut out of the policy making process.

Among the sectors we have surveyed, labor found itself in the worst position. Despite the fact that unions dwarfed all other organizations both in membership and in potential political power (through voting or through strikes), labor remained a weak political force. How do we know this? Simply, in the words of one Ukrainian observer, "If labor unions were really strong, then [because of their sheer size] there would be no need to talk of any other political forces at all."[31]

According to all union leaders, their most important task is to conclude collective agreements with the government, and the leading forum that formally ensures their participation in policy making and implementation is the National Committee of Social Partnership, a tripartite body that was inspired by the social corporatist model. In 1993, the first General Agreement was concluded between the unions, both the FPU and the "independents," and the government, and the Committee of Social Partnership was charged with overseeing implementation and coming up with new economic reform proposals.

How effective were these institutions? If one listened to Stoian of the FPU, one might believe that the FPU had managed to achieve numerous improvements in economic and social policy.[32] Such claims ring hollow, however, when juxtaposed with real conditions for workers and the actual implementation of the agreements. The government repeatedly broke its agreements to consult with unions on the questions of price increases and wage indexations, wages were not paid on time, and the government also began to curtail unions' rights over safety inspections and operation of enterprises. The FPU itself was forced to admit that the government had "practically liquidated the agreed regulation of social-labor relations" and established a government monopoly over wage policy.[33] FPU protests were in vain, "sneezed at" by government officials according to one report.[34]

The National Committee on Social Partnership also failed to live up to expectations. Many union officials complained of lack of goodwill on the government's side, whereas government officials claimed that unions failed to understand what social partnership really meant.[35] A major problem was that the employers' side was poorly developed, since the state continued to own 95 percent of the property. Even the committee's chairman, Anatolii Rybak, conceded that in its first two years of existence the body had yet to produce a really concrete act that had clearly contributed to the reform process.

Despite these problems, the FPU unions have remained, in general, quite passive, unwilling to provoke a direct confrontation with political authorities. Part of the problem can be attributed to the general passivity of the workers, their lack of confidence in the FPU itself, and their fear that labor activism will bring about nothing but a pink slip. But the problem lies deeper, as the FPU itself is essentially part of the system. Many of its unions backed Communist or Socialist Party candidates in the 1994 elections, and Stoian, also an MP, allied himself in a bloc dominated by government officials, former communists, and other remnants of the Party of Power. FPU passivity is also explained by its dependence upon the government, particularly with respect to social insurance funds. Thus far, these remain under control of the FPU, which gives them an advantage in maintaining membership. If they were to lose this (and there have been rumblings that they should), it would be a significant blow. Thus, the FPU has every reason to stay on their "best behavior."

The independent unions, more so than the FPU, have been more willing to act in other forums that are independent of state or government control. They have occasionally resorted to strikes, but by 1994 the support for these measures (as well as strike funds) had largely dried up. Coordinated activity between the NPGU and Lanovy to push for reform led nowhere. In addition to all of their other problems, the independent unions found themselves in a real dilemma. Because they were by orientation in favor of greater economic liberalization, their dilemma consisted of the fact that liberalization could also easily hurt their members by bringing about unemployment. This was especially true among the miners, who work in mines that simply are not economically viable. As a consequence, the independent unions have found it easier to eschew direct political demands and focus on more concrete concerns like wages and pensions. The irony is that the concessions the unions do win on bread-and-butter issues come from the coal industry restructuring fund, meaning that today's "victories" make tomorrow's reform even more difficult.[36]

Ultimately, labor has been politically marginalized. The corporatist structures and social insurance funds give them something so they do not bark so loud, and it is clear that the FPU has been co-opted. Ivan Zinnyk of the FPU Union of Aviation Workers conceded that conditions are very difficult, but "trade unions are in no position to do anything about it." A rival from the independent pilots' union basically agreed, noting that the most fundamental questions of economic and social reform have been taken out of the hands of the unions and placed in those of government ministries "whose interests lie against those of workers."[37]

In contrast, the USPP, the leading industrial-entrepreneurial organization in Ukraine, has been much more of a political player. As mentioned, the USPP was the primary backer of Kuchma's presidential candidacy, several of its leaders found positions in government, and throughout the Kravchuk years its members successfully lobbied the government for more credits for industry, contributing to hyperinflation. Several observers accused the Ukrainian government of being held hostage to the directors, and Kuchma in particular was singled out for serving the directors' interests and abandoning reform during his tenure as prime minister from 1992 to 1993.[38] Although much of the USPP's influence can be attributed to direct, personal connections to the political elite, the USPP was also given a favored institutional role. Kuchma placed many USPP officials on the government's Commission on Entrepreneurship, which was disbanded in 1993 after Kuchma resigned as prime minister. USPP leaders also composed the majority of the employers on the Social Partnership Committee, although no USPP representative with whom I spoke attributed much importance to this body.

Other groups have also tried to find patronage from above. The most successful, next to the USPP, was Babych's VOP, which was supported by Kravchuk and given a limited role in submitting economic proposals to the government. However, it would perhaps be more accurate to view these connections not so much as a means to direct national economic policy but a way to obtain financial favors in return for political support. This sort of mutual back-scratching, familiar to those who study the political economy of post-Soviet states, should not be surprising. Jadwiga Staniszkis dubbed it "political capitalism," a process in which yesterday's elite use their control over economic resources to influence politics and thereby use political power to cement their economic position during the process of economic "reform."[39] The result is the emergence of a new oligarchy, one whose primary roots can be found in the bureaucratic networks of the Soviet period.

This does not mean, of course, that every director has had his way. The USPP or the directors' corps are not homogeneous organizations, and some began to feel that the government was not serving its own interests. This was either because sufficient credits were not forthcoming or because the government dragged its feet on adopting real reforms that would help those well positioned take advantage of market liberalization; hence the support for Kuchma against Kravchuk in 1994 from the USPP. The consensus was that Kuchma would better protect the directors' interests, although these "interests" were often vaguely defined or cast in a pro-reform light. Skeptics, however, suggested that Kuchma, once in office, would abandon the rhetoric of reform and return to his old ways and reward the state industrial sector for its support.[40] As we shall see, things did not turn out quite that way, although it is undeniable that the state directors continue to exercise a very significant political role.

In the agricultural sector, prototypical, institutionalized corporatist structures of participation are lacking. There is no state commission that brings together various organizations to discuss or develop policy. The one exception might be the State Fund to Support Farmers, created by the cabinet of ministers in July 1991. This body brings together representatives of the AFU and the ministry. However, according to its chair, Yurii Bebekh, it works poorly because the state grants farmers only a small fraction of what they really need.

Rather than exercising its power through formalized networks, the major agricultural group, the *Kolkhoz* Council, relies on lobbying and personal contacts. As mentioned, the council's head has virtually unfettered access to the ministry and is regularly consulted on policy matters. Directors of collective farms also have the resources and access to make their voices heard by the ministry. Bebekh claimed that the council *as an organization* had little influence, but he conceded that elements within the council were far more powerful than organizations such as the AFU. For example, in 1994 when the AFU pressed the government to make changes in the law on farming, a special commission was appointed to draft amendments. Not surprisingly, no farmer or representative of the AFU was included. The commission was composed exclusively of officials from the ministry and their council allies. After AFU officials badgered the commission to hear their proposals, they were banned from the proceedings. Consequently, the adopted changes in the law were viewed by the AFU as worse than the original law.

The *Kolkhoz* Council also has extensive power through its close relations with the Peasant Party. In fact, the two organizations are so tightly interwoven that it is impossible to say where one ends and the other begins. The Peasant Party is dominated by the directors of collective farms and until 1995 was wholeheartedly against expanding the private agricultural sector. This party has had tremendous success in rural areas, and many attributed this to the machine tactics of the collective farm directors. In the Verkhovna Rada, its faction has been *the* voice on agricultural issues, and it has managed to reject, delay, or water down various reform proposals. The AFU has no equivalent ties to any single party, and no faction was able to convince the rather conservative parliament to adopt genuine land reform.

Another important means of influence that the *Kolkhoz* Council has at its disposal is its de facto control over the implementation of Ukraine's land policy. As mentioned, local councils are charged with implementation of the law on farmers, and the result is that these bodies, dominated by collective farm representatives, have been hostile to those who endorse genuine land reform. One report in the official press outlined the abuse of power by these local officials, who act without regard to the law and encourage anti-farmer propaganda. One locally organized farmer support group lodged repeated protests, but it was told that "Sliuzalek [the group's name] exists only in Kyiv, not in the village."[41] This responsibility for implementation is not per se corporatist, because the responsible body is the local government, not the organization. However, because *kolkhoz* directors dominate these bodies and thus wear two hats, they are in fact enlisted as the agents of implementation. Again, this is "corporatist in content, if not in form," meaning that land policies, as carried out, help ensure the continued domination of the ministry's implicit ally, the *Kolkhoz* Council.

In addition to blocking privatization, the collective farm directors have adopted a number of "reforms" to correspond to their interests. For example, collective farms have not only received the overwhelming majority of agricultural credits but have also been granted privileges in regard to export of products and imports of machinery. These policies are unlikely to stimulate structural reform and reinvestment, but instead will line the pockets of the *kolkhoz* directors and perpetuate the current inefficient system by shielding them from competition at home or abroad. The *kolkhozy* were also granted special privileges on the foreign exchange (they are exempt from having to exchange 50 percent of hard currency earnings at deflated rates), thereby violating the law on property, which declares all forms of property, legally equal.

Land reform in Ukraine is a vital issue affecting the whole of society. Serious reform, however, was not on the immediate post-Soviet agenda, as the *kolkhoz* directors remained firmly entrenched in Ukrainian politics. Until their dominance is somehow broken—which will not be an easy task—prospects for agricultural reform look very bleak.

By and large, many aspects of the initial post-Soviet system corresponded to the corporatist model: groups tied to or co-opted by the state had near monopoly control over interest representation. The overall effect is clear: a focus on stability and maintenance of the status quo, what one writer called a "bad peace."[42] The old structures were essentially preserved, and new actors found their path to political influence blocked. Fundamental change of the underlying socioeconomic system was therefore not forthcoming.

Developments under Kuchma

The election of Leonid Kuchma in July 1994 as the second president of Ukraine must be considered a watershed event. Kuchma bucked the predictions that he would cozy up to Russia and be the plaything of the "red directors." Instead, under his leadership Ukraine has embarked upon a long-delayed program of economic reform, which included budget austerity, tax reform, market liberalization and gradual privatization, backed by IMF financial assistance. Inflation, raging at 10,000 percent in 1993, has been brought down to double digits, the budget deficit has been reduced, the *hryvna* was finally introduced, and real wages have gone up. True, production continued to decline until 1997, living standards could hardly be called good, and corruption is still rampant, but clearly there has been some progress under Kuchma.

How have these reforms been influenced by and affected interest associations? Let's start with the business/industrial sector, which was candidate Kuchma's primary constituency. As mentioned, the conventional wisdom was that Kuchma would serve the interests of the industrial lobby and not undertake radical economic reform. While it would be an exaggeration to say that Kuchma has completely abandoned the directors, he nonetheless has managed to push through some economic reforms. How was this possible? The answer is that splits emerged within the USPP itself, and these splits were reflected in the parliament, as groups more amenable to reform formed a "Center" faction and provided Kuchma with crucial support in his battles with more conservative forces in the legislature. This pro-reform group within the USPP emerged from the directors' corps but gradually became convinced that there would be more money (and power) under a market-oriented system, since they could use their positions to acquire economic assets.[43] This group, many of whose members are now private "owners," are no longer dependent upon state subsidies, and they are interested in freer markets and stable currencies that will facilitate economic growth.

While divisions may have weakened the power of the USPP as an organization, one could also say that "clientelistic" networks and clandestine intrigues have become more important in Ukrainian politics. These, of course, are centered on the state directors-turned-capitalists. Lanovyi, for example, resigned as head of the "Reform" faction in parliament, claiming that his largely academic group was powerless compared to the parties backed by industrialists. By 1996, one saw, as in the case of Russia, the rise of "clan politics," as regionally based groups of industrialists vied with each other for political power. The largest of these clans were from Dnipropetrovs'k and Donets'k, the former headed by former Prime Minister Pavlo Lazarenko and implicitly backed by Kuchma, himself from Dnipropetrovs'k. Lazarenko, enjoying Kuchma's patronage, used his position to enrich himself and his cronies (especially through government contracts in the energy sector), until he began to challenge Kuchma's authority and was sacked in July 1997. Kuchma blamed him for the rise of a "criminal elite," and Lazarenko, commonly thought to be the former richest man in Ukraine, formed an opposition political party, *Hromada,* which campaigned against Kuchma's policies in the March 1998 parliamentary elections.

In addition, it is worth noting that the more conservative elements in the USPP still have substantial political weight. For example, in autumn 1995 their grumblings led to the re-emergence of the "old" Kuchma, who claimed that the government would have to change its course and pay more attention to the state sector. Throughout Kuchma's presidency, reform has moved in fits and starts, as he has had to rely on the political support of "centrists" whose commitment to reform may be more opportunistic than principled.[44] By the end of 1997, the momentum for reform slowed as Kuchma's presidency was adrift amid increasing graft, political indecision, plummeting public confidence in the president and the government, and renewed challenges from a leftist-dominated parliament.

Less has changed in state-labor relations. Work conditions have not dramatically improved, wage arrears totaled some $2.5 billion by the end of 1997, and unions remain as marginalized as ever. There are periodic strikes to demand back pay, especially among the coal miners, but this has not been transformed into a real challenge to the government or assumed a real political character. The FPU itself remains tentative as a political actor, fearing that reprisals by the government might threaten its control over some social benefits and undermine its near-monopoly status among Ukrainian unions. There have been further splits within the FPU among branch and regional unions, but it remains secure in its position. One article in the independent unions' newspaper, conceded that despite predictions by some that the FPU would collapse, it has actually expanded and gained strength, while the independent union movement is far less active and powerful than it once was.[45] During the March 1998 parliamentary elections the FPU created an All-Ukrainian Party of Workers.

The independent unions suffer not only from internal squabbles, worker apathy, and difficulties in articulating a pro-reform, pro-worker policy, but also from continued government assaults on their rights. In 1996, for example, government officials used provisions in the law on strikes to declare the Donets'k Workers' Committee and strikes organized by the NPGU illegal. The primary demand of the striking miners was that they be paid their wages, which in some cases had not been paid in months. Nonetheless, many in Kyiv saw the strike as a political campaign by the "Donets'k Clan" against the government. Strike leaders were arrested and Mykola Krylov of the NPGU accused the government of an orchestrated clampdown on the independent union movement, and even charged Lazarenko with purposely withholding wages to provoke the miners into striking. Others might question whether the unions were the real target or were the pawns in Kyiv's battle with Donets'k governor Volodymyr Shcherban, an opponent to Lazarenko and Kuchma. In any event, these events testify to the government's continued lack of tolerance of workers' movements.

In the agricultural sector, there has been very little reform. Proposals to implement outright privatization of land have been repeatedly defeated, despite the backing of President Kuchma. In November 1994 Kuchma issued a decree for the immediate privatization of land and ordered the parliament to update legislation on private property rights, including the right to sell and inherit land. Cooperation from the legislature was not forthcoming, and a year later it voted overwhelmingly (245 to 13) against a proposal for land privatization. At the same time, however, parliament approved a plan to hand over, for nothing, over 4,000 agro-businesses to the directors of collective farms, which is both economically and politically an incredible proposition. Kuchma was able to use his powers to overrule parliament, but dogged opposition to privatization of land remains.

Members of the *Kolkhoz* Council, the Agrarian Union, and the ministry do foresee some sort of eventual reform, but it is obviously not akin to that proposed by the AFU. The main idea thus far is to turn the state and collective farms into a "joint stock company" that would be owned by the collective.[46] This strategy would prevent any sort of breakup of the collective farms and would be more cosmetic than real, basically changing little on the farms themselves. The farm would still be "owned" by the collective, and the current bosses would be likely to remain in place. This sort of strategy, one report concluded, is little more than an attempt to serve a very narrow interest of the existing powers-that-be and does not uphold the wider interest of the countryside.[47] In essence, this sort of model would not address the fundamental issue of private property and would be a legalistic maneuver sideways instead of a step forward.

However, the position of the conservative interests was weakened as the Peasant Party split into two factions in early 1995. In some ways, this mirrored the informal split in the USPP, although the split within the Peasant Party was primarily along regional lines and on questions of Ukraine's relationship with Russia.[48] The Agrarians for Reforms, composed of 25 members of parliament, however, were in general support of Kuchma's policies and claimed they were in favor of all forms of property. Like USPP "reformers," one might wonder whether this group's commitment to reforms is one of principle or one of seeing that some liberalization might line their pockets. In November 1996, they formed their own Agrarian Party with the support of Kuchma and then-Prime Minister Lazarenko, and have been loyal supporters of Kuchma in parliament. The Agrarian Party has been dubbed the "rural Party of Power." However, agricultural reform remained stalled.

The 1998 Elections and Beyond

By the time of the March 1998 parliamentary elections, the cracks in the corporatist edifice were becoming clearer. "Business" interests were represented by a variety of parties, and many businesspeople ran as independents in single-member districts. The top five on the party list of the Peoples' Democratic Party in the March 1998 elections, which enjoyed close ties to the Kuchma administration, was led by current Prime Minister Valery Pustovoytenko (another Kuchma crony from the "Dnipropetrovs'k clan") and USPP President Anatolii Kinakh. The Labor/Liberal Bloc (Together), centered in Donets'k, was a pro-reform business party with links to groups within the USPP. Lazarenko heads the Hromada party, and others from the energy sector "hid," ironically enough, in the Green Party. Each of these groups endorses some reforms, although their positions are not as pro-market as that of former Deputy Economics Minister Viktor Pynzenyk's Reform and Order Party (dubbed the "dissident party of power"). Their main differences are based on region and personality, and their battle can best be considered an intra-*nomenklatura* struggle. "New" business interests generally eschewed participating in these blocs, allying instead with the center-right *Rukh* or Pynzenyk. The rural lobby was split into pro- and anti-reform groups, the latter allied with the Socialists. The FPU hastily organized an All-Ukrainian Workers' Party, which is sympathetic to the leftist parties, and some FPU leaders ran on the Communist or Socialist ticket, although they did not rank as prominent figures in these parties. On the whole, one saw, more so than in 1994, that business interests are the dominant force behind the various Ukrainian political parties.

The elections did little to clarify the Ukrainian political landscape. As expected, the leftists did well, winning 37 percent of the proportional representation vote and garnering about 40 percent of the total seats in parliament. Independents won 114 of the 225 single-member district seats, and five center or center-right parties cleared the four percent proportional representation hurdle—*Rukh*, the Greens, the People's Democratic Party, Hromada, and Kravchuk's and former Prime Minister Evhen Marchuk's United Social Democrats. The Workers' Party and the pro-reform Agrarians received no seats from party-list voting. Since the leftists lack a majority in this new parliament, another amorphous centrist bloc will likely be the crucial actor, meaning that the continuation of reform may depend, as it did from 1994 to 1998, upon how much Kuchma can offer the various business factions in parliament.

What can we say at last for interest associations? If current trends hold, it appears that aspects of Ukrainian corporatism, especially those affecting the business sector, will give way to clientelism, as business interests will be represented and served through personal contacts with members of parliament or the government. Unions, on the other hand, show little sign of gaining strength, and are likely to be disregarded as a "social partner" by the government, despite occasional rhetoric to the contrary. Radical reforms in agriculture are unlikely, although collective farm directors may be able to use their position to shape both policies and their implementation to suit their own advantage. In effect, Ukrainian politics shows every sign of still being run by a bureaucratic-oligarchical stratum, one that is ostensibly "pro-reform" but not substantially different than the Soviet-era *nomenklatura*. This group still has the political wherewithal to protect its narrow interests, to the detriment of both democracy and economic reform in Ukraine.

Notes

1. Arkady Misuno, "Pro kontseptsiiu natsional'no-demokratychnoyi ideologii dlia suverennoiyi Ukrayiny, yak peredmovu derzhavotvorchoho protsesu," *Ukrayins'kyi Chas*, vol. 1, no. 11 (Fall 1993), pp. 27–29.
2. *Vysoky Zamok*, December 8, 1992.
3. See Mykola Ryabchuk, "Authoritarianism with a Human Face?" *Eastern European Reporter*, vol. 5, no. 6 (November-December 1992), pp. 52–56, and "Between Civil Society and the New Etatism: Democracy in the Making and State Building in Ukraine," in Michael D. Kennedy (ed.), *Envisioning Eastern Europe: Postcommunist Cultural Studies* (Ann Arbor: University of Michigan Press, 1994), pp. 125–148. See also my "Dynamics of Contemporary Ukrainian Nationalism: Empire-Breaking to State Building," *Canadian Review of Studies in Nationalism*, vol. 23, nos. 1–2 (1996), pp. 39–50.
4. David Ost, "The Politics of Interest in Post-Communist Europe," *Theory and Society*, vol. 22, no. 4 (August 1993), pp. 453–485.
5. The classic discussion distinguishing between the two can be found in Philippe Schmitter, "Still the Century of Corporatism?" *Review of Politics*, vol. 36, no. 1 (January 1974), pp. 85–131.
6. For an elaboration of corporatism as a system of policymaking, see Philippe Schmitter and Gerhard Lehmbruch (eds.), *Patterns of Corporatist Policymaking* (Beverly Hills: Sage, 1982).
7. The most useful source on this remains op cit., P. Schmitter, 1974.
8. For examples, see Laszlo Bruszt, "Transformative Politics: Social Costs and Social Peace in East Central Europe," *East European Politics and Societies*, vol. 6, no. 1 (Winter 1992), pp. 55–72, and Peter Rutland, "Thathcerism, Czechstyle: Transition to Capitalism in the Czech Republic," *Telos*, no. 94 (Winter 1992–1993), pp. 103–129.
9. Yurii Pokal'chuk, "Real'nist' zahrozy: 'Latinoamerykanizatsiia; Ukraïny," *Universum*, no. 1 (December 1993), pp. 10–11.
10. Vasyl' Tkachenko, "Dovhy shliakh do hromadians'koho suspil'stva," *Politychna Dumka*, no. 2 (1994), p. 21.
11. Volodymyr Cheriak, "Svitovy dosvid pidkazue," *Uriadovyi Kur'er*, March 26, 1994.
12. Yurii Buzduhan, Chairman of Parliamentary Committee on Social and Labour Policy, interview in *Mist*, July 4, 1994.
13. Valentin Pozhydaev, First Deputy FPU Chairman, in *Profspilkova hazeta*, May 25, 1994.
14. Interview with Volodymyr T'otkin, Head of FPU Membership and Branch Relations Department, June 1994, Kyiv. Unless otherwise noted, all quoted sources are from interviews conducted by the author in Kyiv, June-August 1994.
15. Interview with Semen Karikov of the Independent Railroad Machinists' Union, Kyiv, July 1994.

16. *Mist,* July 11, 1994.
17. In July 1993, after a wave of labor unrest, 2.7 percent of respondents in one survey said they completely trusted unions, 40.7 percent claimed absolutely no trust. By December 1993, the figures were 11.3 percent and 47.6 percent, respectively. See *Ukrayins'ky Ohliadach* no. 2 (February 1994). While this survey was not exclusively of FPU members, given the scope of FPU membership, it is fair to say that a plurality of union members do not trust trade unions.
18. *Profspilkova hazeta,* May 11, 1994.
19. *Post-Postup,* May 4–10, 1993.
20. Interview with Anatolii Shirokov, Kyiv, June 1994.
21. As one might expect, there is no documentation for these allegations other than reports in the independent unions' newspaper, *Mist/Most.* Incidents were also reported in all conversations I had with representatives of 13 independent trade unions.
22. *Mist,* June 12–18, 1995.
23. "I Kongres VPU pochatok chy kinets?" *Profspilkovi vidomosti,* no. 3 (August-September 1995), pp. 19–25.
24. Tamara Svirus, interview, Kyiv, July 1994.
25. *Post-Postup,* January 30 December 1993–5, 1994.
26. Valery Yuzba, interview, Kyiv, July 1994.
27. This, I was told by Arnold Romanenko of the Union of Cooperatives, was why Babych of VOP was in the USPP structure, because without the USPP he was a "nobody."
28. When I asked Mozgovoi about his organization's achievements, I was shown an impressive chart with the names of various subsidiaries they had formed. When pressed about what these organizations had done, his answer was evasive, qualified with the disclaimer, "Well, first you must understand our difficult situation . . ."
29. *Holos Ukrayiny,* August 5, 1993.
30. *Liberal'naia gazeta,* January 27-February 4, 1994.
31. Maria Chorna, "Try trampoliny," *Post-Postup,* February 2–8, 1994.
32. Oleksandr Stoian in *Profspilkova hazeta,* July 6, 1994.
33. *Profspilkova hazeta,* June 15, 1994.
34. *Demokratychna Ukrayina,* January 15, 1994.
35. For more on this body, see Paul Kubicek, "Variations on a Corporatist Theme: Interest Associations in Ukraine and Russia," *Europe-Asia Studies* vol. 48, no. 1 (January 1996), pp. 27–46.
36. *Mist,* April 24–30, 1995.
37. Valentin Pvachev in *Mist,* May 16, 1994.
38. For example, see Taras Stets'kiv, "Try tsviakhy v domovynu ukraïns'koï nezalezhnosti," *Post-Postup,* August 25, 1993.
39. Jadwiga Staniszkis, *The Dynamics of Breakthrough* (Berkeley: University of California Press, 1991).

66

40. *Post-Postup*, August 11–18, 1994.
41. *Holos Ukrayiny*, December 9, 1993.
42. Evhen Holovakha, "Suchasna politychna sytuatsiia i perspektyva derzhavno-politychnoho ta ekonomichnoho rozvytku Ukrayiny," *Politychnyi Portret Ukrayiny*, no. 4 (December 1993), p. 5.
43. Chrystyna Lapychak, "Back on Track," *Transition*, vol. 1, no. 3 (March 15, 1995), pp. 44–45.
44. One Western diplomat called them "opportunist scum." See *The Economist*, March 28, 1998.
45. *Mist*, June 12–18, 1995.
46. Pavlo Haiduis'kyi, "Ne shukaiemo osoblyvoho shliakhu," *Polityka i chas*, vol. 3, no. 7 (July 1995), pp. 25–29.
47. *UNIAN-Biznes*, May 10–16, 1994, pp. 5–6.
48. Andrew Wilson, "The Ukrainian Left: In Transition to Social Democracy or Still in Thrall to the USSR," *Europe-Asia Studies*, vol. 49, no. 7 (November 1997), pp. 1309–1310.

CHAPTER FOUR

The Impact of Domestic Divisions on Ukrainian Foreign Policy: Ukraine as a "Weak State"

Paul D'Anieri

Since becoming independent in 1991, Ukraine has been severely constrained by its economic dependence on Russia. In Russia's use of energy supplies to coerce Ukraine, in coping with decreased trade with Russia, and in managing affairs with the Commonwealth of Independent States (CIS), Ukrainian leaders have come to recognize that economic security is the primary problem facing the country.[1] In that sense domestic policy has become Ukraine's most significant foreign policy. Yet Ukraine has adopted no coherent strategy to deal with the problem and has done little to rectify the underlying domestic economic problems that exacerbate its vulnerability to Russia.[2]

It would seem that given a clear notion of the problem facing it, Ukraine's leadership would adopt a coherent policy for economic security. The question that motivates this chapter is: why has Ukraine been unable to devise (let alone implement) a strategy to deal with such a "clear and present danger" to its interests. In answering this question, I seek to assess the impact of the institutional problems analyzed in this book on the making of foreign policy.

Two important parts of the answer focus on the difficult international situation in which Ukraine finds itself, and in the societal (ethnic, linguistic, and regional) divisions in Ukrainian society. International relations theory tells us that states with relatively little power have less latitude for action than do others. For Ukraine, constraints emanating from its position vis-à-vis Russia mean that many potential options are simply unavailable. Equally relevant, the ethnic, regional, and political divisions in Ukraine help account for the inability to reach consensus. Survey research indicates, for example, that the question of relations with Russia is the major disagreement underlying regional differences in Ukraine.[3]

However, these explanations, while undoubtedly valid, leave some questions unanswered. First, the international structure argument explains why Ukraine has a narrow range of options but not why it has been unable to choose among them. Thus Simon Johnson and Oleg Ustenko contend that the blame for Ukraine's dismal economic performance lies primarily with "a lack of a government strategy of economic adjustment" rather than with external pressures.[4] Second, the domestic society argument assumes that leaders are unable to bridge domestic gaps. Because in many states leaders are able to build coherent foreign policies in divided societies, we must look further to understand why Ukraine has failed to do so.

This chapter examines the impact of Ukraine's institutional fragmentation on the country's foreign policy. To understand fully Ukraine's passivity in its relations with Russia, it is necessary to consider the structure of the Ukrainian state and state-society relations in Ukraine. The primary argument is that institutions of the Ukrainian state make it nearly impossible to adopt and implement a coherent policy, even within the narrow range of choices left by international and societal constraints. Ukrainian society is divided, and its institutions do little to resolve those divisions. Indeed, the government may be even more divided than the society. It follows that it is extremely difficult for such a divided government to implement the domestic measures that would support an active foreign policy. In short, Ukraine has a "weak state," where weak describes not the power of the state relative to other states but the ability of the government to adopt a policy and implement it in the society.[5]

This chapter describes Ukraine's institutional divisions, showing how they have eroded Ukraine's ability to cope with its economic vulnerability, and proceeds in four stages. First, a brief overview of the literature on state strength demonstrates how this concept has been used elsewhere and how it applies to contemporary Ukraine. Second, a review of the formation of the Ukrainian state in 1991 traces Ukraine's current institutional problems to the legacy of Soviet institutions and to the chaos surrounding Ukrainian independence. Third, an examination of Ukraine's electoral law and of the division of powers highlights the institutional barriers to foreign-policy consensus. Finally, institutional stalemate is linked to the problems of nuclear disarmament and energy dependence in order to show how the weakness of Ukraine's state affects its foreign policy.

Small States and Weak States

A considerable body of research in comparative politics and comparative foreign policy addresses the question of state strength.[6] While defined differently by different scholars, the concept refers to strength of the state relative to its society and may be defined both in terms of the state's ability to remain impervious to pressure from society and in terms of its ability to enact its programs within society. The United States, the most powerful country in the world, is regarded as a "weak state" in this literature, because the government is institutionally divided, is highly penetrated by interest groups, and has relatively few institutional mechanisms to micro-manage society. In contrast, France is the quintessential "strong state," because it has a more unified state structure and considerable formal control over a wide range of issues that are beyond the reach of other states.

"Small" states, in contrast, are those that are comparatively weak vis-à-vis other states. The terminology can be a bit confusing, but the point is to be able to address two separate but related concepts: the capabilities of a state relative to other states versus the capability of the state vis-à-vis its own society. For the study of foreign policy, the connection is important: some states may have enormous capabilities relative to other states but be unable to use them due to domestic opposition or stalemate. Others may have relatively little power internationally but be successful in the international realm because they are able to choose policies, implement them, and change them as circumstances require.

In particular, the concept of state strength has been used to explain why some states deal more successfully with interdependence than do others. While strategies for avoiding economic vulnerability are relatively clear, states vary in their abilities to implement different strategies. Stephen Krasner and Peter Katzenstein, among others, attribute states' different abilities to cope with interdependence to different state structures and state-society relations. Various studies of the small states of Western Europe explain those states' ability to be economically dependent but still politically autonomous in terms of their ability to adjust decisively to new conditions in the international political economy. In a sense, they survive along with larger actors because their agility offsets their small size.[7] The same question can be asked about the post-Soviet states: how do the strength of the state and the nature of its institutions enable or impede the development and implementation of a successful strategy for reducing economic vulnerability?

Ukraine, while not "small" in any conventional sense is indeed "small" compared to its primary trade partner, Russia, and compared to the western states (Germany and the United States) that it hopes to engage. Unlike the small states of Western Europe, Ukraine is entirely lacking in agility, due to two related factors, its institutional make up and the state's inability to create change against societal inertia. This explains why throughout the period of its independence, Ukraine has responded to the challenges Russia has presented it primarily in international arenas rather than domestically. Ironically, Ukraine has been much more successful in dealing with other governments than in handling its own internal problems. Increasingly, however, those internal problems will constrain Ukraine from effectiveness in the international arena, as Sherman Garnett's chapter in this volume indicates. As a Ukrainian scholar complains, "Ineffective socio-economic policy and the *nomenklatura*-tinged patriotism of the ruling elite made the country so weak that it has to make new and dangerous concessions in its bilateral relations with Moscow, bringing it closer to the Belarus status of a model younger brother."[8]

Katzenstein has shown that the small states of Western Europe have succeeded in large part because of corporatist arrangements that enable the state and elite representatives of key interests to hammer out agreed-upon measures to deal with economic shocks from abroad. These arrangements, he argues, rely on "strong oligarchic tendencies. Political power is concentrated in the hands of few decision-makers and rests with strong parties or strong interest groups."[9] This chapter suggests that contrary to these needs, Ukraine has no concentration of power and weak political parties (and few organized interest groups).[10] Recent reforms have significantly increased the power of the president, but it remains to be seen whether these changes will make the Ukrainian state more effective—because the conditions for presidential-parliamentary cooperation are still absent.

Origins of the Modern Ukrainian State: 1991

Borrowing from the literature of historical institutionalism, this section shows briefly how the origins of the Ukrainian state affect its current form and capacities. Ukraine had been gradually establishing greater autonomy from Moscow during the Gorbachev years, but the August 1991 coup and the collapse of the Soviet system were completely unexpected. The opportunity to break away from the Soviet Union was seized, but there had been little preparation for establishing a Ukrainian state. "That Ukrainian independence came so abruptly and so unexpectedly has enormous consequences for the future of the country. Virtually no one in or out of the government was prepared for independence or its aftermath."[11] The Ukrainian state was created almost spontaneously in a rush of pronouncements in the late summer and fall of 1991.

Consequently, the government consists of a mix of institutions that were held over from the communist era because there was no time to create new ones (such as the Verkhovna Rada), and institutions that had to be devised in great haste (such as the presidency and cabinet system) without sufficient consideration of how they might work. Most fundamentally, there was no time to write and debate a new constitution before independence, so the new state was launched with a heavily modified version of the Soviet constitution, which created problems throughout the political system. It is not yet clear how well the 1996 Constitution will remedy the defects of the old one.

It is particularly important that the events of 1991 are not viewed as a revolution that overthrew the existing elite. Elster and his colleagues contend that this non-revolutionary change is one of the most important characteristics of the collapse of communism in East Central Europe.[12] Politically, the establishment of independent Ukraine papered over a fundamental conflict of interest between the opposition nationalists and the government that existed in Ukraine at the time of the coup. Throughout history, Ukraine had been dominated from outside because it had been divided internally. So when the nationalists sought independence, they made a deal with the *nomenklatura* in Kyiv: If the government broke with the Soviet Union, the nationalists would not attempt to remove the government from power in its drive for independence. Hence the *nomenklatura* obtained its primary goal, remaining in power, and the nationalists achieved their goal, an independent Ukraine.[13] Thus the *nomenklatura* "managed to preserve real power and property quite easily after 1991 by means of a peculiar political deal—by recruiting to its ranks the most conformist leaders of the former counter-elite and by a timely change in its slogans for the sake of a new 'legitimacy.'"[14]

The consequences of this deal were significant. "Kravchuk's victory . . . in essence signified the retention of the dominant societal position of the *nomenklatura*."[15] By agreeing to let the communist-era government retain power under a new label, the opposition made political and economic change in the country extremely difficult. None of the people in government had an interest in the rapid changes that political and economic reformers sought. And if the reformers thought the old guard would gradually be swept from power, they were mistaken.

The old *nomenklatura* became known as "the party of power," because its members were in power and saw their primary interest as staying in power. The Communist Party of Ukraine had been at least as rigid and conservative as Russia's (some say that Ukrainian communists sought independence so that Boris Yelsin would not force reform upon them). And this group of people was responsible, along with a handful of transplants from the nationalist and reformist camps, for governing the new Ukraine. While the new institutions were devised spontaneously, there was a powerful built-in opposition to change. A temporary solution has become to some extent permanent.

Ukraine's Electoral Law and Nascent Political Parties

For a variety of historical, political, and institutional reasons, organized political parties have played only a minor role in post-independence Ukrainian politics, though that role seems to be increasing under the new election law. The main result has been the absence of a majority party in parliament, a group of deputies able to put forward a coherent program and defend it before the opposition. It is impossible for the parliament to adopt a policy, which as a result of being passed by a majority, commands legitimacy in the government and in society. As much as Americans may lament their political parties, they play an essential role in structuring the political debate in a country and allowing legislation to be formed in a coherent manner. In Ukraine, Alexander Motyl asserts, "the absence of an institutionalized party system means that . . . effective parliamentary rule is virtually impossible."[16] Equally significant, Ukraine's presidential-parliamentary system means that even a parliamentary majority might not be enough for decisive policy if the policy were opposed by the president and/or the prime minister.

There are two primary reasons for the absence of powerful parties in Ukraine, one historical and one institutional. On the historical side, the connection of political parties in general with the Communist Party of the Soviet Union in particular has made many leery of party politics.[17] Because they attained their political freedom only recently, most Ukrainians put a low value on party loyalty. Party affiliation therefore does not guarantee votes. Moreover, party leaders who fall out over political issues have tended to divide and create new parties rather than compromise for the sake of unity. Party discipline, an important component of strong parties, seems to be equated in many Ukrainians' minds with "democratic centralism," the principle by which communists were expected to toe the party line. Thus in the 1994 parliamentary elections, many prominent reformists in the west ran under the banner of the political movement *Nova Khvilya* (New Wave). This movement was not a party, its candidates emphasized, because it had no platform or set of principles to which candidates had to subscribe. While this prevented the candidates from having to compromise their positions, it also meant that voters did not know what the banner stood for and that the candidates were essentially independents.

The tendency of parties to fragment had its biggest effect on the national-democratic movement, *Rukh*, which was the primary organization promoting Ukrainian independence and reform. With the ban on the Communist Party following independence, it appeared that *Rukh* would become a dominant force in the country, but it rapidly disintegrated. The nationalists were unable to decide whether to continue in opposition or to support the government, as well as whether to focus on nation-building or economic reform.[18] Those who wished to remain in opposition, led by the late *Rukh* leader V'iacheslav Chornovil, sought to keep the government of *apparatchiks* honest and promote reform. Others argued that the nationalists should support Ukraine's government even if they disagreed with it.[19] In addition, they believed that by providing Kravchuk with support in the West, they could wean him away from his reliance on the "party of power." In mid-1992 *Rukh* split, as Mykhailo Horyn, Ivan Drach, and Larysa Skoryk, all prominent nationalists, left *Rukh* to form the Congress of National Democratic Forces.[20]

Ukraine's two presidential elections have emphasized the lack of importance of political parties. In the first, in December 1991, Kravchuk, who had recently abandoned the communist party and ran as an independent, easily defeated Chornovil, who was at that time the leader of Ukraine's largest quasi-party, *Rukh*. In 1994, none of the major contenders ran with political party backing. The closest thing to a party any candidate had was Kuchma's Interregional Bloc for Reform, which had managed to win only four seats in the parliament. Having a party is not essential for the presidential election itself. However, in such a system, a situation in which the chief executive and parliamentary majority are in the same party, and therefore working together, is impossible. Such a situation precludes the sort of decisive action needed to cope with extreme economic vulnerability.

Institutional factors also play an important role in fragmenting Ukraine's political parties, and it is within the parliament that the problem is greatest. Under Soviet election law, candidates were elected by majority vote from single-member districts. The Communist Party won all the seats until 1990, when nationalists were able to win many seats in the west under the Democractic Bloc umbrella. Because the candidates had only to win a majority in their districts, they did not need to rely on a national political organization for their positions.

This independence from parties was reinforced when the Communist Party was dissolved, and its members remained in the parliament with no party affiliation or discipline.

When, in the fall of 1993, new elections were scheduled for March 1994, the key question became the election law. Reformers advocated a party list system, such as that used in Poland and the Czech Republic, and in part in Germany. In that system, voters choose a party rather than a candidate, and seats in the parliament are distributed to all parties receiving a minimum threshold (typically five percent) according to their percentage of the vote. The virtue of this system is that it puts the focus on parties; individual candidates can get nowhere by themselves. Because individuals rely on parties for their re-election hopes, the party can maintain discipline in the parliament.

More significantly, if the threshold to get into parliament is sufficiently high, there is a great incentive for small parties to join together and for blocs within larger parties to negotiate their differences rather than split. When a party splits, both of the new parties may fall short of the minimum required and gain no seats. At best, they suffer reduced influence in the parliament.[21] Thus with the important caveat that the threshold for a party's receiving seats in parliament be high enough, proportional representation promises a greater chance of a working majority in parliament. The majority party or coalition should then be able to present and pass its program, and stalemate is avoided.

This plan for proportional representation was opposed on two grounds. First, many genuinely feared making individuals so dependent on their parties in a state in which the Communist Party was so recently defeated. More significantly, the new election law had to be passed by the old parliament, which meant that its interests were pre-eminent. Deputies in the pre-1994 parliament had been elected from single-member districts, so all had strong local support networks, due either to their personal prestige or to their positions as heads of large enterprises. In a system based on proportional representation and party lists, local power bases would be much less important as political assets. Most were unwilling to surrender their most valuable asset in the hope of forcing a consolidation of Ukraine's political parties. Ukraine's new Verkhovna Rada was therefore elected under a law quite similar to the old Soviet law.

The 1994 parliamentary elections were therefore indecisive and served to transmit Ukraine's atomized political spectrum into parliament rather than prompting some consolidation.[22] Because elections were based on local popularity, there was little that national-based parties (especially brand-new ones) could do to help candidates. On the other hand, anyone with local notoriety or popularity had a decent chance of winning. Over 5,800 candidates ran for 450 seats (roughly 13 candidates per seat). Only eleven percent of these candidates came from political parties.[23] The result was chaos in the elections, as runoffs were still being held months after the original election.[24]

The one strong political party in the country—the Communist Party, which has retained its organizational network—managed to do well but not well enough to form a working majority or a majority coalition. Together with its allies, the socialists and the peasants, the communists controlled 118 seats after the first two rounds. The next largest coalition was the national democrats (*Rukh* and its allies) who together controlled just 35 seats. The largest bloc of candidates was the 163 unaffiliated candidates who had been elected solely on their local power base. This group was referred to in the Ukrainian media as "the swamp" due to its amorphous character.[25] Moreover, 113 seats, almost exactly one fourth, remained unfilled until a lengthy series of by-elections were held.[26] Because few others were willing to work with the communists, no one was able to muster a working majority. There was some coalescing of individuals and small groups into larger "factions," but these tended to be unstable and have shown signs of becoming genuine parties only since the revision of the election law in 1997 (see below).

The 1994–1998 parliament therefore could do little more than oppose the executive. Under President Kravchuk, parliament opposed the president's policies on relations with the CIS and nuclear weapons. President Kuchma has been much more active than Kravchuk and has run into concerted opposition to his economic reform plans (for example, control of privatization was moved from the State Property Committee to a parliamentary committee, and then a outright ban was passed). In the end, however, parliament's internal division has led to a partial resolution of another problem: the division of power between the president and parliament (see below). As parliamentarians recognized that their body was incapable of legislating coherently, more and more deputies were amenable to shifting power toward the president, and after a long struggle that has been done. It has not, however, resolved the more basic problem: Ukraine is a democratic country without a functioning legislature.

The election law adopted in late 1997 changed this system for the 1998 parliamentary elections. Ukraine adopted a "German" system in which half the parliament was elected according to party lists and half was elected in single-member districts. This system (also adopted in Russia) balances political interests and also balances the principle of local representation with the desire for stronger parties.

The election had much of the intended effect on party formation and consolidation. Eight parties passed the four-percent threshold, and the new parliament had a much smaller number of independents (elected in single-member districts) than the old one. There is a clear division between the left-ist parties and the center-right that will likely structure debate and competition for the allegiance of wavering parties and deputies.

The new laws, however, did not lead to the election of a majority coali-tion, reinforcing the fact that in a deeply divided society, producing a ma-jority coalition may be exceedingly difficult. Tinkering with election rules can do only so much. The 1998 parliament is so evenly divided that for three months it could not even elect a speaker. The Communist Party in-sisted that as the largest vote-getter, it should be able to name the speaker, while the center-right parties united to bloc the communists but were un-able to elect a candidate of their own.

As was predicted by many, the choice of a four-percent rather than a five-percent threshold was crucial, as four of the eight parties admitted to parlia-ment received between four and five percent of the vote. At the same time, however, both the left and the right consolidated, with their biggest parties (the Communist Party and *Rukh* respectively) gaining votes at the expense of smaller parties. It may take several more election cycles before the evolution of the Ukrainian party system stabilizes. At this point we can say only that the parliament is gaining some structure due to the new election law. It is too early to say whether at some point a majority will be produced, or whether Ukraine will follow the Italian route of perpetual minority governments.

Division of Power

In many western governments, the constitution defines which branches of government are allowed to perform which functions.[27] Typically, functions are divided between executive, legislative, and judicial branches. According to liberal theory, the three branches are supposed to check each other to pre-vent tyranny but allow sufficient differentiation of authority so each can do its job unimpeded and the government can function.[28] Executives have lit-tle legislative authority, and legislatures lack the power to implement the laws they enact. While practice often blurs these functions, the principle of separation is held by many to lead to effective but restrained government. Others, however, criticize separation of powers for inviting stalemate, and it is this problem that has arisen in Ukraine's state.[29]

Under the Soviet Union, Ukraine had a unified government. While all se-rious decisions were made in Moscow, Ukraine did have its own institutions, which focused not on the separation of powers but on the monopoly of power in the Communist Party, which controlled the government as the realization of Lenin's "dictatorship of the proletariat." The problem in Ukraine and in the other former Soviet states is moving from a system in which power is monopolized to one in which it is divided. In Ukraine, the situation has evolved in such a way that power is divided, but the powers of the various organs are not defined. The various organs can check each other effectively, but almost no duties are clearly held for one branch—and beyond the reach of the others. Therefore tyranny is averted, but effective policymaking is nearly impossible.

Ukraine has four centers of power at the top of its government: the parliament (Verkhovna Rada), the speaker of the parliament, the prime minister, and the president. Because each has had sufficient power to check the others, finding a policy that all approve of has been nearly impossible, especially as the four are struggling for power and have little incentive to do anything that might increase the prerogatives of their rivals.

This institutional setup evolved due to the peculiarities of the disintegration of Soviet power, as discussed above. The Verkhovna Rada was (theoretically) the main organ of government under communism, and the president and prime minister did not exist. The speaker of the Verkhovna Rada was technically the head of government. As Ukraine moved toward independence prior to 1991, it became more and more necessary to have an individual figure who represented the embryonic state. This figure was created by the elevation of Leonid Kravchuk as speaker of the Verkhovna Rada and as the head of state, while no longer performing the duties of prime minister. It was Kravchuk who, by virtue of his position as speaker, took the lead in declaring independence in 1991, and it was his position of authority as speaker that made him a natural candidate for president.

As Ukraine became independent, the one branch of government that it already had was a parliament. This institution has continued in its previous form and has adopted more or less the function of a western legislature. However, because until 1996 there were no clear circumscriptions on its authority, it often became involved in running the day-to-day affairs of the government, especially under Kravchuk, who tried to be apolitical and remain above the fray of daily political issues. This tendency is a holdover from the late Soviet era, when "the [republic] Supreme Soviets, gradually accumulating power at the expense of the Union center . . . in essence combined representative and executive functions."[30] Institutional continuity was emphasized by one writer who stated in 1993 that "political conditions remain almost the way they were over two years ago."[31] This ability to interfere in executive functions, however, does not mean that Ukraine has a strong parliament. Not only is it badly divided internally (it is much better at blocking what it opposes than deciding what it supports), but the president has his own decree powers of legislation as well as veto powers. The president's ability to initiate legislation through decree gives him little incentive to compromise with the parliament.

Ukraine created a head of government in the form of a prime minister and a head of state in the form of a president but, by failing to distinguish their powers, achieved only a watering down of leadership at the top of the state. The president was important to those (especially nationalists) who sought the presence of a strong symbolic leader of the Ukrainian state. In addition, the presidency ended the parliament's monopoly on power.[32] However, many members of the Verkhovna Rada were concerned about potential tyranny and about diluting their own influence, and they insisted on dividing executive power between the president and a prime minister.

The Verkhovna Rada maintained important levers of influence over the president, including the elimination of the position of vice-president (which was initially proposed), the parliamentary right to veto executive decrees, the simple majority vote to override a presidential veto (which in essence means no presidential veto), the right to reject appointment of key ministers, and the right to dismiss the government. The president had no right to dissolve the parliament or call new elections.[33]

Neither president nor prime minister was made primarily responsible for policy (in contrast to the British and German systems, in which the Queen and president are symbolic figures and the prime minister and chancellor are responsible for policy). Some Ukrainians have compared the system to that of France, which it superficially resembles, a comparison that appeals to nationalists because of France's very strong state. In the French system, however, immense authority is vested in the presidency in order to prevent the system from stalemating. And even when France has had "cohabitation" of president and prime minister of different parties, they have successfully worked together.

The Ukrainian parliament, in modifying the Soviet constitution, was unwilling to vest that much authority in the president, because it would greatly reduce the relevance of the parliament and because genuine fear of authoritarianism remained. Quite unlike the French Fifth Republic, Ukraine has a system that is very prone to stalemate, and Italy is the more relevant analogue for the functioning, if not the structure, of the Ukrainian government.

Authority to make and implement laws has been hopelessly diluted. The Verkhovna Rada had the primary authority to legislate. But both the president and the cabinet had prerogatives to issue decrees under certain circumstances. The president had the authority to appoint the prime minister and cabinet of ministers, but the parliament could reject his nominees. The cabinet of ministers was in charge of actually running the government, but there were no official limits on the ability of the parliament or the president to micro-manage the bureaucracies. Because the cabinet of ministers and prime minister were dependent on both the president and the parliament for their continuance in office, there was no way to resist such encroachments. The speaker of parliament retained little statutory authority by himself, but through his control of the legislative agenda he had significant ability to initiate legislation and to block legislation (and executive decisions).[34] The kernel of the problem is that the prime minister and cabinet, who were presumably most responsible for devising a policy program, getting it enacted, and then implementing it, were at the mercy of both the president and the parliament.

In essence the Ukrainian cabinet prior to the 1996 Constitution was a part of the executive branch but responsible to the parliament.[35] Both the authority to legislate and the authority to execute laws were spread across the three primary institutions, and each of them as well as the speaker had a de facto veto power over others' initiatives.

Since the stalemates of 1993, debate in Ukraine has focused on strengthening the office of the president, which promised both to break the stalemate between the executive and the legislature and to make the stalemate within the legislature less significant. The lack of concentrated power in the Ukrainian system was severe enough that some advocated decidedly antidemocratic measures to solve the problem. Kravchuk put forth South Korea as an example in an interview in late 1993, and the example of Pinochet was cited so frequently that Ukrainians began speaking of "Pinochuk" as the solution to their political impasse. There is sufficient support for democracy in Ukraine that authoritarian sentiments have not been taken seriously, but the belief that Ukraine needs a more unified and powerful state has had a significant effect.

After his election, Kuchma made strengthening the presidency a priority issue:

> Without a doubt, the conditions, without which reforms or any movement forward are impossible, are the formation of a strong and effective state power. This envisages strengthening of a single executive vertical structure as the fundamental instrument for implementing statewide policy. At the same time, relations between all branches of power should be stabilized.[36]

Eventually he was able to succeed to some degree. Even under a new president with a clear program and a strong electoral mandate, parliament was able to foil action, most notably when it passed a moratorium on all privatization in late 1994 in order to prevent Kuchma from initiating reform while parliament was in recess. The prime minister's power to check the president became a problem in early 1995 when, until he was forced out, Vitaliy Masol resisted many of the reforms that Kuchma was attempting to implement as president.[37] Thus the Ukrainian presidency has been hampered not only by executive-legislative conflict, but by intra-executive conflict between the president and prime minister.[38]

The 1996 Constitution should resolve some of the problems that have plagued its institutions for the first five years of independence. How this constitution will function in practice remains to be seen, but it should be noted that one considerable shortcoming persists—the lack of a functioning court system. While Ukraine now has a constitution, it does not have an effective mechanism for resolving disputes over the constitution's provisions. Many of the same conflicts over prerogative have therefore continued even under the new document. Moreover, despite the augmentation of the president's powers, the Ukrainian president still lacks some of the most important levers others have over parliaments, including the power to dissolve parliament.

Kuchma's campaign to strengthen the presidency has represented an important shift in Ukrainian politics by transforming the presidency into a partisan position. Kravchuk saw himself as the leader of all Ukrainians and saw his primary job as playing a unifying role in a divided society. This was perhaps crucial in the early stages of independence. But it meant that Kravchuk declined to take a firm stand on many issues of the day, because that would mean choosing sides rather than unifying. As a result, the lack of authority in the government was exacerbated. The one official who might have had the juridical authority and the political strength to try to advance a political program chose to stand aside.

Kuchma has taken a much more political role. He is well aware of the limits on his policies created by Ukraine's divisions, but he does not attempt to stand above politics, as Kravchuk did. He has therefore put forth relatively clear domestic and foreign policy plans, even if he has taken account of political necessity in doing so. Moreover, he clearly allied himself with two of the parties running in the 1998 parliamentary election (the National Democratic Party and the Agrarian Party), forsaking the view that the president was "above party politics." Whether Kuchma's reforms will succeed and how long he will last as president remain to be seen. The important point for this analysis is that Ukraine's institutional setting is changing, such that it might be more possible in the future than it has been in the past to devise and enact a coherent strategy to reduce economic vulnerability.

Giving the president increased power over the Verkhovna Rada should help end stalemate in the government, but one must be cautious. Research on semi-presidential systems in the former Soviet Union indicates not only that such systems tend toward authoritarianism but that they tend toward conservatism. More significantly, perhaps, laws passed by executive decree lack the legitimacy of those passed by legislatures and hence are more difficult to enforce on society. The Ukrainian president has the power to rule by decree on a wide range of issues, but without support from the Verkhovna Rada, the underlying domestic conditions for change cannot be created.

It is not necessary simply for the president to be able to overrule the parliament; the president must be able to work *with* the parliament. The 1996 Constitution, by increasing the president's powers, does not necessarily create the impetus toward an agreed program approved by the legislature and implemented by the executive. In this context, the absence of a "presidential" party in parliament and more broadly the absence of a strong party system have hampered effective rule as much as has the weakness of the presidency.[39] Even in Russia, where Boris Yeltsin's constitutional powers are extensive, parliament has been able to block many reforms, and many others have simply been unenforceable. Thus,

> In some countries (Poland, for instance) only governments with democratic legitimacy have had the strength to institute economic reforms that entailed a period of sacrifice before the benefits arrived. Hence the equation of authoritarianism with stability is at least as misleading as the equation of democratization with instability.[40]

Creating a strong presidency is not equivalent to creating a strong state. Indeed, there are examples throughout the third world of leaders with near-dictatorial powers that are barely in control of their state's territory.[41]

Moreover, even with a less divisive institutional structure, political disagreement could still impede a coherent foreign policy. While institutional confusion has been an important constraint on Ukraine's economic security policy, it is not the only one, and reforming Ukraine's institutional structure is not by itself a sufficient condition for reducing economic vulnerability. If Ukraine's other internal divisions, especially disagreement over economic reform, persist, stalemate may continue due to political rather than institutional reasons. Similarly, even if Ukraine does adopt a coherent strategy to deal with its economic vulnerability, the success of the policy will depend on the content of the policy. Ukraine needs not just a coherent policy, but a sensible one.

Ukraine as a "Weak State": Nuclear Weapons and Energy

Ukraine's institutional and political divisions help create a situation that places important constraints on Ukraine's ability to deal with its economic vulnerability: the state is very weak relative to the society. It is therefore limited in its ability to implement policies that might alleviate its economic vulnerability. Because the state is so divided, it is relatively easy for aggrieved societal actors to block policies that they oppose. Just as the weakness of the prime minister makes it easy for the parliament to foil his program, the overall weakness of the government makes it easy for societal actors to obstruct certain policies. This is especially true as different branches of government at odds with one another will gladly adopt some group's cause if it will help them win an institutional battle.

While Ukraine has been successful in those issues where successful policy required nothing from Ukrainian society, it has failed on the more fundamental issue of creating a domestic economy strong enough to resist foreign pressure. Two examples illustrate the problem: First, institutional fragmentation severely hampered the state's ability to adopt a coherent policy on nuclear weapons. Second, the state, largely due to its internal divisions, had little ability to change the country's energy consumption patterns to meet a severe challenge from Russia. These were not isolated incidents but rather are representative of the problems in forming and implementing policy in a weak state.

The concrete consequences of Ukraine's institutional fragmentation were visible initially in policymaking over nuclear weapons. It was never clear in Ukraine or in the West who had the authority to negotiate on behalf of Ukraine and what sort of ratification of agreements was necessary. Repeatedly, Kravchuk reached agreements on nuclear weapons only to find that he had no support in the Verkhovna Rada. Because he and other governments assumed he had the authority to negotiate for Ukraine, the repeated need to put previously reached agreements back on the bargaining table created the impression that Ukraine was reneging on its agreements and finally had the effect of undermining Kravchuk's bargaining position, because he clearly could not deliver what he promised.[42]

When the Trilateral Agreement was reached in early 1994, Kravchuk tried an end run by asserting that as a "statement" by executives, not a treaty, the deal did not need to be ratified by the parliament (American presidents have made similar attempts with "executive agreements").[43] *Rukh* Leader V'iacheslav Chornovil responded: "President Kravchuk has no authority to sign such an agreement. Nuclear policy is for parliament to work out."[44] Despite the gravity of the debate, there was no way to decide the issue on legal grounds: the constitution was unclear, and there was no court to make a decision.[45] In the end, the Verkhovna Rada won the war (it did get to vote on the agreement) but Kravchuk won the battle (the Verkhovna Rada ratified the treaty after Kravchuk left office).

These problems were also demonstrated at the Massandra Summit in September 1993, the most significant case of Ukraine's economic weakness causing foreign policy repercussions. At this summit, Ukraine apparently agreed to trade its share of the Black Sea Fleet and its nuclear weapons for relief from its debts for Russian energy. The deal was plagued from the beginning by institutional controversy. First, it was not clear who had the authority to negotiate, Kuchma or Kravchuk (both of them signed agreements). Kuchma and Kravchuk were primarily concerned with solving Ukraine's economic woes. Parliament had other priorities, and it bitterly opposed the deals. Kravchuk immediately distanced himself from the agreements, even though he was as responsible as Kuchma for their existence. Parliament's opposition ensured that the agreements would never be fulfilled. Ukraine was in the position of having signed the agreements and then refusing to be bound by them, because the authority to sign was unclear.

More fundamentally, Ukraine has had great difficulty dealing with its economic dependence on Russia and with its overall economic weakness. Ukraine's economy—and the problem of energy in particular—is not just a domestic problem but in fact has become the largest source of its international weakness. Economic issues were crucial in the policy of economic isolation adopted in early 1992 and in the struggle over energy supplies. A weak economy, and one tied closely to Russia, will continue to limit Ukraine's foreign policy options. Yet the government's success in implementing austerity and efficiency measures has been limited. Because the state controlled the energy supply and distribution, it was theoretically possible to cut off gas to delinquent consumers when times got bad. But the government could not withstand the inevitable unrest that would result. The state could not cut off its delinquent customers. Consequently, it has sought to privatize much of the gas industry, in order to put the gas supply in the hands of an entity that might have the ability to force payment.[46]

Essentially, Ukrainian leaders admitted the weakness of their state when they recognized that private firms could do what the state could not: cut supplies to customers who do not pay their bills. In promoting efficiency, the state was even less successful, because the interests it had to take on were well organized and well represented in Kyiv. An energy austerity bill prepared by the Ministry of Power Engineering and Electrification during the energy crisis in November 1993 was "torpedoed" quickly in the Verkhovna Rada, apparently due to the opposition of "the directors' lobby," even as schools were being closed for lack of heat and light.[47]

It was therefore nearly impossible to close those factories that were the most profligate wasters of energy. In many cases, the factories were not only wasting energy but also losing money; still, they could not be closed. Factory directors remained influential actors in the political system, able to deliver (or deny) large blocs of votes (and large bribes). "Top level executive officials acknowledge that the Government does not even have control over the public sector of the economy, for enterprises which have separated from the State have no responsibilities to it."[48] The need to reduce energy waste was widely acknowledged, and energy supplies to many industries were cut in the short term, but there was insufficient government unity to deal with the long-term issue by closing even unprofitable plants. Moreover, much administration is still conducted by the local Soviets, which have largely resisted efforts by Kyiv to reduce their power, and which are largely unreformed since the Soviet era.[49]

The state's weakness was also a key issue in the retraction of the policy of isolation from Russia. If the ability to extract sacrifice from society is a measure of state strength, the Ukrainian government was proven to be weak. Protests from citizens and industries in eastern Ukraine caused Kravchuk to slowly back down on that policy, even as he moved toward the nationalist end of the political spectrum. At the same time however, the agreement to join the CIS economic union as an associate member in 1993 had to be reconsidered due to opposition from nationalists. Kuchma's resignation was prompted by the public outcry caused by that decision and the Massandra agreements. The government's inability to resist being caught in the middle of this tug of war indicates its weakness in Ukraine as well as the degree of political bifurcation within society. Together, those two characteristics (divided society and weak state) prevented action to deal with economic vulnerability and many other problems.

Conclusion

Ukraine's state structure has had an important impact on how it has dealt (or rather not dealt) with its economic security. Because the country is divided politically and the state is divided institutionally, Ukraine has been unable to devise or implement a strategy to cope with economic vulnerability ever since its initial strategy of isolation failed. The inability to formulate a policy is not unique to economic security but endemic to Ukrainian politics. This is most notable in the realm of economic reform, which would have entailed ending some of the practices that made Ukraine most dependent, especially in terms of energy. The link between political reform, economic strategy, and Ukrainian independence was captured by Kuchma when he resigned as prime minister: "It is my belief that Ukraine badly needs substantial political reforms, without which economic reforms are impossible, and without which we risk losing our independence."[50]

Ukraine of course is not the only country in the world with a stalemated political system. However, as a state in dire economic and political straits, challenged both from within and outside the country, Ukraine has seen the effects of such a political stalemate magnified. Advanced industrial states with economies that basically function, fundamental political questions that get resolved, and little external threat can flourish with relatively little adjustment in policy, and in some cases the continuity provided by such a system is beneficial. Ukraine's system did ensure a large degree of continuity in policy—in a way. But since previous political arrangements had been shattered, and Ukraine had no established patterns of government, the continuity provided was continuity of chaos.

If the essence of Russia's power over Ukraine is the ability to narrow Ukraine's range of feasible economic options, Ukraine's internal political situation narrows the range of possible choices even further. In the worst of times during the first few years of independence, these constraints have combined to prevent any real choices at all from being made. More recently, however, it appears that Ukraine's domestic ability to make choices to deal with its economic vulnerability is increasing.

Such improvement will be badly needed as Ukraine faces the foreign policy challenges looming on the horizon. Relations with Russia have stabilized in large part due to American support for Ukraine. Similarly, domestic economic stability, such as it is, has depended on help from western financial institutions, most notably the IMF. It is not clear how long those benefactors will continue to pour resources into a state that is seen as largely ineffective (not to mention corrupt, a problem I have not addressed here). Ukraine's foreign policy successes to date have occurred in interstate arenas and did not require much capacity vis-à-vis society. Ukraine's future foreign policy challenges will increasingly overlap with problems of domestic economic reform, and success will depend on strengthening the Ukrainian state. As long as Ukraine has a weak state and a divided society, it will continue to find itself the passive victim of forces beyond its borders.

Notes

1. Ukraine's economic vulnerability and its relations with Russia are covered in detail in Paul D'Anieri, *Economic Interdependence in Ukrainian-Russian Relations* (Albany: SUNY Press, 1999).
2. Ihor Buryakovskyi describes Ukraine as a "passive" respondent to others' policies, due to its own lack of strategy. See "On the Way to 'Guided' Integration?" *Politychna Dumka/Political Thought*, no. 3 (1994), pp. 190–191.
3. Dominique Arel and Valeri Khmelko, "The Russian Factor and Territorial Polarization in Ukraine," *The Harriman Review*, vol. 9, nos. 1–2 (Spring 1996), pp. 81–91.
4. Simon Johnson and Oleg Ustenko, "Ukraine," in Michael L. Wyzan (ed.), *First Steps Toward Economic Independence* (Westport, CT: Praeger, 1995), pp. 51–52.
5. A brief analysis of the concept of state strength is in Stephen D. Krasner, *Structural Conflict: The Third World Against Global Liberalism* (Berkeley: University of California Press, 1985), pp. 38–39. He refers to a state's "internal capacity to modulate and adjust to the pressures emanating from an uncertain international environment."
6. Prominent works in this literature include: Peter J. Katzenstein (ed.), *Between Power and Plenty* (Madison: University of Wisconsin Press, 1977); Stephen D. Krasner, *Defending the National Interest* (Princeton: Princeton University Press, 1978); Stephen D. Krasner, "Domestic Constraints on International Economic Leverage," in Klaus Knorr and Frank Trager (eds.), *Economic Issues in National Security* (Lawrence: Regents Press of Kansas, 1977), pp. 160–181; Joel S. Migdal, *Strong Societies and Weak States* (Princeton: Princeton University Press, 1988); and Robert H. Jackson, *Quasi-States: Sovereignty, International Relations, and the Third World* (New York: Cambridge University Press, 1990).
7. Peter J. Katzenstein, "The Small European States in the International Economy: Economic Dependence and Corporatist Politics," in John G. Ruggie (ed.), *The Antinomies of Interdependence* (New York: Columbia University Press, 1982), pp. 91–130. It might seem odd to compare Ukraine to the small European states. The theory as constructed, however, is not meant to be limited to a particular set of states, as Katzenstein emphasizes when he states that: " . . . the domestic structures of the small European states, far from being unique, can aid in the analysis of the domestic structures of other states, the analysis of the structures . . . should shed light on the more general political correlates of successful economic strategies," and he specifically cites the communist states in this regard (pp. 128–130). And while Ukraine is as large in

population and area as the large western European states, it is relatively small compared to its main trading partner, Russia.

8. Oleksandr Dergachov, "Geopolitical Constellations in the Postcommunist World," *Politychna Dumka/ Political Thought,* no. 1 (1995), p. 168.

9. Katzenstein, op. cit., "The Small European States," p. 121.

10. On Ukraine's lack of organized interests, see Volodymyr Polokhalo and Anatoliy Slyusarenko, "Political Process and Political Elite," *Politychna Dumka/Political Thought,* no. 1 (1993), p. 110.

11. Alexander J. Motyl, *Dilemmas of Independence: Ukraine After Totalitarianism* (New York: Council on Foreign Relations, 1993), p. 50; see also his chapter 2.

12. Jon Elster, Claus Offe, and Ulrich K. Preuss, *Institutional Design in Post-Communist Societies* (New York: Cambridge University Press, 1998), chap. 1.

13. Ihor Markov, "The Role of the President in the Ukrainian Political System," *RFE/RL Research Report,* vol. 2, no. 48 (December 3, 1993), p. 32.

14. V. Polokhalo, "The Neo-Totalitarian Transformations of Post-Communist Power in Ukraine," *Politychna Dumka/Political Thought,* no. 3 (1994), pp. 133–134.

15. Op cit., I. Markov, p. 32.

16. Op cit., A. J. Motyl, p. 173.

17. After being elected president, Kuchma said: "It is good that not a single political party supported me during the elections, as I am going to serve the people and not the party." See Oksana Holovko, "The Economy and Law and Order Are in the Foreground," *Uriadoviy Kur'er,* July 16, 1994.

18. Steven J. Woehrel, "Political-Economic Assessments: Ukraine," in Richard F. Kaufman and John P. Hardt (eds.), *The Former Soviet Union in Transition* (Armonk, N.Y.: M. E. Sharpe, 1993), p. 964.

19. This view was characterized by one observer in terms of the following thesis: "To support the President of Ukraine, who was elected by the whole nation, is to support independent state building . . . Opposition to the President would lead to destroying the independent state." See Valentyn Yakushyk, "Establishment of the Multi-Party System," *Politychna Dumka/Political Thought,* no. 1 (1993), p.122.

20. Op cit., A. J. Motyl, p. 166.

21. If thresholds are established at a low level, as they were in Poland's first postcommunist election, the system encourages party fragmentation, because any group that can get a tiny share of the vote (such as the Polish Beer Drinkers' Party) can be represented.

22. Ivan Besiada, "Pershyi Parlament Nezalezhnoyi Derzhava Obrano," *Za Vil'nu Ukrayinu,* April 12, 1994.

23. These statistics are from "Settling in for More of the Same," *The Economist,* March 19 1994.

24. In Ukrainian, like Soviet, election law, a candidate had to win 50 percent of the vote to be elected. The Ukrainian law also specified that 50 percent of registered voters had to turn out for an election to be valid. In the first round, with so many candidates, only the most prominent national politicians won a

majority. In the second round, which had only the top two in each district, many elections were invalidated by low turnout. Successive rounds were held, but some seats have not been filled due to voter apathy and the election law.

25. Oleg Shmid, "Vybory Staly Pomstoiu," *Post-Postup,* April 15–24, 1994.
26. Data are from "Lonely at the Top," *The Economist,* April 16, 1994. A slightly different breakdown is provided by John Lloyd and Jill Barshay, "Moscow Starts Crisis Talks with Kyiv," *Financial Times,* April 13, 1994.
27. For a detailed account of Ukraine's presidential-parliamentary conflict, see Andrew Wilson, "Ukraine: Two Presidents But No Settled Powers" in Raymond Taras (ed.), *Postcommunist Presidents* (Cambridge: Cambridge University Press, 1997), pp. 67–105.
28. The doctrine of separation of powers and the position of its critics are concisely summarized in R. Taras, "Separating Power: Keeping Presidents in Check," in op cit., R. Taras (ed.), *Postcommunist Presidents,* pp. 15–37.
29. Ibid., R. Taras, "Separating Power," pp. 26–27.
30. Op cit., I. Markov, p. 31.
31. Op cit., V. Polokhalo and A. Slyusarenko, p. 109.
32. Op cit., I. Markov, p. 31.
33. Op cit., I. Markov, p. 32. Kravchuk complained about his lack of power almost from the beginning, saying of the parliament: "You want to put the president in a position where he would be walking around like a puppet, consulting with everyone about what he should do. That is not appropriate." See Kravchuk's interview in *Pravda,* February 11, 1992, translated in FBIS-SOV-92–029; February 12, 1992, p. 71.
34. One commentator states that "the first microphone is better than the English crown." See Oleh Shmid, "Ivan Pliushch zmushenyi vybyraty mizh synytseyu I zhuravlem. Obydva ptakhy v nebe," *Post-Postup,* April 22–28, 1994.
35. Op cit., I. Markov, p. 34.
36. See "Inauguration Speech by President Leonid Kuchma at the Supreme Council in Kyiv—live relay," *Radio Ukraine World Service,* July 19, 1994, translated in FBIS-SOV-94–139, July 20, 1994, p. 36.
37. *OMRI Daily Digest* part II, March 2, 1995.
38. On intra-executive conflict, see op cit., R. Taras, "Separating Power: Keeping Presidents in Check," pp. 23–24; and op cit., A. Wilson, "Ukraine: Two Presidents But No Settled Powers," p. 89, specifically referring to Ukraine.
39. Op cit., A. Wilson, p. 92.
40. Barnett R. Rubin, "Conclusion: Managing Normal Instability," in Rubin and Jack Snyder, (eds.), *Post-Soviet Political Order: Conflict and State Building* (London: Routledge, 1998), p. 177.
41. On this point see op cit., R. H. Jackson, *Quasi-States,* and J. S. Migdal, *Strong Societies, Weak States.*
42. This problem of "involuntary defection" is the subject of an increasing literature on "two-level games," in which a state leader must negotiate simultane-

ously with other states and with elements within his or her own state that can block an agreement. See Robert Putnam, "Diplomacy and Domestic Politics: The Logic of Two-Level Games," *International Organization,* vol. 42, no. 3 (Summer 1988), pp. 427–460.

43. The assertion that the Trilateral Agreement was a "statement," not an agreement or treaty, was made by Foreign Minister Zlenko. *RFE/RL Daily Report,* January 17, 1994.

44. J. Lloyd, "Ukraine Nuclear Pact in Doubt," *Financial Times,* January 12, 1994.

45. Note that this discussion has not included a discussion of the third branch of government, the judiciary. At the criminal and civil levels, the Ukrainian judicial system is in shambles, and until the adoption of the 1996 Constitution, there was no notion of judicial review in Ukraine nor any "supreme court" to try to assert that authority. The new constitution provides for judicial review by a Constitutional Court, but the system is not yet functioning. See Bohdan A. Futey, "Comments on the Constitutional Court of Ukraine," *The Harriman Review,* vol. 10, no. 1 (Spring 1997), pp. 15–23.

46. See "Kravchuk Presents Economic Program to Parliament," *Radio Ukraine World Service,* November 11, 1993, translated in FBIS-SOV-93–218, November 15, 1993, p. 65.

47. Leonid Dayen, "Ukraine is Freezing, But, It Seems, People's Deputies Couldn't Care Less," *Demokratychna Ukrayina,* December 1, 1993, translated in FBIS-SOV-93–231, December 3, 1993, pp. 44–45; "Energy Famine Hits Schools," *Izvestiya,* December 1, 1993, translated in FBIS-SOV-93–231, December 3, 1993, pp. 45.

48. Voldymyr Volovych and Serhiy Makeyev, "Social Stratification and Politics," *Politychna Dumka/Political Thought,* no. 1 (1993), p. 113.

49. On the struggle between Kravchuk and the local soviets, see Vladimir Skachko, "Three Centers of Power: Leonid Kravchuk Has Shared Power with the Government and He Is Now Prepared to Share It with Parliament and the Local Soviets," *Nezavisimaya Gazeta,* November 7, 1992, translated in FBIS-USR-92–155, December 4, 1992, pp. 111–112.

50. "Text of Leonid Kuchma's Resignation Statement," *Radio Ukraine World Service,* September 9, 1993, translated in FBIS-SOV-93–174, September 10, 1993, p. 42.

CHAPTER 5

Like Oil and Water: Ukraine's External Westernization and Internal Stagnation

Sherman W. Garnett

Despite constrained resources and a complex international environment, the Ukrainian leadership has, throughout 1997 and into 1998, achieved several notable foreign policy successes: long-delayed agreements with Russia on key aspects of the bilateral relationship including the division and basing of the Black Sea Fleet, the lifting of a Russian-imposed VAT on sugar and other Ukrainian consumer goods, the signing of a long-term economic agreement with Russia, a treaty with Romania, and a "Charter on Distinctive Partnership" with NATO. Ukraine also intervened in the long-standing dispute between Moldova and the breakaway region of Transdniestr, becoming a co-guarantor with Russia of a May 1997 memorandum that outlined basic principles for resolution of the conflict. Kuchma has also offered to deploy Ukrainian peacekeeping troops once a final political agreement is reached.

In part, these successes can be traced to the influence of NATO enlargement, which clearly affected the calculations of both Moscow and Bucharest with regard to Kyiv. But Ukraine has itself gained enormous confidence in its foreign policy from successfully managing widespread international recognition for the fledgling state, a difficult trilateral negotiation on nuclear disarmament, and difficult relations with Russia and the Commonwealth of Independent States (CIS).[1]

The West, once seen largely as a support for internal reforms and Ukraine's eastern policy, has steadily expanded in the Ukrainian leadership's conception of Kyiv's long-term national interests. The removal of the question of Ukraine's nuclear intentions in 1994 allowed U.S.-Ukrainian relations to expand to a full-fledged strategic partnership in October 1996. In 1995, after initial skepticism toward NATO enlargement, Kuchma announced Ukraine's desire to form a special partnership with the Atlantic Alliance. Later that year, in September, Foreign Minister Udovenko led a high-level delegation to Brussels to begin defining a special relationship with NATO. In October, Ukraine entered the Central European Initiative with Poland's help. In April 1996, addressing the Council of Europe Parliamentary Assembly in Strasbourg, President Kuchma announced Ukraine's aim of becoming a full-fledged member of the European Union some day. In recent months, some senior Ukrainian officials have even intimated their long-term interests in NATO membership, though official policy declares "no intention" of applying for NATO membership.[2] Underlying Ukraine's outreach to the West is a vision Kuchma articulated during a February 1996 visit to Washington of Ukraine's need for integration, not within a closed and backward Commonwealth of Independent States, but with the world economy and the advanced states of the West.

Yet in proclaiming these ambitious goals, the Ukrainian foreign policy leadership has created a long term dilemma for itself and its policy. For while it pursues westernization abroad, it appears content with political and economic stagnation at home. These two things, like oil and water, simply do not mix. For a time Ukraine may muddle through, but ultimately the basic disparity between foreign and domestic policy will take a toll. The internal problems that have produced this internal stagnation are threefold:

1. The political class is deeply divided over basic policy. More important, it is too distracted by its pursuit of wealth and power in a new Ukraine to sustain basic economic and political reforms. There is no consensus within the political class for a tilt toward the West of this magnitude. Among broad sections of political leadership in the regions, legislative branch, and middle levels of the executive bureaucracy, the old and largely bankrupt ways remain the good ways.

2. There is certainly no broad-based public support for such a foreign policy. Although the country has not broken in two, as many analysts feared in the early days of independence, the people as a whole are divided along political, regional, and ethnic lines that have domestic and foreign policy implications. These divisions do not influence the

day-to-day conduct of foreign policy, but they represent a significant constraint on that policy's overall strategic direction.

3. More troubling, Ukraine's political institutions are weak. Its economy simply is not in a condition to support these ambitions and would not stand sustained scrutiny from a West that takes Ukraine's aspirations seriously. A Euro-Atlantic foreign policy needs political and economic reform to sustain momentum.

This chapter will examine the implications of the disparity between Ukrainian foreign ambitions and domestic realities. It will do so by first reviewing the basic domestic constraints on sustaining such a policy, including the divisions among the political elite, regional and ethnic divisions in the country at large, and the failure of internal reforms to keep pace with external ambitions. It will then return to examine Ukraine's strategic challenges, particularly relations with Russia and long-term integration in the West, in light of these constraints.

Domestic Constraints

In the period since independence, Ukrainian foreign policy has been made almost exclusively by the presidents, prime and foreign ministers, and a small group of senior advisers. This group has factored in public and elite opinion, of course, in their deliberations, but that opinion appears to have played a larger role in the rhetoric surrounding a particular policy course than in the decision for or against it. The big issues have been debated in the Verkhovna Rada and the press, but the actual decisions have been made and implemented by a very small group.[3]

Large-scale strategic decisions, however, have internal consequences and are subject to internal constraints. The Ukrainian leadership cannot sneak the country into the European Union. It cannot alter its fundamental security orientation. The founding acts of the Ukrainian state and subsequent constitutional provisions bind the country to formal neutrality. This policy has been proclaimed in part to acknowledge the fact of Ukrainian geography and history and in part to address internal divisions within the Ukrainian political elite and the nation as a whole. Living within or overcoming these divisions is the test of the Ukrainian leadership's management of not only the nation's foreign policy but its basic political and economic soundness. These internal constraints must be directly addressed. This section looks at them as they are expressed in Ukrainian elite politics and in society at large.

Division and Distraction at the Top

Both the formal divisions and informal preoccupations of Ukrainian politics place limits on any sustained foreign policy strategy, particularly a Euro-Atlantic one. The formal struggle is an ideological divide of an old left, a moderate and extreme nationalist right, and a muddled center. The informal struggle is the unfinished competition for power and property among a small number of competing economic, regional, and political groupings. Both processes have gone on since before independence and have deeply affected the ability of the state to defend itself and its policies.

Left, Right, and Center

Even a superficial observer sees the ideological conflict in Ukrainian politics. The Ukrainian left has emerged from the old Communist Party structures, though the new circumstances have produced variations on the old theme. There are of course old-line communists, suspicious of Ukrainian statehood, political and economic reform, and the West. But there are also newer national communists and socialists who combine a suspicion of private property with Ukrainian patriotism. Indeed, the speaker of the Ukrainian parliament from 1994 to 1998, Oleksandr Moroz, is a Socialist, and one of the most nationally well-known politicians. The left is strongest in the east of the country, where old mining and manufacturing structures remain, but both communists and socialists have supporters throughout the country (though both are weak in the far west). The left makes up approximately one-third of the Rada, having improved its position in the March 1998 elections as a result of the 1997 revised "Law on Elections" that called for half the parliament to be elected from party lists.

However, the Ukrainian left has so far not undergone the reconstruction of its organization and attitudes to key political and economic questions that characterize the rebuilt socialists and former communists in Poland or Lithuania. It largely opposed the Law on Power and 1996 Constitution, though deals were struck and both pieces of legislation passed with left-wing votes. On foreign policy, this group is oriented toward close cooperation within the Commonwealth of Independent States (CIS) and holds deep suspicions of the West and NATO. Moroz has repeatedly stated his opposition to NATO enlargement, calling instead for efforts to create a new all-European security structure. Even as Ukrainian-NATO negotiations proceeded toward the conclusion of a special charter, Moroz denied the need for such a special relationship. He and his left-wing colleagues were the driving force behind the formation of the "Ukraine Outside NATO" bloc within parliament.[4]

The Ukrainian right, regionally based in western Ukraine, Kyiv, and scattered outposts elsewhere, are strong supporters of Ukrainian state power, favorable toward a presidential system, desirous of taking Ukraine out of the CIS and forging stronger ties with the West. The right is divided itself into various moderate and more extreme nationalist parties and groupings. They favor the revival of the Ukrainian language, culture, and political primacy. For some on the extreme edge of Ukrainian politics, this agenda has become a demand for ethnic Ukrainian supremacy.

The right's orientation on securing Ukrainian statehood and their fear of long-term Russian hostility toward this project makes many on the right, particularly among the moderate nationalists in *Rukh,* advocates of accelerating Ukraine's integration into key western institutions, including NATO. *Rukh's* main foreign policy strategist and deputy chairman of the Rada Committee on Foreign and CIS Affairs, Ivan Zayets, noted in mid-1997 the inherent contradiction between Ukraine's stated policy in favor of such integration and its inability to make a serious claim on the key western institutions. He argued that Ukraine must submit applications for membership in NATO, the European Union, and the Western European Union to signify "the political will to come closer to European democracy."[5]

The center is an amorphous mix of reformists and opportunists. The key blocs and factions often arise around leading politicians and are not as broadly based in the public at large as either the old left or the nationalist parties. However, the most significant Ukrainian political force occupies the center: the so-called Party of Power. First and foremost, this party includes President Kuchma and his supporters, who have formed the People's Democratic Party; but the center also includes Kuchma's main rivals, former Prime Ministers Yevhen Marchuk and Pavlo Lazarenko, who were associated with the United Social Democratic Party and the *Hromada* Union respectively.

This mix has made for an odd legislative process, one that often begins with deep and seemingly irreconcilable divisions but usually ends in passing the legislation in question with a lopsided majority in favor. Although the left and right resemble much more real political parties, in the sense that the views of parliamentary representatives from these wings resonate with constituencies back home, few have real knowledge or experience on key foreign policy issues. A large number from right, center, and left are ready to be persuaded, pushed, or rewarded to change their position. As a result, the executive branch has usually obtained what it wants—often after long and painful negotiations—on key issues such as economic reform, constitutional change and the ratification of START I and the Nuclear Non-Proliferation Treaty. Nevertheless, though suitable for fashioning individual deals and making incremental progress, this political landscape will not as yet support a sustained and serious effort at Euro-Atlantic integration, one that will also require serious internal reform efforts to make credible Ukraine's claim to participate in western institutions. Senior Ukrainian officials acknowledge this.[6]

The Informal Struggle for Power and Wealth

More debilitating than the current ideological squabble to any Ukrainian effort at Euro-Atlantic integration is the current state of Ukraine's informal political process.[7] In Ukraine, political institutions are still not well defined, despite the adoption of a new constitution in June 1996. Tensions between the executive and legislative branches continue, with both seeking to expand their powers. However, the most intense struggles in Ukrainian politics take place not between parties, ideologies, or branches of government but among the political and economic leadership in Kyiv and the regions. Various coalitions of leading politicians, bankers, and new- and old-style business leaders struggle for control over the state's wealth and for positions of power that will control its divestiture into private hands. As long as these elites are distracted by the still unfinished competition for power and property, there will be little energy left over for sound policy.

An informal Party of Power still makes most of the decisions. The weakness of Ukrainian civil society, particularly of the mechanisms of press and public opinion that must operate in the intervals between elections, means there is no effective constraint on governmental decision-making. It may in fact be one of the characteristics of post-communist states such as Ukraine that for some time to come the old state decision-making structures will exist side by side with new forms of civil society and public opinion. While the state no longer dominates civil society, civil society has barely begun to stand on its own feet; the press, public opinion, and democratic structures such as elections are not yet much of a force in influencing governmental decisions.

The men who run Ukraine come from the Soviet ruling class, the so-called *nomenklatura*. The biographies of the sitting and former presidents, prime ministers, and key executive-branch and legislative-branch officials show their roots in the large industrial enterprises, the old republican ministries, and the Ukrainian Communist Party.[8] These backgrounds should not be seen as either destiny or indictment, but they do indicate that the Ukrainian independence movement was not simply a collection of nationalist or dissident groups but became co-opted by the former *nomenklatura*. In a situation in which the need for qualified bureaucrats, managers, diplomats, and soldiers was great and the pool from which to choose them was relatively small, it is not surprising that the old provincial ruling class in large measure became the new national ruling class.

Presidents Kravchuk and Kuchma brought to power their former associates, friends, politically important patrons, and potential rivals. Such personnel policies are as old as politics itself, but they tend to be corrupting if unlimited by broader social forces of public opinion and the press, or by a fixed set of laws and institutions that regulate political life. Without such constraints, politics tends to become increasingly focused on the struggle for position, influence, and wealth rather than on basic policy options.

Under President Kravchuk, large sections of the former *nomenklatura* were included in the power and spoils of office. Power and influence were distributed across a wide range of regional and sectoral elites, and a rough balance was maintained among these groups. Under President Kuchma—with the beginnings of real reform and thus of the potential to upset the scheme for the distribution of power and control of resources—this formerly cozy era has given way to a struggle among various groups. There has been a mass migration to Kyiv of the former *nomenklatura* of Dnipropetrovs'k, where Kuchma served as the director of *Pivdenmash,* the largest missile factory in the former USSR. By one count, there were over 60 *Dnipropetrovtsy* in the executive branch in April 1995. By mid-1996, there were over 160.[9] They have come to Kyiv for a variety of reasons, though they were brought there principally to shore up the president against potential rivals, particularly former Prime Minister Marchuk. In May 1996, this group succeeded in ousting Marchuk and replacing him with one of their own, Pavlo Lazarenko, who was himself ousted in summer 1997.

This group from Dnipropetrovs'k is by no means monolithic. The intense rivalry between Lazarenko and Kuchma demonstrates this fact. Groups like those from Dnipropetrovs'k are important because they control the state and key sectors of the economy, but the state they control is weak. Thus the great danger posed by their dominance is not a return to authoritarianism, for they are no more venial or less patriotic than any other group, but rather the reduction of politics at the highest level to a constant management of elite competition for wealth and power. The emergence of one group brings forth other rivals and brings about coalitions among them. After all, groups from Donets'k or Poltava want their share. They are willing to stall crucial privatization and other reforms to restore a balance. Mid-level bureaucrats, who owe their livelihood to the old system and its confusing regulations, also have a vested interest in avoiding systemic change.

While this competition among leading individuals and groups has at times been bitter for control of individual media outlets, energy companies, or industrial plants, it has largely taken place outside the public view. But this is changing. The disputes that were once handled behind closed doors are now at the center of Ukrainian presidential politics. With major newspapers in the hands of each of the main contenders, and the government controlling the television, charges of corruption aimed at discrediting rivals appear frequently. Kuchma and his opponents have all played key roles in Ukrainian political life in the past several years. Moroz was the speaker of the Rada (1994–1998). Marchuk and Lazarenko are former prime ministers under Kuchma. They have worked together on large issues of public policy as well as less public questions of managing the competition among rival financial industrial groups. There is little they do not know about one other.

This public process of campaigning for the presidency is ushering in a new phase in Ukrainian politics by bringing the nature of elite politics before the wider citizenry. The major contenders are reluctant to embrace this kind of openness, but elections require it, at least in part. The major contenders try to limit its extent by refraining from raising anti-corruption and populist themes that might mobilize the general public in ways that would be difficult to predict and which might very well threaten incumbents. However, as this presidential race takes shape, it is simply impossible for Kuchma to run the kind of campaign he might wish, given his low standing in the polls and the still unfilled promises of economic reform. He cannot run simply on his record. He also cannot portray the major divide in Ukraine as between communists and anti-communists, as President Yeltsin did in 1996, and place himself as the leader of the anti-communists. His strongest opponents are men like him. He must distinguish himself on matters of policy and results (or lack thereof), or fear being indistinguishable from them.

Most of the ruling elite, perhaps even the candidates themselves, would prefer a colorless campaign. They remain distrustful of elections. They do not want to risk their positions before a people with reason to be angry. Kuchma and his advisers have occasionally speculated out loud how much easier it would be to make progress if elections were delayed for a year or so, as President Kravchuk himself did in 1994. However, elections have become a fact of Ukrainian political life. In time, elections, a stronger civil society, and the growth of independent media and non-governmental organizations might even force the candidates to differentiate themselves on the basis of policy and performance. Marchuk has embraced the weak Ukrainian variant of European social democracy. Lazarenko has set his sights on the emerging business class, which he himself represents with all its virtues and vices. Kuchma has at times shown himself adept at cultivating both business and moderate Ukrainian ethnic constituencies.

There is no sign of this kind of transformation yet. Instead, Ukrainian politics has come out partly in the open, while also remaining partly in the shadows. There are still no popularly based party organizations, no real labor unions or business organizations of the kind we in the West understand. There is certainly no deep popular support for any party or political figure that would ensure a grass roots base. Finally, once the election season has passed, there are still no lasting sources of popular influence on the day-to-day policy process. Ethnic and regional divisions set out broad constraints, but public opinion still has not matured to the point that it is a force to be reckoned with between elections.

Ethnic and Regional Divisions

Ethnic and regional divisions also constrain Ukrainian foreign policy. These divisions have not turned out to be the "great divide" many predicted—one that would pit the Russian and "russified" eastern regions against the western regions. There are, however, a number of deep ethnic and regional divisions that constitute basic constraints on Ukrainian foreign policy.

The first task is to explain why the apocalyptic vision of a country divided in two has not come to pass. The true ethnic and regional constraints on long-term foreign policy can be understood only against this backdrop. Many observers saw an additional source of instability from Ukraine in its large and territorially concentrated Russian minority.[10] In his July 1994 inaugural address, President Kuchma underscored the potential dangers arising from the ethnic divisions in the country: "[W]e must understand that Ukraine is a multiethnic state. Any attempts to ignore that fact threaten a deep schism and the collapse of the idea of Ukrainian statehood."[11] His predecessor, Kravchuk, justified key foreign economic and security policies, particularly his compromises on the CIS, as a way of avoiding the emergence of "two Ukraines."[12] Voices in Russia have pronounced Ukraine "a fragile, artificial, heterogeneous ethno-political formation lacking any real chance for the formation of its own statehood."[13] A chorus of western analysts, including the CIA, noted with alarm the great ethnic split, added to the dangers of a nuclear Ukraine, economic collapse, and hyperinflation, which reached its peak from 1993 to 1994, and concluded that Ukraine might not survive.[14]

As Dominique Arel has argued, when one looks at the division within Ukraine on the basis of language of first preference rather than ethnicity, the Russophone population (ethnic Russians and Ukrainians who speak Russian as their language of choice) is more or less equal to the Ukrainophone. From this point of view, the "divide" is even more significant than the census numbers suggest. Moreover, surveys conducted by Arel and his colleagues from 1994 to 1995 show a strong correlation between language of preference and positions on key issues such as relations with Russia and the internal structure of the state.[15] These and other surveys have shown marked regional differences on fundamental social issues such as private property and market reform, the preservation of the Russian language, the need for integration with Russia, and close cooperation with the EU or NATO. The need to ensure balance between different regions and ethnic groups has loomed large in every important political issue in Ukraine from constitutional and legal change to economic reform. In the nuclear debate as well, Ukraine's internal divisions played a decisive role.[16]

Yet a bifurcated Ukraine has failed to appear. Ethnic and regional divisions are real and of political consequence, but they have never constituted the imminent danger to Ukrainian statehood that many analysts have predicted. According to the 1989 Soviet census, ethnic Ukrainians make up roughly 73 percent of the total population (over 37.4 million of 51.4 million). Ethnic Russians comprise roughly 22 percent (11.4 million).[17] Only in Crimea do Russians make up the majority, and even there they are concentrated in the eastern and southern regions. Ethnic Russians account for over 30 percent of the population in Kharkiv, Donets'k, Luhans'k, and Zaporizhzhya, and for over 20 percent in Dnipropetrovs'k, Kherson, Odesa, and the city of Kyiv.[18] In these regions, the presence of ethnic Russians and the political and cultural influence of Russia has deeply affected the language and overall orientation of the majority Ukrainian population. Moreover, Moscow has influenced the economic development and settlement patterns of these regions—first under the Romanovs and then under the Soviets—with larger ends in mind than the autonomous development of Ukraine and the people who live there. The question really is whether these policies have produced two separate Ukraines.

Several factors mitigate these regional and ethnic divisions:

Ukraine is made up of several important regional, economic, and cultural divisions that cut across the "great divide." The country does not divide on every issue between Russians and Ukrainians, or Russian and Ukrainian speakers, at the Dnipro River. In looking at key social and political attitudes, there are at least five important regional divisions: the eastern, central, southern, and western regions and Crimea. The east includes four *oblasts* that are the most Russified and highly industrialized: Dnipropetrovs'k, Donets'k, Luhans'k, and Zaporizhzhya. Crimea is a region unto itself. The west includes the most ethnically conscious Ukrainian regions of Galicia-Volhynia (L'viv, Ternopil, Ivano-Frankyvsk, Volyn, and Rivne) as well as Zakarpattia and Bukovyna, which historically have a much looser connection to Ukraine as a whole. The south includes the *oblasts* of Odesa, Kherson, and Mykolayiv—an area opened up to settlement only after the Russian conquest of Crimea in 1783 and formerly known as Novorossiya. Odesa and other southern *oblasts* exhibit distinct social and political features, although they are often lumped under the Russian and Russified east. The center includes the remaining, highly diverse *oblasts*—ranging from Kharkiv in the east to Khmel'nyts'kyi in the west. It would be easy to expand this list to seven by subdividing the center into the east-central and the west-central regions and making Kyiv its own region.

Intense intraregional competition normally erodes potential unity on ethnic, linguistic, or political issues. The eastern regions share concerns about economic, cultural, and political questions at the heart of state building, but they also must compete politically with one another for scarce resources and political influence. The eastern regions are also economic competitors—for government support as well as for international aid and investment. The government must regularly respond to pressures from key interest groups, such as the miners or collective farmers. But even Kravchuk understood the limits of appeasing these interests, particularly after experimenting with massive subsidies in the summer of 1993. Kuchma has adopted a tougher approach, mixed with some "carrots." But the basic condition of the Ukrainian budget, the necessity of sustaining economic reform, and outside pressures from international financial institutions and key Western governments have effectively put an end to hopes that the subsidy pie can be expanded or that it will be spread widely over the eastern regions.

The Russian Federation has not provided significant support for ethnic and regional political movements within Ukraine. Russia currently enjoys a great deal of eastern sympathy in public opinion polls, but it is in no condition to take on new economic challenges of the size and magnitude desired by Ukraine's Russia-oriented politicians. They and their constituents conceive of a future Russian-Ukrainian relationship largely in old-fashioned terms. Yet experience has shown that leaders in Dnipropetrovs'k and Luhans'k can do better by playing the regional card in Kyiv than by joining the long line for subsidies in Moscow. Integrationist schemes to return to the old prosperity through the restoration of socialist economic ties must confront the fact that Russia's industries are also engaged in a furious competition for scarce resources. The debate within Russia over the defense budget and subsidies for crumbling high-technology industries illustrates that even if the Ministry of Defense wanted to pursue a strategy of military integration with Ukraine, there would be little to spread around to Ukrainian industries.

Despite problems and failures, the Ukrainian state has successfully addressed and continues to work on the challenges posed by basic divisions within society. The laws, policies, and actions of the Ukrainian government have to date secured the rights of minorities in Ukraine. The basic provisions for citizenship and participation in the country's institutions have been defined from the very beginning in political, not ethnic terms. The combination of this tolerance and the communist-era pre-eminence of the eastern regions within the Soviet system has meant that ethnic Russians and Russophones from the east have played a preponderant role in the founding and running of the Ukrainian political system. It is they, and not the nationalists of western Ukraine, who run the country. The demographic and industrial weight of the east ensures it will remain an important place in both electoral and informal political calculations. Of even greater importance is the fact that the weight of the east also shapes Ukrainian state building in fundamental ways.

This inheritance places *positive* as well as negative constraints on state building. No serious Ukrainian statesman who hopes to govern can advocate an ethnic state. The inheritance likewise limits the center's ability to concentrate power, ensuring that the regions have a voice of their own and are players in Ukrainian political life. Any political scenario that defies these limits must rely either on foreign help or on an internal coup. While such a political scenario can easily be imagined, it is more difficult to visualize how those responsible for seizing power could govern a state like Ukraine over the long term without an anti-democratic transformation: under ordinary political circumstances, the divisions within Ukrainian society are an effective restraint against extremist politics.

Processes already at work in Ukraine are slowly creating a political community that is more than the sum of its parts. Instead of looking for simple expressions of loyalty to Kyiv, analysts must understand the multiple and even contradictory sources of attachment to the Ukrainian state beyond language, ethnicity, or culture. Opinion polls show that the number of people favoring Ukrainian independence have continued to climb even as large segments of the population favor integration with Russia.[19] These multiple sources of identification, allegiance, and tolerance range from passionate nationalism to support of the central government's control of political and economic wealth. The test will be whether the Ukrainian state can build a unifying allegiance to, and tolerance of itself despite these multiple and contradictory sources of identification. The wisdom or good fortune of the Ukrainian government to date is that it has not pursued policies that bring potential conflicts between those identifications into the open. The "great divide" thus remains a decisive factor in shaping Ukrainian politics but does not threaten its demise.

The current divisions are not immutable. The distribution of Russophone and Ukrainophone populations is not something established by nature. There is in fact evidence that ethnic re-identification is under way.[20] Linguistic orientations are subject to similar erosions over time. The present divisions are the result of who ruled, who settled where, and how people made their living. The historical circumstances that created the current ethnic and regional divisions have been profoundly disrupted and are unlikely to be reestablished. The forces that Russified ethnic Ukrainians or made Dnipropetrovs'k a center of military production have weakened—probably forever. They have little hold over the young. Every year of Ukraine's existence increases the number of its citizens who know little or nothing of the Soviet past. It has been ten years since Mikhail Gorbachev's loosening of the Soviet system and five years since the disappearance of the USSR altogether. Those under thirty know no other existence. Those under forty came of age during the Leonid Brezhnev years and have now spent nearly half of their adult lives under Gorbachev's Soviet Union and in an independent Ukraine.

New forces of opportunity and cruel necessity are at work reshaping the Ukrainian polity, and state building itself is one of these forces. The current political geography of Ukraine must be respected, but it is by no means immutable. Of course, these divisions could also harden or perhaps even become deeper under conditions of economic and political failure in Kyiv. It is the task of this generation of Ukrainian statesmen to find a way to build upon the positive legacy of this geography yet create a state and society that is no longer held captive by its most serious divisions.

Although the vision of Ukraine as a bifurcated society has not come to pass, regional and ethnic divisions remain that do constrain long-term Ukrainian strategic policy. Uniting the various regional and ethnic perspectives is a widespread ignorance of foreign and security policy choices, notions of Russia and the West that have been nurtured by Soviet and Diaspora writings and long decades living without the free flow of information. The weakness of civil society means that these constraints do not operate as day-to-day pressures on particular decisions. Rather, they function like gutters in a bowling alley. They place hard boundaries on the left and right but permit the ball freedom of movement in between. They create powerful incentives for a foreign policy that balances between the eastern orientation of some in Ukraine and the western orientation of others. Ukraine's careful balancing act on relations with Russia and integration within the CIS reflects these divisions. Ukraine's policy on nuclear weapons similarly reflected these broad constraints: it would have been difficult to pursue the policy of becoming an openly nuclear state, a policy that many western experts believed Ukraine was in fact pursuing, without having profoundly destabilizing internal consequences.

Polling in Ukraine has its pitfalls beyond those ordinarily complicating public opinion surveys. Yet polls illustrate the problem facing Ukrainian statesmen in their quest for a sustained strategic posture. There remain serious regional and ethnic divisions in Ukrainian society that could have significant strategic consequences. Moreover, in nearly all the polls cited below, there is a large number of people responding simply that they do not know or are not well informed. There also remain highly contradictory tendencies among the population at large that at times embraces independence yet shows consistently high numbers for integration or even unification with Russia:

- A Kyiv International Institute of Sociology (KIIS) poll from October to November 1996 found that 56 percent of Ukrainians say that Ukraine should unite with Russia in a single state; 36 percent disagree with the statement; 86 percent of the ethnic Russians polled favored unification with Russia.[21]
- A December 1996 poll conducted by Sotsis-Gallop and Democratic Initiatives found a total of 36 percent of respondents agreeing that Ukraine should become a member of NATO; 19 percent believed Ukraine should not join NATO; 45 percent could not provide an answer either for or against membership in NATO.[22]
- A 1997 KIIS poll reported by *Interfax* found that 32 percent of Ukrainian citizens believe their country's security would best be preserved "if Ukraine joins a CIS military alliance." In this poll, only 18 percent supported NATO membership. Over a quarter of those polled (26 percent) found it difficult to give any answer at all.[23]

- A Democratic Initiatives poll from January 1997 found 38 percent in favor of NATO membership (19 percent as soon as possible and 19 percent "not right away"). There were 21 percent opposed; 42 percent found it "difficult to say." Yet when asked about which option best served Ukraine's national interest, the same group favored neutrality (20 percent), with NATO gathering 19 percent. A further 10 percent favored the option of Ukraine joining NATO with other CIS countries. Only 11 percent favored the creation of a military alliance with CIS countries as an alternative to NATO membership. Some 41 percent found it "difficult to say." When given yet another set of choices on the kind of Ukraine they would prefer, 25 percent favored an independent neutral state, 19 percent a bloc with Russia and Belarus, and 14 percent preferred being a member of a "new USSR." CIS membership (9 percent) and becoming part of Russia (3 percent) received even lower support; 15 percent favored being part of a bloc with Western countries. Only 15 percent found it "difficult to say." Finally, this same poll found that 24.7 percent of respondents found Russia the biggest threat to Ukraine. The United States was second at 4.6 percent. Over 65 percent of respondents did not know which country represented the biggest threat to Ukraine.[24]
- Another Socis-Gallup poll conducted in May 1997 asked, "which variant of a foreign policy course is best for Ukraine?" Some 46 percent of the respondents favored unification of CIS countries into a single state; 13 percent favored the current status quo, while 26 percent wanted a course of secession from the CIS, firm independence, and orientation toward countries outside of CIS. Only 15 percent found it hard to respond.[25]
- A June 1997 poll of residents of Donets'k, a large city in eastern Ukraine, also asked about possible ties to NATO: 28 percent of respondents were positive; 33 percent were negative; 16 percent said they were neither positive or negative; 23 percent did not provide an answer. In these and other questions relating to key security issues, the pollsters found a substantial difference between the young and the old. On Russian-Belarusian integration, for example, only 12.2 percent of young respondents (23 to 29 years old) expressed approval. 57.2 percent of those in their fifties and sixties thought Russian-Belarusian integration a positive thing. In the overall poll on the Russian-Belarusian integration question, not broken down for age groups, "the majority of the respondents either were poorly acquainted with the situation, either had heard something, but found it difficult to determine their orientation, or relate to events in Belarus neutrally."

A similar generational divide was found in questions regarding the favored model of development for Ukraine. Among those 17 to 22 years old, models based on Germany (29.4 percent) and the United States (20.6 percent) were favored. Models based on the USSR (1.5 percent) and Russia (2.9 percent) fell far behind. For those over 60, the USSR was the preferred model of development (25.1 percent), with Germany second (16.5 percent), Russia third (10.1 percent) and the United States well back (2.8 percent).[26]

It is, of course, difficult to compare polls. The questions do not match, even when they are focused on NATO and its alternatives. Technical aspects of the survey may have varied widely. However, these and many other polls do seem to suggest the existence of important constraints on Ukrainian foreign policy. The first and most obvious is that many in the society at large do not really understand the options. This conclusion emerges from the high numbers of respondents who cannot answer the question at all, as well as from the polls that show conflicting or divided tendencies. The number of people who support Ukraine's immediate membership in NATO is relatively small, around 20 percent in several of the polls above. Numbers for a Russian or CIS alternative to NATO vary wildly. On some polls, large numbers appear indifferent to Ukrainian independence. Those who do not know or do not wish to answer are often nearly half those surveyed. One suspects that many who choose one or another concrete alternative did so less out of profound conviction and more out of falling in with the general ideological tenor of their town or region. Deep divisions exist, but so do large elements of uncertainty

There are also divisions within divisions, as the Donets'k polls show, in which the young are less entrenched in their Russian or even Soviet orientation and more inclined to view NATO favorably than the very old. The high support among pensioners in this poll for the USSR and Russia—including preference for the USSR as a model of development—is more likely to reflect their difficult economic status than a sustained reflection on strategic alternatives. These numbers reflect real and long term doubts among the population regarding a Euro-Atlantic course for Ukraine, but they are far from showing a society split right down the middle. The leadership has some immediate room to maneuver, particularly if it can keep its policies focused on practical cooperation that does not require formal treaties or publicly visible and controversial steps. A serious long-term effort to do something more ambitious, especially embracing NATO membership as a long-term goal, would require in turn a much more serious and sustained effort to address the divisions and questions that remain in the public at large.

Economic Stagnation

No discussion of the internal constraints on Ukraine's foreign policy options would be complete without underscoring the country's current economic stagnation. This stagnation also doubtless contributes to the divisions and distractions discussed above. Economic hardship plays upon ethnic and regional differences, giving the left a boost in the east and, at times, giving the Russian nationalist parties a boost in Crimea.

Ukraine's economic reforms have largely been limited to price liberalization and macroeconomic stabilization. The commitment to privatization has been fitful, but the process has moved forward gradually. President Kuchma's 1994 reforms brought the economy back from the verge of collapse in 1993, reducing inflation from over 10,000 percent a year in 1993 to perhaps less than 20 percent in 1997. Kuchma's reform package included a sweeping set of measures designed to produce financial stabilization, privatization, and price liberalization.

Despite serious internal opposition, at times extending to the executive branch itself, and occasional lapses in the form of credit emissions, the package succeeded in freeing most prices and bringing real financial stabilization. Privatization remained slow and subject to insider deals, official corruption, and rent seeking. The economy continued to contract in 1997, the GDP down by perhaps 3 percent. The best that can be said here is that the rates of decline in GDP and industrial production have slowed.[27] Official statistics do not capture the still unmeasured dynamism of the "informal sector" of the economy, estimated by one study to provide the "main source of income for 2.5 million people, including up to 40% of youth in urban and border regions."[28]

The real problem remains the lack of commitment to a real market economy. There has been little deregulation or structural reform apart from privatization. The state remains the majority or largest shareholder in many cases. Many of the best deals are divided ahead of time by insiders. The lack of a clear legal base, weak courts, and bureaucratic corruption scare off most foreign investors. Opposition to privatization, particularly in the communist and socialist-dominated stronghold in the eastern part of the country, remains strong. This reform process remains vulnerable to reversal, but the more likely danger is that of the reform simply entering a long-term hiatus, leaving Ukraine somewhere between old-style socialism and a market system.

The Asian economic crisis and internal political considerations exacerbated the economic problems in the country. Although the Ukrainian government responded with additional budget cuts and other measures to defend the currency, Ukraine is not out of the woods. In fact, as the March 1998 parliamentary election neared, the government released back wages and pensions, forcing a treasury already strapped for cash to seek it abroad at a penalty. Ukraine was forced to pay "the highest spread ever for a sovereign borrower—12 percentage points above German government bonds—" for its February 1998 Eurobond issue.[29] Its currency, the *hryvna,* lost 6 percent of its value against the dollar in February 1998 alone. In the past year, Ukraine has fallen behind in its energy payments to Russia, running up a debt of over $1 billion dollars. The weakness of the Ukrainian state and the preoccupations of the political class with the division of property and the long political season, beginning with the March 1998 parliamentary elections and ending only with presidential elections in the fall of 1999, promise to exacerbate these problems as the government turns to populist gestures—such as massive emissions—rather than reforms to keep its hold on power.

Impact on Ukraine's Strategic Challenges

The great disparity between Ukraine's stated strategic course and its internal problems is unlikely to go away soon. Despite what many senior Ukrainian officials believe, they can not simply take a year or two off from the business of managing the economy.[30] If anything, the internal challenges are likely to grow in the near future, deeply altering both Ukraine's ability to pursue a westward-oriented foreign policy and external assessments of such a policy's viability. Internal stagnation threatens to unravel the hard-fought gains of Ukrainian foreign policy in its relations with both Russia and the West, leaving Ukraine in the end fewer options for the future than the current leadership now contemplates.

Ukrainian-Russian Relations

Ukraine's greatest external challenge remains the normalization of its relations with Russia. Normal and friendly relations between these states would be a substantial contribution to European stability. These two states have the greatest military potentials of any of non-NATO Europe. Conflict between these two states, over Crimea or other issues, would have an immediate and chilling effect on European stability. There is another aspect to Russian-Ukrainian relations that has European-wide significance. The Russian-Ukrainian relationship reveals much about Russia itself, particularly whether Russia is reconciled to its current borders and to exerting its influence in a way that is compatible with the stability and independence of its new neighbors. Key issues of Russia's long-term evolution are bound up in its relations with Ukraine. Ukraine is perhaps the greatest single external factor in Russia's definition of itself as a state and international actor.

Despite mutual suspicions and a conflicting sense of where the relationship ought to be headed, both sides have shown a high degree of moderation and pragmatism when it mattered most. These qualities coexist with real disagreements as well as symbolic gestures and hard rhetoric that periodically suggest the relationship is on the verge of a great crisis. The several Yeltsin-Kravchuk summits and the successor meetings between Yeltsin and Kuchma remain a prime example of how the two sides found ways to steer the relationship through rough waters. Until May 1997, the two leaders regularly announced agreements in principle on issues such as the Black Sea Fleet or the Friendship Treaty that never materialized or soon dissolved in follow-up technical negotiations. The leaders probably knew these agreements would not hold up and intended to use them to reduce the pressures of the moment and restore a sense of normalcy, not obtain a long-term resolution of the issues.

The May 1997 Yeltsin-Kuchma summit represented an important step forward, leading to concrete and long-delayed agreements on the basic principles underlying the bilateral relationship, including the first legal acknowledgment of the legitimacy of Ukraine's borders, and a settlement of the Black Sea Fleet issue.[31] Agreements in late 1997 and 1998 furthered this trend, ending a dispute over value added taxes and proclaiming a ten-year plan of economic cooperation. Unlike the period from 1991 to 1997, the two sides are now concluding finished agreements, not agreements in principle. However, these texts face skeptical voices in both Russia and Ukraine and the hard task of successful implementation by cash-strapped and internally distracted countries. In fact, several Russian observers have noted that these agreements come on the eve of an election season in Ukraine, when good relations with Russia are considered good politics in the more populous eastern regions of Ukraine. Several observers in Moscow have argued that the current goodwill from Ukraine will last only until the day after the presidential elections.[32]

Even with these cautionary notes, the 1997–1998 agreements provide a chance for an enduring resolution of the problems that have heretofore plagued bilateral relations. They are the beginnings of normal, state-to-state ties regulated by treaties and respect for sovereignty. Such a resolution of the relationship is needed, but it ultimately requires that Russia and Ukraine go even further in resolving existing ambiguities.

The greatest ambiguity of all remains the two sides' different views of the goal of the relationship itself. Many in Russia are reluctant to put the relationship once and for all on a true state-to-state footing, hoping that, over time, the two sides will return to something more intimate—a notion Yeltsin adviser Dmitriy Riurikov once described as "a fraternal Slavic compromise."[33] Ukraine would like an unambiguous state-to-state relationship. But Ukraine by itself is too weak to impose such a relationship on Russia. The West, particularly the United States, has been a crucial instrument of Ukraine's Russian policy. Once the nuclear issue was resolved, Kyiv used its expanding western ties and the impending prospect of NATO enlargement to its advantage in relations with Moscow. Russia, to its credit, responded with greater flexibility, not hostility, to these changing circumstances. The resulting agreements contain individual provisions that benefit Moscow, of course, but as a package they represent a victory for Ukraine's insistence on developing a bilateral, treaty-based relationship that is no different from that between close neighbors anywhere in the world.

However, all that is put at risk by Ukraine's internal stagnation. Ukraine's internal weakness could become the decisive factor in the next stages in Russian-Ukrainian relations. In a sense, the recent history of this relationship has been defined by the exhaustion and preoccupations of both sides. Russia has been too burdened by its own internal problems; its basic institutions are too chaotic and fragmented to provide the basis for a sustained assertive policy. In this condition, Russia could not manage a serious crisis within Ukraine, let alone carry out interventionist policies. However, there are real dangers in assuming that dual exhaustion can endure indefinitely. Russian consolidation of its political and economic system over time will increase its capacity to conduct a more ambitious Ukrainian policy. The key is not in Russia's size or strength but the size of the gap between it and Ukraine. If Ukraine remains stuck in its current stagnation, not only will the gap between it and Russia widen but the leverage of Kyiv's western policies could well diminish as the West closes the door to Ukraine's Euro-Atlantic ambitions. A stronger Russia, a stagnant Ukraine, and an indifferent West make for a much less stable Russian-Ukrainian relationship.

Ukraine's Westpolitik

Ukraine has to date successfully used its growing ties with Washington, Warsaw, and other western capitals and institutions to support state consolidation, the early stages of economic reform, and the management of relations with Russia. Ukraine's overall western policy has greatly expanded beyond this instrumental function, especially since mid-1995. Before that, Ukraine had trouble sustaining a serious dialogue with the West because of the unresolved status of Soviet nuclear weapons on Ukrainian soil. The securing of the Soviet nuclear arsenal under a single Russian command and control was a western strategic priority.

Until Ukrainian nuclear intentions were clarified, a process that lasted until at least 1994, there were few takers in the West for a policy of engagement. There were, however, important voices, especially in Poland and the United States, arguing for deepening ties with Kyiv if it began nuclear disarmament. The January 1994 Trilateral Agreement, Kuchma's economic reform package and Ukraine's adherence to the Nuclear Nonproliferation Treaty later that same year generated the momentum needed to sustain serious ties between Kyiv and western nations and institutions.

United States-Ukraine ties have steadily improved since the signing of the Trilateral Agreement in January 1994. President Kravchuk came to Washington within weeks of its signing, leading to new agreements of economic and other assistance that in 1997 made Ukraine the third largest recipient of U.S. foreign aid. In May 1995, President Clinton visited Kyiv. Senior ministerial and deputy ministerial visits have been common. During one of these visits, Foreign Minister Udovenko's meetings in Washington in October 1996, the two sides publicly declared their relationship a full-fledged strategic partnership. The United States has also supported Ukraine's efforts to expand its ties with other western nations and institutions. The United States, for example, was the driving force behind the language in the December 1996 NATO ministerial communiqué stating the alliance's support for Ukrainian political and economic reform and acknowledging that "the maintenance of Ukraine's independence, territorial integrity and sovereignty is a crucial factor for stability and security in Europe."[34] Washington played an equally central role in the negotiation of the Ukrainian-NATO charter.

Although ties with the United States have always been the cornerstone of Ukraine's western policy, in mid-1995, the Ukrainian leadership embarked on a policy designed to expand its links with other western nations and key institutions. In September 1995, Foreign Minister Udovenko led a high-level delegation to NATO to begin to define a special relationship between Ukraine and the alliance. In October 1995, with Poland's strong support, Ukraine became a member of the Council of Europe. Poland was also crucial to Ukraine's invitation to join the Central European initiative in June 1996. In that same month, a Warsaw summit between Polish and Ukrainian presidents produced strong statements of mutual support, with Kuchma giving a ringing endorsement of Poland's desire to join NATO. In September 1996, German Chancellor Kohl visited Kyiv, as did the Secretary General of the Western European Union, José Cutileiro. Cutileiro and Kuchma agreed that for membership purposes, Ukraine would be treated like the six former non-Soviet Warsaw Pact countries and the three Baltic states. Ukraine would not have to wait for associate status in the European Union but could apply after ratification by all parties of the June 1994 cooperation agreement between Ukraine and the European Union.[35]

Yet despite the undoubted successes of Ukraine's western policy, particularly in relations with Washington, Warsaw, and Europe's key institutions, Ukraine has still not succeeded in convincing the majority of its European neighbors that it wants or deserves a place in Europe. Many of the key European states, such as France, have yet to recognize Ukraine's strategic importance. For these states, Ukraine seems more like Turkey, a state on the edge of Europe, a player on the European scene but certainly not of Europe itself. In the chancelleries of Europe, little thought is given to Ukraine, except in regards to Chornobyl.

Ukraine's internal problems and historic ties to Russia and the former Soviet space are taken as justification for this neglect. Many of these states believe that the crucial task after NATO expansion will be to rebuild ties with Russia, not expand them with other states Russia regards as crucial to its own security. There is thus an incompleteness and fragility to Ukrainian-Western ties. Kyiv's gains could be easily reversed by its own internal problems, its failure to make economic progress, or simply Western anxiety about Russia. They require further broadening and deepening to sustain them.

Ukraine's continuing stagnation comes at a crucial time and could decisively alter its prospects for long term participation in Europe. Ukraine's Euro-Atlantic policies invite Western consideration, not merely of the utility of an independent Ukraine but of Ukraine's fitness for Europe. There is essentially no disagreement on Kyiv's short-term prospects. Ukraine is simply not qualified to be a member of the EU or NATO now or in the near term. However, the current internal situation raises questions in some Western countries whether Ukraine will ever be qualified for a role in Europe. It raises fundamental questions about the intentions of the Ukrainian leadership and the directions that the Ukrainian state and society are taking overall. These questions are coming up at a time when Europe itself is preoccupied with monetary union, the enlargement of the EU to central Europe, Estonia, and Cyprus, and the crisis in the Balkans, with little energy left over for a state that does not appear to want to help itself.

Ukrainian internal stagnation also corrodes relations with the United States. There is little chance that Washington will rethink its recognition of the importance of an independent Ukraine. Yet many important voices are emerging that criticize corruption, the lack of a predictable investment climate, and problems in controlling high tech and defense exports. The U.S.-Ukrainian partnership cannot be built on geopolitics alone. Similarly, Polish-Ukrainian cooperation cannot become as broad and deep as both sides want if the two countries retain two incompatible economic systems. The old-fashioned economic relations fostered by the Soviet system between portions of the Russian and Ukrainian economy, continued energy dependence, personal ties, and the distribution of rents do not need market reform. Indeed, they will not survive it. Thus, Russia has an inherent advantage in a stagnant Ukraine, while Ukraine's ties to the West require reform to move toward their full development.

Conclusion

Oil and water do not mix. Ukrainian internal stagnation and external westernization are just such a combination. Yet why should the West care? The Ukrainian leadership might well continue its preference for "muddling through" or even trim its westward ambitions. Why would this matter in Washington, Paris, or Berlin?

Ukraine's problems are man-made. They can and must be addressed and resolved by Ukrainians themselves. If the Ukrainian leadership is able to avoid the hard choices, why not let them enjoy their spoils on Europe's periphery? After all, Ukraine is a stable enough place. Does the West really have much of a stake in Ukraine, especially a Ukraine that appears to have no real intention to take the steps necessary to show it wants to belong to Europe? As tempting as such a conclusion is, Ukraine's choice between Europe and Europe's periphery matters to the continent as a whole.

A choice in favor of the status quo in Ukraine does not merely perpetuate the country as it is today. It undermines the foundations that have made the current situation bearable inside the country and less dangerous for Ukraine's neighbors. It would certainly put in danger the policies that have dramatically lowered inflation and brought Ukraine a stable currency. It would exacerbate economic deprivation in the country as a whole, particularly along crucial ethnic and regional fault lines, such as Crimea. A stagnant Ukraine will grow weaker and less coherent as a government, depriving it of the ability to handle future crises, whether inside the country or with its neighbors.

Finally, it would convince the many skeptics in the West that they were right all along about Ukraine—that it does not belong in Europe. The current momentum in Ukraine's ties with the West would erode in a way that would undermine the most important external supports for the political and economic reforms that are hanging on in the country. A western disengagement from Ukraine would adversely influence the course of Ukrainian-Russian relations, which have stabilized in no small measures because of the current strategic context provided by U.S. and Western interest in their normalization.

A peripheral and stagnant Ukraine would increase the danger that enlarging European institutions like NATO and EU would find themselves on a much more unpredictable and unstable frontier. The West of course cannot force the Ukrainian leadership to act against its immediate political interests. It cannot impose sound economic reforms or more transparent politics. It can, however, remain a strong stimulus for these reforms by reminding Ukraine of the choice it faces and the basic requirements for participation in Europe. It can also make plain that its long-term support will be there for whichever leader, whether President Kuchma or one of his opponents, who understands the choices and acts in a constructive manner to get the country moving in the right direction.

Notes

1. There is a growing list of book and book-length studies of Ukrainian security policy. See, for example, Tor Bukkvoll, *Ukraine and European Security* (London: The Royal Institute for International Affairs, 1997); John Jaworsky, *Ukraine: Stability and Instability,* McNair Paper No. 42 (Washington, DC: National Defense University, 1995); Taras Kuzio, *Ukrainian Security Policy* (Washington, DC: The Center for Strategic and International Studies, 1995); and Arkady Moshes, *Vnutripoliticheskoe razvitie i vneshnaya politika Ukraïny v 1991–1995 gg.,* Occasional Paper of the Institute of Europe No. 27 (Moscow: Russian Academy of Sciences, 1996). See also the author's own recent work, *Keystone in the Arch: Ukraine and the Emerging Security Environment of Eastern and Central Europe* (Washington, DC: The Carnegie Endowment, 1997).

2. For example, the flap over press reports that Foreign Minister Udovenko was seeking "associate membership" in NATO led to a Kuchma statement that associate membership is "absent from our political vocabulary" (ITAR-TASS, June 26, 1996).

3. The Ukrainian negotiating team for the January 1994 trilateral agreement, for example, included Presidential Adviser Anton Buteyko, Deputy Prime Minister Valeriy Shmarov, First Deputy Foreign Minister Borys Tarasiuk, and the Head of the Disarmament Division of the Ministry of Foreign Affairs, Konstantyn Hryshchenko. Buteyko, according to interviews the author conducted in Kyiv in April and October 1995, drafted the basic text of ratification the

Rada adopted in November 1993, ensuring that while it focused on Ukrainian demands and interpretations for the disposition of nuclear weapons, it also kept open negotiating options with Washington.

4. ITAR-TASS, May 30, 1996; ITAR-TASS, February 22, 1997; and *Interfax,* May 7, 1997.

5. *Interfax,* July 18, 1997.

6. See, for example, Volodymyr Horbulin's statement that "Ukraine is not ready to join NATO, even if it wanted to . . ." (*Interfax,* July 18, 1997).

7. For a fuller discussion see op cit., S. Garnett, *Keystone in the Arch.*

8. See, for example, the biographical entries for Kuchma, Kravchuk, Marchuk, and Lazarenko in *Khto ie khto v ukrains'kiy politytsi, Vypusk 2* (Kyiv: KIS, 1995).

9. On the influence of the *Dnipropetrovtsy* in the Kuchma government, see the articles by V'yacheslav Pikhovshek in *Most,* no. 46, (translated in *FBIS Daily Report: Central Eurasia,* December 19, 1995) and in *Kievskiye vedomosti,* May 28, 1996 (translated in *FBIS Daily Report: Central Eurasia,* May 28, 1996).

10. This section is adapted from op cit., S. Garnett, *Keystone in the Arch,* pp. 11–26.

11. "Leonid Kuchma Prinyos Prisyagu Na Vernost' Ukrainskomu Narodu," *Holos Ukrayiny,* July 21, 1994.

12. For example, on the CIS charter and economic union, Kravchuk had spoken of the danger of "the creation of a situation in which Ukrainian society is divided into two defined groups" and of the need to avoid the emergence of "two Ukraines" (*Holos Ukrayiny,* January 20, 1993 [translated in *FBIS Daily Report: Central Eurasia,* September 22, 1993, pp. 26–27]).

13. Andranik Migranyan, "Rossiya i blizhnee zarubezh'e," *Nezavisimaya gazeta,* January 18, 1994.

14. For examples of predictions of Ukraine's imminent collapse, see Daniel Williams and R. Jeffrey Smith, "U.S. Intelligence Sees Economic Plight Leading to Breakup of Ukraine," *The Washington Post,* January 25, 1994; Rowland Evans and Robert Novak, "West Is Still Unsure How to Aid Ukraine," *Chicago Sun-Times,* June 9, 1994; Eugene B. Rumer, "Will Ukraine Return to Russia," *Foreign Policy,* no. 96 (Fall 1994), pp. 129–144; and F. Stephen Larabee, "Ukraine: Europe's Next Crisis?" *Arms Control Today,* vol. 24, no. 6 (July-August 1994), pp. 14–19. For a recent Russian argument about the dangers of a "nationalizing" Ukraine, see Aleksey Miller, "Ukraina kak natsionaliziruyuschesya gosudarstvo," *Pro et Contra,* vol. 2, no. 2 (Spring 1997), p. 85-98.

15. See Dominique Arel, "Ukraine: The Temptation of the Nationalizing State," and Zenovia Sochor, "Political Culture and Foreign Policy: Elections in Ukraine 1994," in Vladimir Tismaneanu (ed.), *Political Culture and Civil Society in Russia and the New States of Eurasia* (Armonk, NY: M. E. Sharpe, 1995), pp. 157–188 and pp. 208–226.

16. On the link between Ukrainian domestic policy (including the ethnic and regional divisions) and nuclear policy, see the author's essay, "The Sources and

Conduct of Ukrainian Nuclear Policy: November 1992 to January 1994," in George Quester (ed.), *Nuclear Challenges for Russia and the New States of Eurasia* (Armonk, NY: M. E. Sharpe, 1995), pp. 125–151.

17. USSR 1989 census figures are provided in *Natsional'nyi sostav naseleniya SSSR, po dannykh perepisi naseleniia* (Moscow: Finantsy i statistika, 1991). For breakdowns by region, see also F. D. Zastavnyy, *Heohrafiya Ukrayiny* (Lviv: Svit, 1994), pp. 411–417; and the summary table based on the 1989 census in Taras Kuzio and Andrew Wilson, *Ukraine: Perestroika to Independence* (New York: St. Martin's Press, 1994), p. 30.

18. Op cit., T. Kuzio and A. Wilson, p. 30.

19. *Nezavisimaya gazeta*, March 1, 1994 and *OMRI Daily Digest*, January 10, 1995. These and other polls seem to capture general moods of satisfaction and dissatisfaction, not deep-seated convictions that are translated into political action. For example, a 1994 poll conducted in 24 Ukrainian regions by the Kyiv International Sociological Institute found 40 percent of the respondents expressing preference for Ukraine and Russia being a single state. However, a January 1995 poll by the same organization found 64 percent of Ukrainians polled declaring their support for the country's independence.

20. Stephen Rapawy, *Ethnic Redentification in Ukraine*, IPC Staff Paper No. 90 (Washington DC; U.S. Bureau of the Census, August 1997).

21. USIA, Opinion Analysis, January 12, 1997, p. 4.

22. In this poll, 15 percent stated that Ukraine should join NATO as quickly as possible; 21 percent preferred a later date for membership. See *Molod' Ukrayiny*, January 24, 1997; *Holos Ukrayiny*, January 25, 1997; and *Uriadoviy Kur'er*, January 30, 1997.

23. *Interfax*, February 4, 1997.

24. *A Political Portrait of Ukraine*, no. 8 (1997), as cited by *The Ukrainian Weekly*, February 9, 1997.

25. *Den'*, May 30, 1997.

26. *Izuchenie obshchestvennogo mneniya kak sotsialnogo faktora Donetskoy oblast* (Donetsk: Tsentr politologicheskikh issledovanii, June 1997).

27. *Ukraine. Country Focus* (London: Economist Intelligence Unit, 26 March 1998).

28. These and other figures in this section are taken from *Ukraine. Country Focus* (London: Economist Intelligence Unit, May 6, 1996); and a report of the Kyiv Office of The World Bank, "On the Pillars of Economic Reform in Ukraine," March 1996.

29. *The Wall Street Journal Europe*, March 9, 1998.

30. A very senior Ukrainian official assured me in May 1997 that the government could in fact do that, surviving even a communist victory in the parliament, because "they do not have any ideas." While perhaps true, it struck me that few people in Ukraine had much faith in the government's intellectual power, either.

31. Previous Russian-Ukrainian agreements and Russian statements provisionally recognized Ukrainian borders by recognizing boundaries "within the framework of the Commonwealth of Independent States." For an extended discussion of the border issue, see op cit, S. Garnett, *Keystone in the Arch,* pp. 57–61.
32. Author's interviews in Moscow, January and March 1998.
33. *Kievskiye vedomosti,* April 28, 1995.
34. *Final Communiqué of the Ministerial Meeting of the North Atlantic Council,* December 10, 1996, NATO Press Office.
35. James Sherr, *Ukraine, Russia and Europe* (Sandhurst: Conflict Studies Research Centre, October 1996), p. 10.

CHAPTER 6

The Law on the Civil Service: A Case Study of Administrative Reform in Ukraine

Bohdan Krawchenko

The civil service is the administrative machinery of government, and its development is central to the state building process. This institution merits particular attention in the case of transitional societies. As N. R. Nyzhnyk recently noted, "The fate of the Ukrainian democratic state depends on whether it will succeed in overcoming the weighty heritage of bureaucratism, corruption, and create the conditions that will facilitate the employment of talented civil servants, and secure their promotion in the bureaucratic hierarchy."[1]

The Ukrainian civil service has many detractors and few defenders. Yet what is often overlooked when evaluations are made is that this institution is barely five years old. It came into being on January 1, 1994 when the primary legislative instrument—the law on the civil service—came into force. The events leading to the birth of this institution are the subject of this chapter. We examine how the civil law was written, the debates surrounding the passage of the bill, and the act's shortcomings, and point to some of the major tasks that remain to be accomplished.

The Civil Service Prior to 1991

Shortly after the fall of communism, almost all central and Eastern Europe states passed legislation establishing a civil service. The aim was to provide a legal framework for the establishment of a state civil service that was, "politically neutral but designed to provide efficient and cost effective administrative support services to elected government in the achievement of its economic and social objectives."[2] In Ukraine the law on the civil service was passed by parliament—the Verkhovna Rada—in December 1993. Ukraine was the first country in the former USSR to adopt this legislation.[3]

In Western countries, civil service systems that crystallized at the turn of this century did not come into being overnight. They were the culmination of developments lasting hundreds of years. Central Europe and the Baltics, had pre–World War II administrative traditions that could be drawn upon in fashioning new institutions.[4] Ukrainians also sought inspiration from the past. As two young Ukrainian civil servants put it, "as we face the need to introduce radical changes in the public service in Ukraine, we turn to the historical road that Ukraine has travelled to understand traditions and specificity of the development of [our country's] public administration."[5] History bequeathed a legacy that could be easily ignored.

Just as in Western Europe, the first civil servants on the territory of Ukraine originated in seigniorial households and performed purely personal and military functions. The establishment of a unified Kyivan Rus' state in the ninth century meant that the sovereign needed a new category of servants, those responsible for broader tasks such as the collection of tributes, registration, and arbitration of disputes. These too were considered the personal servants of the ruler. The collapse of Kyiv Rus' ended this period of indigenous administrative development. Prince Danylo Halyts'kyi attempted to establish an administrative system on his territory inspired by European models of the High Middle Ages, but his kingdom was short-lived. In Western Europe, it was the organizational principles of the Roman Catholic Church that played such a decisive role in the development of state bureaucracy. This influence was absent in Ukraine. It was only at the end of the seventeenth century, under the Hetmanate, that the country saw the rise of a group of functionaries who held clear and specialized offices and whose senior members were increasingly recruited from the newly established academies.[6]

Ukraine's absorption into the Russian Imperial system put an end to this development of a Ukrainian state service. By the end of the eighteenth century Ukraine was incorporated into the Russian Imperial bureaucratic system with its Table of Ranks (established 1722), fourteen ranks of service that spelled out in detail its order and conditions. The rule of Russian *chinovnik,* characterized by servility to the autocracy, and unchecked authority marked administration in Ukraine until 1917. During the revolution of 1917, there

were several attempts to establish a modern civil service. The most conse-
quential was made by the government of Hetman Pavlo Skoropads'kyi
(which existed for less than a year in 1918), who enacted a civil service law.[7]
This chapter also closed when the Soviet regime established itself in Ukraine.

Under the Soviet regime, firmly established in Ukraine from 1920, there
was no civil service as such. The bureaucratic apparatus was characterised by
Communist party patronage and cronyism, and personnel management was
highly politicized. Although the Soviet Union was often called a "bureaucratic behemoth," its administrative machinery possessed few of the characteristics one associates with bureaucratic organization. (These would include
a division of labor based on functional specialization, a well-defined hierarchy of authority, a system of rules governing rights and duties of employment, a system of procedures for dealing with work situations, impersonality
of interpersonal relations, and promotion and selection based on technical
competence.)[8]

The very concept of a unified civil service as a body of professional administrators did not exist. Each ministry and state committee (and there
were over 100 in total) had its own management system. As a reformer of
the *perestroika* period put it, when it came to managing state functionaries,
"The leadership . . . at all levels . . . acted according to their own understanding of things, by happenstance."[9] The only legislation governing civil
servants was the labor code. It was clear even under Gorbachev that a radical administrative reform was needed, and indeed a draft law on the civil service was prepared on the eve of the collapse of the USSR.[10]

First Steps Towards Civil Service Reform

Throughout 1991 the Ukrainian political leadership was preoccupied with
wresting sovereignty from Moscow. The entire focus of attention was on asserting Ukrainian control over spheres of activity hitherto monopolized by
union and union-republic ministries. Little thought was given to broader issues of public administration. The August 24, 1991 declaration of independence and the banning of the Communist Party of Ukraine changed things
dramatically. There was no understanding as yet that the country needed to
develop civil service legislation and reform. It was, however, understood that
Ukraine would need an institution to train public servants—a structure to
replace the Higher Party School, which had been disbanded. The first step
in civil service reform was thus the establishment of the Institute of Public
Administration and Local Government, Cabinet of Ministers (IPALG), by a
March 4, 1992 decree of President Leonid Kravchuk.[11]

The institute was patterned after the French Ecole Nationale d'Administration (ENA). The choice of a continental model was consciously made and found support during a visit to France in late December 1991 by a group of advisers to President Kravchuk. The institute was mandated to train those who would occupy senior positions in the bureaucracy and to develop policy recommendations for the improvement of public administration in the country. If Ukraine passed a civil service law in December 1993 it was because the institute had started to function in the spring of 1992, as an institution that had a mandate, duty, and a vested interest in lobbying for a civil service law. As was noted in the "First Annual Report," when the institute was established, "Ukraine did not have a civil service law nor a modern civil service organisation. . . . Thus the relationship between training at IPALG, and the recruitment into the civil service and promotion within that body, remained ad hoc in nature."[12]

The very nature of the IPALG project required the development of a modern civil service structure in Ukraine.[13] IPALG's initiatives in this respect were supported by senior civil servants in the Cabinet of Ministers, especially Ihor Kharchenko (head of the department of labor and social welfare), and Anatolii Bohomolov (deputy head of the department of education, culture, and health), who understood the need to professionalize Ukraine's bureaucracy and who played a major role in all subsequent events.

It was the study mission to France in May 1992 by Volodymyr Piekhota, Minister of the Cabinet of Ministers, (accompanied by IPALG senior management) that served as the catalyst. Among the institutions visited was the Ministry of the Civil Service. During the return flight the major lessons learned from the visit were discussed, and among the points raised was the need to establish civil service institutions in Ukraine. A few days later, a meeting was held in Mr. Piekhota's office to discuss the report he had to file on his mission to France, and the main recommendation was that work had to commence on a civil service law.

Documents motivating this move were submitted to the cabinet, and on June 27, 1992, the Cabinet of Ministers Writ Number 384 established the "Working Group to Write the Draft Law on the Civil Service in Ukraine," which consisted of 13 people. The group was given the unrealistic deadline of August 15, 1992 to submit the law for consideration by the Cabinet of Ministers, a deadline that was pushed back by more than six months.[14] All in all, it should be noted that at a time when hundreds of Ukrainian dignitaries were being invited to visit Western institutions, the Piekhota mission to France was one of few to produce tangible results. It did this because it was prepared by Ukrainian officials and institutions with a clearly formulated reform agenda, which capitalized on the opening created when a senior decision-maker gained new knowledge.

The Working Group consisted of senior civil servants and legal scholars drawn from the Institute of State and Law, the Ukrainian Academy of Law, and IPALG. The legacy of Ukraine's communist-imposed isolation weighed heavily on the group. None of the Ukrainians knew foreign languages, nor had any first-hand experience of Western institutions; yet this group was charged with writing a fundamental law to fashion a modern institution. Moreover, in Ukraine, legislative drafting and work on policy was dominated by a "fire-fighting" approach. There were no permanent units in government concerned with policy. People were simply mobilized to form a working group, which disbanded once the document was written. Documents were usually written in the splendid isolation of a government dacha with no reference library or other resources at hand. IPALG was determined that this Working Group would function in a different regime.

Rather than retreat to a dacha, sessions of the Working Group were held at IPALG. Translators were put at the disposal of the group so that materials from IPALG's reference library could be used. Indeed, in a matter of months, a number of important publications were issued in Ukrainian translation.[15] Western technical assistance was mobilized and members of the Working Group visited the following countries: Canada, France, Germany, Great Britain, Hungary, Spain, and Sweden. The fact that individual members of the group learned about widely different types of civil service systems provided a much-needed comparative perspective. Drafts of the law were translated into English and submitted to Western experts for comment.[16] In the final analysis, it is not surprising that the civil service systems of unitary continental states (France and Spain) were the primary sources of inspiration for the Ukrainian law.

The first draft of the law was ready by early November 1992. It was presented to a seminar held at IPALG on November 24, 1992 whose participants included the major stakeholders who needed to be convinced of the merits of such a law. Attending the seminar were deputy ministers responsible for personnel policy, members of the Verkhovna Rada, and academics and journalists whose constructive comments were incorporated into subsequent versions of the law. On April 5, 1993, the law was presented to the Cabinet, which approved the document and allowed a month for final revisions before the bill was submitted to parliament. The prime minister (Leonid Kuchma) sent the Law on the Civil Service to the Verkhovna Rada on June 12, 1993.

The Rada's Commission on Legislation and Legality examined the law three times, and in July 1993 the bill received first reading. The young deputy Serhii Soboliev played an important role as liaison between the Commission of Legislation and Legality and the Working Group. Prior to its final reading the law was examined by a number of parliamentary committees. The Rada's Presidium allocated the role of "lead" commission in parliamentary hearings to the Commission on Social Policy and Labour (headed by Mykola Biloblots'kyi). That is, it was charged with reconciling the views expressed by all of the commissions examining the law. The act was passed December 16, 1993, and took effect January 1, 1994.

The Debate in Government

The civil service law is a concise piece of legislation—38 articles divided into eight chapters. The authors of the law resisted the tendency toward over-regulation that characterizes so much of Ukraine's legislation. The law was to serve as a basic framework for a country in transition and a situation in which one had to return constantly to the Rada for amendments of tertiary importance that had to be avoided. The Working Group knew that civil service regulations in Western countries filled many tomes. It was obviously impossible and inadvisable to write the entire regulatory framework at once. Indeed, the Working Group estimated that some 90 substantial regulatory documents would have to be written once the law was adopted.[17]

The passage of the civil service law was anything but smooth sailing. Before the law was sent to parliament in June 1993, it was discussed in the executive branch of government and with key stakeholders such as the trade unions. Voices were raised opposing the very idea of a civil service act. A number of important ministers and the Ukrainian Federation of Trade Unions were the chief opponents.

Those heading branch ministries (such as coal and agriculture) with responsibility for hundreds of enterprises, and the minister of education (who had custody over thousands of schools and post-secondary institutions) voiced strong opposition to the very notion of civil service legislation. At the November 24, 1992 seminar (mentioned above) ministerial representatives argued that the proposed civil service act was premature and unnecessary at this stage of Ukraine's development and that it represented an unwarranted intrusion on the prerogatives of the minister to hire and fire staff at will. They understood the intention of the draft law correctly: the whole point of the legislation was to end the arbitrariness of the "one-man management" (*edinonachalie*) approach that dominated Soviet bureaucratic culture.

Opponents of the bill also advanced the sensible argument that hundreds of separate units were under their jurisdiction and they feared that the civil service law would eventually extend to enterprises and establishments under their control, thus stymieing reform of these sectors. The authors of the civil service legislation pointed out that the act was restrictive in nature and did not extend to state enterprises or educational establishments (see below). The argument that ministers wished to retain unrestricted authority in the employment and dismissal of their staff could not be sustained because it was incompatible with the new discourse of rule of law and building modern state institutions.

Ministers hostile to the civil service law eventually withdrew their opposition in principle to focus their resistance to the idea of establishing a separate institution to manage the civil service act, namely the Ministry of the Public Service. Without a *central* management authority, with policy making and secondary legislation powers for the whole civil service, the act would have no teeth. The minister of education, Petro Talanchuk, wrote:

> Establishing a Ministry of the Civil Service serves no purpose, since it will hardly have the capacity to fulfill the functions which are foreseen for it with respect to ministries and *central* government agencies and having appropriated these functions it will deprive the heads of ministries and agencies the opportunity to form their apparatus, and recruit needed employees. Moreover if such a structure is established it will promote the further growth of the state apparatus and this can evoke negative social and psychological reaction from the public who consider the state administration to be too large as it is. The functions foreseen by this Ministry [of the Civil Service] can be performed by existing units of the Cabinet of Ministers.[18]

The argument advanced by Talanchuk could not be dismissed too easily. If the Ministry of the Civil Service proved to be a an ineffective institution (and this was a real possibility given the weakness of other regulatory agencies), then it made sense not to strip existing institutions of their power over personnel policy. On the other hand, it was clear to the authors of the law that unless a cross-governmental management unit was established, the civil service act would be stillborn. Members of the Working Group started actively lobbying ministers to build support for the creation of a separate institution, and the culmination of this campaign was the publication of a lengthy article in the official government newspaper on why a Ministry of Public Service was needed.

Establishing systems for evaluation of work performance, promotion by merit, maintaining political neutrality, cross-ministerial job classifications, adjudication of conflicts, and many other functions required such a body. The article written by Donald Fuller, an American expert consulting the Working Group, ended with the observation that "Even in the Chinese People's Republic decisions on personnel matters has been delegated to a Ministry of Public Service."[19]

Trade unions opposed the law for different reasons. They argued that provisions of the act duplicated the labor code and paid undue attention to a specific category of employees. In the words of V. V. Pozhydaiev, First Deputy Head of the Federation of Trade Unions of Ukraine, "The law foresees the introduction of numerous secondary regulations . . . and in our view such attention to a relatively small number of employees, when the problems of other workers are ignored, is simply unacceptable." Developing the theme that the civil service law creates special conditions for public servants, the trade unions opposed the modest privileges to be awarded to civil servants, provisions of security employment, and the establishment of a separate agency such as the Ministry of the Civil Service to manage the implementation of the norms of the law.[20]

Notwithstanding detractors, the law won the cabinet's endorsement. It was embraced by senior members of government—such as the minister of the cabinet of ministers—and by key staff of the cabinet office who lobbied their colleagues intensely. Most recognized that the bureaucracy of a modern democratic state needed a set of well-defined norms and institutions. In the words of one official, the law was needed so that "The legal basis for the institution of a public service in our country can be created."[21]

All in all, the discussion of the law by ministries showed there was little understanding of modern notions of public administration and human resource management. However, an important step had been taken and the act was sent to the Rada.

The Debate in the Verkhovna Rada

The law was discussed by parliamentary committees from July to December 1993. There were relatively few outright opponents of the act. The views of one deputy from Crimea, a retired admiral, that Ukraine did not need a civil service because this was a Western import were not widely shared. The former Prime Minister Vitold Fokin (who was a member of parliament) repeated the opinions of some ministers, namely that civil service legislation would infringe on the right of heads of ministries and agencies to shape the administration of the organizations as they saw fit. The majority of deputies, however, accepted the intent of the legislation but challenged many provisions. It is to the major points of contention that we now turn.

The first chapter of the law introduced concepts such as "civil servant" and the "civil service." The chapter described the basic principles that were to govern the civil service (devotion to service and to democratic norms, the rule of law, respect for human rights, integrity, and professionalism). It provided for equal opportunity for employment in the public service and outlined the ethical code, which was to guide the behavior of bureaucrats.[22]

The first and the third chapter of the law restricted the civil service to functionaries of the state apparatus. It excluded technical and support staff, employees of state enterprises, teachers, employees in state-provided medical services, state-provided educational services, national transport, and communication services, and employees of parastatal authorities or agencies. It covered the judiciary, procuracy, diplomatic service, customs staff, intelligence, and internal security services until such time as separate laws were adopted for these structures. It also encompassed municipal employees, a provision that became problematic when the Law on Local Self-Government was adopted in 1997, which raised the need for the development of a separate statute on the status of municipal civil servants.[23] All in all, some 250,000 public employees became subject to the terms of the act.

The debate in parliamentary committees focused, in the first instance, on whether employees of state enterprises were to be included in the provisions of the law. In 1993 there were still thousands of enterprises controlled by ministries. Members of the Commission on the Primary Branches of Industry were particularly insistent on their inclusion.[24] The Commission on Economic Reform, headed by the pro-market-oriented Volodymyr Pylypchuk, also desired their incorporation, albeit for different reasons. State enterprises had an uncertain status at that time. Opponents of market reform undoubtedly thought that fixing their status as civil servants would hamper their privatization, while pro-reform forces hoped this would introduce a measure of control and prevent practices such as the stripping of assets. Pylypchuk suggested that since the country had a vast public sector, the law should be all-encompassing, having special provisions for those in: (a) state administrative organs, (b) state enterprises, and (c) public (state-funded) organizations. Indeed, he argued that the current draft law should be scrapped and that three separate laws should be written, covering each of the above.[25]

Most deputies, however, realized that the process of the adoption of a civil service law would be paralyzed for many years if legislation regulating personnel relations in the public sector was a precondition of its passage. Some considered Pylypchuk's proposal as an example of "regulation mania."

Fortunately, Ihor Kharchenko, head of the Working Group, had established an excellent working relationship with the Commission on Social Policy and Labor, the "lead" commission. This commission recommended that the abovementioned objections not be considered and concluded that "this law does not preclude the possibility of future laws on public enterprises and public organisations."[26]

Interestingly, no one advanced the argument that the technical and administrative staff of public administration should be included in the provisions of the law. This was a major shortcoming of the draft law, which the Working Group was aware of. As Vadym Averianov, one of the authors of the law, wrote, "Entire categories of public servants actually fell by the wayside, in particular, technical and support staff."[27] These are categories typically regulated by Western civil service legislation.[28] The reason for this omission in the Ukrainian law lay in the fact that their inclusion presupposed the existence of detailed job classifications, a difficult task that would have seriously delayed the passage of the law.

The law's authors were aware that prior to writing law on the civil service, they ought to have established a classification system, that is, the categorization of positions according to the type of work performed, the type of skill required, and other job-related factors. Ideally, this ought to have happened prior to the writing of the act since normally this precedes all other human resource planning processes. This task, however, was beyond the resources of the Working Group. It was difficult enough to develop a nomenclature of positions (*posady*), which formed the basis of the law (see below). It was hoped that the future Ministry of the Public Service would tackle job classification as its first order of business. This basic weakness in the civil service law was not noticed by the Rada's commissions, and members of the Working Group were not keen to point it out.

Provisions of the act governing principles and ethical norms of the civil service proved uncontroversial and were readily accepted. This was not so in the case of provisos stipulating equality of employment. Deputies from the democratic opposition argued the law should ban "functionaries of the former totalitarian regime" and "former employees of the KGB" from the civil service (amendments proposed by P. Osadchuk and F. Sviders'kyi respectively). The militant nationalist Stepan Khmara insisted that employment in the civil service be limited to citizens of Ukraine. The "lead" Commission on Social Policy and Labor rejected the former on the grounds that it denied the principle of the presumption of innocence and contravened universal norms of human rights. The latter was rejected because the employment of foreign nationals on the basis of fixed-term contracts helped the reform process and had become acceptable with the advent of Western technical assistance.[29] The attempt to introduce principles of lustration two years after independence was not seriously pursued by the opposition. Had it done so, the result would have upset the basic political settlement that enabled Ukraine to achieve independence.[30]

Another major source of contention was the act's provisions establishing a governmental agency to regulate and manage the civil service (chapter 2 of the law). The Working Group advocated the creation of a Ministry of the Public Service with strong powers of cross-governmental management. It was argued that only a properly empowered authoritative body could deal with issues such as equity of treatment between different parts of the civil service and guarantee standards of quality throughout the public service. Other areas that could not be properly addressed included: fair treatment for all civil servants, professional and loyal execution of governmental policy decisions throughout the public service, mobility of civil servants within the service, proper oversight of economic costs of the civil service, some *central* control over its size and distribution, and the independent monitoring of implementation of the civil service legislation.[31]

Not a single parliamentary commission spoke in favor of the creation of a Ministry of the Public Service. The proposal was actively opposed by the Commissions on Education and Research, on Economic Reform, on Human Rights, on Agriculture, and individual deputies from all sides of the political spectrum. Here they were backed by many ministers. One would have thought that deputies from the national-democratic camp would have supported a strong institution charged with implementing the civil service act. This was not the case. What dominated was hostility toward bureaucracy and any increase in the size of government. Democrats, like others, argued that there were too many ministries as it was, and given the dismal records of performance, they had no confidence that this new ministry would make a difference. In this respect they were supported by their colleagues from the other side of the ideological divide who viewed with suspicion any innovation that strayed too far from familiar Soviet forms of management.[32] The connection between state building and building up capacity in government was poorly understood at that time.

A compromise was reached and instead of a ministry, a Directorate General of the Public Service was created as part of the *apparat* of the Cabinet of Ministers. In other words, this would not be a separate ministry answerable to the cabinet and the prime minister but a division of the apparatus of the Cabinet of Ministers. The Directorate General had many of the rights of a ministry, but its status placed a serious limitation on its independence. As

Anatolii Bohomolov noted in hearings before the Commission on Legislation and Legality, "We need an independent body and not one that is subordinated to another structure."[33]

The Directorate General was given significant statutory rights: monitoring the implementation of legislation, human resource planning and policy formulation, introduction of secondary legislation, co-ordination and initiation of measures to improve effectiveness, and co-ordination of training and education. It came into being sometime after the passage of the act, on April 2, 1994 (Cabinet of Ministers Regulation Number 209).[34] However, it was limited in its ability to tackle cross-governmentally the above-mentioned issues suggested by the Working Group. Recently, there have been calls to give greater empowerment to the national civil service agency.[35]

The third major bone of contention was the distinction between political officials and non-political civil servants. At issue were two articles of the bill: article 9, chapter 3, "The Specificity of the Legal Status of Civil Servants in State Organs and their Administration"; and article 24, chapter 5, "Classification of Public Positions."

Draft article 9 provided that "The judicial status of the President of Ukraine, the Head of Verkhovna Rada and his deputies, the Prime Minister of Ukraine, members of the government, the head of the Constitutional Court of Ukraine, the Head of the Supreme Court of Ukraine, and the General Procurator are regulated by the Constitution and other laws of Ukraine."

Draft article 24 stipulated that "The following categories of public positions are established: highest—President of Ukraine, Head of the Verkhovna Rada, Prime Minister, Head of the Constitutional Court of Ukraine; upper-deputy heads of the Verkhovna Rada, members of the government, Head of the Supreme Court of Ukraine, Head of the High Arbitration Court of Ukraine, the Procurator General."[36]

These are highly unusual formulations for a law on the civil service. The above cited section of article 24 was not included in the bill that was passed by parliament; article 9 became part of the law on the civil service that is in force today.

Drawing the boundaries between the political and non-political realm was not an easy task in 1992 and 1993. The country, for all intents and purposes, had no structured political life. There were no stable parties in the Rada, and neither the president nor the prime minister or members of his cabinet were members of any political party. The highest positions of the country were occupied by people who acted as individuals, and they often thought of themselves as holders of positions at the highest rungs of state service rather than as political figures. While the situation of the president, head of the Rada, and the prime minister was clear enough, ministers were in a highly ambiguous situation.

There was no cabinet as such, nor could there be with over 120 ministries and state committees (whose status was similar to that of a ministry). Ministers thought of themselves as "professionals," not politicians. This self-definition was reinforced by the curious machinery of government that Ukraine had inherited, namely a structure called the *apparat* of the Cabinet of Ministers, comprised of hundreds of civil servants operating in departments charged with co-ordinating the work of ministries. Thus a civil servant could give binding orders to a minister, reversing the functions that are commonly understood in representative democracies.[37] Given Ukraine's political instability and frequent changes in government, ministers wanted some form of security and therefore lobbied for their inclusion in (at least) some of the provisions of the civil service law.

Terms as they are used in the Ukrainian language added to the confusion (a lexicon of English-Ukrainian terms in public administration was published only in 1996).[38] In English, the word "public" has many meanings, among them as in "open and shared by all the people," "a service provided by local or *central* government," or "a person in government" (occupies a *public* office, or is a *public* servant). In Ukrainian, "public" (*publichnyi*) has only one meaning—open or shared by the public; neither can one use "civil servant" in Ukrainian. The Ukrainian term for "public servant" or "civil servant" is *derzhavnyi sluzhbovets* ("state servant"), defined as a *posadova osoba* ("position holder") in *derzhavni orhany ta ikh aparatu* ("state organs and their apparatuses").[39] The terminology was confusing and led many to expect the Law on State Service (to use Ukrainian terms) to establish legal norms for all "position holders" in state administration (*derzhavne upravlinnia*), starting with the upper echelons. This expectation was reinforced by the legislative vacuum that existed.

The Law on the Civil Service was one of the first pieces of legislation dealing with the executive branch of government. The new constitution had not yet been adopted; there was no Law on the Cabinet of Ministers defining the status of ministers, no Law on Local Government; and institutional practice was in its infancy. Hence there was pressure to have the civil law deal with issues that were best handled by statute.

The Working Group was aware of the distinction between politicians and civil servants and hoped to resolve the question by simply stating that the "juridical status" of the holders of political office would be dealt with by other legislation (article 9, as adopted). However, there was enormous

pressure from several ministers in support of draft 24, which included political officer holders in the classification of positions. Rada deputies, many
of whom had international experience, opposed this measure. For example,
during hearings of the bill before the Commission on Legislation and Legality the following exchange took place (verbatim report):

> *Tkachuk, A.* [deputy]: Regarding ranks, and categories. Article 24 classifies
> positions and then we have civil service ranks. And here we have an interest-
> ing situation. We have political figures in other countries the list of political
> figures is not included in the list of civil servants . . .
>   *Bohomolov, A.* [Working Group]: All of your points are well taken but ex-
> cluding [political figures] cannot be resolved at our level . . . A certain cate-
> gory of our country's leadership thinks they should be included . . .
>   *Makar, I.* [deputy]:. I understand you, that you are under pressure . . .
> Who is putting pressure on you to include [these] people in the list?
>   *Soboliev, S.* [deputy]: When there will be an article of the law protecting
> civil servants from pressure, he will tell you who it is . . . [40]

Other Rada commissions also opposed the inclusion of the contentious section of article 24, chapter five, and it was dropped from the final version.

However, there were two other problems raised by chapter five (classification of positions). According to the articles of this chapter, the civil service
was divided into seven categories, ranging from category one (for example,
first deputy ministers) to category seven (junior administrators in local government and the like), and fifteen ranks. Positions in categories one and two
were exempt from the general rules of competitive recruitment established
by the law. Instead, appointments at this level and the confirmation of ranks
were the prerogative of the president or the Cabinet of Ministers.

In effect, the law initiated the establishment of a Top Management System (TMS), which is a structured and recognized system of personnel management for the higher non-political positions in government.[41] However, a
clearer definition of rules and the additional legislative framework needed
for a Top Management System to be properly implemented were not established. The Working Group recognized that this was beyond its capacity and
hoped that the issue would be tackled at a future date.[42]

Another critically important issue not adequately addressed by the law
was the so-called "patronage service" (article 15), or the status of the personal staff of the prime minister, vice prime ministers and ministers. The intention was to draw a distinction between political appointees and
professional civil servants. What the law did not do is draw up a list of posts
that can be distinguished as political positions and removed from the defin-

ition of the civil service. As subsequent experience showed, the "patronage service" of some vice prime ministers and ministers became substantial structures and often supplanted the functions of public servants.

Neither of the above-mentioned problems were discussed at commission hearings. The institutional experience of the participants was too limited at this stage of Ukraine's development to contemplate these questions.

The law's provisions on issues such as the duties and rights of a civil servant, political neutrality and limitation on political activity, declaration of assets, oath of loyalty, procedures for dismissal, and open competitive recruitment evoked little debate in the Rada's commissions. This was not the case with chapter seven, which dealt with remuneration, housing, medical services, and pensions.

When the law was debated in the Rada (December 1993), Ukraine was in the throes of an economic nightmare—annual inflation (consumer price increases) was 10,155 percent; the nominal monthly wage in the state sector of the economy was the equivalent of $31. The average civil servant earned less than $50 a month, and a minister earned $100. Under conditions of extreme economic crisis, legislators were totally unresponsive to any idea of increasing expenditures on public administration. Salary settlements are, of course, not the subject of legislation. However, the Working Group succeeded in having a clause adopted stating that civil service salaries had to be competitive in order to attract competent staff. The draft law proposed modest improvements in the remuneration package: free health services for public servants and their families in government clinics, government credits to purchase housing, subsidized communal housing charges, and access to the state housing fund for those eligible. The costs of these benefits were estimated at $16 million in 1994.[43]

The privileges were hotly debated in commissions. Some wanted all privileges struck out of the act, others to have them reduced. Working Group members provided deputies with sobering facts. For example, in December 1993, out of 6,000 positions in central government agencies covered by the civil service law, one third were vacant. Working Group members argued that the emerging private sector would attract the brightest civil servants, and unless urgent measures were taken, government would be deprived of the skills of lawyers, accountants, economists, and other professionals whose market value had risen. Legislators agreed to the package suggested (but not to subsidies for housing charges), but these measures were ineffectual in stemming the tide of resignations from civil service, and the growth of corruption in the bureaucracy, bred in good measure by appallingly low wages.

Conclusion

The first World Bank mission to study the civil service in Ukraine noted that the law "is comprehensive and refers to all the major issues to be covered in respect of a civil service—definition; recruitment; promotion; rights and obligations of civil servants; classification of posts; ranks of civil servants; remuneration; leave, discipline, suspension, resignation, retirement and pensions."[44] This is a reasonable report card given that the law was written and passed under difficult circumstances, at a time when Ukraine was just emerging from its totalitarian past and there was a limited understanding of public administration issues.

The Law on the Civil Service was a milestone in the development of public administration in Ukraine.[45] It is true that "As a framework legislation, and with the experience of the last few years, it now requires some changes."[46] At the regulatory level, enormous work remains to be done. The law on the civil service is only a prelude in creating the institutions of a modern public administration. The most difficult task remains to be accomplished—changing institutional culture and practices.

Notes

1. N. R. Nyzhnyk, "Etyka upravlinnia," *Komandor,* no. 3, 1995, p. 28.
2. Paul Collins, "Civil Service Reform and Retraining in Transitional Economies: Strategic Issues and Options," *Public Administration and Development,* no. 4, 1993, p. 331.
3. *Local Governments in the CEE and CIS, 1994: An Anthology of Descriptive Papers* (ILGPS: Budapest, 1994).
4. Joseph C. N. Raadschelders and Mark R. Rutger, "The Evolution of Civil Service Systems," in Hans A. G. M. Bekke, James L. Perry, and Theo A. J. Toonen (eds.), *Civil Service Systems in Comparative Perspective* (Bloomington: Indiana University Press, 1996), pp. 67–92; and Gyorgy Jenei, "Administrative Reform in Hungary and Central and Eastern Europe: Constraints and Prospects," in Jak Jabes and Mirko Vintar (eds.), *Public Administration in Transition* (Bratislava: NISPACEE, 1995), pp. 69–79.
5. S. I. Terebun and D. Iu. Iakovliev, "Administratyvni metody i orhany upravlinnia v sferi derzhavnoi sluzhby," Masters in Public Administration thesis, Institute of Public Administration and Local Government, Cabinet of Ministers, Kyiv, 1994, p. 49.
6. See *Dilova dokumentatsiia Het'manshchyny XVIII st.* (Kyiv: Naukova dumka, 1993), pp. 5–22. For an interesting discussion of the administrative apparatus of the Zaporozhzhian Cossack Host, see V. L. Andrushchenko and V. M. Fe-

dosov, *Zaporiz'ka sich iak ukrains'kyi phenomen* (Kyiv: Zapovit, 1995), pp. 57–61.

7. See O. L. Kopylenko and M. L. Kopylenko, *Derzhava i pravo Ukrainy 1917–1920* (Kyiv: Lybid', 1997), pp. 193–194.

8. Ken E. McVicar (ed.), *Lexicon of Terms and Concepts in Public Administration, Public Policy and Political Science* (Kyiv: Osnovy, 1994), p. 42.

9. F. Nazarenko, "Printsipy gosudarstvennoi sluzhby," *Narodnyi deputat,* no.2, 1992, p. 9.

10. Ibid., pp. 7–13.

11. Bohdan Krawchenko, *First Annual Report, 1992–1993; Institute x of Public Administration and Local Government, Cabinet of Ministers, Ukraine* (Kyiv: ILGPS, 1993). This and other documents cited below are to be found in the library of the Academy of Public Administration, Office of the President of Ukraine, successor of IPALG.

12. Ibid.

13. For a discussion of the implications of adopting various models of public administration educational systems (Anglo-American or continental European traditions), see Bohdan Krawchenko, "Organizing an Institute of Public Administration: A Case Study of Ukraine," in Jak Jabes and Stephen McCormick (eds.), *The Education and Training of Public Servants* (Bratislava: NISPACEE, 1995), pp. 10–12.

14. Kabinet Ministriv Ukrainy, *Rozporiadzhennia vid 27 chervnia 1992,* no. 384-r. The author of this paper was a member of the Working Group.

15. Among these works published by IPALG in 1992 and 1993 were: Jerzy Stepien (Senator, Poland), *Reforma derzhavnoi administratsii. Osnovyni porady;* Cabinet Office, Great Britain, *Pytannia protsedury dlia ministriv;* Government of France, *Pravove rehuliuvannia derzhavnoi sluzhby u Frantsii;* Ministry of the Public Service, Spain, *Orhanizatsiino-pravovi aspekty derzhavnoi sluzhby Ispanii.*

16. Important contributions were made by Jim Dixon, Public Service Commissioner, Alberta Provincial Government, Canada; Donald Fuller, University of Southern California; and the staff of the French Ministry of the Public Service.

17. Ihor Kharchenko and Bohdan Kravchenko, June 10, 1993 Memorandum to A. K. Lobov, Minister of the Cabinet of Ministers, "Perelik aktiv zakonostavstva shchodo riznykh aspektiv derzhavno-sluzhbovnoii dial'nosti, shcho neobkhidno rozrobyty pislia pryniattia Zakonu Ukrainy 'Pro derzhavnu shluzhbu.'"

18. Letter to the Cabinet of Ministers, P. Talanchuk, "Zauvazhennia pro proekty Zakonu Ukrainy pro derzhavnu sluzhbu," April 14, 1993.

19. *Uriadoviy Kur'er,* May 27, 1993.

20. Letter to the Cabinet of Ministers, V. V. Pozhydaiev, "Lyst Federatsii profesiinykh spilok Ukrainy pro poekt Zakonou pro derzhavnu sluzhbu," June 23, 1993.

21. *Stenohrafichnyi zapys zasidannia Komisii u pytannia zakonodavstva i zakonnosti 7 lypnia 1993 r.*, p. 14.

22. "Zakon Ukrainy pro derzhavnu sluzhbu," *Visnyk derzhavnoi sluzhby Ukrainy,* no. 1, 1995, pp. 9–30.

23. See Fond spryiannia mistevomu samovriaduvanniu Ukrainy pry Prezydentovi Ukrainy, "Kontseptsiia Zakonu Ukrainy 'Pro munitsipal'nu szluzhbu v Ukraini," July 1997.

24. Verkhovna Rada Ukrainy, *Zakon Ukrainy pro derzhavnu sluzhbu. Zmist propozytsii i zauvazhen'. Vysnovky Komisii u pytanniakh sotsial'noi polityky ta pratsi. Tekst proektu shcho vynosyt'sia na rozhliad Verkhovnoi Rady Ukrainy* (Kyiv:, n.p. 1993). Cited hereafter as *Zmist propozytsii.*

25. Letter to the prime minister of Ukraine, Leonid Kuchma, from V. Pylypchuk, Commission on Economic Reform, September 16, 1993.

26. *Zmist propozytsii.*

27. V. Aver'ianov, "Zakonodavche rehuliuvannia derzhavnoi sluzhby: Stan i problemy," *Visnyk derzhavnoi sluzhby Ukrainy,* no. 1, 1995, p. 36.

28. See Svitlana Ozirs'ka, "Derzhavna sluzhba v Ukraini: novi perspektyvy v konteksti svitovoho dosvidu," Masters in Public Administration thesis, Institute of Public Administration and Local Government, Cabinet of Ministers, Kyiv, 1995.

29. *Zmist propozytsii.*

30. See Bohdan Krawchenko, "Ukraine: the politics of independence," in Ian Bremmer and Ray Taras (eds.), *Nations and Politics in the Soviet Successor States* (Cambridge: Cambridge University Press, 1993), pp. 76–98.

31. The views of the Working Group are very close to the recommendations made by SIGMA (Support for Improvement in Governance and Management in Central and East European Countries) in *Civil Service Legislation Contents Check-List,* January 1994. See *Uriadoviy Kur'er,* May 27, 1993.

32. *Zmist propozytsii.*

33. *Stenohrafichnyi zapys zasidannia Komisii u pytannia zakonodavstva i zakonnosti 7 lypnia 1993 r.*, p. 12.

34. Kabinet Ministriv Ukrainy, *Postanova vid 2 kvitnia 1994,* no. 209.

35. See Derzhavna komisiia z provedennia v Ukrainy administratyvnoi reformy, *Kontseptsiia administratyvnoi reformy v Ukraini* (Kyiv: n. p. 1998).

36. *Zmist propozytsii.*

37. See B. Krawchenko, *Administrative Reform in Ukraine: Setting the Agenda,* Discussion Papers, no. 3 (Budapest: Local Government and Public Service Reform Initiative, 1997).

38. *English-Ukrainian Lexicon of Terms and Concepts in Public Administration* (Kyiv: Osnovy, 1996).

39. Op. cit., "Zakon Ukrainy pro derzhavnu sluzhbu," article two.

40. *Stenohrafichnyi zapys zasidannia Komisii u pytannia zakonodavstva i zakonnosti 7 lypnia 1993 r.*, pp. 13–14.

41. See *Top Management Service in Central Government,* SIGMA (Support for Improvement in Governance and Management in Central and East European Countries), Paper no. 1, 1995.
42. *Stenohrafichnyi zapys zasidannia Komisii u pytannia zakonodavstva i zakonnosti 7 lypnia 1993 r.,* p. 19.
43. Ibid., p. 12.
44. World Bank, "Aide Memoire of the Preparation Mission for the Public Administration Reform Loan: Civil Service Issues," April 23, 1997.
45. See Viktoriia Borysova, "Stanovlennia ta funktsionuvannia derzhavnoi sluzhby v Ukraini," Masters in Public Administration thesis, Academy of Public Administration, Office of the President of Ukraine, 1996, pp. 19–33.
46. Op cit., "Aide Memoire."

CHAPTER 7

The Quest for Balance:
Regional Self-Government and
Subnational Fiscal Policy in Ukraine

Robert S. Kravchuk

Regionalism in the Ukrainian Context

State-building in Ukraine has been laggard along a number of significant dimensions since the country achieved its independence in 1991. According to almost any reasonably acceptable definition of statehood, Ukraine rates as a "weak state."[1] This is especially apparent in Ukraine's inability to raise taxes and its still nascent rule of law regime. Another critical dimension concerns the internal organization of the Ukrainian state: its regional structure and the relations between Ukraine's diverse regions and the central government.

It is increasingly recognized by both indigenous and foreign observers alike that Ukrainian politics are driven considerably by regional interests.[2] Vast differences in regional preferences and political orientations were observed in voting patterns during both the 1994 and 1998 parliamentary elections, as well as during the 1994 presidential race.[3] Further, much has been made of the apparent East/West ethnocultural divide; it has even been mentioned as a potential cause of Ukraine's ultimate disintegration and break-up.[4] Despite fears that Ukraine's regional divergencies would fuel radical secessionist movements, it was clear by late 1996 that Ukraine is in no real danger of collapse.[5] It remains an integral whole at year-end 1999.

From 1992 to 1995, however, attention focused on the increasingly vociferous demands of certain regions for economic autonomy and calls for
Kyiv to reestablish trade ties with Russian enterprises. Such sentiments have
been especially strong in eastern Ukraine. Industry in the Don River Basin
(or, "Donbas") was largely subordinated to all-union ministries prior to independence. Consequently, this region was highly dependent upon links
with Russian industry. In an expression of dismay at the precipitous fall in
output following independence, the Donets'k and Luhans'k *oblast* councils
in June 1993 voted in favor of regional autonomy. These were "straw votes"
that nonetheless encapsulated the general sentiment in these *oblasts*. In related developments, special (free) economic zones have from time to time
been proposed for Odesa, Kharkiv, Kherson, Donets'k, Zakarpattia, Sevastopol, and the Crimean Republic.[6]

Clamorings for closer ties with Russia have been based, at least in part,
on regional evaluations as to the relative strength of the Ukrainian versus the
Russian economy.[7] With the exception of certain key metallurgical, chemi-
cal, and trading enterprises, much of Donbas industry still finds its most lu-
crative markets in Russia, especially among those in the military-industrial
complex.[8] However, from 1995 to 1997, whatever romanticism for renewed
ties with Russian industry still existed, the regions have gradually come to a
more realistic assessment of their situation.[9] Further, economic disparities
with Russian border regions narrowed considerably after 1994, lessening
support for regional autonomy, even in eastern Ukraine.[10]

By 1997, it was clear that the forces of cohesion were stronger than the
centrifugal tendencies that appeared to predominate during Ukraine's
early formative period. The more heavily industrialized regions and their
representatives in parliament employed fears of a geographic divide in
combination with their superior economic strength to dominate the national policy agenda, carrying other, poorer regions with them, however
reluctantly. The plain truth is that several poor regions in western and central Ukraine are highly dependent upon the budgetary subsidies that orig-
inate largely in taxes paid in the east. The eastern region thus plays the
west off against the center. This placed serious constraints on President
Leonid D. Kuchma's ability to reform the economy, insofar as the eastern
and southern regions have been able to preserve their stream of enterprise
and agricultural subsidies, effectively stifling substantive economic restructuring (i.e., large-scale privatization, private land ownership, new enterprise governance structures, etc.).

As will be seen below, the center, for its part, has rendered all regions
increasingly dependent, but especially the poorer western and central

oblasts. This has served political stabilization objectives but places certain limits on Kyiv's ability to maintain macroeconomic stability. Regional dependency also reinforces disparities in economic and social development across Ukraine and intensifies regional competition over increasingly scarce budgetary resources and investment capital. The paradoxical result, in the words of Birch and Zinko, has been that, "the desire for greater autonomy in Ukraine's regions often coincides with the greatest need for help from Kyiv."[11]

This chapter begins with a brief examination of the sources of Ukraine's regional diversity, then moves to a discussion of Kyiv's piecemeal efforts from 1992 to 1997 to establish regional policy. It concludes with an analysis of the regions' generally deteriorating fiscal condition and the implications for the future.

Ukraine's Broad Regional Diversity

Numerous authorities have examined sources of regional differentiation in Ukraine.[12] The general consensus is that the regional diversity appears to be the result of intertwining strands of historical development, having significant sociocultural and economic dimensions.

Historical Sociocultural Developments

At the outbreak of the First World War, the territory of modern Ukraine was split between Russian and Austro-Hungarian rule. All but the western Galician regions were ruled by Russia; eastern and southern Ukraine were settled by ethnic Russians from the north, establishing in the nineteenth and early twentieth centuries the industrial centers of "New Russia" (*Novaya Rossiya*). Russian tends to be the dominant language spoken in these regions; however, ethnic Russians are a minority throughout the east. Further, many Russian speakers are ethnic Ukrainians, and many ethnic Russians are "passively fluent" in Ukrainian (i.e., they understand Ukrainian but do not necessarily speak it very well). Thus the question of ethnolinguistic heritage in Ukraine is quite a complicated matter.

The western Ukrainian province of Galicia, under Polish administration in the interwar period, was invaded by the Red Army during the Second World War; it was annexed by the Soviet Union in 1945. Ethnic Ukrainians in the west are the overwhelming majority, with small Hungarian and Rumanian minorities in the Zakarpattia (Trans-Carpathia) and Bukovina regions. Ukrainian is the dominant language in the west, and it is here that ethnic nationalism has taken on its most virulent forms. By contrast, in the east a form of democratic nationalism has come to characterize domestic politics, except in the Crimean Republic, which can be regarded as something of a special case. Transferred to Ukraine from the Russian Federation by former Communist Party boss Nikita Khrushchev only in 1954, ethnic Russians form a majority of Crimea's population. Crimea has thus had the shortest social and political association with Kyiv, and it is here that secessionist tendencies have been most pronounced.[13]

These historical sociocultural factors have significantly influenced modern Ukrainian political orientations.[14] Western Ukraine has long been oriented toward Europe, viewing a return to the "common European home" as the means to secure Ukraine's permanent independence from Russia. Eastern Ukraine has had a longer association with Russia, which makes easterners less fearful of closer economic, social, and cultural ties to that country. Eastern regions have been especially anxious to renew economic ties with Russian border regions.

Modern Public Opinion Differences

Regional differences in socioeconomic development have been linked to important differences in public attitudes toward the regional distribution of power and the internal structure of the Ukrainian state. In a useful and stimulating article concerning regional opinion in Ukraine, Hesli explored the geographical dispersion of support for devolution of political power.[15] She examined Ukraine's internal divisions over the assignment of governmental responsibilities between Kyiv and regional governments (*oblasti*). Her basic proposition was that the question of state sovereignty is linked regionally to the question of state structure. She tested her proposition using data from a June-July 1992 opinion poll conducted in Ukraine by the University of Iowa.

Hesli regressed opinion data across demographic characteristics that previously have been found to be relevant for the fourteen *oblasts* in which interviews were conducted, with controls for region, degree of Russification, and levels of industrialization, social and agricultural development, and relative population growth rates. In constructing her control variables, Hesli employed Soviet-era socioeconomic statistics, organized into five sets of indicators, employing a methodology that grouped and weighted measures according to their prevalence in the literature, timeliness, and demonstrated reliability. Hesli's standard scores for development indices (ranging from 0 ("least developed") to 25 ("most developed") are presented in Table 7.1. As

Table 7.1   Hesli's Standardized Scores for Regional Development Indices
[Scale: 1.00 (*Low*)–25.00 (*High*)]

Oblast	Russification Score	Industrial Development Score	Social Development Score	Agricultural Development Score	Population Strength Score
Crimean Republic*	25.00	5.15	12.10	18.55	16.76
Vinnytska Oblast	1.37	3.60	5.13	23.79	1.72
Volynska Oblast	0.78	0.18	1.20	8.29	11.58
Dnipropetrovska Oblast	8.39	20.88	14.04	25.00	13.09
Donetska Oblast	18.29	25.00	8.24	20.35	4.09
Zhytomyrska Oblast	2.13	1.71	1.52	15.94	7.38
Zakarpattska Oblast	0.78	1.05	0.07	0.01	17.45
Zaporizhzhia Oblast	11.82	8.42	10.74	19.82	9.78
Ivano-Frankivska Oblast	0.69	1.44	3.62	3.05	14.41
Kyivska Oblast**	2.04	15.16	25.00	22.34	25.00
Kirovohradska Oblast	3.06	1.97	6.88	17.04	2.30
Luhanska Oblast	17.05	12.62	7.48	14.58	6.51
Lvivska Oblast	1.51	13.75	13.10	12.94	21.41
Mykolaivska Oblast	7.57	3.00	6.26	15.32	8.59
Odesska Oblast	11.43	8.37	18.94	24.56	9.21
Poltavska Oblast	2.57	6.74	7.41	22.49	1.07
Rivenska Oblast	0.89	0.01	3.03	6.89	14.76
Sumska Oblast	4.65	2.51	3.66	15.48	0.82
Ternopilska Oblast	0.22	1.45	4.92	9.77	7.35
Kharkivska Oblast	11.56	10.07	24.60	23.33	3.73
Khersonska Oblast	6.86	2.01	6.24	16.69	10.37
Khmelnytska Oblast	1.33	2.48	2.84	16.00	4.59
Cherkasska Oblast	1.90	2.47	5.23	15.97	2.69
Chernivitska Oblast	1.73	1.63	4.68	1.21	9.46
Chernihivska Oblast	2.66	0.03	3.43	21.20	0.00

Notes: *Including city of Sevastopol
**Including city of Kyiv
Source: Vicki L. Hesli, "Public Support for the Devolution of Power in Ukraine: Regional Patterns." *Europe-Asia Studies* vol. 47, no. 1 (1995), Table 2, p. 100.

to region, Hesli adopted Arel's thoughtful classification of Ukrainian *oblasts* into four larger regions. (See Table 7.2.)

Contrary to expectations, Hesli found no strong support in any region for a significant devolution of authority to the regions. Most interestingly, western Ukraine stands out as more significantly for pro-regional autonomy than eastern or central *oblasts*. This counterintuitive result shows the strongest support for regionalism emanating from the more pro-nationalist

Table 7.2   Arel's Classification of Ukrainian *Oblasts*

East	South	Central	West
Karkiv	Crimea	Chernhiv	L'viv
Donetsk	Odessa	Sumy	Ivano-Frankivsk
Luhansk	Mykolaiv	Poltava	Ternopil
Dnipropetrovsk	Kherson	Kyiv	Volyn
Zaporizhzhia		Cherkassy	Rivne
		Vinnytsya	Chernivtsy
		Zhytomyr	Zakarpattia
		Khmelnytskij	
		Kirovohrad	

Source: Dominique Arel, "Federalism and the Language Factor in Ukraine." Paper presented at the Annual Meeting of the American Association for the Advancement of Slavic Studies, November 1992.

west. In fact, strong support for regionalism was found to be more directly related to a region's level of industrialization, with the most industrialized *oblasts* favoring regional power structures, regardless of section of the country. This would appear to account for the strong centralizing sentiments found in the west, centered on L'viv.

Finally, no distinctive patterns emerge in Hesli's analysis of the relationship between the degree of social or agricultural development and opinion on her pro-regional power scale. This is not difficult to understand, insofar as these same regions tend to vary considerably according to their relative levels of industrialization and geographic locale. (See Table 7.3.) Overall, Hesli found that the most Russified and industrialized regions have quite different public attitudes about the proper division of political authority than others in Ukraine.[16]

Vast Economic Disparities

In terms of the regional economy, wide disparities in economic and industrial development characterize Ukraine's regions.[17] The six extreme eastern *oblasts* constitute the industrial heartland of Ukraine, accounting for 48.2 percent of Ukraine's 1989 industrial output, and 36.3 percent of the 1991 GDP. Western, central, and southern *oblasts* tend to be economically much weaker, except L'viv *oblast,* which was the industrial center of Soviet western Ukraine. Soviet-era investment policies thus produced a pattern of broadly divergent regional social and economic endowments throughout Ukraine.[18] As a result, living standards vary widely, with wages in the west lower than

Table 7.3 Categorization of *Oblasts* by Helsi's Scale Values

Scale Scores	Russification Score	Industrial Development Score	Social Development Score	Agricultural Development Score
High	Crimea Donetsk Luhansk	Donetsk Dnipropetrovsk	Kyiv Kharkiv Odessa	Dnipropetrovsk Odessa Vinnytsya Kharkiv Poltava Kyiv Chernihiv Donetsk Zaporizhzhia Crimea
Medium High	Zaporizhzhia Kharkiv Odessa	Kyiv L'viv Luhansk Kharkiv Zaporizhzhia Odessa	Dnipropetrovsk L'viv Crimea Zaporizhzhia	Kirovohrad Kherson Khmelnytskij Cherkassy Zhytomyr Sumy Mykolaiv
Medium Low	Dnipropetrovsk Mykolaiv Kherson	Poltava Crimea Vinnytsya	Donetsk Luhansk Poltava Kirovohrad Kherson Mykolaiv Cherkassy Vinnytsya	Luhansk L'viv Ternopil
Low	Sumy Kirovohrad Chernihiv Poltava Zhytomyr Kyiv Cherkassy Chernivtsy L'viv Vinnytsya Khmelnytskij Rivne Zakarpattia Volyn Ivano-Frankivsk Ternopil	Mykolaiv Sumy Cherkassy Khmelnytskij Kherson Kirovohrad Zhytomyr Chernivtsy Ivano-Frankivsk Ternopil Zakarpattia Volyn Chernihiv Rivne	Ternopil Chernivtsy Sumy Ivano-Frankivsk Chernihiv Rivne Khmelnytskij Zhytomyr	Volyn Rivne Ivano-Frankivsk Chernivtsy Zakarpattia

Source: Vicki L. Hesli, "Public Support for the Devolution of Power in Ukraine: Regional Patterns." *Europe-Asia Studies* vol. 47, no. 1 (1995), Table 3, p. 102.

in other regions, price subsidies more extensive, and, as we shall see, budgetary support from the center greater in western than in southern and eastern *oblasts*.

Further, owing to their relative economic strength, eastern *oblasts* have generated and transferred to the consolidated state budget a greater proportion of total national tax revenues than other regions. The subsidization of western *oblasts* by Eastern Ukraine has been a source of continuous griping in parliament. However, despite their complaints, from the very beginning of Ukrainian statehood, the intergovernmental system of budgetary transfers has proven advantageous to eastern *oblasts* in dominating the national domestic policy agenda.

An examination of Table 7.3 reveals little uniformity in the grouping of *oblasts* according to Hesli's scale values, except among the least developed regions, which tend to be in western and south-central Ukraine. Interestingly, the most industrialized regions possess very large territories, which also correlates strongly with their high levels of agricultural development. Consequently, there tends to be a strong association between attitudes favoring greater regional autonomy, devolution of political authority to the regions, and levels of industrial and agricultural development. Consequently, it comes as no surprise that eastern *oblasts* have been the most vociferous in their demands for greater autonomy, and most active in their efforts to dominate national economic policy. As argued below, however, Kyiv's response has been a rather piecemeal series of reactions to regional political agitation rather part of a coherent strategic design.

The Struggle over Local Self-Government

Ukraine's policy toward its regions has lacked clarity, coherence, and consistency. Kyiv's policy from 1992 to 1997 was actually an admixture of actions that have both helped and hindered regional development and independence from the center. There is no decentralization policy to speak of. Indeed, the effective pattern of Kyiv's actions has been to render regional governments increasingly subordinated to and fiscally dependent upon the center. Rather than pursuing a "grand design," however, Kyiv has proceeded in a thoroughly ad hoc fashion, oscillating between actions that support regional improvement in some areas, only to be followed by steps which detract from regional autonomy in others.

As early as 1992, regional and municipal government in Ukraine was caught up in the general struggle between the president and parliament over the definition and control of the executive power. At times, control over local government itself appeared to be the prize. At other times, the objectives appear more vague. The legislative basis for local self-government has therefore been subject to a fairly continuous series of revisions, reversals, and shifts in focus, beginning in 1992, and continuing even in the period following adoption of the June 1996 Constitution of Ukraine, which ought to have resolved the basic issues. The struggle was to continue well into 1997, however.

Initial Problems with the Legislative Basis

The fundamental basis for local government in newly independent Ukraine was established in February 1992, with enactment of the Law on Local Self-Government.[19] This act amended the 1991 Law of the Ukrainian SSR by granting substantial new powers to local governments. Indeed, article 12 stipulated specifically that "higher-level bodies [of government] may not interfere in the development, approval and execution of local budgets."[20] Further, the act separated local budgets from those of higher-level units, stipulating that, "local budgets of single administrative and territorial units may not be included in the budgets of other units and in the state budget of the republic." In practice, however, as we shall see, Ukraine's regions have little fiscal independence.

Both the letter and spirit of the 1992 law contradicted the centralizing approach embodied in existing legislation at the time. The 1991 Law on Budget System, for instance, authorized higher-level governments to determine annually the types and levels of responsibilities they would assign to their subordinate governments.[21] This provision of the law has been used fairly aggressively in a manner that has compromised almost completely the fiscal autonomy of Ukraine's regions. The Law on Budget System was amended in 1995 to give clearer definition to regional and local tax and expenditure responsibilities.[22] However, a significant narrowing of local revenue sources combined with a substantial devolution of expenditure responsibilities has placed subnational governments into a virtual financial "vise grip."[23]

The System of President's Representatives

Frequent changes to the legislative regime began early in Ukraine's post-Soviet existence. In a dramatic turnaround of legislative fortunes, in the month following enactment of the 1992 law, President Leonid M. Kravchuk issued a decree establishing the office of President's Representatives, who were to become the titular heads of the *oblast* administrations in each region, acting in the name of the president.[24] In April 1992, Kravchuk issued another decree, pursuant to the first, that formalized the President's Representatives' role as head of the state administrations in *oblasts* and in the cities of Kyiv and Sevastopol.[25] At the same time, Kravchuk terminated the activities of the previously existing state administrations, and in the process he usurped even those powers previously exercised by the *oblast* Councils of People's Deputies but now legally exercised by President's Representatives. Later the same year, another presidential edict subordinated all local state administrative units to the President of Ukraine and the Cabinet of Ministers on all matters falling within the latter's jurisdiction.[26] Parliament had some complicity in this case, by enacting, on March 5, 1992, the Law on the Representatives of the President of Ukraine effectively formalizing Kravchuk's dominance of local government.

Despite this act, regionalism was on the rise throughout 1993 as discontent over Kyiv's management of the economy set in, becoming all the more intense during that year. Eastern Ukraine and Crimea were especially adamant in the view that regions should be permitted to reestablish economic links with regions in other former Soviet republics, unimpeded by Kyiv. The President's Representatives were widely viewed as an obstacle to the fulfillment of some regions' economic aspirations. Thus, in late 1993, following the June Donbas coal miners' strike, and that summer's agitation for a national referendum of confidence in president and parliament, Kravchuk issued a decree granting greater autonomy to the administrations of certain eastern *oblasts* for a two-year period, ending December 31, 1995.[27] Privileges granted to these *oblasts* included the right to manage property owned by the state. This decree was widely seen as intended to counter separatist tendencies in the East.

Kravchuk's Waning Power, 1994

As the 1994 elections approached, when Kravchuk's grip on power was in its waning moments, popular discontent with the system of President's Representatives became universal.[28] Taking advantage of its opportunity to "play the regions card," parliament passed the Law on Formation of Local Government Bodies, establishing an entirely new structure of local government throughout Ukraine.[29] The act undermined direct presidential control of regional and local government, eliminating the office of President's Representatives effective June 26, 1994, the date on which new elections to subnational office were to be held.[30] Far from bolstering regional indepen-

dence, however, by this act parliament introduced a new system of subordination of representative bodies, whereby *oblast* and *rayon* councils were effectively converted into adjuncts of the national parliament. This set the
stage for conflict between higher-level councils and their now-subordinated
councils, and between the legislative and executive branches at all levels of
government.

In an apparent effort to strengthen his electoral appeal throughout the regions, Kravchuk in 1994 undertook two measures that were seen at the time
as preludes to a future state restructuring. In February he issued a decree extending property and entrepreneurial legislative powers to the four *oblasts* of
eastern Ukraine that had been subject to his November 29, 1993 grant of
increased autonomy.[31]

In a more far-reaching action in March, Kravchuk ordered the wholesale
transfer of the ownership of all state assets in housing and communal services, personal services, trade, public restaurants, urban roads, education,
culture, fitness and sports, health care, and other social welfare functions to
the *oblast* capital city governments by July 1, 1994.[32] *Oblasts* were directed
to do the same for their subordinate local governments by September 1,
1994. (Crimea was not affected.) Lists of specific objects subject to transfer
were to be developed by the Cabinet of Ministers. The general purpose of
the decree was to improve the economic strength of subnational governments, however much it might add to their administrative burdens. At the
time, Presidential Adviser Vasyl Rudenko described these actions as "serious
steps towards decentralization and power-sharing between ministries and
oblast administrations."[33]

Kuchma Reestablishes Presidential Primacy

Kravchuk's efforts to placate the regions were to prove unsuccessful, however. In July 1994, running on a platform of greater regional autonomy,
closer economic ties with Russia, and a looser official language policy, former Prime Minister Leonid D. Kuchma defeated the president's bid for re-
election. Upon taking office, however, both the new president and
parliament were to make control over local government an issue of continuing contention between them. Parliament was to make the first move. In
the shadow of the presidential election, the recently elected parliament in
July approved in its first reading a new Law on Local Councils. The act—
which was never to become law—was a fairly transparent attempt by the socialist plurality in parliament to reestablish the former Soviet system of
"rule by people's soviets." Kuchma responded to this threat to his executive

prerogatives in August with a decree subordinating all heads of *oblast* councils to the president.[34] Acting during a parliamentary recess, the president thus asserted his direct control over both the parliamentary-appointed Cabinet of Ministers, and all independently elected regional authorities.

In order to demonstrate openness on matters of regional concern, however, and to facilitate closer cooperation between his administration and regional leaders, in September 1994 Kuchma established a new Council of Regions.[35] Composed of the heads of regional councils, this body was to serve in an advisory capacity to the president.[36] But Kuchma soon became frustrated with the ability of the independently elected regional chairmen to stifle his efforts at economic reform. This propelled the president in December to introduce a draft Law on Power, which contained provisions that would clearly establish what he termed "the vertical structure of legitimate executive power."[37] Kuchma's draft would strengthen the executive by abolishing the hierarchy of legislative authority, putting an end to soviet power in Ukraine.[38] The president's draft also served to counter a parliamentary draft already in circulation, which would remove executive structures from power altogether, instituting "people's rule" at all levels, including enterprises, regardless of their form of ownership.[39] At year-end 1994, the two sides appeared headed for collision.

The 1995 Law on Power and Constitutional Accord

Adopted in its first reading on December 28, 1994, the draft Law on Power would be continuously revised throughout the winter of 1995. In the process, over 900 amendments were made to its 56 articles. Consequently, the second reading did not take place until April 1995. The process of designing the governmental power structure became so contentious that representatives of eight parliamentary factions and deputies' groups proposed that an interim Constitutional Agreement be executed between president and parliament, until such time that a new constitution could be adopted and ratified. To work out the details of the Law on Power as a basis for the agreement, a Conciliatory Commission was established, with members equally representing parliament and the executive branch.[40] By April, the commission was able to agree on all substantive points save the major one: the competence of heads of regional state administrations. The Law on Power was adopted on May 18, 1995, but implementation had to await the constitutional amendments and other legislative changes necessary to implement the law.[41] The mandatory two-thirds parliamentary majority required to amend the constitution, and thus to implement the Law on

Power, proved to be an elusive objective, however. The process rapidly bogged down.

Exasperated, Kuchma threatened to hold a national plebiscite on confidence in parliament.[42] In the face of this threat, and fearing that Kuchma enjoyed broad popular support, parliament finally relented, enacting the power-sharing agreement in late May. The president had maneuvered parliament into effectively formalizing his actions of the previous year, rendering regional councils accountable solely to the president.[43] In order to avoid the plebiscite, which it would surely have lost, parliament had no choice but to accept considerable restrictions on its ability to influence the exercise of executive power.[44] On June 8, at a formal signing ceremony, the Constitutional Accord was ratified by the president and the speaker of parliament. In effect for one year as an interim "petite constitution," the accord restricted parliament's formal powers to the approval of the budget, ratification of the government's program, and drafting of ordinary legislation.

The president, on the other hand, received the exclusive right to form a government, issue decrees, appoint elected chairmen of local and regional councils as heads of their respective state administrations (article 46), and to dismiss the heads of local administrations for violations of the law, the constitution, or presidential decrees (article 58).[45] Pursuant to his new powers, in July Kuchma appointed all chairmen of local councils to the position of head of their respective state administrations. This action unified regional legislative and executive powers under the president's overall direction.

In August, Kuchma issued two further decrees, placing local (municipal, *rayon*, and settlement) councils under the president, securing to himself the right to dismiss council chairs from their executive position, and to hold new elections.[46] Parliament vetoed Kuchma's decrees on November 2, however, asserting that they contradicted at least seven existing laws. Kuchma responded with a new decree in November, challenging parliament's right to veto presidential edicts, and, in the absence of a constitutional court, setting himself up as the "guarantor of the constitution."[47] Matters were again at an impasse.[48]

In a further effort to strengthen the "vertical structure of power," Kuchma clarified the executive powers of village, settlement, and city council chairs on January 4, 1996.[49] Previously, the executive councils of these bodies and their chairmen possessed no state executive authority. After this decree, council chairs at all levels would be accountable to the president for the administration of state executive authority within their respective jurisdictions. Kuchma thus took steps that would consolidate his grip on the executive power.

The 1996 Constitution and After

On November 17, 1995, Kuchma transmitted to parliament a draft Constitution of Ukraine. Kuchma's draft envisioned a two-house legislature: one-third of the upper house, or "senate," was to be represented by the heads of the regional state administrations, which the president could dismiss under his August 21 decree. All but one parliamentary faction opposed Kuchma's two-chamber body, which was rejected in favor of the unicameral legislature already in place.[50] Adopted on June 28, 1996, the new constitution rejected the concept of federalism as an internal structure for Ukraine, in favor of a unitary state.[51] The constitution contains no provision for regional powers or prerogatives; there is no decentralization approach embodied in the document; regional councils are granted relatively limited powers. The political competition of 1992 to 1996 clearly has worked against the interests of the regions. As Birch and Zinko have observed, "the fact that Ukraine's constitution-making process dragged on as long as it did probably benefited Ukrainian centralists."[52]

The result has been that well into 1997, regional interests were still seeking vehicles for political expression at the center. Kuchma continued to press for an all-embracing Law on Local Self-Government that would clarify regional prerogatives and assign a well-secured revenue stream to subnational bodies.[53] Passed on its second reading on May 21, 1997, despite his lingering objections to the lack of clarity in the assignment of expenditures and revenues to local government in the law, it was endorsed by Kuchma.[54] The law contains general provisions for the organization and operation of local and regional governments in Ukraine, fixes their legal status and competencies on a firmer basis than the 1992 law, and guarantees the exercise of self-government in accordance with the 1996 constitution.

The 1997 law does guarantee budgetary independence and spending discretion to subnational governments (articles 16 and 61), permitting a greater degree of fiscal flexibility to local governments in the fulfillment of their designated functions, including the right to issue debt instruments (article 70). However, the law also contains an extensive list of "general and specific competencies (functions)" of local governments (title II, articles 25–41). The principle of subordination of lower-level governments is preserved (article 4). For instance, central legislative clearance is provided for, insofar as registration of statutory acts of local governments with the Ministry of Justice can be refused on the basis of nonconformance with the constitution and laws of Ukraine (article 19).

Budgetary discretion is largely shared with the central government, which approves the minimum local budgets sufficient to provide residents with services at the "minimum state social standards level" (article 61), on the basis of per capita "budgetary norms" (article 62). In an important concession, the central government guarantees that all subnational governments will be provided with funds necessary to achieve minimum spending levels (article 62). Further, unfunded mandates are specifically disallowed (article 67), and local governments have unrestricted use of off-budget funds (article 68).

As a matter of continuing concern to the regions and localities, however, revenue assignment remains unclear under both the 1996 constitution and 1997 law. Intergovernmental revenues are shared on a combined retention/subvention basis, just as in Soviet times. As we shall see below, many poor regions remain highly dependent upon the central government for necessary revenues. Budgetary decisions made in Kyiv therefore have considerable effects on the regions and localities. In their turn, *oblast* governments continue to make decisions concerning the intraregional allocation of funds emanating from the center (1997 law, article 63), as well as the division of functional expenditure responsibilities among their subordinate governments. Consequently, regional and local governments remain largely "captive" to budgetary politics at higher levels. Under current law, however, local governments have much greater flexibility to develop own-source revenues, levy and collect taxes, and control expenditures.

These measures may have been too little, too late for many regions; by 1996, the fiscal deterioration had reached rather dramatic proportions, the combined effects of a devolution of functions from above and an eroding revenue base. In the midst of the five-year-long struggle to define the status of Ukraine's regions, many of them had become ever more subordinated and fiscally dependent upon the central government.

Expenditure Responsibilities at Various Levels

As late as 1996, the assignment of expenditure responsibilities at various levels of government in Ukraine remained very similar to the former Soviet framework. Since the collapse of the former USSR, the Ukrainian public sector has remained rather robust, proving difficult to shrink even in the face of chronic fiscal pressures.[55] To a great extent, the central government's ability until mid-1996 to engage in inflationary budget finance postponed the difficult social priority-setting and attendant budgetary cutbacks that have accompanied the economic transition process in other post-communist countries. Thus, significant microeconomic restructuring (i.e., privatization of enterprises of state and local subordination) has not taken place, so that many functions that could be privatized remain responsibilities of the state sector.

Analysts have observed that in general, "the current assignment [of functions] respects to a large extent the basic principle of assigning expenditure responsibilities according to the benefit area for the public service."[56] Central government ministries tend to specialize in activities of national economic significance: defense, law and order, foreign relations, major public works, and unemployment and pension outlays.

Subnational governments focus mainly on the social and cultural spheres. However, during the years 1993 to 1996, in response to fiscal retrenchment at the center, subnational governments increasingly assumed responsibility for "social protection of the population," other "social safety net" programs, and housing and communal services. Municipal governments especially undertook many functions previously performed by enterprises, as the latter cleansed their cost structures of functions that were unrelated to their core industrial activities. Such devolution of functions from above and below acted as a "vise" upon the increasingly meager fiscal capacities of Ukraine's subnational governments.

The Public/Private Distinction

Expenditure assignment has two dimensions. First, there is the public/private division of activities that ought to be the prerogative of government and that are best left to the private sector. Second, there is the question of the proper allocation of functions among the various levels of government. Ukraine has had difficulty in addressing issues along both of these dimensions, following very much an ad hoc process of shifting costs between sectors and levels of government.

Concerning the public/private distinction, there is no uniform pattern across Ukraine. The roles of government and enterprises remain considerably blurred, as in Soviet times. Under the former regime, much infrastructure spending (roads, housing, and public works such as electric power-generating stations) was undertaken by enterprises. Further, in the former USSR, the quality of housing, health care, employment training, and even access to cultural and recreational facilities depended more on one's place of employment than on the place of residence. Vast disparities have been noted both between and within regions as a result of these former Soviet expenditure policies.[57]

Municipal enterprises provided generous subsidies to their workers for housing and communal services (utilities), which varied considerably across enterprises and regions. Large subsidies have been allotted for heat and hot water. However, these have diminished as rates were progressively raised by the central government since 1994, in order to increase cost recovery levels. Cross-subsidization from enterprises to households continues, however, but the extent and level of subsidy is very uneven across Ukraine. Further, to the extent that many enterprises continued to receive operating subsidies in the years 1992 to 1996, this amounted to an implicit national subsidization of households from the state budget.[58]

State enterprises' ability and interest in continuing to provide their traditional menu of social and cultural services has diminished markedly since 1993, the result of falls in production and sales, decreasing operating subsidies from the budget, and the persistent payments crisis. For instance, many previously enterprise-operated services, such as kindergartens and daycare facilities, have either been transferred to local governments or been closed permanently.[59] The long-term trend is clearly one of shifting functions to the state sector, where the problem becomes one of assigning functions to the appropriate level of government.

Major Expenditure Assignments

Table 7.4 outlines the major expenditure assignments among levels of government in Ukraine. In order to understand the *oblast*-level functions properly, it should be observed that the main fiscal function of the *oblasts* is to redistribute and redirect the expenditure of national taxes shared with regional governments and direct budgetary transfers from the center. *Oblasts'* direct service provision activities are actually much more limited. In accordance with the "benefit principle," *oblasts* do tend to fund services whose impacts are primarily felt on a regional basis. For instance, *oblasts* are the primary providers of health, education, and housing and communal services. *Oblast* expenditures for social safety net programs increased sharply (to 65 percent) in 1994, mainly owing to increases in price subsidies rather than direct transfers to individuals and organizations. Subnational governments thus account for a large share of price subsidies, whose apportionment between *oblast* and municipal governments varies broadly.

Individual *oblasts* have the power to reassign expenditures among *oblast*, municipal, and *rayon* (district) governments, which has resulted in a highly checkered pattern of subnational expenditure assignments across Ukraine. *Oblast* and lower-level governments account for over one-third of all spending on public administration, and this share may be expected to rise with the

Table 7.4 Major Expenditure Assignments Among Levels of Government in Ukraine

Expenditure Category	Central (State) Government	Oblast (Regional) Government	Cities and Towns of Regional Subordination	City Districts (Ravons)	Rural Settlements and Townships
Legislative bodies Foreign affairs	Own expenses Diplomatic service Embassies abroad Foreign economic relations	Own expenses Limited autonomy for foreign trade in some Oblasts	Own expenses	Own expenses	Own expenses
National security	Armed forces Intelligence services Border troops				
Public safety/Law & Order	National militia Criminal justice Procurator General Internal affairs State Bureau of Investigation	Traffic police (DAI) Fire protection	Local police & security Some volunteer and enterprise-financed fire companies	Some volunteer fire companies	Township, Kolhosp, and volunteer fire companies
Public works	Roads, Tunnels, and Bridges National highway maintenance Railroad construction Aqueducts and reservoirs Mass transit systems Sewer system construction	Maintenance of regional roads, tunnels, bridges, and canals School construction	Maintenance of city and Rayon roads and bridges Operations and maintenance of sewage facilities	Operations and maintenance of sewage facilities	Maintenance of communal roads

(continues)

Table 7.4 (continued)

Expenditure Category	Central (State) Government	Oblast (Regional) Government	Cities and Towns of Regional Subordination	City Districts (Ravons)	Rural Settlements and Townships
Public transportation	Airports and sea terminals Airport operations Sea terminal operations Railroad operations Mass transit subsidies	Subsidies to subordinate level governments	Mass public transit systems operations and maintenance		
Sanitation services			Trash collection	Trash collection	Trash collection
Public health and welfare	Medical research institutes Medical schools Universal health care benefits	Tertiary health care facilities Veterans hospitals Psychiatric hospitals Specialty clinics All capital expenditures on health care	Some primary health care facilities Secondary health care facilities	Primary health care facilities	Local clinics and paramedic services
			Emergency and trauma services	Emergency and trauma services	Emergency and trauma services
Social protection of the population	Pension benefits	Family allowance Orphanages	Child allowance Bread allowance		
Public education	All state universities Research institutes Kyiv Polytechnic Institute Technological institutes Pedagogical institutes Technical schools	Some vocational training schools Schools for orphans Schools for the handicapped Capital expenditures	Local teacher salaries Kindergarten operations School maintenance	Local teacher salaries Kindergarten operations School maintenance	Local teacher salaries Kindergarten operations School maintenance

(continues)

Table 7.4 (continued)

Expenditure Category	Central (State) Government	Oblast (Regional) Government	Cities and Towns of Regional Subordination	City Districts (Rayons)	Rural Settlements and Townships
Communal services (housing and public utilities)	Construction and development Implicitly subsidizes public utilities via price controls Construction and operation of electric power grid	Operation and maintenance of some facilities	Maintenance and renovation Direct household subsidies for public utilities	Small-scale construction and some maintenance Some enterprises may construct housing units for some employees	Kolhosps construct and maintain much of their own housing
Mass media and public communications	Telephone & postal system Television and radio operations National news service (UkrInform)				
Culture, parks & recreation	National museums National opera National theater National libraries Botanical gardens	Some museums, theaters, and operas	Local museums, libraries, and zoos Music schools Stadiums and sports facilities Parks and concert facilities		

Sources: Law of Ukraine, "On the Budget System;" 1992–1996 State Budget Laws of Ukraine; Interviews with Ministry of Finance Officials; Supplementary information from Jorge Martinez, et al., "Subnational Fiscal Decentralization in Ukraine," ch. 8 in Bird, Ebel, and Wallich (1995, pp. 281–319).

devolution of functions from above. The share of subnational expenditures in other functional areas is relatively low.

As to their unique functions, despite recent improvements in the rate of privatization, *oblasts* and municipalities own and manage hotels and tourist camps, run restaurants, operate shops, and provide other services that are typically privately owned and operated in market-based economies. For instance, in 1994 the city of Kharkiv operated more than two-thirds of all retail and consumer shops in that city.[60] A similar situation exists in all large cities; however, small-scale privatization has reduced the proportion of municipal shops, restaurants, and services since 1994.

Municipal governments primarily serve the local population, providing public transit, primary education, basic health and medical care, communal services, and sanitation. In addition, devolution of new functions from above has been quite extensive since 1993. Starting with the 1994 budget, *oblast* and municipal governments became responsible for certain expenditures that were previously the functional responsibility of the central government, including those for the "social protection of the population" (child allowance, bread allowance, and housing); "social safety net" (retirement homes, aid to families with blind and disabled children, additional allowances for families with children); and further price subsidies for items as disparate as school lunches and housing construction. Housing and communal services were largely provided by municipal enterprises. These are quasi-public entities, possessing a measure of fiscal independence from the local governments to which they are subordinated. Until quite recently, communal services were heavily subsidized (by as much as 88 percent, or 20 percent of GDP).[61]

Problems with Expenditure Assignments

There are several serious shortcomings of the current assignment of expenditure responsibilities. First, a fragmentation of functions produces inefficiency and unevenness across regions, which militates against policy success. A classic example is in basic education, where *oblast* governments pay to build schools, *rayons* pay teachers' salaries, and city districts and settlements pay wages of support staff and maintenance personnel. Unified school budget management has thus proved to be elusive.

Second, the central government has shifted expenditure responsibilities to subnational governments on a fairly ad hoc basis, with little longer-term planning. City and regional finance officials are almost universal in their opinion that Kyiv tends to shift the most unpopular funding cuts down to the lower echelons of government. Similarly, *oblasts* have shifted functions to *rayon* or city governments in order to meet momentary fiscal and political objectives. This has resulted in a third problem, in which social safety net programs, a national responsibility in most market-based economies, have been funded since 1994 on a highly decentralized basis. Fourth, and as a consequence of the above, the present system does not serve expenditure equalization objectives. Fifth, the continuing devolution of expenditure functions from both above and below (i.e., from enterprises) have worked against effective budgetary planning in the regions. Finally, as already noted, the legislative basis for regional and local fiscal management has been ever changing, internally contradictory, and subject to selective implementation.

In general, expenditure needs and responsibilities at the municipal and *oblast* levels increasingly exceeded the available resources throughout 1992 to 1996. One indication of the desperately acute nature of the subnational fiscal situation is that despite the shifting of expenditure functions to subnational governments in recent years, the subnational share of public expenditure shrank in real terms, owing to both the inflation of 1993 to 1996 and to falling tax receipts generally. Due to the dwindling real value of budget resources transferred from higher-level governments, cities, towns and settlements have been under considerable pressure to maintain service levels. According to interviews conducted by the author from 1993 to 1995, most city and *oblast* officials expect a continued decline in service levels in the foreseeable future. These expenditure pressures are made all the more severe by a deteriorating intergovernmental revenue situation.

Revenue Assignment among Levels of Government

The essence of regional independence from the center is the attainment of some measure of fiscal independence from Kyiv. The need to develop such regional "own-source" revenues has been noted by President Kuchma's former regional policy adviser, Volodymyr Hry'niov, who views "serious and profound financial-budget reform in general, and taxation reform in particular," as "certain preconditions" for regional independence.[62] In fact, Hry'niov would "overturn the taxation pyramid to place its foundation not in the center but in the regions." Hry'niov's remarks are largely reflective of the regional sentiment. In order to appreciate and understand his view that Ukraine's intergovernmental fiscal system is "a mill working in vain," we must describe in some detail the basic framework and operation of the system as it has evolved since 1992. Several noteworthy problems present themselves:

- Unclear distinctions exist between national ("regulating") and subnational ("fixed") revenue sources;
- Continually shifting tax-sharing rates complicate fiscal planning;
- Fluctuating budgetary transfers to subordinate levels accompany shifting tax-sharing rates; and,
- *Oblast* revenue structures deteriorated from 1992 to 1996.

Unclear Distinctions between Fixed and Regulating Revenues

Subnational (*oblast* and municipal) governments derive their revenues from so-called fixed (i.e., local) sources and from tax-sharing and budgetary transfers from the central government. Local governments in turn may also receive transfers from the *oblast* administration. Intergovernmental fiscal relations in Ukraine retain many vestiges of the former Soviet budgetary system, especially the distinction between "fixed" revenues and state "regulating" revenues. Fixed, or own-source revenues, include taxes, charges, and fees that have been assigned by law to subnational governments. "Regulating" revenues are central government taxes that are shared with *oblasts* on a derivation basis, with varying rates of retention set according to the total tax anticipated to be collected in each *oblast*.

A serious problem afflicting subnational governments has been that the central government has periodically changed the definition of "fixed" revenues since 1992, diminishing both their number and value to subnational governments. To cite two such instances, until the 1994 budget law, the personal income tax and land tax were defined as fixed revenues, with 100 percent assigned to *oblast* and municipal governments.[63] They have since been shared with the center on a percentage basis. Effective with the 1995 budget, the tax on profits of enterprises of communal subordination was also redefined as a state regulating revenue, which significantly diminished the already poor fiscal strength of subnational governments.[64]

Exclusively subnational revenue sources are now much more limited, including taxes on motor vehicles, payments for water employed by industry, housing and communal services (utility) fees, revenues from privatization of communal property, and other non-tax revenues (hotel occupancy, parking fees, apartment occupancy, pet licenses, advertising, lotteries, auctions, market stall rentals, etc.).[65] Unfortunately, these taxes have very nominal yields, with little growth potential. Table 7.5 provides the conceptual framework for *oblast* revenues prior to the 1994 and 1995 changes in the composition of "fixed" and "regulating" revenues.

Table 7.5   *Oblast* **Revenue Framework, 1993**

	E.g., Autonomous Republic of Crimea—1993 Revenues	
	Millions of Nominal KBV	*Percent of Total*
Regulating revenues (derived from national taxes):		
Value-added tax	512,211,831	36.5
State enterprise income tax	229,068,738	16.3
Excise taxes	111,218,689	7.9
Total regulating revenues	852,499,258	60.7
Fixed (i.e., own source) revenues:		
Personal income tax[1]	101,860,758	7.3
Income tax on communal property enterprises[2]	70,689,651	4.9
Other fixed revenues	367,270,538	26.3
Total fixed revenues	539,820,947	38.3
"Pure revenues"	1,392,320,205	99.3
Transfers from (extractions to) state budget	9,701,000	0.7
Subventions	0	0
Total Oblast Revenues	1,402,021,205	100

Notes: [1]Effective with the 1994 budget, the personal income tax became a state "regulating revenue," distributed on a retention basis at a flat rate of 50 percent.
[2]Effective with the 1995 budget, the income tax on profits of enterprises of all forms of ownership and subordination became subject to distribution on a retention basis at a flat rate of 70 percent.

The central government also has routinely violated legal norms when doing so suited its fiscal convenience. For instance, the provisions of both the 1994 and 1995 laws on state budget, which changed the composition of *oblast* fixed revenues, contradicted provisions of both the then-effective Law on Local Self-Government and the Law on the Budget System, which fully assigned these taxes to subnational governments, and made the fiscal relationship between *oblasts* and their subordinate municipal jurisdictions solely a matter of *oblast* policy.[66] Far from serving as the basis for a rational distribution of resources, legal requirements have not prevented Kyiv from acting in its own fiscal interest at the expense of the regions.

Shifting Tax-Sharing Rates

Regulating revenues are shared between the central government and subnational governments according to tax retention rates, which entitle the regions to retain a proportion of the tax raised on their territory. (The 27 "regions" that are subject to retention rates include Ukraine's 24 *oblasti,* the Crimean Republic, and the strategically important cities of Kyiv and Sevastopol.) Retention rates have been set annually in the Law on State Budget. *Oblasts,* in their turn, assign a proportion of their respective tax-sharing rates to their subordinate governments, which do the same for their districts and settlements. Retention rates have varied considerably by type of tax (e.g., value-added tax, personal income tax, enterprise profits tax, and excises), and between the regions for each type of tax.[67]

A problem that rendered budgetary planning all but impossible at the subnational level throughout the years from 1992 to 1995 was the rather dramatic shift in retention rates from year to year, especially for the value-added tax (VAT), which has been the "workhorse" of Ukraine's intergovernmental revenue system.[68] Table 7.6 provides the *oblast*-level detail for regulating revenue retention rates from 1992 to 1996. Note that the VAT and state enterprise income tax, which together accounted for between 40 to 60 percent of total *oblast* revenues during this period, were subject to the widest variation in retention rates. This obviously injected great uncertainty and stress upon the annual budget process at all levels of government, wreaking havoc upon the efforts of *oblast* and municipal budget officials to pursue a rational and consistent fiscal policy.

To illustrate the problem in a more direct fashion, weighted-average regulating revenue retention rates for each subject tax are presented in Table 7.7. Such broad fluctuation in average retention rates militates against multi-period fiscal planning. The problem appears to be only more acute at the *oblast* level. It can be seen in Table 7.8 that weighted-average retention rates across taxes have also varied significantly among *oblasts.* The rationale for the differential *oblast* retention rates has been to equalize differences in per capita expenditure between Ukraine's regions. However, as will be seen below, it is not clear that lower-income *oblasts* benefit from higher retention rates, or that per capita expenditure levels are significant determinants of an *oblast's* level of fiscal contribution from the central government.

Fluctuating Budgetary Transfers to Subordinate Levels

In addition to regulating revenues, the central government provides budgetary transfers, or "subventions," to its regions. In principle, such transfers are intended as a supplementary device to achieve revenue equalization objectives. The evidence suggests that budgetary subventions actually have been increasingly used for this purpose, becoming more selective (i.e., targeted)

Table 7.6 Oblast Regulating Revenue Retention Rates (Norms), 1992–96

Oblast	Value-Added Tax					State Enterprise Income Tax					Excise Taxes					Personal Income Tax		
	1992	1993	1994[1]	1995[3]	1996[4]	1992	1993	1994[1]	1995[3]	1996[4]	1992	1993	1994[1]	1995[3]	1996	1994[1,2]	1995[3]	1996[4]
Republic of Crimea	58.6	100	20	100	100	50	100	50	70	70	50	100	20	20	100	50	50	100
Vinnytsya	82	89.7	20	97.6	100	50	100	50	70	70	50	50	20	20	20	50	50	50
Volyn	82.7	100	20	100	100	50	100	50	70	70	50	100	20	20	20	50	50	50
Dnipropetrovs'k	15.8	24.3	20	46.4	24.2	40	25	50	70	70	50	10	20	20	20	50	50	50
Donets'k	15.5	22.1	20	30.7	23.4	20	25	50	70	70	50	10	20	20	20	50	50	50
Zhytomyr	84.3	100	20	100	100	70	100	50	70	70	50	100	20	20	20	50	50	50
Zakarpattia	89.5	100	20	100	100	100	100	50	70	70	100	100	20	20	20	50	50	50
Zaporizhzhia	14.5	60.3	20	22.9	20	20	50	50	70	70	50	50	20	20	20	50	50	50
Ivano-Frankivs'k	81.5	68.9	20	100	89	50	50	50	70	70	50	50	20	20	20	50	50	50
Kyiv oblast	43.8	100	20	100	91.6	70	100	50	70	70	50	100	20	20	20	50	50	50
Kyiv city	41.9	36.1	20	20	20	50	50	50	70	70	50	50	20	20	20	50	50	50
Khirovohrad	100	95.7	20	100	100	100	100	50	70	70	100	50	20	20	20	50	50	50
Luhans'k	15.5	35.7	20	78.1	72.8	35	50	50	70	70	50	50	20	20	20	50	50	50
L'viv	44	38.6	20	93.9	59.6	50	50	50	70	70	50	50	20	20	20	50	50	50
Mykolaiv	72.6	62.1	20	100	100	50	100	50	70	70	50	50	20	20	20	50	50	50
Odesa	54.3	41.1	20	56.5	45.3	50	50	50	70	70	50	50	20	20	20	50	50	50
Poltava	38.7	35.6	20	24.7	20	50	25	50	70	70	50	10	20	20	20	50	50	50
Rivne	92.9	100	20	100	100	70	100	50	70	70	70	100	20	20	20	50	50	50
Sumy	66	100	20	53.8	53.1	50	100	50	70	70	50	100	20	20	20	50	50	50
Ternopil	93.7	90.7	20	100	100	70	100	50	70	70	70	50	20	20	20	50	50	50
Kharkiv	57	27.1	20	76.7	44.7	50	25	50	70	70	50	50	20	20	20	50	50	50

(continues)

Table 7.6 *(continued)*

Oblast	Value-Added Tax					State Enterprise Income Tax					Excise Taxes					Personal Income Tax		
	1992	1993	1994	1995[5]	1996[4]	1992	1993	1994	1995[5]	1996[4]	1992	1993	1994	1995[5]	1996	1992[1,2]	1992[3]	1992[4]
Kherson	97.2	74.2	20	100	100	100	100	50	70	70	100	100	20	20	20	50	50	50
Khmel'nyts'kyi	79.4	63.3	20	100	100	50	50	50	70	70	50	100	20	20	20	50	50	50
Cherkasy	65.7	76.5	20	100	78.8	50	50	50	70	70	50	50	20	20	20	50	50	50
Chernivtsi	93.6	100	20	100	100	100	100	50	70	70	100	100	20	20	20	50	50	50
Chernihiv	56.3	23.1	20	86.6	86.3	70	50	50	70	70	50	50	20	20	20	50	50	50
M. Sevastopol	n.a.	100	20	100	100	n.a.	100	50	100	100	n.a.	100	20	100	100	100	100	100

Notes: [1] Effective with the 1994 budget, the intergovernmental fiscal system was changed, providing for an across-the-board, flat retention rate for regulating revenues in all *oblasts*, supplemented by a more "targeted" system of budgetary subventions. This short-lived experiment was partially terminated in 1995, when the Value-Added Tax was again distributed on the basis of differential retention rates.

[2] In 1994, the Personal Income Tax became a state regulating revenue, distributed on a retention basis, at a flat rate of 50 percent.

[3] The 1995 Budget Law contradicted a requirement of the December 28, 1994, Law of Ukraine, "On Taxation of Profits of Enterprises" (No. 334-94-VR), which was effective January 1, 1995, that the tax on profits was to be allocated to budgets of villages, settlements, and towns (i.e., below the oblast level). All other regulating revenues were to be shared on the usual retention basis. Also in 1995, oblasts were to retain 70 percent of the Income Tax from enterprises and organizations of all forms of ownership and subordination. This is a change from 1991–94, when 100 percent of the profits tax on communal property enterprises was retained as fixed revenue. In addition, the 1995 budget of the Autonomous Republic of Crimea was formed on the basis of an agreement with the central government in Kyiv. Funds in the amount of 12,877,284.4 million KBV were to be transferred from the Budget of Crimea to the State Budget of Ukraine.

[4] The 1996 Budget Law, Article6, specifically directs that Enterprise Income Tax receipts are to be allocated to the appropriate budgets in accordance with the 1995 Law of Ukraine, "On the Budget System" (i.e., 70 percent to budgets of of oblasts and subordinate levels of government). However, the March 22, 1996, Decree of Verhovna Rada, "On the Enactment of the Law of Ukraine 'On the State Budget of Ukraine for 1996,'" Article 8, establishes the principle of the distribution of revenues at sub-oblast levels in proportion to population. Further, Article 9 of the decree effectively expands the revenue base of local councils, specifying that oblasts shall retain 50 percent over and above revenues from Value-Added Taxes, Excise Taxes, and Income Taxes on State Enterprises of National Subordination.

Source: Ministry of Finance of Ukraine; 1992, 1993, and 1994 Budgets of Ukraine (source documents in the author's possession); 1995 Budget is from *Holos Ukrayiny*, April 21, 1995, pp. 3–5 [FBIS-SOV-95-102-S (Original in Ukrainian)]. 1996 Budget is from *Holos Ukrayiny*, April 6, 1996, pp. 3–5 [FBIS-SOV-96-084 (Original in Ukrainian)]. Supplementary information from Inna Lunina, "Probleme des regionalen Finanzausgleichs in der Ukraine," Berichte des Budesinstituts fur ostwissenschaftliche unde internationale studien, 11/1994, Tabelle 13, p. 24.

Table 7.7   Weighted Average Regulating Revenue Retention Rates, 1992–1995[1]

Budget Year	Value Added Tax	Excise Taxes	Enterprise Income Tax[2]	Personal Income Tax[3]	Weighted Average Excluding Subventions	Weighted Average Including Subventions
1992	42.90%	53.20%	45.50%	n.a.	44.90%	n.a.
1993	49.40%	54.70%	54.50%	n.a.	51.60%	52.50%
1994 Budget	20.00%	20.00%	50.00%	50.00%	30.80%	37.80%
1995 Budget	62.50%	21.00%	72.10%	52.40%	63.80%	65.80%

Notes: [1]1994 and 1995 calculations may be subject to further revision, based on actual budget outturn data.
[2]In 1995, the Enterprise Income Tax base subject to the 70% retention norm was expanded to include enterprises and organizations of all forms of ownership and subordination, including communal property enterprises.
[3]The Personal Income Tax became a state regulating revenue with the 1994 budget. Previously, it was a fixed revenue of oblast and local governments only.
Source: Author's calculations.

from 1992 to 1996. Indeed, in the 1994, 1995, and 1996 budgets, in a clear break with past practice, wealthier regions (such as Donets'k, Dnipropetrovs'k, Zaporizhzhya, Kyiv city, and Poltava) either received no subvention or were subject to an additional exaction from their budgets to the state budget.69 (See Table 7.9.)

The level and pattern of subventions/exactions has been changed annually in order to reflect the level of regulating revenues authorized to be retained by *oblasts* each year. For instance, effective with the 1994 budget, the central government introduced a system of uniform tax retention rates for all *oblasts,* supplemented by a more extensive (and generous) set of budgetary subventions, especially to *oblasts* with relatively narrow tax bases. This short-lived experiment was abandoned the following year, however, in favor of variable retention rates.[70] It may be argued that revenue equalization objectives may be more readily achieved with variable rather than fixed rates.[71] However, the vast inherent differences between *oblasts'* natural endowments, industrial development, population, and income result in significant differences in *oblast* revenue capacities. These differences are of such magnitude that they limit the potential beneficial effects of a derivation-based revenue system, necessitating supplementary transfers from the central (state) budget to many needy regions.

In general, as Martinez-Vazquez et al. point out, the goal of revenue equalization is "undermined by the lack of objective rules or principles for

Table 7.8 Ukraine—Average Regulating Revenue Retention Rates, 1992–1995
(Percent Retained for All Regulating Revenue Items)[1]

Oblast	Actual 1992	Actual 1993	Budget 1994		Budget 1995	
			Excluding State Budget Transfers	Including State Budget Transfers	Excluding State Budget Transfers	Including State Budget Transfers
Republic of Crimea	55.6	100	28.6	57.9	90.1	48.6
Vinnytsya	70.8	87.4	28.8	57.4	74.8	74.8
Volyn	70.5	100	26.8	63.4	75.9	124.4
Dnipropetrovs'k	24.1	24.2	33.2	32.5	58.1	58.1
Donets'k	18.7	22.7	32.3	26.8	52.2	52.2
Zhytomyr	77.3	100	28.3	58.8	77.1	129.9
Zakarpattia	93.1	100	27.4	78.9	77.1	140.6
Zaporizhzhia	20.1	54.9	30.3	21.6	49.9	49.9
Ivano-Frankivs'k	67.6	59.4	27.9	39.8	75.6	81.2
Kyiv *oblast*	49.3	100	28.9	37.1	76.4	82.7
Kyiv city	45	56.2	33.2	28.6	46.5	35.4
Khirovohrad	100	92.1	29.6	66.9	76.2	93.1
Luhans'k	23.2	41.1	36.3	39.4	69	69
L'viv	46.6	43.5	28.8	39.9	84.1	84.1
Mykolaiv	62.7	78.1	32	40.3	75.3	79.5
Odesa	52.2	45.6	33.3	39.1	60.5	60.5
Poltava	43.6	35.9	28.9	20.9	41.5	41.5
Rivne	85.7	100	31.6	67.1	76.8	87.1
Sumy	60.9	100	29.8	47.5	58.5	58.5
Ternopil	81.9	85	27.2	69.9	75.2	91.9
Kharkiv	54.5	27.7	29	31.9	69.8	69.8
Kherson	98.2	86	31.7	54.9	76.7	85.9
Khmel'nyts'kyi	68.7	62.4	28.6	47.7	76.1	91
Cherkasy	59.4	63.2	27.7	41.7	74.9	89.7
Chernivtsy	96.1	100	28	63.9	75.6	97.7
Chernihiv	59.1	36.5	26.7	37.8	69.8	69.8
M. Sevastopol	100	100	30.1	64.1	100	130.9
Ukraine—Average	44.5	51.6	30.8	37.8	63.1	65.1

Note: [1]1994 and 1995 calculations may be subject to further revision, based on actual budget outturn.
Source: Author's calculations, based on data from source documents.

determining sharing rates and subventions."[72] Absence of such rules has had the effect of placing *oblast* budgets very much at the mercy of political decisions made in Kyiv. Further, as a consequence of inflation, the falling real value of *oblast* revenues has placed unprecedented fiscal pressures upon

Table 7.9 Budgetary Subventions (Exactions) and Other Transfers, 1992–1996 (millions of nominal KBV)

Oblast	1992	1993	Budget 1994	Budget 1995	Budget 1996
Republic of Crimea	11815.5	9701	1657068	−12877284.1	−13086000
Vinnytsya	5223.4	3122	1197749.3	0	8195500
Volyn	3099.5	7940.5	866227.6	5274858.5	7473800
Dnipropetrovs'k	10831.2	32532	−109042	0	0
Donets'k	14045.8	0	−1473286.3	0	0
Zhytomyr	4434.4	22634	1080103.6	10929436.1	12318400
Zakarpattia	4230.4	0	1099705.1	6948711.9	12623000
Zaporizhzhia	7767.4	16373	−983808.9	0	−1553500
Ivano-Frankivs'k	3492.8	1945.6	481521.4	1182507.1	0
Kyiv oblast	4453.7	42120	471655.5	2151047	0
Kyiv city	11235.2	0	−695180.4	−14079656.1	−32249700
Khirovohrad	3925.7	21320	1082500.2	3409231.7	7143600
Luhans'k	7207.9	0	282816.4	0	0
L'viv	7004.2	0	940304.2	0	0
Mykolaiv	4193.9	0	358756.8	1202757.5	1311200
Odesa	6529.4	12211	402544.2	0	0
Poltava	4688.9	0	−758890	0	−1445800
Rivne	3070.6	5090	799445.8	1686545.5	2014800
Sumy	4031.3	0	699285.4	0	0
Ternopil	3196.7	2060.7	960652.5	2100332.3	6504000
Kharkiv	8862.6	46430	340620.2	0	0
Kherson	3720.8	6954	787729.6	2069612.9	9264500
Khmel'nyts'kyi	4027.9	15542	716747.8	3369485.4	7082800
Cherkasy	4561.9	10128	753350.1	4095699.2	0
Chernivtsy	2428.9	9395	722278.3	2808147.5	5625100
Chernihiv	4312.3	0	494691.3	0	0
M. Sevastopol	3100	10083	337998.3	2600317.5	1550800

Source: Ministry of Finance of Ukraine; 1992, 1993, and 1994 budgets of Ukraine (source documents in the author's possession); 1995 Budget is from Holos Ukrayiny, April 21, 1995, pp. 3–5 (FBIS-SOV-95-102-S [Original in Ukrainian]). 1996 Budget is from Holos Ukrayiny, April 6, 1996, pp. 3–5 (FBIS-SOV-96-084 [Original in Ukrainian]).

subnational governments, magnifying the impact of the central government's fiscal policies upon the regions.

Deteriorating Oblast Revenue Structures

The revenue structures of oblasts fluctuated widely from 1992 to 1995, but the general pattern was clearly one of increasing regional budgetary dependence upon the center. Table 7.10 illustrates that oblasts were generally more

Table 7.10 *Oblast* Revenue Structure, 1992–1995

Budget Year	Value Added Tax	Excise Taxes	Enterprise Income Tax	Personal Income Tax[1]	Fixed Revenues	Budgetary Subventions and Transfers	Total
1992	29.11%	4.27%	14.01%	n.a.	32.67%	20.94%	100%
1993	33.30%	5.25%	22.81%	n.a.	37.57%	1.07%	100%
1994 Budget	17.78%	5.10%	23.69%	8.39%	32.44%	12.58%	100%
1995 Estimated	34.79%	1.19%	25.48%	10.34%	25.38%	2.82%	100%

Note: [1]The Personal Income Tax became a state regulating revenue with the 1994 budget. Previously, it was a fixed revenue of *oblast* and local governments only. Accordingly, it has been included in the "Fixed Revenues" column for 1992 and 1993.

Source: Author's calculations, based on data from source documents.

Table 7.11   Fluctuating Real Value of *Oblast* Fixed Revenues

Year	Nominal Fixed (Own Source) Revenues (millions of KBV)	Nominal GDP (billions of KBV)	Fixed Revenues as Percent of GDP	Net Change (%)
1992	242698.3	5168	4.69%	n.a.
1993	9690880.7	141916	6.83%	45.60%
1994	9170000	1080307	0.84%	−87.70%
1995	12502000	5083061	0.25%	−70.20%
1996	28768000	8051000	3.57%	1328%

Source: Consolidated budget results reported by the Ministry of Finance; GDP reported by the Ministry of Statistics; author's calculations.

dependent upon regulating revenues in 1995 than in previous years. This is also reflected in the falling share of consolidated government (central plus subnational) revenues going to subnational governments (38 percent in 1992 versus under 25 percent in 1994 and thereafter). Further, according to Table 7.11, fixed revenues have been grossly insufficient to fill the gap left by falling regulating revenues, even in real terms. Fixed revenues fell from 4.69 percent of GDP in 1992 to just 0.25 percent by 1995. There is some improvement noted in 1996 (to around 3.6 percent), owing to the falling inflation rates that year. If this trend continues, it will provide much welcome relief to regional and municipal budgets.

Unfortunately, the falling real value of fixed revenues has been paralleled by falls in real state regulating revenues and budgetary transfers. Although the inflation-driven compound annual growth rate from 1992 to 1995 reached the astonishing level of 1,043 percent, in real terms per capita regulating revenues and subventions fell 77.7 percent from 1992 to 1994. As can be seen from Table 7.12, no *oblast* was spared deterioration in the real value of budgetary receipts from Kyiv.

This has effectively placed regional finances in a double bind: even as the real value of the *oblasts'* share of regulating revenues and budgetary transfers declined, the fiscal dependence of Ukraine's regions on the center increased to more than two-thirds (measured as the proportion of *oblast* revenues accounted for by regulating revenues plus budgetary transfers). Table 7.13 presents the *oblast*-level estimates of levels of fiscal dependence on the central government from 1992 to 1994. The unpalatable result is that competition between Ukraine's regions for fiscal relief from Kyiv has become all the more intense, even as the purchasing power of such relief has fallen. Further, due to the progressive redefinition of "fixed" revenues as state "regulating" revenues from 1994 to 1995, even the higher-income *oblasts* of eastern Ukraine, which were relatively fiscally independent of the central government in 1992, by 1995 approached or even exceeded the average for regional budgetary dependence upon Kyiv. As one would expect, the less wealthy regions were even more utterly dependent upon the center throughout this period.

Political Economy of Fiscal Relations

Despite the apparent convergence of regions with respect to their relative levels of fiscal dependence upon the central government, there is evidence to suggest that more heavily industrialized *oblasti* remained relatively less dependent on Kyiv. In order to estimate the effects of industrial development and other socioeconomic factors upon fiscal dependence, the level of *oblast* budgetary dependence was regressed over industrial output (percent of total); the proportion of a region's enterprises that were subordinated to all-union (USSR) ministries in 1989 (and that reverted to republican control in 1991); levels of *oblast* urbanization (percent of population residing in cities); proportion of population classified as ethnically Russian (based on one's internal Soviet passport in 1989); and *oblast* per capita expenditures for 1993. The 1993 expenditure data were employed in order to filter out the possibility of a real decline in *oblast* per capita expenditure in response to the falling real revenues that occurred in 1994 and subsequent years. The results are presented in Table 7.14.

As can be seen, industrial output is strongly and inversely related to the level of fiscal dependence on Kyiv. Also significant is the proportion of an *oblast*'s enterprises that were subordinated to the center, but with a much smaller beta-coefficient than output. As to the other variables, neither level of urbanization nor proportion of ethnic Russians was significant, indicating that neither the more extensive service demands of cities nor the possible presence of ethnic politics exerted a significant influence upon intergovernmental fiscal relations in Ukraine.

Most interesting for present purposes is the utterly insignificant effect of *oblast* per capita expenditures, indicating the absence of any direct, measurable link between revenue sharing from the center and actual *oblast*-level expenditures. These results are doubly significant when one considers that *oblast* expenditure norms are developed annually by the Ministry of the Economy on a per capita basis precisely in order to equalize social expenditure across Ukraine's entire population. It appears obvious, then, that other,

Table 7.12   Ukraine—Value of State Regulating Revenues and Budgetary Transfers,

Oblast	Billions of Nominal KBV				Compound Growth Rate (1995–1992)
	1992	1993	Budget 1994	Budget 1995	
Republic of Crimea	25.197	862.2002	3276.8103	15100.8	753.10%
Vinnytsya	19.5034	571.878	2401.7811	17506.6	864.64%
Volyn	9.2505	306.6005	1501.341	13557.9	1035.91%
Dnipropetrovs'k	34.8106	796.3428	4968.7258	71913.6	1173.60%
Donets'k	35.743	840.0635	7173.0747	77818.2	1196.07%
Zhytomyr	14.5993	588.2595	2081.8632	26874.9	1125.57%
Zakarpattia	12.0272	294.2127	1685.4088	15384.9	985.53%
Zaporizhzhia	17.0126	973.469	2453.1223	33197.2	1149.62%
Ivano-Frankivs'k	12.6295	328.6778	1617.5235	17128.2	1006.90%
Kyiv *oblast*	13.611	966.3582	2146.1886	28402.1	1177.87%
Kyiv city	41.8801	1453.6786	4275.2888	44987.4	924.14%
Khirovohrad	13.807	436.9643	1943.608	18739.8	1107.19%
Luhans'k	17.1627	679.5977	3636.8435	43020.2	1258.40%
L'viv	26.3388	744.3882	3366.8143	49376.3	1133.03%
Mykolaiv	11.2425	559.8859	1749.6407	22624.9	1162.53%
Odesa	24.3156	680.5782	2720.343	33144.3	1008.77%
Poltava	23.3488	542.0669	1967.0849	20631.8	859.60%
Rivne	11.1108	445.0298	1508.9236	14330.5	988.53%
Sumy	14.1034	757.1015	1880.4638	16051.8	944.08%
Ternopil	11.4197	315.8853	1573.249	11500.1	902.34%
Kharkiv	34.4036	675.5214	3762.9308	54824.5	1068.04%
Kherson	17.1961	490.7714	1866.686	19092.3	935.48%
Khmel'nyts'kyi	12.5398	393.9834	1792.6718	20558.2	1079.14%
Cherkasy	15.2114	511.6871	2247.1317	25010.5	1080.28%
Chernivtsy	9.624	349.4513	1286.2623	12397.5	988.08%
Chernihiv	13.8277	280.4069	1691.3608	17968.3	991.24%
M. Sevastopol	7.3673	228.2793	637.9891	10993.2	1042.72%
Totals/Averages	499.8835	16103.3402	67213.1312	747133	1043.34%

Memorandum: CPI[2]

Notes: [1]Ukraine's population is shrinking. Standing at 52.1 million at independence, by January 1, 1997, the [2]Average annual CPI for the year.

Source: Author's calculations, based on data from source documents.

1992–1995

Inflation Adjusted KBV Per Capita				Percent Change		Memo: 1-1-92 Population (000s)¹
1992	1993	Budget 1994	Budget 1995	1992 to 1994	1992 to 1995	
1008	667	218	222	−78.4	−77.9	2156.1
887	503	182	292	−79.5	−67.1	1896.6
746	478	201	401	−73.1	−46.2	1069.9
769	340	182	583	−76.3	−24.2	3907.2
578	263	193	462	−66.6	−20.1	5332
842	656	200	569	−76.2	−32.4	1495.9
694	388	191	385	−72.5	−44.5	1264.9
699	773	168	500	−75.9	−28.4	2100.7
756	381	161	376	−78.7	−50.2	1441.2
608	860	159	466	−73.8	−23.4	1932
1379	926	234	544	−83	−60.6	2620.8
964	599	226	480	−76.6	−50.2	1236.2
516	395	182	474	−64.7	−8	2871.7
826	452	176	568	−78.7	−31.2	2751
719	693	186	531	−74.1	−26.1	1348.5
802	434	149	401	−81.4	−50	2616.1
1146	514	160	372	−86	−67.6	1758.5
815	631	184	386	−77.4	−52.6	1176.2
854	886	189	357	−77.9	−58.2	1425.5
841	450	193	311	−77.1	−63.1	1172.2
937	356	170	548	−81.8	−41.5	3168.3
1212	646	211	477	−82.6	−60.6	1267
714	434	170	430	−76.2	−39.8	1515.9
859	559	211	519	−75.4	−39.6	1527.6
880	618	196	416	−77.7	−52.7	943.3
855	335	174	408	−79.6	−52.3	1394.9
1544	925	222	846	−85.6	−45.2	411.7
833	519	186	457	−77.7	−45.1	51807.9
1159	59922	696972	3157181			

total population had diminished to some 50.9 million.

Table 7.13 Ukraine—Estimated *Oblast* Budgetary Dependence on the Central Government, 1992–1994 (Regulating Revenues and Budgetary Transfers as a Percent of *Oblast* Budget)

	Actual 1992		Actual 1993		Actual 1994	
Oblast	*Excluding State Budget Transfers*	*Including State Budget Transfers*	*Excluding State Budget Transfers*	*Including State Budget Transfers*	*Excluding State Budget Transfers*	*Including State Budget Transfers*
Republic of Crimea	58.5	72.6	61.2	61.5	34.4	64.8
Vinnytsya	70.2	76.3	72.7	72.8	34.8	69.4
Volyn	64.8	73.5	69.5	70.1	30.1	71.1
Dnipropetrovs'k	47.3	56.6	44.9	45.9	64.9	63.6
Donets'k	36.4	48.5	35.4	35.4	83.9	69.6
Zhytomyr	66.5	73.9	73.2	73.9	32.2	66.9
Zakarpattia	70.4	78.6	67.9	67.9	25.7	74.1
Zaporizhzhia	42.4	57.5	67.3	67.7	81.9	58.5
Ivano-Frankivs'k	67.6	74.3	68.8	69	47.1	67
Kyiv *oblast*	53.1	62.8	79.6	80.3	51.5	66
Kyiv city	61.8	68.9	56.2	56.2	70.9	61
Khirovohrad	68.9	75.6	75.4	76.3	31.4	70.9
Luhans'k	37.1	50.4	60.4	60.4	65.4	70.9
L'viv	67	73.5	67.4	67.4	51.8	71.8
Mykolaiv	56.6	67.5	70.3	70.3	52.9	66.5
Odesa	63.5	70.4	63.7	64.1	48.2	56.6
Poltava	68.2	72.9	63.6	63.6	93.7	67.6
Rivne	68.2	74.7	67.4	67.7	32.8	69.7
Sumy	65.4	72.4	79.8	79.8	45.8	72.8
Ternopil	69.9	76.4	73	73.1	28.3	72.7
Kharkiv	64	70.5	55.2	57	61.9	68.1
Kherson	71.7	76.2	71.7	72	39.2	67.8
Khmel'nyts'kyi	59.9	68.8	63.4	64.3	41.5	69.1
Cherkasy	66.9	74.3	71.8	72.2	47.9	72
Chernivtsy	74.5	79.6	79.9	80.3	31.3	71.4
Chernihiv	66.9	74.6	54.9	54.9	50.5	71.4
M. Sevastopol	81.4	88.3	55.5	56.6	34.4	73.1
Ukraine—Average	58.7	67.3	62	62.4	54.9	67.6

Source: Author's calculations, based on data from source documents.

more overtly political factors have intruded upon intergovernmental revenue policy.

The politics of public expenditure has had some weak equalization effects since 1992. Further analysis reveals the apparent decreasing dispersion of per capita *oblast* revenues after 1993. Appendix Tables A-7.1 through A-7.4 pre-

Table 7.14 Determinants of Degree of *Oblast* Revenue Dependency Upon Kyiv, 1993 (Dependent variable is proportion of *oblast* budget accounted for by regulating revenues)

Independent Predictors	Regression Coefficients				
	Model 1	Model 2	Model 3	Model 4	Model 5
Industrial output	−2.8338**	−4.1086**	−3.7889**	−3.8118**	−4.1699**
	(.4156)	(.6762)	(.7332)	(.7022)	(.6906)
Subordinated enterprises (%)		.2866*	.3412*	.2945*	.2784*
		(.1253)	(.1342)	(.1232)	(.1274)
Level of urbanization			−.1334		
			(.1212)		
Ethnic Russians (%)				−.1189	
				(.0881)	
Expenditures per capita (%)					.0161
					(.0241)
Constant	76.9569	68.9952	73.3677	69.4943	65.5052
R-square	.6595	.7226	.7371	.7439	.7282
Adjusted R^2	.6453	.6985	.7013	.7089	.6911

Notes: [1]Standard errors are given in parentheses beneath regression coefficients.
[2]Significance levels are: *$p < .05$; **$p < .01$.

sent the estimated total *oblast* revenues from all sources for the years 1992 through budget 1995, and on a per capita basis. Standard deviations of the inflation-adjusted per capita *oblast* revenues have been calculated for the years 1992 to 1995. The dispersion narrows somewhat from 1992 to 1993 and 1994 to 1995, consistent with the above-noted convergence of the *oblasts'* levels of fiscal dependence on the central government:

Standard Deviation of Per Capita Revenues

Year	Nominal Data	Real Data
1992	2,875.610	248.1113
1993	171,076.103	285.4979
1994	222,971.170	31.9914
1995	3,484,572.500	110.3697

Source: Author's calculations, based on data from Appendix Tables A-1 through A-4.

It seems clear that although significant differences in per capita revenues between Ukraine's *oblasti* remain the case, there has been some narrowing of the gap between wealthy and poor regions.

The relative improvement in intergovernmental fiscal equity turns on parliamentary politics. Despite the existing system of proportional representation, owing to its regional economic strength, Peoples' Deputies from the five *oblasts* of eastern Ukraine have a marked advantage in the crucial budget decision-making process, an advantage that has permitted them to exert a disproportionately greater influence on domestic policy making in general.[73] Analysis of the fiscal strength of the eastern *oblasts* indicates that per capita regulating revenues generated on their territory amounted to some 41.8 percent of the all-Ukraine total in 1995 (and 13 percent for Donets'k *oblast* alone). In fact, despite rapid inflation and falls in industrial output, between the years 1992 to 1995, the east consistently produced between 40 to 45 percent of total regulating revenues. Table 7.15 provides estimates of the "fiscal clout" among deputies of Verkhovna Rada from various *oblasts*, grouped into broad regions of the country. As can be seen, the relative wealth of eastern Ukraine has provided deputies from these *oblasts* with a marked negotiating advantage in legislative deliberations vis-à-vis deputies from poorer regions, which have tended to be concentrated mainly in western Ukraine.

It is estimated that between 1992 and 1995, eastern Ukrainian deputies represented regulating revenues on a per member basis of between 168 and 191 percent of that of the poorest regions and between 121 and 134 percent of the Ukrainian average (including the east). (See Table 7.16.) This represents a fiscal dominance of vast proportions respecting the less economically developed and consequently more fiscally dependent *oblasts* in central and western Ukraine. It creates the potential for deputies from the east to trade votes with deputies from the poorer regions, ceding budgetary transfers in return for the recipient *oblasts'* cooperation on other policy issues. Obviously, this sets the stage for the eastern Ukraine policy agenda to dominate national politics.

Conclusions

In the long run, it is in the mutual interest of both the center and the regions to develop appropriate levels of regional autonomy. This implies, at a minimum, the assignment of secure revenue sources to subnational governments, a rational distribution of functional responsibilities among the levels of government, and establishment of an effective means to represent regional interests within the new constitutional system. A solid foundation may be built with a well-structured new Law on Local Self-Government. However, until Ukraine's tax system is subject to comprehensive reform, local govern-

Table 7.15 Ukraine—Regional Fiscal "Clout" Among Members of Parliament (Organizaed by oblast)

Oblast	1992 Population (000s)	Members of Parliament (Okruhs)	Population Per Member (000s)	Estimated Total National Tax (Regulating) Revenues Raised (billions KBV)[1]				Inflation-Adjusted Regulating Revenues Generated Per Member (millions KBV)			
				Actual 1992	Actual 1993	Budget 1994	Estimated 1995	Actual 1992	Actual 1993	Budget 1994	Estimated 1995
Totals/Averages	51801.9	450	115115	774.064	30666.0513	177720.6	1147451.9	148.4161	113.7258	56.6635	80.7649
Center & North—											
Summary	15803.9	148	113540	235.6195	10505.2967	58406.58	379079.7	137.3618	118.4569	56.6219	81.1277
Vinnytsya	1896.6	17	111565	20.1666	650.599	4186.901	23390.1	102.3529	63.8672	35.3369	43.5796
Zhytomyr	1495.9	13	115069	13.1549	565.6255	3539.605	20686	87.3094	72.6105	39.0657	50.4004
Kyiv oblast	1932	17	113647	18.5801	954.2382	5788.485	34339.8	94.3009	93.6745	48.8541	63.9808
Kyiv city	2620.8	23	113948	68.0515	3450.191	14964.75	127093.6	255.2857	250.3393	93.3526	175.0235
Kirovohrad	1236.2	11	112382	9.8813	451.3147	2906.972	20124.3	77.5068	68.47	37.9169	57.9467
Poltava	1758.5	16	109906	42.8201	1507.8051	9434.097	49768.9	230.9108	157.2675	84.5996	98.5232
Sumy	1425.5	13	109654	16.5453	757.1015	3959.309	27459.1	109.8115	97.1906	43.5041	66.9026
Khmel'nyts'kyi	1515.9	13	116608	12.3888	606.4639	3760.538	22583	82.2247	77.8529	41.5041	55.0223
Cherkasy	1527.6	13	117508	17.9286	794.0766	5387.91	27888.2	118.9925	101.9372	59.465	67.9482
Chernihiv	1394.9	12	116242	16.1023	767.8812	4478.015	25746.7	115.7773	106.7889	53.5413	67.958
South—Summary	7799.4	68	114697	87.9854	3816.3485	21362.32	144909.1	111.6396	93.6597	45.0738	67.4974
Republic of Crimea	2156.1	19	113479	24.0656	852.4992	5662.254	31052	109.28	74.88	42.758	51.765
M. Sevastopol	411.7	4	102925	4.2673	218.1963	995.33	8392.9	92.047	91.0335	35.7019	66.4588
Mykolaiv	1348.5	11	122591	11.2331	716.4579	4344.205	28465.3	88.1097	108.6955	56.6634	81.9641
Odesa	2616.1	23	113743	34.087	1466.6844	6960.243	54797.4	127.8726	106.4198	42.4191	75.4628
Kherson	1267	11	115182	14.3324	562.5107	3400.289	22201.5	112.4198	85.3398	44.3514	63.9279

(continues)

Table 7.15 *(continued)*

Oblast	1992 Population (000s)	Members of Parliament (Okrubs)	Population Per Member (000s)	Estimated Total National Tax (Regulating) Revenues Raised (billions KBV)[1]				Inflation-Adjusted Regulating Revenues Generated Per Member (millions KBV)			
				Actual 1992	Actual 1993	Budget 1994	Estimated 1995	Actual 1992	Actual 1993	Budget 1994	Estimated 1995
East—Summary	17379.9	152	114341	351.467	12522.4363	74457.23	480189.9	199.5067	137.4861	70.2826	100.0622
Dnipropetrovs'k	3907.2	34	114918	99.4508	3154.4825	15308.55	123797.7	252.375	154.833	64.6011	115.328
Donets'k	5332	47	113447	116.1594	3699.8484	26778.44	149027.7	213.242	131.371	81.747	100.4314
Zaporizhzhia	2100.7	18	116706	46.1093	1742.0036	11354.44	66478.3	221.0205	161.5094	90.5061	116.979
Luhans'k	2871.7	25	114868	42.9221	1655.6727	9231.824	62346.7	148.1349	110.5219	52.9825	78.9903
Kharkiv	3168.3	28	113154	46.8254	2270.3991	11783.98	78539.5	144.2913	135.3187	60.3836	88.8445
West—Summary	9818.7	82	119740	99.0471	4003.4498	23494.44	143272.2	104.2184	81.4769	41.1089	55.3412
Volyn	1069.9	9	118878	8.7256	298.66	2368.891	10899.4	83.6506	55.3794	37.7648	43.5796
Zakarpattia	1264.9	10	126490	8.3757	294.2127	2134.885	10946	72.2666	49.0993	30.6309	34.6702
Ivano-Frankivs'k	1441.2	12	120100	13.5173	550.4949	4059.154	21090.3	97.1908	76.5571	48.5332	55.6675
L'viv	2751	23	119609	41.5215	1711.0479	8420.487	58691.9	155.762	124.1504	52.5284	80.8259
Rivne	1176.2	10	117220	9.3782	439.9398	2247.983	16458.9	80.9163	73.4187	32.2536	52.1316
Ternopil	1172.2	10	117220	10.0449	369.0382	2249.45	12502.2	86.6687	61.5864	32.2746	39.5993
Chernivtsy	943.3	8	117913	7.4839	340.0563	2013.589	12683.5	80.7151	70.9373	36.1132	50.2169
Memorandum: CPI (Average Annual CPI, 1991 = 100)				1159	59922	696972	3157181				

Note: [1] A24 columns may not sum precisely to totals due to rounding.

Source: Author's calculations, based on data from source documents provided by the Ministry of Finance of Ukraine.

Table 7.16   Index of Regulating Revenues Generated Per Member of Parliament
(percent of poorest region)

	1992	1993	1994	1995
Center & North	131.8	145.4	137.7	146.6
South	107.1	114.9	109.6	121.9
East	191.4	168.7	170.9	180.8
West	100.0	100.0	100.0	100.0
Standard deviation	56.816	104.943	18.043	29.951
Eastern Ukraine versus Ukrainian average	+34.4%	+20.9%	+24.0%	+23.9%

Source: Author's calculations.

ments will lack the assured revenue source necessary to realize true democratic self-government. Without attention, the process of development is likely to proceed in the same ad hoc fashion as in the past. Ukraine's "regional problem" is not without precedent in other countries, where various means to balance regional and state interests have been devised.

The situation, as difficult as it may seem, is not desperate. Rather, as Birch and Zinko astutely observe, "regionalism in Ukraine is not so much a problem to be solved as a condition to be lived with, recognized, and dealt with in the most rational way possible."[74] The quest for balance will therefore likely continue for quite some time, as Ukraine searches for a uniquely "Ukrainian way" to deal with regional issues.

Notes

1. For instance, see Charles Tilly (ed.), *The Formation of National-States in Western Europe* (Princeton: Princeton University Press, 1965), concerning the minimum requirements of sovereign statehood.
2. See Sarah Birch and Ihor Zinko, "Ukraine: The Dilemma of Regionalism," *Transition,* November 1, 1996, pp. 22–25; Sherman Garnett, *Keystone in the Arch: Ukraine in the Emerging Security Environment of Central and Eastern Europe* (Washington, DC: Carnegie Endowment for International Peace, 1997); Taras Kuzio, *Ukraine Under Kuchma: Political Reform, Economic Transformation and Security Policy in Independent Ukraine* (London: Macmillan, 1997); David Marples, "Ukraine After the Presidential Election," *RFE/RL Research Report,* vol. 3, no. 37 (August 12, 1994), pp. 7–10; Vyacheslav Pikhovshek, *Most* 46 (December 19, 1995), p. 1 (translated in FBIS Daily Report: Central Eurasia, December 19, 1995), and *Kievskiye vedomosti,* May 28, 1996, pp. 3–4 (translated in FBIS Daily Report: Central Eurasia, May 28, 1996); and

Zenovia Sochor, "Political Culture and Foreign Policy: Elections in Ukraine, 1994," in Vladimir Tismaneanu (ed.), *Political Culture and Civil Society in Russia and the New States of Eurasia* (Armonk, NY: M. E. Sharpe, 1995), pp. 208–226.

3. See Dominique Arel and Andrew Wilson, "The Ukrainian Parliamentary Elections," *RFE/RL Research Report,* vol. 3, no. 26 (July 1, 1994), pp. 6–17; Sarah Birch, "Electoral Behavior in Western Ukraine in National Elections and Referendums, 1989–91," *Electoral Studies,* vol. 14, no.1 (1995), pp. 1145–1176; Marko Bojcun, "The Ukrainian Parliamentary and Presidential Elections of 1994," *Europe-Asia Studies,* vol. 47, no. 2 (March-April 1995), pp. 229–249; Taras Kuzio, "The Implications of the Ukrainian Elections," *Jane's Intelligence Review,* vol. 4, no. 6 (June 1994); and Roman Solchanyk, "Ukraine: The Politics of Reform," *Problems of Post-Communism* (November/December 1995), pp. 46–51.

4. See Paul S. Pirie, "National Identity and Politics in Southern and Eastern Ukraine," *Europe-Asia Studies,* vol. 48, no. 7 (1996), pp. 1079–1104; Roman Solchanyk, "The Politics of State-Building: Centre-Periphery Relations in Post-Soviet Ukraine," *Europe-Asia Studies,* vol. 46, no. 1 (1994), pp. 47–68 and "Ukraine: A Year of Crisis," *REF/RL Research Report,* vol. 3, no. 1 (January 7, 1994), pp. 38–41; F. Stephen Larrabee, "Ukraine: Europe's Next Crisis?," *Arms Control Today* (July/August 1994), pp. 14–19; Tim Weiner, "C. I. A. Head Surveys World's Hot Spots," *New York Times,* January 26, 1994, p. A5; and Samuel P. Huntington, *The Clash of Civilizations and the Remaking of the World Order* (New York: Simon & Schuster, 1996).

5. Birch and Zinko, "Ukraine: The Dilemma of Regionalism."

6. On October 13, 1992, parliament enacted the Law of Ukraine, "On General Principles on the Creation and Functioning of Special (Free) Economic Zones," VR-2673–12, establishing a general framework for the creation of such zones in Ukraine. Several regions and cities have taken advantage of this legislation. See Myron Rabij, "Free Economic Zones in Ukraine," *Ukrainian Legal and Economic Bulletin,* vol. 1, no. 7 (July 1993), pp. 5–8; Natalia A. Feduschak, "Odesa Closes the File on Soviet Past, Opens One Full of Hope for the Future," *Wall Street Journal,* May 13, 1994, p. B4; "Prospects for Establishing Free Trade Zone in Kharkov," *Kharkiv Vremya,* May 23, 1996, p. 2 (translated in FBIS-SOV-96–110); Chrystyna Lapychak, "Sevastopol Seeks Free-Trade Zone Status," *OMRI Daily Digest,* vol. 2, no. 150 (August 5, 1996), p. 2.

7. Vicki L. Hesli, "Public Support for the Devolution of Power in Ukraine: Regional Patterns," *Europe-Asia Studies,* vol. 47, no. 1 (1995), p. 96.

8. Kuzio, *Ukraine Under Kuchma.*

9. There is increasingly a uniformity of opinion across Ukraine as to the priority of building the Ukrainian economy from the regions up. See, for instance, the interview with Lyubomyr Kraynyk, Deputy Chair of the L'viv

Oblast Council in *Za Vilnu Ukrayiny,* January 12, 1995, p. 1 (translated in FBIS-SOV-95–024-S). These sentiments intensified in L'viv throughout 1995 and 1996. See the interview with L'viv *Oblast* State Administration Head Mykola Horyn, *Ukrainian Weekly,* September 22, 1996, p. 3. For similar sentiments in eastern Ukraine, see the interview with Aleksandr Maselskiy, Kharkiv *Oblast* Chairman, in Kharkov *Vremya,* March 2, 1995, pp. 1–2 (translated in FBIS-SOV-95–047), and the 1997 interview with Dnipropetrovs'k *Oblast* State Administration Head Ivan Derkach in *Dneprovskaya Panorama,* May 7, 1997, p. 1 (translated in FBIS-SOV-97–143, May 23, 1997).

10. See Chrystia Freeland, "Eastern Ukraine Turns Its Back on Russia," *Financial Times,* July 23, 1997, p. 3.

11. Birch and Zinko, "The Dilemma of Regionalism," p. 25.

12. See Birch, "Electoral Behavior"; Birch and Zinko, "Ukraine: The Dilemma of Regionalism"; Hesli, "Public Support"; Sochor, "Political Culture and Foreign Policy"; Solchanyk, "The Politics of State-Building" and "Ukraine: The Politics of Reform." See also Andrew Wilson, "The Growing Challenge to Kiev from the Donbas," *RFE/RL Research Report,* vol. 2, no. 33 (August 20, 1993), pp. 8–13; "The Donbas Between Ukraine and Russia: The Use of History in Political Disputes," *Journal of Contemporary History* 30, pp. 265–289; and *Ukrainian Nationalism in the 1990s: A Minority Faith* (Cambridge: Cambridge University Press, 1997).

13. See Maria Drohobycky (ed.), *Crimea: Dynamics, Challenges, and Prospects* (London: Rowman & Littlefield).

14. See Wilson, *Ukrainian Nationalism in the 1990s.*

15. Hesli, "Public Support for the Devolution of Power in Ukraine: Regional Patterns."

16. Hesli, "Public Support," pp. 104–107.

17. Mariian Dolishnii, "Regional Aspects of Ukraine's Economic Development," in I. S. Koropeckyj (ed.), *The Ukrainian Economy: Achievements, Problems, Challenges* (Cambridge, MA: Harvard University Press, 1992).

18. See Inna Lunina, "Problemi Rehionalnoyi Budjetnoyi Politiki Ukrayiny," *Ekonomika Ukrayiny,* vol. 8, no. 393 (August 1994), pp. 30–36, and "Probleme des Regionalen Finanzausgleichs in der Ukraine" (Koln: Bundesinstitut fur Ostwissenschaftliche und Internationale Studien, 1994).

19. Law of Ukraine, "On Local Radas of People's Deputies and Local and Regional Self-Government," February 7, 1992. The legislative basis for local self-government in Ukraine can be traced from the former Soviet period. For an enumeration, see Y. Sayenko, A. Tkachuk, and Y. Privalov, *Misetseve Samovraduvannya B Ukrayini: Problemi I Prognozi* ("Local Self-Government in Ukraine: Problems and Outlooks") (Kyiv: Institute of Sociology, National Academy of Sciences of Ukraine, 1997), pp. 86–87.

20. In the act, "local" is understood also to mean "regional."

21. Law of the Ukrainian SSR, "Law on the Budget System," December 5, 1990. VR-513–12.
22. Law of Ukraine, "On Amendments to the Law of the Ukrainian SSR," "On the Budget System of Ukraine," April 19, 1995.
23. The current tax and revenue assignments are quite restrictive. See the Law of Ukraine, "On the Introduction of Amendments to the Law of Ukraine, On the System of Taxation," February 18, 1997. VR-77–97. See also *Golos Ukrainy,* March 25, 1997, pp. 6–7 (translated in FBIS-97–070).
24. Decree of the President of Ukraine, "On the Representatives of the President of Ukraine," March 20, 1992. The text of the decree was published in *Holos Ukrayiny,* March 20, 1992.
25. Decree of the President of Ukraine, "On Regulations Concerning Local State Administration," April 14, 1992.
26. Decree of the President of Ukraine, "On Subordination of Local State Administrations," October 27, 1992.
27. The decree was enacted November 29, 1993, and the eastern *oblasts* affected were Dnipropetrovs'k, Donets'k, Luhans'k, and Zaporizhzhia. See *Ukrainian Weekly,* December 19, 1993, p. 2, and *IntelNews,* February 28, 1994, p. 1.
28. So frustrated with direct presidential rule were officials in the Crimean city of Sevastopol that on November 4, 1993, the city council asked the Ukrainian president and parliament to eliminate the presence of President's Representatives in the city. The council expressed its desire to manage and control local executive powers unimpeded by interference from above. The council's letter to President Kravchuk indicated that it would take preliminary steps toward regaining control of the municipal state administration within a month if it failed to receive a response from Kyiv. See *IntelNews,* "In Brief," November 5, 1993, p. 4.
29. Law of Ukraine, "On the Formation of Local Power and Self-Governing Bodies," February 3, 1994. VR-3917–12.
30. Will Ritter, "Elections to Local Radas Set for June 26," *IntelNews,* February 6, 1994, p. 1.
31. Decree of the President of Ukraine, "On Additional Measures for Delegating More Powers for Dnipropetrovs'k, Donets'k, Zaporizhzhia, and Luhans'k Regional State Administrations in Managing All-State Property," February 21, 1994. See also "Decentralization on the Way," *IntelNews,* February 28, 1994, p. 1.
32. Decree of the President of Ukraine, "On the Strengthening of the Economic Basis of the Municipal Self-Government in Ukraine," March 12, 1994. See the text in *Uriadoviy Kur'er,* March 15, 1994.
33. Victor Zubaniuk, "Kravchuk Signs Decentralization Decree," *IntelNews,* March 17, 1994, p. 3.
34. Decree of the President of Ukraine, "On Ways to Ensure Appropriate Management of Local Structures of State Executive Authorities," August 9, 1994.

See also "Ukraine's Leader Issues Decrees to Expand Hold on Parliament," *New York Times,* August 11, 1994, p. A12.

35. The Council of Regions was formally established on September 20, 1994. See *Holos Ukrayiny,* September 23, 1994.

36. Some saw the Council of Regions as the basis for the formation of an upper house in a new bicameral parliament. In fact, Kuchma was to place the regional leaders in the core of a "Senate" in the draft constitution of Ukraine that the president submitted to parliament on November 17, 1995.

37. For a chronicle of the evolution of the 1995 Law on Power, see Viktor Tkachuk, "President Pushes for Real Power," *UPressA Weekly,* Ukrainian Press Agency, November 6–12, 1995.

38. Draft Law of Ukraine, "On the State Powers and Local Self-Government," introduced December 2, 1994. See the text in *Uriadoviy Kur'er,* December 1994.

39. Draft Law of Ukraine, "On Local Councils of People's Deputies," November 10, 1994. See the text translated from Kiev *Most,* November 10, 1994, in FBIS-USR-94-131, December 5, 1994, p. 34. According to the draft, enterprises were to be under the control of and accountable to the soviets in the territory where they were located.

40. See "Kuchma, Deputies to Coordinate Political Reforms," Moscow INTERFAX News Service, December 16, 1994. FBIS-SOV-94-243.

41. Implementation of the Law on Power required the suspension of some 60 of the 170 articles of the constitution of 1978, as well as changes in certain other laws. See Kuzio, *Ukraine Under Kuchma,* p. 101.

42. Decree of the President of Ukraine, "On Holding Plebiscite to Ascertain the Trust Citizens of Ukraine Place in the President of Ukraine and the Verkhovna Rada of Ukraine," May 31, 1995, no. 413–95. See also "Kuchma Interviewed on Parliament Session," Moscow INTERFAX News Service, May 14, 1995. FBIS-SOV-95-093.

43. Marta Kolomayets, "Ukraine's Parliament Passes Law on Powers," *Ukrainian Weekly,* May 28, 1995, p. 1. See the text of the law in *Holos Ukrayiny,* June 6, 1995, p. 2.

44. The text of the Constitutional Accord was published in English translation by *IntelNews,* "On the Books," June 7, 1995. It is also available in English over the World Wide Web at <www.kiev.sovam.com:70/00/UPRESA/WEEKLY/06.07.95–06.12.95/Documents>. For a summary of the major points, see "Some Aspects of the Constitutional Agreement Between the Supreme Council and the President," *Ukrainian Economic Monitor,* no. 2 (1995), p. 20. For the political implications, see Chrystyna Lapychak, "Showdown Yields Political Reform," *Transitions,* July 28, 1995, pp. 3–7.

45. Both of these provisions were to be incorporated into the executive authority of the president in the June 1996 Constitution of Ukraine.

46. Decree of the President of Ukraine, "On the Basic Organization and Functioning of State Power and Local Self-Government in Ukraine," August 8,

1995; and Decree of the President of Ukraine, "On the Status of *Oblast*, Kyiv and Sevastopol and Regional Government Administrations," August 21, 1995. The purpose of holding new elections in the case of dismissal of council chairs was to preserve their dual roles as heads of the local administration and chairs of their respective councils.

47. Kuchma has referred to the president as the "guarantor of the constitution" on a number of occasions. For instance, see the text of his speech before the Ukrainian Association of Local and Regional Authorities on June 19, 1997, in *Urayadoviy Ku'rer,* June 21, 1997, pp. 3–4. FBIS-SOV-97–147-S. See also Kuchma's message to parliament concerning his veto of the enacted Law on Local State Administrations" in *Urayadoviy Ku'rer,* August 14, 1997, p. 3. FBIS-SOV-97–266.

48. Despite the conflict of laws, it seems that parliament was more concerned that Kuchma's innovation might set the precedent for a new two-house parliament, with the upper chamber a "Council of Regions" represented by the elected chairmen of regional councils, all accountable to the president.

49. Decree of the President of Ukraine, "On Delegating State Executive Authority Powers to Chairmen and Executive Committees Headed by Them of Village, Settlement and City Councils," January 4, 1996. See "Kuchma Issues Decree Delegating State Executive Authority," Moscow INTERFAX News Service, January 4, 1996. FBIS-SOV-96–004.

50. According to former President Leonid Kravchuk, Kuchma's bicameral legislature failed for two reasons. First, leftist forces feared that a pro-executive upper chamber would dilute their power. The Council of Regions at the time was functioning as an "embryo Senate," with a pro-reform membership. Second, eastern Ukraine eventually withdrew support for an upper house, fearing that equal representation of all *oblasts* in the proposed Senate would shift the dominance of national policymaking away from the east. At the end, the only faction that supported a two-chamber Rada was Statehood, a center-right faction from western Ukraine. Kravchuk made his remarks to Dr. Taras Kuzio at the conference on "Soviet to Independent Ukraine: A Troubled Transformation," University of Birmingham, June 13–15, 1996. (I am indebted to Dr. Kuzio for these observations.)

51. An official English language translation of the June 1996 Constitution of Ukraine has been published in *Ukrainian Quarterly,* vol. 52, nos. 2–3 (Summer-Fall 1996), pp. 223–289. The text is also available in an official English language translation over the World Wide Web at <www.Rada.Kiev.UA/const/conengl.htm>, and in Ukrainian (CP1251 Cyrillic Coding) at <www.Rada.Kiev.UA/const/constl.htm>. A broad overview of the highlights of the new basic law of Ukraine is provided in the *Ukrainian Economic Monitor,* vol. 3, nos. 8–9 (August-September 1996), p. 30.

52. Birch and Zinko, "Ukraine: The Dilemma of Regionalism," p. 24.

53. See Kuchma's remarks before a meeting in Kyiv of the Association of Towns of Ukraine, "President Kuchma on Local Self-Government Law," Kyiv UT-1 Television Network, 1900 GMT, January 25, 1997 (translated in FBIS-SOV-97–017).

54. Law of Ukraine, "On Local Self-Governments in Ukraine," May 28, 1997. VR-280–97.

55. Robert S. Kravchuk, "The Challenge of Fiscal Reform in Ukraine, 1991–97," paper presented at the international conference, "Institutional Reform in Ukraine: Exploring Links Between the Market and State." Sponsored by the Yale Ukrainian Initiative, Russian and East European Studies, Yale University, New Haven, CT, April 24–25, 1998.

56. Jorge Martinez-Vazquez, Charles E. McClure, Jr., and Sally Wallace, "Subnational Fiscal Decentralization in Ukraine," in Richard M. Bird, Robert D. Ebel, and Christine I. Wallich (eds.), *Decentralization of the Socialist State: Intergovernmental Finance in Transition Economies* (Washington, DC: The World Bank), p. 290.

57. See Donna Bahry, *Outside Moscow: Power, Politics, and Budgetary Policy in the Soviet Republics* (New York: Columbia University Press, 1987); "Perestroyka and the Debate Over Territorial Economic Decentralization," *Harriman Institute Forum,* vol. 2, no. 5 (May 1989), pp. 1–8; and "The Union Republics and Contradictions in Gorbachev's Economic Reforms," *Soviet Economy,* vol. 7, no. 3 (1991), pp. 215–255. See also Daniel Berkowitz and Beth Mitchneck, "Fiscal Decentralization in the Soviet Economy," *Comparative Economic Systems,* vol. 34, no. 2 (Summer 1992), pp. 1–18; and Martinez-Vazquez, McClure, and Wallace, "Subnational Fiscal Decentralization in Ukraine."

58. While the central government sets maximum rates that can be charged, public utility pricing has been a complex undertaking. Governments at all levels are able to provide exceptions, exemptions, and special deals for certain customers, apparently irrespective of the revenue impact on service providers. No specific data concerning regional disparities was available to the author, but interviews with finance officials at all levels indicate the presence of enormous regional variation. Martinez-Vazquez, McClure, and Wallace, "Subnational Fiscal Decentralization," make similar observations.

59. Martinez-Vazquez, McClure, and Wallace, "Subnational Fiscal Decentralization," p. 289.

60. Martinez-Vazquez, McClure, and Wallace, "Subnational Fiscal Decentralization," p. 289.

61. In 1994, the cost recovery rate for heat and hot water was a mere 12 percent; gas, 3 percent; water, 15 percent. None of these services was metered. Electricity consumption by industry is metered, but consumption by households is not. Cost recovery for electric power consumption—mostly by industry—averaged about 50 percent. In the prevailing fiscal environment, these rates

became unsustainably low. At the urging of Anatoliy Dron, chairman of the State Committee on Housing and Communal Services, in 1994 the Cabinet of Ministers issued a decree calling for long-term, progressive tariff increases to achieve cost recovery levels of 20 percent in 1994, 40 percent in 1995, and 60 percent in 1996. These targets were largely achieved on schedule. In October 1994, tariffs were raised to recover costs for heat, hot water, sewage, and gas at a rate of 15 percent. Tariffs were raised again in February 1995 to 20 percent cost recovery, June 1995 to 30 percent, and September 1995 to between 40 and 50 percent (International Monetary Fund, 1996, p. 97).

62. See the interview with Hryniov in *Kyivska Pravda,* translated as "Kuchma Aide Outlines Regional Policy Concept," FBIS-SOV-95–176, September 7, 1995, pp. 1–2.

63. Law of Ukraine, "On State Budget for 1994," February 1, 1994. Original document in the author's possession. (Also published in *Uradoviy Kur'er,* February 19, 1994, pp. 6–8.

64. Law of Ukraine, "On State Budget for 1995," April 6, 1995. See the translated text of the 1995 budget law from *Holos Ukrayiny,* April 21, 1995, pp. 3–5, in FBIS-SOV-95–102-S.

65. Law of Ukraine, "On the Introduction of Amendments to the Law of Ukraine," "On the System of Taxation," February 18, 1997, no. 77–97-VR, articles 14 and 15. See also *Golos Ukrainy,* March 25, 1997, pp. 6–7, in FBIS-97–070.

66. It should be noted that the "Law on Local Self-Government" and the "Law on the Budget System" also contradicted each other in several crucial respects. See Law of Ukraine, "On Local Radas of People's Deputies and Local and Regional Self-Government," February 7, 1992; and Law of the Ukrainian SSR, "Law on the Budget System," December 5, 1990, VR-513–12. Both laws have subsequently been amended several times (and since July 1996 are a matter of constitutional governance).

67. In the case of the personal income tax, the taxpayer's "tax home" is the place of employment, not his or her place of residence.

68. Other significant factors contributing to the region's fiscal planning difficulties have been the wildly swinging basic tax rates, frequent redefinition of the tax base, devolution of expenditure responsibilities from the center to the subnational level, and parliament's consistent failure to pass the state budget until well after the start of the fiscal year.

69. In 1994, the "Law on State Budget" formalized a previously ad hoc practice whereby some *oblasts* were periodically required to pay additional exactions to the central government, even though such transfers lacked a legal basis (see Martinez-Vazquez et al., "Subnational Fiscal Decentralization").

70. In the interests of "full disclosure," the author confesses that he had pressed the Ministry of Finance for the 1994 approach during his tour from 1993 to 1994 in Kyiv as the U.S. Treasury's Budget Management Adviser to Ukraine. How-

ever, rampant inflation severely depressed the real value of the budgeted sub-ventions, making frequent re-appropriation a necessary feature of budget execution throughout 1991. The regions correctly understood that this placed them at a severe disadvantage to the central government; consequently, they pressed for a return to the pre-1994 variable retention rate regime.

71. Martinez-Vazquez et al., "Subnational Fiscal Decentralization."
72. Martinez-Vazquez et al., "Subnational Fiscal Decentralization," p. 300.
73. The five *oblasts* of eastern Ukraine (Dnipropetrovs'k, Donets'k, Zaporizhzhia, Luhans'k, and Kharkiv) possess 33.6 percent of Ukraine's population (1992 Ministry of Statistics data) and 33.8 percent of People's Deputies in Verkhovna Rada but produce 45 percent of Ukraine's GDP (Ministry of Statistics of Ukraine, *Narodnyeh Hospodarstvo Ukrayini U 1992 Rotsi, Statistichnij Shchorichnik* [Kyiv: Technika, 1993]).
74. Birch and Zinko, "Ukraine: The Dilemma of Regionalism," p. 25.

Appendix Table 7.1   Ukraine—Estimated *Oblast* Revenues—All Sources, 1992 (Millions

| Oblast | Actual Fixed (Own Source) Revenues[1] | Oblast *Share of Regulating (National) Revenues*[2] | | |
		Value-Added Tax	Excise Taxes	State Enterprise Profits Tax[3]
Republic of Crimea	9494.5	9190	1202.1	2989.4
Vinnytsya	6060.9	10754	1088.2	2437.8
Volyn	3340.3	4522.5	590.5	1038
Dnipropetrovs'k	26745.5	10563.2	1890.9	11525.3
Donets'k	37944.1	11939.1	3219.2	6538.9
Zhytomyr	5131	7295.8	702.8	2166.3
Zakarpattia	3271.9	4934.6	864.5	1997.7
Zaporizhzhia	12557.3	3754.9	2412.7	3077.6
Ivano-Frankivs'k	4374	6152.7	718.2	2265.8
Kyiv *oblast*	8079.7	5447.1	1476.1	2234.1
Kyiv city	18906.5	17488.5	2416.3	10740.1
Khirovohrad	4448	6394.2	531.9	2955.2
Luhans'k	16904.5	4293.3	1116.9	4544.6
L'viv	9506.2	10458.5	1774.8	7101.3
Mykolaiv	5408.8	4600.3	692.5	1755.8
Odesa	10233.3	9378.8	2271.9	6135.5
Poltava	8683.9	9418.6	1141.6	8099.7
Rivne	3754.8	6324.6	209.1	1506.5
Sumy	5318.3	7422.7	640.7	2008.7
Ternopil	3536.3	5878.1	738	1606.9
Kharkiv	14363.7	17330.4	1477.8	6732.8
Kherson	5558.6	8924.6	873.4	4277.3
Khmel'nyts'kyi	5677.1	6258.8	167.5	2085.6
Cherkasy	5256.8	7052.1	1127.7	2469.7
Chernivtsy	2458.9	4223.1	1084	1888
Chernihiv	4709.8	5787.4	869.7	2858.3
M. Sevastopol	973.6	2965.9	418.3	883.1
Ukraine—Totals	242698.3	208753.9	31717	103920.1

Notes: [1]For 1992, includes personal income tax and the income tax on enterprises of communal (local)
[2]Regulating revenues are distributed on a retention basis, according to norms established by law (see text).
[3]Includes the tax on profits of enterprises of state subordination only.
Source: Population data from the Ukrainian Ministry of Statistics. All other data are from the Ministry of

Total Regulating Revenues	Total Fixed Plus Regulating Revenues	Transfers from State Budget (Including Subventions)	Total Oblast Revenues	1992 Population (000s)	Revenues Per Capita (KBV)
13381.5	22876	11815.5	34691.5	2156.1	16090
14280	20340.9	5223.4	25564.3	1896.6	13479
6151	9491.3	3099.5	12590.8	1069.9	11768
23979.4	50724.9	10831.2	61556.1	3907.2	15755
21697.2	59641.3	14045.8	73687.1	5332	13820
10164.9	15295.9	4434.4	19730.3	1495.9	13186
7796.8	11068.7	4230.4	15299.1	1264.9	12095
9245.2	21802.5	7767.4	29569.9	2100.7	14076
9136.7	13510.7	3492.8	17003.5	1441.2	11798
9157.3	17237	4453.7	21690.7	1932	11227
30644.9	49551.4	11235.2	60786.6	2620.8	23194
9881.3	14329.3	3925.7	18255	1236.2	14767
9954.8	26859.3	7207.9	34067.2	2871.7	11863
19334.6	28840.8	7004.2	35845	2751	13030
7048.6	12457.4	4193.9	16651.3	1348.5	12348
17786.2	28019.5	6529.4	34548.9	2616.1	13206
18659.9	27343.8	4688.9	32032.7	1758.5	18216
8040.2	11795	3070.6	14865.6	1176.2	12639
10072.1	15390.4	4031.3	19421.7	1425.5	13624
8223	11759.3	3196.7	14956	1172.2	12759
25541	39904.7	8862.6	48767.3	3168.3	15392
14075.3	19633.9	3720.8	23354.7	1267	18433
8511.9	14189	4027.9	18216.9	1515.9	12017
10649.5	15906.3	4561.9	20468.2	1527.6	13399
7159.1	9654	2428.9	12082.9	943.3	12809
9515.4	14225.2	4312.3	18537.5	1394.9	13289
4267.3	5240.9	3100	8340.9	411.7	20260
344391.3	587089.6	155492.2	742581.8	51801.9	14335

subordination.

Finance of Ukraine, or are the author's estimates, based on source documents.

Oblast	Actual Fixed (Own Source) Revenues[1]	Oblast *Share of Regulating (National) Revenues*[2]		
		Value-Added Tax	Excise Taxes	State Enterprise Profits Tax[3]
Republic of Crimea	539821	512211.8	111218.7	229068.7
Vinnytsya	214055.5	322283.9	44836.1	201636
Volyn	130808.9	169492.4	38177.7	90989.9
Dnipropetrovs'k	936369.3	418841	8496.3	336473.5
Donets'k	1534993.4	435773.6	18477.1	385812.8
Zhytomyr	207277	316797.4	53536.9	195291.2
Zakarpattia	139189.5	175622.2	27488.3	91102.2
Zaporizhzhia	464268.9	503939.3	82019.6	371137.1
Ivano-Frankivs'k	147959.7	187687.7	22675.6	116368.9
Kyiv *oblast*	244419.6	508428.3	109520.8	336289.1
Kyiv city	1132854.5	704902.9	96152.2	652623.5
Khirovohrad	135798.2	275465	23293.2	116886.1
Luhans'k	445956	370078.3	30215.9	279303.5
L'viv	360667.6	376301.7	96880.1	271206.4
Mykolaiv	236718.5	218401.1	23280.5	318204.3
Odesa	381099.1	300053.1	75211.5	293102.6
Poltava	309700.7	351938.7	17369.6	172758.6
Rivne	212859.7	237825.4	35002	167112.4
Sumy	192218.4	435237.7	71469.6	250394.2
Ternopil	116224.2	188158.5	35920.6	89745.5
Kharkiv	509897.4	434346.2	55667.6	139077.6
Kherson	190613	226371.2	24959.4	232486.8
Khmel'nyts'kyi	218744.3	209026.4	62581.6	106833.4
Cherkasy	197449.3	301729.8	62597.4	137231.9
Chernivtsy	85661.5	191465	41211.5	107379.8
Chernihiv	230458	88908.1	72109.2	119389.6
M. Sevastopol	174798.2	128063.7	13458.7	76673.9
Ukraine—Totals	9690880.7	8589350.7	1353827.8	5884579.9

Notes: [1]For 1992, includes personal income tax and the income tax on enterprises of communal (local)
[2]Regulating revenues are distributed on a retention basis, according to norms established by law (see text).
[3]Includes the tax on profits of enterprises of state subordination only.
Source: Population data from the Ukrainian Ministry of Statistics. All other data are from the Ministry of

Total Regulating Revenues	Total Fixed Plus Regulating Revenues	Transfers from State Budget (Including Subventions)	Total Oblast Revenues	1992 Population (000s)	Revenues Per Capita (KBV)
852499.2	1392320.2	9701	1402021.2	2156.1	650258
568756	782811.5	3122	785933.5	1896.6	414391
298660	429468.9	7940.5	437409.4	1069.9	408832
763810.8	1700180.1	32532	1732712.1	3907.2	443466
840063.5	2375056.9	0	2375056.9	5332	445435
565625.5	772902.5	22634	795526.5	1495.9	531811
294212.7	433402.2	0	433402.2	1264.9	342638
957096	1421364.9	16373	1437737.9	2100.7	684409
326732.2	474691.9	1945.6	476637.5	1441.2	330723
954238.2	1198657.8	42120	1240777.8	1932	642225
1453678.6	2586533.1	0	2586533.1	2620.8	986925
415644.3	551442.5	21320	572762.5	1236.2	463325
679597.7	1125553.7	0	1125553.7	2871.7	391947
744388.2	1105055.8	0	1105055.8	2751	401692
559885.9	796604.4	0	796604.4	1348.5	590734
668367.2	1049466.3	12211	1061677.3	2616.1	405824
542066.9	851767.6	0	851767.6	1758.5	484372
439939.8	652799.5	5090	657889.5	1176.2	559335
757101.5	949319.9	0	949319.9	1425.5	665956
313824.6	430048.8	2060.7	432109.5	1172.2	368631
629091.4	1138988.8	46430	1185418.8	3168.3	374150
483817.4	674430.4	6954	681384.4	1267	537794
378441.4	597185.7	15542	612727.7	1515.9	404201
501559.1	699008.4	10128	709136.4	1527.6	464216
340056.3	425717.8	9395	435112.8	943.3	461267
280406.9	510864.9	9	510864.9	1394.9	366238
218196.3	392994.5	10083	403077.5	411.7	979056
15827758.4	25518639	275581.8	25794220.9	51801.9	497940

subordination.

Finance of Ukraine, or are the author's estimates, based on source documents.

Oblast	Actual Fixed (Own Source) Revenues[1]	Oblast *Share of Regulating (National) Revenues*[2]			
		Value- Added Tax	Excise Taxes	State Enterprise Profits Tax[3]	Personal Income Tax
Republic of Crimea	1433208	652710.4	154879.4	470672.5	341480
Vinnytsya	1058144	445137.8	147808	434406	176680
Volyn	609660	236093.2	130128.2	179557	89335
Dnipropetrovs'k	2844879	1481617.2	236053.6	2477907	882190
Donets'k	3137039	2660881.8	501758.2	4105181	1377440
Zhytomyr	1025697	398218.2	113810.4	355491	134240
Zakarpattia	589838	217733.2	103426	169699.5	94845
Zaporizhzhia	1738926	1153542.6	339984.6	1460684	482720
Ivano-Frankivs'k	795683	447073	148643.6	390740.5	149545
Kyiv *oblast*	1105173	735877.6	77262	657418.5	203975
Kyiv city	2730681	14113122	261483.2	2511704	784160
Khirovohrad	798690	303553.4	91365.4	332374	133815
Luhans'k	1488378	660733.8	180522.8	1855660.5	657110
L'viv	1320517	883849.8	305305.8	957694.5	279660
Mykolaiv	879882	385011.4	135801	657006.5	213065
Odesa	2086580	481826	293055.8	1111222	431695
Poltava	943501	938144	389238.4	1125147.5	273445
Rivne	654479	231325.4	45017.4	335490	97645
Sumy	701222	418869.8	113447.6	463466	185395
Ternopil	590226	228969.6	112449.4	176317.5	94860
Kharkiv	1760243	1320229.4	326224.2	1271602	504255
Kherson	887983	335468.4	78657	479541	185290
Khmel'nyts'kyi	802833	432895.8	103334.2	372399	167295
Cherkasy	872389	495187	304928.6	537946	155720
Chernivtsy	515012	209818.2	85388.8	185637	83140
Chernihiv	676363	421622	273270	372697.5	129080
M. Sevastopol	235024	107638.4	24144.4	126288	41920
Ukraine—Totals	32282250	17697149	5077388	23573950	8350000

Notes: [1]For 1994, includes income tax on enterprises of communal subordination.
[2]In 1994, includes for the first time the personal income tax. Regulating revenues are distributed on a
[3]Includes the tax on profits of enterprises of state subordination only.
Source: Ministry of Finance of Ukraine, author's estimates, based on source documents.

Total Regulating Revenues	Total Fixed Plus Regulating Revenues	Transfers from State Budget (Including Subventions)	Total Oblast Revenues	1992 Population (000s)	Revenues Per Capita (KBV)
1619742.3	3052950.3	1657068	4710018.3	2156.1	2184508
1204031.8	2262175.8	1197749.3	3459925.1	1896.6	1824278
635113.4	1244773.4	866227.6	2111001	1069.9	1973083
5077767.8	7922646.8	−109042	7813604.8	3907.2	1999796
8645261	117823000	−1472186.3	10310113.7	5332	1933639
1001759.6	2027456.6	1080103.6	3107560.2	1495.9	2071385
585703.7	1175541.7	1099705.1	2275246.8	1264.9	1798756
3436931.2	5175857.2	−983808.9	4192048.3	2100.7	1995548
3436931.2	1931685.1	481521.4	2413206.5	1441.2	1674442
1136002.1	2779706.1	471655.5	3251361.6	1932	1682899
1674533.1	7701150.2	−695180.4	7005969.8	2620.8	2673218
4970469.2	1659797.8	1082500.2	2742209	1236.2	2218329
861107. 8	4842405.1	282816.4	5125221.5	2871.7	1784734
3354027.1	3747027.1	940304.2	4687331.3	2751	1703865
2426510.1	2270765.9	358756.8	2629522.7	1348.5	1949961
1390883.9	4404378.8	402544.2	4806923	2616.1	1837439
2317798.8	3669475.9	−758890	2910585.9	1758.5	1655153
2725974.9	1363956.8	799445.8	2163402.6	1176.2	1839315
709477.8	1882400.4	699285.4	2581685.8	1425.5	1811074
1181178.4	1202822.5	960652.5	2163475	1172.2	1845653
612596.5	5182552.8	340620.2	5523173	3168.3	1743261
3422309.8	1966939.4	787729.6	2754669	1267	2174167
1075924	1878757	716747.8	2595504.8	1515.9	1712187
1493781.6	2366170.6	753350.1	3119520.7	1527.6	2042106
563984	1078996	722278.3	1801274.3	943.3	1909546
1196669.5	1873032.5	494691.3	2367723.8	1394.9	1697415
299990.8	535014.8	337998.3	873013.1	411.7	2120508
54698487.2	86980737.2	12514644	99495381.2	51801.9	1920699

retention basis, according to norms established by law.

Appendix Table 7.4 Ukraine—Estimated *Oblast* Revenues—All Sources, 1995 (Billions

| Oblast | Actual Fixed (Own Source) Revenues[1] | Oblast *Share of Regulating (National) Revenues*[2] | | | |
		Value-Added Tax	Excise Taxes	State Enterprise Profits Tax[3]	Personal Income Tax
Republic of Crimea	555	13309.2	1802.9	7172.3	5693.8
Vinnytsya	409.8	9111.7	290.7	6313.3	1790.9
Volyn	236.1	4404.1	123.8	2848.9	903.2
Dnipropetrovs'k	1101.7	20780.9	275.5	42140.7	8716.5
Donets'k	1214.9	15729.3	599	49319.6	12170.3
Zhytomyr	397.2	8231.6	173.6	6114.7	1425.6
Zakarpattia	228.4	4563.3	89.1	2852.5	931.3
Zaporizhzhia	673.4	4972.8	531.8	23241	4451.6
Ivano-Frankivs'k	308.1	7078.1	147	7287.1	1433.5
Kyiv *oblast*	428	13210.9	355.1	10529.4	2155.7
Kyiv city	1057.5	10147.4	623.5	40868	7428.1
Khirovohrad	309.3	7479.2	151	6143.8	1556.6
Luhans'k	576.4	19854.2	195.9	17490.3	5479.8
L'viv	511.4	23785.8	628.2	16983.2	2979.1
Mykolaiv	340.8	9138.3	150.9	9963.2	2169.7
Odesa	808.1	19717.9	487.7	18354.4	3584.3
Poltava	365.4	6344.8	563.1	10818.3	2905.6
Rivne	253.5	6179.6	113.5	5232.5	1118.5
Sumy	271.6	6084.3	231.7	7839.9	1895.8
Ternopil	228.6	5390.4	232.9	2809.9	966.5
Kharkiv	681.7	31942.3	360.9	17418.4	5102.9
Kherson	343.9	7927.2	80.9	7278.7	1735.8
Khmel'nyts'kyi	310.9	8580.3	202.9	6690	1715.5
Cherkasy	337.9	10248.5	405.9	8593.6	1666.8
Chernivtsy	199.4	4974.9	133.6	3362.1	1118.8
Chernihiv	261.9	8660.6	467.6	7476.3	1363.8
M. Sevastopol	91	3327.6	218.2	3429.6	1417.5
Ukraine—Totals	12502	282175.2	9636.9	348571.7	83877.5

Notes: [1]For 1995, excludes tax on income of enterprises of communal subordination, which has become a
[2]Includes personal income tax and taxes on profits of enterprises of all forms of ownership and subordination.
[3]Tax on income of enterprises of communal(local) subordination included as a state regulating revenue in 1995.
Source: Ministry of Finance of Ukraine, author's estimates, based on source documents.

Total Regulating Revenues	Total Fixed Plus Regulating Revenues	Transfers from State Budget (Including Subventions)	Total Oblast Revenues	1992 Population (000s)	Revenues Per Capita (KBV)
27978.2	28533.2	−12877.3	15655.9	2156.1	7261212
17506.6	17916.4	0	17916.4	1896.6	9446589
8280	8516.1	5274.9	13791	1069.9	12889990
71913.6	73015.3	0	73015.3	3907.2	18687372
77818.2	79033.3	0	79033.1	5332	14822412
15945.5	16342.7	10929.4	27272.1	1495.9	18231232
8436.2	8664.6	6948.7	15613.3	1264.9	12343505
33197.2	33870.6	0	33870.6	2100.7	16123483
15945.7	16253.8	1182.5	17436.3	1441.2	12098460
26251.1	26679.1	2151	28830.1	1932	14922412
59067	60124.5	−14079.7	46044.8	2620.8	17568992
15330.6	15639.9	3409.2	19049.1	1236.2	15409408
43020.2	43596.6	0	43596.6	2871.7	15181463
44376.3	44887.7	0	44887.7	2751	16316866
21422.1	21762.9	1202.8	22965.7	1348.5	17030518
42144.3	42952.4	0	42952.4	2616.1	16418486
20631.8	20997.2	0	20997.2	1758.5	11940404
12644.1	12897.6	1686.5	14584.1	1176.2	12399337
16051.7	16323.3	0	16323.6	1425.5	11450930
9399.7	9628.3	2100.3	11728.6	1172.2	10005630
54824.5	55506.2	0	55506.2	3168.3	17519237
17022.6	17366.5	2069.6	19436.1	1267	15340245
17188.7	17499.6	3369.5	20869.1	1515.9	13766815
20914.8	21252.7	4095.7	25348.4	1527.6	16593579
9589.4	9788.8	2808.1	12596.9	943.3	13354129
17968.3	18230.2	0	18230.2	1394.9	13069181
8392.9	8483.9	2600.3	11084.2	411.7	26923002
724261.3	736763.3	22871.8	759635.1	51801.9	14664232

state regulating revenue. Allocation of 1995 actual regional fixed revenues based on 1994 oblast shares.

CHAPTER 8

Defining the Political Community in Ukraine: State, Nation, and the Transition to Modernity

Taras Kuzio

Some of the scholarly work devoted to state and nation building in Ukraine mistakenly pitches civic against ethnic nationalism. In this dichotomy former President Leonid Kravchuk's support for "ethnic policies" that led to Ukraine becoming a "nationalizing state" are counterpoised to those of President Leonid Kuchma who supports a "civic state." Arel, for example, argued that the "nationalizing state" under Kravchuk "was thus sending mixed signals. In the crucial realm of education, however, the signals were unmistakably at odds with the proclaimed civic conception of the state."[1]

This chapter takes a different approach to this fundamental question. It argues that it would be ill-advised to place the choice for Ukraine's leaders in terms of adopting either a civic *or* an ethnic approach to state and nation building in Ukraine. Purely civic or ethnic states are theoretical ideals to which other states may aspire to one day, fully attain. In reality though, *all* states are composed of *both* civic and ethnic elements. Liberalism and nationalism, Nodia argues, "are joined in a sort of complicated marriage, unable to live without each other, but coexisting in an almost permanent state of tension."[2]

This chapter is divided into three sections. The first discusses civic and ethnic nationalism within a theoretical and comparative perspective. It then investigates how this theoretical and comparative study applies to state and nation building in contemporary Ukraine by looking at the different legacies and approaches favored by elites from different regions. It argues that the concept of "nationalising states" is applicable to *all* civic, inclusive states. The second section surveys the interrelationship between nationalism, popular mobilization, and societal transformation. It argues in favor of a strong link between national identity and civil society. The final section analyzes state and nation building in Ukraine since the early 1990s. It argues that a national consensus as to the definition of the political community and the location of its center and its peripheries is gradually emerging.

A. State and Nation Building in Liberal Democracies

Civic and Ethnic Nationalism: Allies or Opponents?

State and nation building in nineteenth- and twentieth-century Europe and North America turned subjects into citizens with national identities. In 1789 there was no French nation; indeed, the majority of the inhabitants of France did not yet speak "French." But during the next 150 years the French civic nation created by the revolution assimilated others into a new French nation based upon the core Ile de France. "Peasants" in France became *both* citizens and Frenchmen/women. Political emancipation (democracy, civil society) and national identity are therefore both tied to the modern epoch because nation-states have created the only vehicles for democratic polities. In the former USSR the democratic movements were both national and democratic in their aspirations. After all, democracies cannot be built within empires. Within Europe, Krejci and Velimsky defined a clear majority of states as both ethnic and civic (political) in their makeup, including Ukraine. The small number of states that overwhelmingly exhibit political attributes were based in western Europe.[3]

Nationalism has traditionally operated through fascism, communism, or democracy. Within the United Kingdom the Welsh, Scottish, and Irish nationalist parties are all socialist. The Basque separatist movement ETA is also socialist. Yet, nationalism and liberalism are nevertheless often counterposed as two opposites, the former illiberal and "irrational," the other liberal and "rational."[4] In reality, *all* liberal democracies exhibit elements of both civic and ethnic nationalism. Cultural/ethnic and civic/political nations are not antagonistic. They are necessary components of the same "community of consent" without which there cannot be a "community of culture." In a similar manner, "it is difficult to accept a communality of consent without a communality of culture," Bereciartu believes.[5] It is implausible to conceive of nations that are purely political or, in fact, "nations lacking a prior cultural and consensual substratum."[6]

Unless one accepts that Ukraine is a bi-ethnic, eastern Slavic (Russian-Ukrainian) state, then demands for the core ethnic group's language and culture to dominate the state are perfectly in keeping with the state and nation building traditionally found throughout the liberal democracies of Europe and North America. According to the 1989 Soviet census all of Ukraine's regions, apart from Crimea, possessed Ukrainian ethnic majorities. Therefore, only Crimea has been granted group rights in the form of political autonomy and has Russian as the state language (with Ukrainian and Turkish as additional official languages).

The division of nationalism and nation-states into inclusive and exclusive variants does not necessarily divide them into clearly defined groups. *All* of the 15 former Soviet states have now adopted liberally inclusive nationality policies. Initially Estonia and Latvia were the only two states that did not grant their residents automatic citizenship on December 31, 1991, when the USSR ceased to exist. Instead, they adopted citizenship laws similar to those found in most Western countries, which grant citizenship only after a certain period of time and after a language test. Thus, to the evident annoyance of Russian leaders, these two Baltic states were never criticized extensively by the OSCE or the Council of Europe. In some liberal democracies, citizenship is never granted at all unless ethnic ancestry can be proven (for example, Germany). France and Greece, two prominent members of the European Union and NATO, refuse to accept that national minorities can even theoretically exist in their territories.

Therefore, inclusive policies also contain elements of both ethnic and civic nationalism. Inclusive nation and state building policies also promote internal unity through the medium of one (or more) language, culture, and historical myths while institutionalizing boundaries to differentiate the "We" from the "Others."[7] Nations are tied in a mystical manner to their land through historical myths, memories, anniversaries, and monuments. Religion, traditions, symbols, and language remain important even in ostensibly civic states.[8]

Without this external differentiation it would be difficult to construct a separate national identity for the "We" that is required to underpin the legitimacy of the independent state. If the leadership of a country, such as Belarus, has accepted that its country is in fact a bi-ethnic state, then there is little, or no need, to promote a "We" different from all "Others." If Ukraine adopted similar policies, it is unclear how it could continue to argue at the same time that it is an independent state different from Russia, particularly at a time when the majority of Russians still find it difficult to accept that Ukrainians are even a separate ethnic group.

Both inclusive and exclusive nationalism foster cultural unity. Liberal democracies in and of themselves foster common values, institutions, and identities at the expense of regionalism or subcultures. "Nationalism is equated with citizenship and the state with civil society," where all citizens are considered equal. Nevertheless, "Although subcultures are allowed within a common core—culturally, liberal democracy has a clear bias towards ethnic integration and assimilation."[9] Residents of France have a more inclusive choice than residents of Germany because they are at least allowed to automatically apply for citizenship. At the same time, the price for granting this citizenship is assimilation into French culture and language. Which is, therefore, the more democratic? France, where one's national identity is lost to French culture and language; or Germany, where one's identity is maintained, but one can never become a citizen unless one possesses some German ancestry?

Some liberal democracies adopted inclusive nationality policies within an ethnically heterogeneous society. These liberal democracies may, in fact, still adopt policies that discriminate in favor of the titular ethnic group.[10] National minority rights in Ukraine have been largely formulated within the traditional Western European view of the nation-state, which recognizes the centrality of the Ukrainian nation while guaranteeing the rights of national minorities. National interests are identified with civil society rather than with an ethnic group. Needless to say, national minorities traditionally prefer group or "collective rights" over individual rights that, they correctly believe, only serve to foster assimilation.[11]

Multiculturalism in a Ukrainian Setting[12]

Polyethnic rights can—and should—be provided for members of non-titular ethnic groups. Nevertheless, these polyethnic rights, which allow ethnic groups to promote their languages and cultures in the private domain, have to be balanced by support for an overall societal culture promoted by the state within the public domain. In post-Soviet Ukraine, the provision of polyethnic rights has always been supported by the government. There is little argument against their provision to national minorities.

The debate instead has rested upon how to define the societal culture and, more particularly, if Russians are to be defined as a titular nation *or* a national minority. Here the state effectively has three options:

1. A Ukrainian ethnic titular nation with the Ukrainian language as the state language (the definition used in the June 1996 constitution);
2. A Ukrainian ethnic titular nation with two languages defined as state languages (Russian and Ukrainian); and,
3. Ukrainians and Russians both defined as titular nations with their two languages also defined as state languages (Russian and Ukrainian).

The Ukrainian left, Hry'niov's Inter-Regional Bloc of Reforms party (MRBR), Russian and some Western authors prefer to see option three, which they define as "civic," contrasting it to the "ethnic" possibility in option one. But four problems arise with the choice of option three. First, it is actually more "ethnic" (not civic) than option one and ignores the fact that all states are composed of civic and ethnic attributes. Bi-ethnic states always lead to nationalizing policies in their ethnic parts. Secondly, it would be a fictitious equality. Russian, as the former dominant imperial language of Tsarist and Soviet power, would, if granted the status of a state language, prevent any revival of the Ukrainian language.

It is indeed strange that Western and Russian cosmopolitan liberals reject any need for affirmative action for Ukrainian language and culture in post-colonial settings, such as Ukraine (while accepting similar provisions for other peoples who emerged from Western colonialism elsewhere). The best example of this is in Belarus where President Alyaksandr Lukashenka understood perfectly well that granting Russian the status of a second state language would lead to the death of Belarusian. As Kymlicka argues:

> In fact, it is very difficult for languages to survive in modern industrial societies unless they are used in public life. Given the spread of standardized education, the high demand for literacy in work, and widespread interaction with government agencies, any language which is not a public language becomes so marginalised that it is likely to survive only amongst a small elite, or in ritualized form, not as a living and developed language underlying a flourishing culture.[13]

Option three would legalize the legacies inherited as a result of Soviet nationality policies where Russian-speaking peoples became defined as a new *Homo Sovieticus*. Homo Sovieticus cannot be defined as a "people" or "nation"—even if it is Russian-speaking—and could be granted group rights. Demands for group rights have been advanced only by Crimeans, who inhabit the only region of Ukraine with a non-Ukrainian ethnic majority. "Cultures," in Kymlicka's definition, are synonymous with "peoples" or "nations," which refers to an "intergenerational community, more or less institutionally complete, occupying a given territory or homeland, sharing a distinct language and history."[14] Russian speaking *Homo Sovieticus* certainly does not therefore fit Kymlicka's definition of "nations" or "peoples."

Finally, should Russian speakers be defined as a bona fide cultural group? Jackson and Wolczuk, like many other Western cosmopolitan liberals and the Russian government, believe that a provision should have been included within the June 1996 Ukrainian constitution for Russian speakers.[15] But can such a group be clearly defined when so many Ukrainians are *not* monolingual (that is, Ukrainophone *or* Russophone) but actually bilingual? Kymlicka also cautions against adopting such an approach by referring to "Hispanics" in the United States who are merely a statistical category. We should therefore also remain cautious when we hear similar calls to define "Russophones" as anything other than a census or polling statistic.

Elites and "Nationalizing States" in Ukraine and the Former USSR

Brubaker divides nation building into three categories:

- The civic state (all citizens are equal, regardless of ethnic origins, and ethnicity plays little role in the state);
- The biethnic/multinational state (the state is the property of two or more ethnocultural core nations in which ethnicity—not civic elements—plays a dominant role);
- The "nationalizing state" and minority rights.

Of these three options, Brubaker believes that only the third has any real chance of being implemented in the former Soviet bloc, because "Almost all of the new states . . . will be nationalizing states to *some* degree and in *some* form."[16] The question therefore is not whether these newly independent states will be "nationalizing" or not, but how and to what degree they will be.

Brubaker's division of nation building is misleading because in reality there are not three but only two possibilities. All civic states are composed of both civic and ethnic elements. Therefore, all states are "nationalizing states" to some degree where the nontitularly defined ethnic groups are gradually assimilated into the core, titular ethnic group. In reality the choices open to Ukraine's elites are not the three outlined by Brubaker but the three available to all elites constructing states and nations:

1. Creation of a civic/political nation (*Ukrains'kyi narod*) based upon the core Ukrainian ethnic group, its language and culture. The political community would include all members of Ukrainian society who would be granted citizenship;

2. An ethnic democracy in which only ethnic Ukrainians would be granted rights and citizenship.

3. Creation of a loosely defined people of Ukraine (*narody Ukrayiny*) that is based upon two titular ethnic groups and languages (Russian and Ukrainian).

To argue, as do the Ukrainian left and Hry'niov that the third choice is "civic" while the first two are "ethnic" clearly shows a confused understanding of state and nation building in liberal democracies. Only option two, which has not been implemented by Ukraine, is "ethnic." An example of this confusion can be seen in the views of Hry'niov:

> A state is built either on the basis of an ethnic nation or on the basis of a political nation—all the people inhabiting this territory. I am convinced that as soon as we fall into realising the rights of the ethnic nation regarding the ideology of the indigenous people and a single state language as of paramount importance, this may be fraught with disaster for Ukraine.

To prevent Ukraine from becoming an "ethnic state," Hry'niov proposes two state languages. In addition, he believes that "we cannot have a monoethnic state. We are not France or Germany. Our state will always be bi-ethnic."[17] Consequently, in Hry'niov's view Ukraine will be a "civic state" if it has two state languages and two titular nations![18] Brubaker believes Hry'niov is mistaken because option three would prioritize ethnicity (not civility) and thereby conform to the second of his three options.

In reality *all* three options open to Ukraine's elites include nationalizing elements because *all* states, to varying degrees, are nationalizers on behalf of the titular ethnic groups (in options one and two Ukrainians, or in option three Ukrainians *and* Russians). Inclusive and exclusive states both include cultural elements while historically civic states have also been involved in ethnic conflict (e.g., in Latin America and the United States). Many of the liberal reformers in Quebec have also been staunch nationalists.

The difference between civic and ethnic states rests *not* on the absence of any cultural component from the former, Kymlicka argues, "but rather the fact that anyone can integrate into the common culture, regardless of race or colour."[19] Purely civic states are impossible because "The idea that the government could be neutral with respect to cultural groups is patently false."[20] The state is never neutral because it has to make choices regarding the state language, national history and myths, political boundaries, educational curricula, and national symbols. Nation building therefore always privileges the majority culture, which becomes the common culture in the process of the drive to modernity (marketization and democratization).

Within every society individuals hold different views as to the degree to which ethnic or civic elements should be emphasized. Most movements draw support from both ethnic and civic elements in society. As Keating points out, "What matters is the balance between the two."[21] This balance is usually achieved over time. During the early phase of post-Soviet transformation, the civic element remains weak and the strength of the reform process is therefore dependent upon the level of inherited national identity and national consciousness (see below). Over time, as a market economy and a democracy are consolidated, the civic element becomes stronger and the ethnic element is overshadowed. The ethnic element is only usually aroused during times of crisis. George Bernard Shaw wrote that "A healthy nation is as unconscious of its nationality as a healthy man of his bones. But if you break a nation's nationality, it will think of nothing else but getting it set again."[22]

Those who stressed ethnic elements were often the first to come to power in many of the newly independent states of the former USSR. These states had, after all, been largely propelled into independence by movements that were *both* nationalist and democratic. Former Ukrainian President Kravchuk relied upon an alliance with national democrats whose main base of support was to be found within western-central Ukraine. Those leaders, such as Kravchuk and his allies, who stressed the ethnic elements of state and nation building, pointed to historical territory, shared myths and memories, public culture, a single economy, and equal rights and duties.

In Ukraine, as in many other non-Russian regions of the former USSR, these leaders were largely replaced through elections or putsches by the mid-1990s. The leaders who replaced them, such as Kuchma in Ukraine, stressed civic in contrast to ethnic elements (common rights and duties, individual over national rights, a territorial political community).

What these new civic leaders quickly found out was that many of the properties found within civic and ethnic states are not confined to either one or the other but do in fact overlap. This is because civic, territorially based states are

also wedded to the ideal of the shared public culture and language of the historical majority in the state, a public culture in which every citizen must participate and which takes priority over the individual concerns and local cultures of the private domain and home.[23]

The choice open to President Kuchma was therefore either to accept the reality that all states are to some degree a mixture of both civic and ethnic elements or to embrace nationality policies tailored to suit the fact that Ukraine is a bi-ethnic (Russian-Ukrainian) state. In Hryn'iov's view, Ukraine was never a "Russian colony," there were never ethnic conflicts between Ukrainians and Russians, and Russification never took place. (Wilson agrees with Hry'niov on the question of Russification, which he agrees did not take place.)[24] Instead, Hry'niov argues, "the stability and good-naturedness of inter-ethnic relations in Ukraine are based upon the unity of the Ukrainian and Russian components in its ethnic structure and in its national-linguistic community."[25]

Hry'niov counterposes civic to ethnic states and therefore disagree with the concept of prioritizing any one core ethnic group. Ukraine, as an allegedly bi-ethnic (or, in Smith's definition, pluralistic) state, should therefore legally codify two state languages (Russian and Ukrainian) because to promote only one of them (for example, Ukrainian) would be tantamount to discrimination against the other. In other words, Hry'niov supports the prioritization of not one titular ethnic group (which they define as "ethnic") but two (which they define as "civic").

This reflects a lack of understanding of the process of state and nation building in other regions of Europe and North America. First, if the aim of adding Russian as a second state language is to ensure no discrimination against it, then where does the state stop? What of the languages of the other national minorities (Polish, Bulgarian, Yiddish, etc.)? If their languages are not added to these two state languages, cannot speakers of these other languages also complain that the state has adopted discriminatory policies against their languages? Secondly, such a line of argument goes against historical practice elsewhere. In Malaysia and Catalonia the state languages are Malay and Catalan, yet Malays and Catalans account for only 50 and 60 percent of the populations of their country and autonomous regions respectively (Ukrainians account for 73 percent). In the United States only one state language exists, despite large areas of the country where Spanish is spoken. Finally, the Ukrainian language, after over a century of state discrimination against it, is simply not in a position to compete with the Russian language. Liberal policies in the west and in other post-colonial countries would therefore understandably encourage affirmative action to raise its profile, usage, and prestige.

Different Legacies and Approaches

At different times and over long periods, the various components of identity that make up the civic and ethnic elements of the nation are in a process of change, transition, re-interpretation, and re-adaptation. Therefore, in any given instance, a nation "would display a variety of characteristics and understandings, for which we would need more than one set of tools to enable us to analyze and understand their successive re-formation."[26] Because nations always exhibit civic and ethnic elements, they should be viewed "through different lenses, in order to understand their peculiar combination and permutation of elements."[27]

This has particular relevance for the study of state and nation building in post-Soviet Ukraine. Due to the different legacies of nation building and nation destroying under Austrian and Tsarist rule, different regions of Ukraine inherited two distinct concepts of state and nation building. This is what the director of the L'viv-based Institute of Historical Studies, Iaroslav Hrytsak, meant when he asked in his inaugural lecture, "What does being Ukrainian mean today? Is it a national or a territorial concept . . . ?"[28] Ukraine therefore inherited two traditions that roughly correspond with those areas of the country that were under Austrian or Tsarist Russian rule:[29]

1. *Eastern/southern Ukraine (Narod Ukrayiny).*[30] A preference for the French and west European tradition of civic/territorial States (i.e., "State to Nation"). This concept of the nation usually emerged within populations/*ethnies* that possessed states with relatively clear-cut boundaries and where the state played an important role in the nation building project. This concept of the nation stressed common laws, uniform rights and duties, inclusive and equal citizenship (passports, oaths, legal identities).

   But civic/territorial states, such as the United Kingdom and France, also sought to forge common cultures, shared values and historical myths, symbols, a common civic ideology/religion, a standard language, uniform educational system and to stress differentiation from "Others."

2. *Western/central Ukraine (Ukrayins'kyi Narod).* Inherited the German and eastern European tradition of ethnic states based on what Kohn defines as the "organic," "mystical" concepts of the nation where the *ethnie/*nation goes in search of the state (i.e., "Nation to State"). A

pre-existing *ethnie* evolves into a nation with the help of a friendly power (in western Ukraine this was the Austrians) and/or as a consequence of conflict with neighbors (for example, the Poles). Howard traced the emergence of cultural nationalism to identities rooted in difference from "Others" with whom one had been in historical conflict.[31] Pre-modern nations (or *ethnie*) usually have little understanding of who they are beyond being "From Here" (*Tuteishi*) but they do define themselves in terms of what they are not (that is vis-à-vis "Others").

"Nation to State" ethnic nationalism places greater stress upon genealogy, nativism, language, and traditions as substitutes for legal codes and institutes as the cement which binds the nation. Nevertheless, some ethnic nationalisms, as in Ukraine, Latvia, and Estonia, also have to make room for elements of the civic (for example, the granting of citizenship to all members of the political community). Once nationhood was achieved in central and eastern Europe they moved toward the concept of the nation-state more commonly found in western Europe.[32]

These different legacies and preferences for certain approaches to state and nation building in Ukraine are clearly reflected in its two post-Soviet presidents. Former President Kravchuk was allied with center-right national democrats from western-central Ukraine where the "Nation to State" legacy of central-eastern Europe remains stronger. The views of western Ukrainians therefore also resemble the three Baltic states in their approaches to state and nation building and their rejection of Soviet rule which is perceived as imported and alien (i.e., Russian). President Kuchma, in contrast, hails from eastern Ukraine where a Ukrainian ethnie was never allowed to evolve into a modern nation under Tsarist and Soviet rule. The population of eastern-southern Ukraine prefers a "State to Nation" approach which is both less threatening and more similar to the Soviet tradition of respect for statehood, a statehood which was not perceived as imported or alien.

Eastern-southern Ukrainians were also targeted in the Soviet campaign that depicted "Ukrainian nationalism" as evil and murderous for having collaborated with the Nazis. Patriotism is therefore regarded as a perfectly healthy human feeling by eastern Ukrainians. "Nationalism" meanwhile, is branded as "fascistic." In the former USSR, anyone with a Ukrainian national consciousness or even anyone who spoke the Ukrainian language was often branded a "nationalist."[33] But even while preferring the propagation of patriotism to civic nationalism Kuchma's rhetoric still combines elements of civic *and* ethnic nationalism:

> Heartfelt respect for our sources of origin, for our own roots, for the deeds of our grandfathers and fathers, for our parents' graves; love for our land both in glory and distress; aspiration to do good and doing good in the name of the people and the state are all the elements of patriotism, which we badly need now to build a new Ukraine.[34]

Kuchma's initial confusion between civic and ethnic nationalism was also evident in two other areas of his policies. First, state and nation building should be treated separately but nevertheless, in a manner akin to civic and ethnic nationalism in that they cannot be completely divorced. Successful state building policies cannot take place without nation building because a civil society cannot exist without national identity (see below). Borders also play a role in both state and nation building by defining the "Other" from the "We." Similarly, Kuchma understood that the August 1991 declaration of independence was one "of those few historical dates" which, transforms a populace/*ethnie* (*naselennia*) into a people/nation (*narod*), and a territory into a state."[35]

Secondly, on the fifth anniversary of Ukrainian independence he described the establishment of an independent state as the "third attempt" to build such a state. This reflected the need for Ukraine's leaders, as it has for other post-Soviet leaders, to underpin the legitimacy of their states upon historical myths. The Ukrainian leadership continually reiterates that independence came about because of the "natural results of our people's centuries-long aspiration to be masters in their own house" (Kuchma on the fourth anniversary of independence).[36] Until 1991, Kuchma believes, " . . . Ukraine had always maintained its own ferment of independence."[37]

The formulation of these new historical myths necessitated the rejection of the Tsarist and post-Leninist historical scheme, which treated Ukrainians, Belarusians, and Russians as three branches of the one *Rus'kiy narod.* (This historical scheme was also dropped by Belarus between 1990 and the presidential election of 1994. President Lukashenka, in an attempt to underpin his Paneastern Slavic and pro-Soviet policies, reverted back to Soviet post-Leninist historiography.) In stark contrast to Belarus, Ukraine, under both Kravchuk and Kuchma, has continued to formulate a new national history based on Mykhailo Hrushevs'kyi's scheme that argued that Ukrainian history could be traced back separately from Russian history to the medieval proto-Ukrainian state of Kyiv Rus'.[38] To build an independent Ukraine separate to Russia, Kuchma had therefore little choice but to back the continued utilization of a national history based upon Hrushevs'kyi's framework. In addition, a national historiography also supports Ukrainian counterclaims against Russian territorial demands in eastern and southern Ukraine by asserting the right of "first settlement."[39]

B. Nationalism, Mobilization, and Modernization[40]

The majority of the literature dealing with post-communist transition focuses on political and economic reform while ignoring state and nation building. In reality, the four processes are taking place simultaneously in Ukraine and within the remainder of the former USSR. Of the 27 post-communist regimes, only five merely changed regime (Albania, Bulgaria, Hungary, Poland, and Romania). In those new states where state and nation building are accompanying reform a great deal of energy is devoted to creating a "We," defining the "Other," forging a new societal culture, contesting borders, and debating the national idea and policies toward national minorities. Often the energy devoted to these questions distracts the elites from pursuing reform.[41] As Linz and Stepan point out, these questions, "almost pushed matters of democratic crafting off the normative and institutional agenda of politics."[42]

It has long been understood that social mobilization, which is particularly important at a time of rapid change from one system to another, is conditioned upon access to mobilization resources *and* national identities. Although originally pitted as two contrasting opposites it is now usually recognized that *both* play a role in any study of social mobilization.[43]

In the Ukrainian case the two are evidently linked. National identity played the part of an important initial stimulus for social mobilization in western-central Ukraine, a factor that largely removed the Communists from the political map in April 1990 and brought democrats to power. Even prior to the April 1990 parliamentary elections national identity played a role in forcing members of the *ancien regime* in western-central Ukraine to decide where they stood on key questions. Those who sided with their national (and not the Communist Party) identities were able to provide some resources (for example, the printing of *samvydav*). When in power these democrats were then able to provide the full range of institutional resources to political parties and civic groups, thereby opening up public space and reviving civil society in western-central Ukraine.

Therefore, national identity plays an important role in mobilizing populations (assuming, of course, public space allows it to play such a role, something only permitted from the late 1980s in the former USSR). The role of national identity would be especially pronounced in regions of the former USSR where memory of independent statehood and/or civil society was still available (for example, the Baltic states and western Ukraine). Where national identity is weak and amorphous (for example, Belarus), social mobilization is made more difficult. Dawson, in a study of the environmental movements in the former USSR, found that social mobilization was more difficult in regions where territorial identities prevailed over ethnic (that is, in areas such as in eastern Ukraine and Belarus).[44] Support for language, culture, and collective historical memory are therefore important components of the building of a civil society, national identity, and a political community, as well as in mobilizing society in favor of modernization.

Rustow advises us that "national unity" and "agreed boundaries" must "precede all the other phases of democratization" as a critical "background condition."[45] In other words, some aspects of civic nation and state (institutional) building must precede or accompany the transition to a market economy and a democracy, both pitstops along the drive to modernity. Speaking to the All-Ukrainian Council of Businessmen, President Kuchma linked economic growth to "political consolidation" and political stability."[46] Yuriy Yekhanurov, then head of the State Committee on the Development of Entrepreneurship, said:

> I noticed traits that make Poles different from Ukrainians. They are not holding a discussion on whether Poland should or should not exist. Neither do they experience any problems with private property in general and private ownership of land in particular.[47]

Historically there has always been a close link between the rise of nationalism and democracy.[48] In countries such as Ukraine the movement for national emancipation was also one that combined demands for national and human rights. Ukraine, according to President Kuchma, chose the path of reform when it became an independent state. The building of a nation-state is therefore inseparably linked to that of creating a market economy and a democracy. Nation building in Ukraine, Kuchma believes, "can only exist on the basis of the transition to a market economy."[49]

Ukrainian civic nationalism (or national democracy) is supportive of modernization which, in the post-communist context, equates to domestic backing for democratization, marketization, nation and state building.[50] Gellner has pointed to how the rise of nationalism is unavoidable during the drive to modernization, marketization, and democratization. Nationalism, national consciousness, and the forging of national unity are indispensable for the growth of civil society, a market economy, and a democracy. A civil society cannot function in the absence of a national identity to which the citizens have a prior loyalty over and above other loyalties (gender, region, family, class).[51] Will Kymlicka therefore points out:

> So the process of modernisation involves, inter alia, a process of "nation building"—that is, a process of promoting a common language and a sense of common membership in and equal access to the social institutions based on that language.[52]

In societies undergoing dramatic change, "Ethnic communities are created and transformed by particular elites in modernizing and in post-industrial societies undergoing dramatic social changes."[53] In Ukraine the drive to modernization, although undertaken at a time of socioeconomic crisis, is also leading to ethnic re-identification (the proportion of self-declared ethnic Russians having dropped by more than half since 1989).[54]

The civic nationalism of Ukrainian elites is closely tied to the drive to modernization and the commonly felt need to remove the legacies of two calamities that befell Ukrainians—totalitarianism and empire. Civic nationalism is that of peoples who were formerly labeled as "backward" or "unhistoric" by elites who are nationalists only because they recognize this "backwardness" (meaning, the country's historical divorce from the "European path") and their wish to overcome it by "re-joining Europe."[55]

The revolt against the *ancien regime* in Ukraine defined the nation in civic terms as composed of all of its inhabitants who were henceforth described as its citizens. Popular sovereignty replaced that of imperial. The new political community or nation was defined in opposition to the "Other," as one which would seek to modernize the feudal or "backward" state inherited from the previous regime. Civic nationalism is an important ingredient in helping to overcome and to integrate the discrepancy between the actual sense of community and that of which they are to become a part. The creation of a nation-state is therefore a precondition for the creation of a democratic polity and a market economy.

Ukraine embarked upon democratization and marketization in the absence of national unity with inherited weak national consciousness, primary regional loyalties, and no unified cultural communities. These inherited factors played a prominent role in Ukraine in two ways. First, they influenced the starting period, pace, and type of transformation chosen by its elites. Second, they influenced their foreign orientations and attitudes towards "Europe" or Eurasia.

Mobilization of the population to support modernization and endure the inevitable short-term sacrifices is a necessary requirement of the post-communist transformation process. In Ukraine the economic crisis has affected all of society. But in nationally conscious regions of the country, discontent with the socioeconomic crisis has not translated into disillusionment with independence. In contrast, in areas of Ukraine where national identity is weaker the socioeconomic situation has given rise to nostalgia for the past, sentiments which the Communist Party, hostile to independence, is only too willing to back. Support for a backward-looking Eurasian orientation therefore translates into hostility toward modernization (democratization, marketization, nation, and state building).

National Identity and Civil Society

National identity and civil society are closely related.[56] Habermas points out how terms such as "nation" and "people" are used interchangeably as legal and political terms.[57] Anderson also argues that "nation-ness" is inseparable from "political consciousness."[58] Modernity unleashes the logic of identity as in traditional society individuals are not integrated into the larger community.[59] Culture, identity, and political consciousness have long been recognized by Kymlicka, Taylor, Cohen, Gellner, and Seligman as closely linked.[60]

A nation sustains civil society when the civic nation is coterminous with the political community and civil society. Shils, for example, argues that:

> The nation is necessary for civil society. It is one of its main supporters. The crucial collective within the nation-state is the dominant nation. Nationality is a necessary ingredient, perhaps even a precondition for civil society. It is the collective self consciousness which sustains the civil society. Concern for one's nation reinforces the concern for the common good.[61]

Citizenship assumes that the citizen will become a member of the nation, which is defined as that which has precedence over all others (i.e., the titular or core nationality). The nation is bounded by clearly defined borders, within which only its constitution and laws will apply. Individual rights remain paramount in such a state where the dominant core nationality promotes an overall societal culture. Meanwhile, it fosters polyethnic rights in the private domain. Therefore, as argued earlier in this chapter, such a civic state is also composed of ethnic attributes, which cannot be completely neutral because it promotes, and hence also fosters, assimilation into the dominant societal culture.

The adoption of the June 1996 constitution signified two important developments. First, it signaled that there was no going back.[62] As Shils points out, constitution-making since 1776 has been seen "as a major symbol of the formation of the new state." "Having become independent, a population living in a bounded territory becomes a state by the promulgation of a constitution," he continues.[63] Five objectives are usually defined as those of nationalists—territory, state, language, culture, and history.[64] All of these were largely theoretically and juridically resolved during the period 1996 to 1997. A new national currency was also issued in September 1996 (itself based upon the currency of the independent governments of 1917 to 1920), and the last two remaining borders were recognized by Russia and Romania in May-June 1997.

Second, the adoption of the constitution signaled a clear preference for building a nation-state based on the Western European model, which would include *both* civic and ethnic elements. The ethnic elements of the Ukrainian nation-state would be based primarily on ethnic Ukrainians as the core, titular group upon which a common culture and values would be forged and then utilized to unify society. The rejection of Ukraine as a bi-ethnic state also reflected acceptance of the Soviet legacy of assigning each of the fifteen titular Soviet ethnic groups a separate and personalized homeland. National minorities, granted citizenship automatically, would be nevertheless expected to respect and know the Ukrainian language, culture, and history while being able to freely use their own languages and cultures in the private domain.[65]

Why had Kuchma been forced to evolve in his views since 1994? Six factors account for this. First, as argued earlier, national identity, and civil society are closely related and both are products of the modern era.[66] The large numbers of people in eastern-southern Ukraine with low national consciousness, a regional and/or eastern Slavic/ Soviet identity are difficult to socially mobilize.[67] As Wilson has admitted, Russophones in Ukraine are a largely amorphous group that find it difficult to assert their influence within the policymaking community in Kyiv.[68] Civil society and political mobilization are most active in areas of national consciousness—central and western Ukraine.[69] Eastern-southern Ukrainians therefore exhibit elements of pre-modernity as defined by Armstrong: "Anthropological historians have been increasingly obliged to confront the fact . . . that (pre-modern) groups tend to define themselves not by reference to their own characteristics but by exclusion, that is, by comparison to 'strangers.'"[70] Eastern-southern Ukrainians or Russians know that they are not part of the Russian ethnic group whose homeland is the Russian Federation. Nevertheless, they are still in the throes of transition

Table 8.1   To What Population Do You Attribute Yourself (%)?

	Ukrainian	Russians	Others	Total
Ukraine	56.9	28.3	29.2	48.3
CIS	5.3	10.4	8.0	6.7
USSR	15.5	33.0	27.4	20.5
Region	13.2	15.9	23.9	14.5
Russia	1.0	5.3	1.8	2.0
Europe	2.3	2.1	2.6	2.3
Don't know	5.8	6.1	7.1	5.7

Source: Institute of Sociology and Democratic Initiatives, Kyiv.

toward membership in a Ukrainian political nation. According to the data in table 8.1, only 5.3 percent of Russians in Ukraine regard Russia as their "homeland."

Further, as evident from Table 8.2, even when broken down by region Russians in eastern Ukraine and Crimea do not see Russia as their "homeland."

Second, Kuchma was faced with a conundrum. The overwhelming majority of Ukraine's forty political parties and civic groups reject any definition of the country as bi-ethnic and in need of two state languages (none of which call for only Russian to become the sole state language).[72]

If Kuchma had supported these twin concepts (dual state languages and a bi-ethnic state) he would have maintained his alliance with the MRBR, obtained new allies (the communists and Civic Congress), while turning against himself the bulk of Ukraine's democratic parties and civic groups. This, in turn, would have prevented him from launching any political and economic reform. It would have also made him enemies of the intellectual and cultural elites who largely support cultural nationalism. These historians, writers, and artists utilize Ukrainian archaeology, historiography, folklore, philology, language, culture, and topography as "moral innovators" in their zeal to recover national pride and remove the stigma of inherited inferiority complexes.[73] In November 1995 these "moral innovators" grouped together into the powerful lobby group, the Congress of Ukrainian Intellectuals.

Table 8.2   To What Population Do You Attribute Yourself (%)?[71]

	L'viv	Kyiv	Donetsk	Simferopol
Russia	0.5	0.2	2.0	3.5

Source: Institute of Sociology and Democratic Initiatives, Kyiv.

Third, as noted earlier in this chapter, all states combine elements of ethnic and civic nationalism. The propagation of a purely "civic state" by Kuchma's advisers in 1994 was only a theoretical possibility. Any Ukrainian leader would have to decide upon what basis to unite and create a new political community? This, as Ukrainian authors tirelessly stress, could be only on the basis of civic (not ethnic) nationalism with the aim of creating a "modern nation and a highly developed state."[74]

Fourth, Kuchma's evolution also reflected geopolitical developments in central-eastern Europe. To have supported the slogan that Ukraine was a bi-ethnic state would have been tantamount to adopting the Belarusian path where Ukraine, like Lukashenka's Belarus, would be perceived as a Little Russian branch of the to be "re-united" *Rus'kiy narod*. Ukraine could *not* strive to "re-join Europe," implement reform, and build a modern civic nation while accepting that it was also a Little Russia. Ukraine defined as "Little Russia" would, like Belarus, not be treated as a serious entity worthy of equality and respect by either Moscow *or* the West. This is especially the case when the majority of Russians still believe that the Ukrainian *narod* would gladly "re-unite" with Russians but are being allegedly held back in this endeavor by their corrupt, former-communist-turned-nationalist elites.[75]

Sixth, the state and nation building project has therefore been couched in terms of national security. "National-cultural security" is defined as one of the four pillars of Ukraine's national security. Within this realm of national security, Ukraine's leaders see the development of democratic social norms, decline in totalitarian stereotypes, and the "development of national consciousness through a revival of Ukrainian language and culture, and a deeper appreciation of Ukraine's unique history." External threats that hinder the "spiritual and intellectual renaissance of the Ukrainian people" are considered a danger to Ukraine's national security.[76] The only country with the capability to launch such a threat is Russia. The national security doctrine adopted by Parliament in early 1997 also points to the "development of the Ukrainian nation, its historical consciousness and the national pride of Ukrainians" as important elements of the country's security.[77]

Finally, Kuchma would have lost the support of the bulk of the democrats and his reform program would have been difficult, if not impossible, to implement. There are clear difficulties for non-communists in Ukraine to propose any union with Russia because within the population at large any such proposal is usually equated with a lack of patriotism and the revival of the former USSR. This perception, which was understood as early as 1994 by Kuchma's advisers,[78] has steadily grown because the Belarusian-Russian union is so openly nostalgic of the Soviet era. A pro-Russian orientation could therefore only be undertaken by a Ukrainian leader *not* committed to reform. All pro-reform political parties (with the exception of only one, the MRBR) are in favor of Ukrainian as the sole state language and the only titular nation of the state. When asked to name a model for Ukraine to follow on its journey to modernity, few Ukrainian citizens who supported reform named Russia. (See table 8.3.)

C. State and Nation Building in Ukraine

Centers and Peripheries

In all post-colonial countries modernization is linked to the concept of returning to the "civilised world." The new elites desire national unity and total mobilization behind the new drive to modernity. They believe in a strong leadership supported by national consensus which, if not initially present, will gradually emerge after the state provides inducements. Elites who desire to see rapid change become impatient with parliaments that seem to be intent on blocking the drive to modernity.

Unfortunately though, most of the post-colonial states lacked the institutional and financial resources to implement their desired goals (see the chapters by Paul D'Anieri, Robert Kravchuk, and Sherman Garnett in this volume). Ukraine's strategic desire to "return to Europe," which has elite consensus, is prevented by many of its domestic policies that fall far short of the exacting standards required to "re-join Europe."

Table 8.3   Country Named as Model for Ukraine, May 1996 (%)

Country/Region	Political Model	Economic Model
USA	13	9
Germany	8	13
Sweden	4	5
Other Western European	9	15
Subtotal: West	21	33
Russia	3	4
East European	3	6
Other	1	3
No country	8	7
Don't know	51	38
Total	100	100

Source: Elehie N. Skoczylas, *Ukraine 1996: Public Opinion on Key Issues* (Washington, DC: IFES, 1997), p. 32.

Ruling elites feel compelled to provide affirmative action for their language and culture, which suffered at the hands of the former imperial power. In addition, a robust language and culture defines the state and nation as different in relation to "Others," thereby legitimizing the state and the ruling elites. A more robust language and culture also increase the strength of civil society and thereby support for the four aspects of the transformation process.

The legacies that states inherit are not so easily removed; it is therefore difficult to escape from the past completely. The traditionally popular French nation-state model is unlikely to be repeated in the post-communist world. In addition, no state (including France) ever completely assimilated its peripheries into the core nation. Most societies are heterogeneous—not homogenous. Indeed, "Every large integrated society has a dissensual as well as a consensual culture."[79] Peripheries are very differentiated with some more peripheral than others.

No state will ever be completely uniform throughout the country. There will always be differing levels of integration where the incumbents of the center, "are ordinarily more 'national' or more 'patriotic' than the population at the periphery." Therefore "A complete national culture focused exclusively on a single national center is improbable," Shils argues.[80] Pye adds:

> In no society is there a single uniform political culture, and in all polities there is a fundamental distinction between the culture of the rulers or power holders and that of the masses, whether they are merely parochial subjects or participatory subjects.[81]

Most post-communist countries, will, however attempt to undertake two projects. First, they will seek to build an overarching societal culture to act as the cement that holds together the political community. An important aspect of state building remains the evolving domination of the periphery by the center in a process of bringing the rulers and ruled closer together. The greater the degree of the interpenetration of the center and periphery, the further the country has moved away from its inherited quasi-state status and the closer the country is therefore to modernity.[82] Second, they will seek to provide polyethnic rights to members of the non-titular defined nation and group rights to national minorities settled on their territory.

Such a societal culture will be drawn from the Ukrainian nation, its culture, and language (as we have seen earlier, no state is neutral when it makes this choice). All such choices are subjective to varying degrees. This societal culture is composed of language, its image of institutions, moral beliefs, territory, group values, history, and attitudes towards symbols.

Societal culture will be fostered by the center, "to which attention and deference are accorded."[83] The institutionalization and transmission of a common culture will flow out from the center, the repository of values and beliefs that govern society and are espoused by the ruling elites, to the periphery. Central institutional and cultural elites may be in conflict with each other for ascendancy. Nevertheless, as in Ukraine, one needs the other and their interests are mutually reinforced.

Consensus flows out from the center through distribution values and institutional systems. A bounded territory imposes a common culture which is then diffused by the center and created by religion, scientists, writers, artists, journalists, and philosophers through institutions such as the Church, schools, universities, the media, libraries, museums, theaters, and other state institutions.

Who controls the center therefore plays a key role in defining the content of the emerging societal culture. If the center is defined *not* as Kyiv but as Moscow—as in the Belarusian case and that of the Ukrainian left—then this represents an attempt at thwarting the drive to modernity by freezing the political, economic, state, and ethnic legacies of the imperial era. In contrast, those elites who back the drive to modernity aspire to replace the external imperial center (Moscow) with a democratic, modern one (Brussels), which would signify that the goal of "returning to Europe" had been achieved.[84]

Towards a National Consensus

The regional differences pointed out earlier in this chapter in traditions and attitudes largely explain the debates that are still raging in Ukraine over the centrality, or otherwise, of language and the content of the national idea around which Ukrainians should be asked to unite. It also accounts for the confusion evident among some Ukrainian academics and the Kuchma leadership who, like Arel, Wilson, Miller, and Hry'niov, see civic and ethnic nationalism as two polar extremes, only one of which has to be chosen. Upon coming to power in the summer of 1994 President Kuchma initially argued that the "national idea had failed." Asked to elaborate upon this comment Kuchma explained that he had meant a national idea based upon "ethnic" (not civic) elements.

Later in Kuchma's presidency there was greater understanding that both elements (civic *and* ethnic) would play a role in the formulation of any Ukrainian national idea. This evolution of Kuchma's views on state and nation building required him to seek new allies. Hry'niov, who had always supported the contradictory building of a one hundred percent civic polity based on a Belgium-style bi-ethnic state, was therefore largely sidelined. His MRBR never became the "Party of Power," as Kuchma had promised it would become in 1994.

Instead, the People's Democratic Party of Ukraine (NDPU) and the New Ukraine bloc were targeted and co-opted as Ukraine's Party of Power. Why then was the NDPU chosen and Kuchma's 1994 election ally, the MRBR, dropped? The MRBR would always remain a small political party whose influence remained confined to certain urban centers of eastern-southern Ukraine. The MRBR had only managed to collect 3,500 members in contrast to the NDPU's 25,000 by the end of 1997.[85] The MRBR failed to get through the 4 percent threshold on the proportional party lists in the March 1998 parliamentary elections. The policies of the MRBR on state and nation building largely resemble those of the Communist Party and the (International Front-style) Civic Congress. The NDPU, on the other hand, has evolved into a far larger political party spread throughout Ukraine with a firm commitment to both civic *and* ethnic nationalism. Unlike the MRBR, which advocates two state languages and a bi-ethnic state, the NDPU and New Ukraine back only one state language (Ukrainian) and do not agree with the concept of Ukraine created by two ethnic core groups (Russians and Ukrainians).[86]

Kuchma's support for state and nation building premised upon a "political-national" basis (in contrast to an "ethnic-national" basis) has gained him the support of the bulk of the social, liberal, and the national democrats—all constituencies whose support he needs in the drive to modernity. This made him more supportive of the usefulness of the national idea in state and nation building because, as one Ukrainian author put it, "A national state is the alpha and omega of the Ukrainian idea."[87] With Kuchma's evolution away from Hry'niov a compromise between Ukraine's inherited legacies and preferences will be easier to find, particularly, as Ukraine's national democrats had always themselves preferred the French to the German model.[88]

In the June 1996 constitution the Ukrainian political nation is defined as "citizens of Ukraine of all nationalities" (that is, the French, not the German concept). Article 11 defines Ukrainians as the core ethnic titular group whom the state should promote through raising its historical consciousness, traditions, language, and culture. Article 10 defines Ukrainian as the only state language and obligates the state to ensure "the comprehensive development and functioning of the Ukrainian language in all spheres of social life throughout the entire territory of Ukraine."

Russians are therefore not considered as one of the core titular nationalities in Ukraine and, like their language, are therefore defined as another national minority. Article 10 guaranteed the "free development, use and protection of Russian, and other languages of national minorities of Ukraine . . ." Unlike in the 1989 law "On Languages," Russian is no longer singled out as the "language of international communication" because this could, and is increasingly likely, to become English. The right to use any language is guaranteed by the constitution. These views within the Ukrainian Constitution had clearly found their resonance within the central Ukrainian elite and were not only confined to western Ukrainian-based national democrats.

Kravchuk and Kuchma

Although there have undoubtedly been different approaches made by Kuchma within the realm of state and nation building there have also been important continuations of earlier strategic policies. Instead of the "national romanticism" of the Kravchuk era, Ukrainian leaders now support "the state as a call to the creation of a strong, paternalistic and, within reasonable confines, a national state."[89] Ukraine's elites no longer believe that the "national idea never worked" but accept that it, like state ideology, are central components of any nation and state. This new approach to Ukraine's national idea emphasizes, as in the Kravchuk era, symbols, borders, historiography, and other attributes of a state. Unlike in the Kravchuk era, however, it also lays important stress upon socioeconomic factors.

State and nation building is now therefore combined in a new approach that lays equal stress upon the development of civic ("European") and ethnic (Ukrainian) ideals. Civic attributes for the Ukrainian democratic state and market economy, as argued earlier, are therefore to be found only in the West (and not in the former USSR). State policies in the humanities focus upon greater individual self-reliance, improving standards of living, health, security from crime, and spirituality. Society will be consolidated on the basis of a broad range of ideas and values lying within the entire democratic spectrum found between the extreme left and right. These values and ideals would be bound together within one national idea and create the basis for a new state building ideology. Ukraine's leaders now understand the close connection between national identity and societal integration as the "key factor in the formulation of the main orientation of the advance of (Ukrainian) society."[90]

It has long been recognized that the Ukrainian language is one of the few defining characteristics of a Ukrainian national identity that is different from Russian. When Kuchma became president he learned the Ukrainian language, and he uses it on every occasion. (President Lukashenka derides the Belarusian language and prefers to use Russian.) As Kuchma himself acknowledged, "Without Ukrainian books there cannot be Ukrainian culture and our own state."[91]

The co-ordination of state and nation building policies within the humanities is divided into six parts—academia, education, culture, the formation of national consciousness, international ties, and financing of the program. Regional leaders are to be held accountable for the implementation of various programs within their *oblasts*. The number of school children taught in the Ukrainian language would be gradually expanded to the proportion of ethnic Ukrainians in each *oblast* and autonomous republic, starting at the elementary level. A new generation of textbooks in historiography and the classics that are to be published are orientated to improving knowledge of national and world culture. The revival of spirituality and national consciousness are believed to be human rights and are directly linked to whether Ukraine would become a "highly civilised state."[92]

Conclusion

All states are constructed from both civic and ethnic elements. In Ukraine the choice, contrary to what some Western scholars and Kuchma advisers initially believed,[93] was never between embracing either a completely "civic" or a fully "ethnic" state. Instead, the choice was always between building a nation-state based upon civic and Ukrainian ethnic elements *or* a bi-ethnic (Ukrainian-Russian) state mistakenly portrayed as a "civic" state. Left-wing and MRBR support for a bi-ethnic state with two state languages is actually more ethnic than the civic state they are rejecting.

The adoption of a bi-ethnic model for Ukraine would not be the panacea for Ukraine because, as Brubaker has pointed out, bi-ethnic states emphasize ethnic (not civic) elements in each of their two components. The experiences of both Canada and Belgium have shown that bi-ethnic states merely end up introducing nationalizing policies within each of their two ethnic regions. These, in turn, lead to the growth of separatism (as seen in Flanders and Quebec). If Ukraine were defined as a bi-ethnic state, in the manner of Belgium or Canada, four negative consequences would be likely to accrue. First, no united Ukrainian political community and civic nation which encompassed the entire country would be created. Second, it would be practically impossible for the Ukrainian leadership to overcome inherited legacies of regional disparities and discrimination against the Ukrainian language. Third, it would lead to the creation of "two Ukraines" where Ukrainian and Russian ethnic nationalism would grow within each component part, which would eventually stimulate separatist tendencies. Fourth, national identity and civil society would not be allowed to grow. This, in turn, would hamper the drive to modernity through the creation of a nation, state, market economy, and democracy.

Ukraine inherited two different legacies of state and nation building common to western ("State to Nation") and eastern ("Nation to State") Europe. After a transition away from the confused program promoted during the 1994 elections President Kuchma no longer gave his support for two state languages or Ukraine's definition as a bi-ethnic state. The June 1996 constitution clearly defined Ukrainians as the core titular group and Ukrainian as the only state language throughout its territory where Russians are classified as a national minority. This evolution was a reflection of the weak and amorphous identity found among Russian speakers in eastern-southern Ukraine who find it difficult to articulate their interests as a coherent, unified lobby group. Therefore the inhabitants of eastern and southern Ukraine have found it difficult to socially mobilize to articulate their interests.

The definition in the Ukrainian constitution of an inclusive political community created from all of its citizens whose societal culture will be based upon the titular Ukrainian ethnic group and one state language is perfectly in line with traditional civic states and liberal democracies. In actual fact, Ukraine's provision in its constitution of polyethnic rights for members of the non-titular ethnic groups and group rights for the Crimeans is more civic and liberal than four western states commonly referred to as both civic and liberal democracies (the United States, France, Greece, and Germany). In these four states national minorities or group rights are either not officially recognized, or citizenship is based upon ethnicity.

Notes

1. Dominique Arel, "Ukraine: The Temptation of the Nationalizing State" in Vladimir Tismaneanu (ed.), *Political Culture and Civil Society in Russia and the New States of Eurasia* (Armonk, N.Y.: M. E. Sharpe, 1995), p. 177. Andrew Wilson also argues that " . . . Kravchuk and his colleagues were sending out political messages that undermined the credibility of their commitment to a multi-ethnic civic state." By the 1994 presidential elections, therefore, "Kravchuk was widely seen as a partisan of the 'nationalising state.'" See *his Ukrainian nationalism in the 1990s: A minority faith* (Cambridge: Cambridge University Press, 1997), p. 112. Understandably perhaps, Alexei Miller, a Russian historian, agrees with the view that Ukraine is a "nationalising state." See his "Ukraina kak natsionalizirushcheesia gosudarstvo," *Pro et Contra*, vol. 2, no. 2 (Spring 1997), pp. 85–98.

2. Ghia Nodia, "Nationalism and Democracy," *Journal of Democracy,* vol. 3, no. 4 (October 1992), p. 4.

3. Jaroslav Krejci and Vitezslav Velimsky, Civic and Ethnic Nations" in John Hutchinson and Anthony D. Smith (eds.), *Ethnicity* (Oxford: Oxford University Press, 1996), pp. 212–219.

4. John Plamenatz argues that that "there is nothing illiberal about cultural nationalism as such . . . A human being becomes an individual, a rational and a moral person capable of thinking and acting for himself, in the process of acquiring the language and the culture of his people." See his "Two types of nationalism" in Eugene Kamenka (ed.), *Nationalism: The nature and evolution of an idea* (Canberra: Australian National University Press, 1974), p. 27.

5. Gurutz J. Bereciartu, *Decline of the Nation-State* (Reno/Las Vegas: University of Nevada Press, 1988), pp. 144–145.

6. Ibid., p. 144. See also Duara Prasenjit, "Historicizing National Identity, or Who Imagines What and When" in Geoff Eley and Ronald G. Suny (eds.), *Becoming National: A Reader* (New York: Oxford University Press, 1996), p. 158.

7. See David Little, "Belief, Ethnicity and Nationalism," *Nationalism and Ethnic Politics,* vol. 1, no. 2 (Summer 1995), pp. 284–301.

8. See Jan Penrose, "Essential Constructions? The 'cultural bases' of nationalist movements," *Nations and Nationalism,* vol. 1, no. 3 (November 1995), pp. 391–417.

9. Sammy Smooha and Theodor Hanf, "Conflict-Regulation in Deeply Divided Societies" in op cit., J. Hutchinson and A. D. Smith (eds.), *Ethnicity,* p. 333.

10. Rogers Brubaker, "Nationhood and the national question in the Soviet Union and post-Soviet Eurasia: An institutionalist account," *Theory and Society,* vol. 23, no. 1 (February 1994), p. 69.

11. See Tamara J. Resler, "Dilemmas of Democracy: Safeguarding Minorities in Russia, Ukraine and Lithuania," *Europe-Asia Studies,* vol. 49, no. 1 (January 1997), pp. 987–998.

12. This section draws on my "The Perils of Multiculturalism: A Theoretical and Area Studies Approach to the Former USSR," *Contemporary Political Studies,* vol. 1, 1998, pp. 108–123.

13. Will Kymlicka, *Multicultural Citizenship* (Oxford: Clarendon Press, 1996), p. 78. See also p. 111.

14. Ibid., p. 96.

15. Louise Jackson and Kataryna Wolczuk, "Defining Citizenship and Political Community in Ukraine," *The Ukrainian Review,* vol. 44, no. 2 (Summer 1997), p. 25.

16. R. Brubaker, "Nationalizing States in the Old 'New Europe'—and the New," *Ethnic and Racial Studies,* vol. 19, no. 2 (April 1996), p. 433.

17. Interviewed in *Kievskiye vedomosti,* January 30, 1998.

18. To be fair to Hry'niov this misperception is common. Michael Ignatieff and William Pfaff both mistakenly pitted liberal "civic" against illiberal "ethnic"

states. See the critical reviews of their two books by W. Kymlicka in his "Misunderstanding Nationalism," *Dissent,* Winter 1995, pp. 130–135.

19. Op cit., W. Kymlicka, *Multicultural Citizenship,* p. 24.

20. W. Kymlicka, "The Sources of Nationialism" in Robert McKim and Jeff McMahan (eds.), *The Morality of Nationalism* (New York: Oxford University Press, 1997), p. 58.

21. Michael Keating, "Stateless nation-building: Quebec, Catalonia and Scotland in the changing state system," *Nations and Nationalism,* vol. 3, part 4 (December 1997), p. 691.

22. Quoted from W. Kymlicka, "The Sources of Nationalism" in Robert McKim and Jeff McMahan (eds.), *The Morality of Nationalism,* p. 65.

23. A. D. Smith, "Civic and Ethnic Nationalism Revisited: Analysis and Ideology," *The ASEN Bulletin,* no. 12 (Autumn-Winter 1996–97), p. 10.

24. Op cit., A. Wilson, *Ukrainian Nationalism in the 1990s,* pp. 214 and 246. In contrast, studies by David Saunders concluded that Russification policies in Ukraine under the Tsarist regime served to prevent the Ukrainian *ethnie* from evolving into a nation by 1917. See his "Russia and Ukraine under Alexander II: The Valuev Edict of 1863," *The International History Review,* vol. XVII, no. 1 (February 1995), pp. 23–50 and "Russia's Ukrainian Policy (1847–1905): A Demographic Approach," *European History Quarterly,* vol. 25, no. 2 (April 1995), pp. 181–208.

25. V. Hry'niov, *Nova Ukrayina: Iakoiu ia ii Bachu* (Kyiv: Abrys, 1995), p. 61.

26. Op cit., A. D. Smith, *The ASEN Bulletin,* p. 11.

27. Ibid.

28. *The Ukrainian Weekly,* May 23, 1993.

29. This division between civic and ethnic nationalism is taken from A. D. Smith, *The Ethnic Origins of Nations* (Oxford: Basil Blackwell, 1989), pp. 134–138. Brubaker also divides this into the French (Civic) and German (ethnic) approaches to state and nation building. See R. Brubaker, "Civic and Ethnic Nations in France and Germany" in op cit., J. Hutchinson and A. D. Smith (eds.), *Ethnicity,* pp. 168–174.

30. Kuchma clearly preferred the multiethnic definition of *narod Ukraiiny.* See his inaugural address to Parliament in *Holos Ukrayiny,* July 21, 1994.

31. Michael Howard, "Ethnic Conflict and International Security," *Nations and Nationalism,* vol. 1, no. 3 (November 1995), pp. 285–295.

32. David B. Knight, "Identity and Territory: Geographical Perspectives on Nationalism and Regionalism," *Annals of the Association of American Geographers,* vol. 72, no. 4 (1982), p. 519.

33. See the discussion on this question by Heorhiy Kas'ianov, "Ukraiins'kyi Natsionalizm: Sproba Pereosmyslennia," *Viche,* no. 1, 1997, pp. 135–136 and 141.

34. *Holos Ukrayiny,* August 28, 1995.

35. Ibid.

36. Ibid.

37. *Uriadoviy Kur'er,* August 29, 1996.

38. See chapter 9 on "History, myths and symbols" in my *Ukraine: State and Nation Building* (London: Routledge, 1998), pp. 198–229.

39. See T. Kuzio, "Borders, Symbolism and Nation-State Building: Ukraine and Russia," *Geopolitics and International Boundaries,* vol. 2, no. 2 (Autumn 1997), pp. 36–56.

40. The importance of ethnicity and national identity to the strength of the reform process can be found in my "The Sultan and the Hetman: Democracy Building in a Grey Security Zone" in Jan Zielonka and Alex Pravda (eds.), *Democratic Consolidation in Eastern Europe: International and Transnational Factors* (forthcoming).

41. Karen Dawisha, *Post-Communism's Troubled Steps Toward Democracy: An Aggregate Analysis of Progress in the 27 New States* (College Park, MD: Center for the Study of Post-Communist Societies, University of Maryland, 1997).

42. Juan J. Linz and Alfred Stepan, *Problems of Democratic Transition and Consolidation: Southern Europe, South America and Post-Communist Europe* (Baltimore: John Hopkins University Press, 1996), p. 387.

43. See Jean L. Cohen, "Strategy or Identity: New Theoretical Paradigms and Contemporary Social Movements," *Social Research,* vol. 52, no. 4 (Winter 1985), pp. 663–716; and J. Craig Jenkins, "Resource Mobilization Theory and the Study of Social Movements," *Annual Review of Sociology,* vol. 9 (1983), pp. 527–553.

44. Jane I. Dawson, *Eco-Nationalism: Anti-nuclear Activism and National Identity in Russia, Lithuania and Ukraine* (Durham, N. C.: Duke University Press, 1996), p. 24.

45. Dankwart Rustow, "Transitions to Democracy: Towards a Dynamic Model," *Comparative Politics,* vol. 2, no. 3 (April 1970), pp. 350–351.

46. *The Ukrainian Weekly,* February 15, 1998.

47. *Uriadoviy Kur'er,* March 18, 1998.

48. See Edward Mansfield and Jack Snyder, "Democracy and War," *Foreign Affairs,* vol. 74, no. 3 (May-June 1995), pp. 79–97.

49. Kuchma speaking to a conference to discuss the "Concept of a Strategy for Economic Growth, 1999–2005," *Ukrainian Television–1,* March 17, 1998.

50. See E. Kamenka, "Political Nationalism—The Evolution of an Idea" in op cit., E. Kamenka (ed.), *Nationalism. The nature and evolution of an idea,* p. 16.

51. Nicos Mouzelis, "Modernity, Late Development and Civil Society" in John A. Hall (ed.), *Civil Society: Theory, History, Comparison* (Cambridge: Polity Press, 1996), p. 237.

52. Op cit., W. Kymlicka, "The Sources of Nationalism" in R. McKim and J. McMahan (eds.), *The Morality of Nationalism,* p. 57.

53. P. R. Brass, *Ethnicity and Nationalism: Theory and Comparison* (New York: Free Press, 1991), p. 25. Quoted from Jan Nederveen Pieterse, "Deconstructing/

reconstructing ethnicity," *Nations and Nationalism,* vol. 3, no. 3 (November 1997), p. 367.

54. Stephen Rapawy, *Ethnic Reidentification in Ukraine.* IPC Staff Paper No. 90 (Washington, DC: US Bureau of Census, August 1997).

55. Op cit., J. Plamenatz, "Two Types of Nationalism" in E. Kamenka (ed.), *Nationalism: The Nature and Evolution of an Idea,* pp. 34–35.

56. See chapter 7 on "National identity and civil society" in T. Kuzio, *Ukraine: State and Nation Building* (London: Routledge, 1998), pp. 144–166.

57. Jurgen Habermas, "The European Nation-State—Its Achievements and its Limits. On the Past and Future of Sovereignty and Citizenship" in Gopal Balakrishan and Benedict Anderson (eds.), *Mapping the Nation* (London: Verso, 1996), p. 282.

58. Benedict Anderson, *Imagined Communities* (London: Verso, 1991), p. 135.

59. Stuart Hall, "Ethnicity: Identity and Difference" in G. Eley and R. G. Suny (eds.), *Becoming National,* p. 341.

60. Op cit., W. Kymlicka, *Multicultural Citizenship,* pp. 18 and 89; Charles Taylor, *Sources of the Self* (Cambridge, MA: Harvard University Press, 1990); Jean L. Cohen, "Strategy or Identity: New Theoretical Paradigms and Contemporary Social Movements," *Social Research,* vol. 52, no. 4 (Winter 1985), pp. 663–716; Ernest Gellner, "The Importance of Being Modular" and Adam B. Seligman, "Animadversions upon Civil Society and Civic Virtue in the Last Decade of the Twentieth Century," in John A. Hall (ed.), *Civil Society: Theory, History, Comparison* (Cambridge: Polity Press, 1996), pp. 32–55 and 200–223.

61. Edward Shils, "Nation, nationality, nationalism and civil society," *Nations and Nationalism,* vol. 1, part 1 (March 1995), p. 116. See also his "The Virtue of Civil Society," in *Government and Opposition,* vol. 26, no. 1 (March 1991), pp. 3–20.

62. See the views of V. H. Kremen et al. in *Sotstial'no-Politychna Sytuatsiya v Ukraiini: Postup P'iaty Rokiv* (Kyiv: National Institute of Strategic Studies, National Security and Defense Council, 1996), p. 10.

63. Edward Shils, *Center and Peripheries: Essays in Macrosociology* (Chicago: University of Chicago Press, 1975), pp. 456–457.

64. Op cit., J. Krejci and V. Velinsky, "Civic and Ethnic Nations" in J. Hutchinson and A. D. Smith (eds.), *Ethnicity,* p. 209.

65. Arel had mistakenly utilized Brubaker's theory by applying it to Russian-speaking Ukrainians (not non-Ukrainians). See R. Brubaker, "National Minorities, Nationalizing States and External Homelands in the New Europe," *Daedalus,* vol. 124, no. 2 (Spring 1995), pp. 107–132.

66. See op cit., E. Shils, "Nation, nationality, nationalism and civil society," p. 93, and Stuart Hall, "Ethnicity: Identity and Difference" in op cit., G. Eley and R. G. Suny (eds.), *Becoming National,* p. 341.

67. See T. Kuzio, "National Identity in Independent Ukraine: An Identity in Transition," *Nationalism and Ethnic Politics,* vol. 2, no. 4 (Winter 1996), pp. 582–608.

68. Op cit., A. Wilson, *Ukrainian Nationalism,* pp. 77 and 154–155, and Graham Smith and Andrew Wilson, "Rethinking Russia's Post-Soviet Diaspora: The Potential for Political Mobilization in Eastern Ukraine and North-east Estonia," *Europe-Asia Studies,* vol. 49, no. 5 (July 1997), p. 855.

69. *Kievskiye vedomosti,* February 19, 1998.

70. John A. Armstrong, *Nations before Nationalism* (Chapel Hill: University of North Carolina Press, 1982), p. 5.

71. Both tables were prepared by the Kyiv-based Institute of Sociology and Democratic Initiatives in May-June 1995 and are reprinted from Irina Bekeshina, "Citizenship and National Identity in Ukraine in the Transitional Period of State Building," Paper presented at the workshop "Long-Term Historical Events and Actual Social Research Data Relating to Future Developments in Eastern Europe." A copy is in the author's possession.

72. Volodymyr Alekseyev, "Osoblyvyi poriadok dlia movy. Rosiys'koii," *Holos Ukrayiny,* February 20, 1997.

73. See J. Hutchinson, "Cultural Nationalism and Moral Regeneration" in J. Hutchinson and A. D. Smith (eds.), *Nationalism* (Oxford: Oxford University Press, 1994), pp. 122–132.

74. H. Kas'ianov, "Ob'iednaty ukraiins'ke suspil'stvo mozhe hromadians'kyi natsionalizm," *Den',* May 20, 1997.

75. See A. I. Miller, "Obrazy Ukrainy i Ukraintev v Rossiiskoi presse posle raspada SSSR," *Polis,* no. 2, 1996, pp. 130–135.

76. Leonid Kistersky and Serhiy Pirozhkov, "Ukraine: policy analysis and options" in Richard Smoke (ed.), *Perceptions of European Security: Public opinion and expert assessments in Europe's new democracies* (Manchester: Manchester University Press, 1996), p. 215. Pirozhkov was director of the National Institute of Strategic Studies, the think tank of the National Security and Defense Council.

77. *Holos Ukrayiny,* February 4, 1997. See also Hryhorii Musienko, "Khto i shcho zahrozhuye ukraiintsem?" *Vechirnyi Kyiv,* April 24, 1997.

78. Dmytro Vydrin, his former domestic adviser, and Dmytro Tabachnyk, his former head of the presidential administration, complained that attempts by "the President to clearly define Ukraine's national interests (especially geo-economic) in the post-Soviet space is classified is an attempt at the 'restoration of the empire.'" See *Ukraiina na porozi XXI stolittia: Politychnyi Aspekt* (Kyiv: 'Lybid', 1995), p. 136.

79. Op cit., E. Shils, *Centers and Peripheries,* p. 177.

80. Op cit., E. Shils, *Centers and Peripheries,* p. 63 and 84. See also pp. 4, 10, 24–25, and 80.

81. Lucian W. Pye, "Introduction: Political Culture and Political Development" in L. W. Pye and Sidney Verba (eds.), *Political Culture and Political Development* (Princeton: Princeton University Press, 1965), p. 15.

82. Charles Tilly, "Reflections on the History of European State-making," in C. Tilly (ed.), *The Formation of National States in Western Europe* (Princeton: Princeton University Press, 1975), pp. 3–83.

244 • Taras Kuzio

83. Op cit., E. Shils, *Centers and Peripheries*, p. 78.

84. See T. Kuzio, "Europe or Eurasia? National Identity, Transformation and Ukrainian Foreign Policy," forthcoming.

85. Interview with presidential administration and New Ukraine bloc head, Ievhen Kushnariov, in *Demokratychna Ukrayina*, June 7, 1996.

86. *Narodno-Demokratychna Partiya: Deklaratsiya, Prohrama, Statut* (Kyiv: n.p., 1997), pp. 16–18.

87. Iuriy Kanyhin and Zenoviy Tkachuk, *Ukrayins'ka Mriya* (Kyiv: Leksykon, 1996), p. 117.

88. See the views of Kravchuk's former minister for culture, Ivan Dziuba, who argued in favor of nation building based upon statehood—not ethnicity—in his "Ukraiina na Shliakhu Derzhavotvorenni," *Viche*, October 1992, p. 59. Iuriy Badzio, the former dissident and well-known ideologue of the Democratic Party, also preferred the French model whereby all citizens of Ukraine belong to the Ukrainian political nation. See his "Ukraiina—ne dlia Ukraiintsiv? Ukraiins'ka natsiya 'ethnichna' chy 'politychna'?" *Chas*, June 14, 1996. An editorial in the national democratic *Vechirnyi Kyiv* (July 8, 1997,) entitled "Khto yeh patriot Ukraiiny" argued that a "Ukrainian patriot" did not have to be an ethnic Ukrainian. The editor pointed to many Ukrainians who were certainly not "patriots" while he knew citizens from among national minorities (e.g., Russians, Jews, Armenians) who were *both* "Ukrainian patriots" *and* representatives of their own ethnic groups.

89. Vasyl' Tkachenko and Vasyl Holovatiuk, "Vid Natsional'noho Romantyzmu do Natsional'noii Derzhavnosti," *Demokratychna Ukrayina*, January 30, 1996.

90. Oleksiy Valevs'kyi, Vasyl' Kremen', Borys Parakhons'kyi, and S. Pirozhkov, "Humanitarna Polityka Dlia Ukraiiny: Stratehichnyi Vybir," *Viche*, August 1996, p. 25.

91. *Narodna Armiya*, April 3, 1997.

92. "Utverdzhuvaty ukraiins'ku dukhovnist'" (interview with Deputy Prime Minister I. Kuras), *Uriadoviy Kur'er*, May 14, 1996.

93. On the Kuchma era, see T. Kuzio, *Ukraine under Kuchma: Political Reform, Economic Transformation and Security Policy in Independent Ukraine* (London and New York: Macmillan-St. Martin's Press, 1997).

CHAPTER 9

Corruption in Ukraine: Between Perceptions and Realities

Roman P. Zyla

Corruption is similar to an opportunistic virus. Kept under control and monitored, a virus can be contained to the point that it exists in the test tubes of a laboratory. That same virus can and likely does exist in nature, occasionally infecting someone. If by some chance the laboratory is destroyed and the virus is set free, it is very possible that the conditions for its propagation are perfect in the immediate bio-geographical area. This however, does not in and of itself result in every being in the area becoming infected; instead, a merely normal level of natural infection would ensue. Simply put, conditions may exist that support the virus but do not lead to an epidemic.

The first part of this chapter seeks to question the alarm raised over increased corruption in eastern Europe and the former Soviet Union, as documented by a number of scholars. The aim of this chapter is to offer a different perspective on the issue and to question the general conclusions derived from "proof" of increased corruption activity, as often argued in literature about corruption. The second part of the chapter investigates the impact upon state building of heightened perceived corruption.

A. Corruption in Post-Soviet Countries

Realities versus Perceptions

Since the break-up of the USSR, there has been a growth of information concerning the subject of corruption which itself has led to increased speculation about the growing incidence of the phenomenon in the former Soviet republics. Examined herein is the legitimacy of government in light of the perceptions of increased corruption. There is little argument that people's perceptions affect the role and the position of the government and the state within society. The question then is, does the state lose its legitimacy to corrupt forces? If their higher profile is merely a perception, as this chapter argues, where does this leave the government and what does it have to undertake in order to reclaim its authority?

This chapter will not question the published figures used by writers on the subject, which indicate the presence of extensive corruption. Clearly the malevolence exists. Nor will this chapter suggest the reasons why perceptions of the population appear as they are reported in various social surveys; our task is not to bring these studies into question. The task here is to ask whether Ukrainian's perceptions of increased corruption are well founded and what possible effects these perceptions will have. Furthermore this chapter is not interested in violent criminal acts or petty theft, both of which have seen a meteoric rise in the last few years. Corruption here is viewed as something undertaken at an *official* level for the private benefit of the actor.

Corrupt forces are impossible to describe as a unified body of thought or the action of a single group, or center of power. Rather, we understand that many problems facing Ukraine are the result of decisions, actions, and power of a vague group of people known in that country as the *mafiya* or *biznismeny*.[1] This vague group, which will be referred to as "corrupt forces," plays an important role in the daily lives of the people of Ukraine, be it through the corrupt forces' ability to control the price of meat, to supply car engine parts, or to obtain a license to export goods to Poland.

Changes in the former Soviet Union over the last decade have shown an increase in focus from all corners on the matter of increasing corruption. What does this mean? Has there indeed been a rise in corruption in the former USSR, or is it simply a perceived increase? There exist no concrete studies that demonstrate a real increase in corruption,[2] which could lead one to argue that the reality of the situation is that there has been a significant increase in the *perception* of growing corruption more than in the overall actual incidence of the phenomenon.

Corruption in the Soviet Union

In the Cold War era, there is strong anecdotal and statistical evidence that corruption existed in the Soviet Union. According to historian Dmitry Shlapentokh, select periods of Soviet history are regularly identified as being characteristically corrupt, among them during the NEP and the Leonid Brezhnev eras. Individuals close to General Secretary Brezhnev, notably his son-in-law, Yuri Churbanov and Sharaf Rashidov, the party boss of Uzbekistan and a close ally of Brezhnev's, were implicated in corrupt activities. Churbanov and Rashidov were involved in a scam that involved cheating Moscow out of billions of rubles for non-existent cotton.[3] Examples such as this are not uncommon and give a good indication of how the affairs of the state were run during these periods. Despite such examples, the Soviets managed to keep a certain degree of control over the level of crime and corruption and the information pertaining to it. The extent to which they were successful in doing so is not as important as the fact that laws were enforced and a functional judiciary existed. The question of whether the USSR was able to make inroads in the fight against crime is only as relevant as the question would be about the United States or Britain. However, control of corruption was successful to the extent that the bulk of it during the Cold War period occurred within a particular strata of society: the *nomenklatura*.

The authoritarian central government confined the spread of corruption to a class of people who were effectively working for the government in the sense that they were in occupations controlled by the public sector. By doing so they could skim off the top and gain material advantages for themselves, as exemplified by countless instances similar to the Uzbekistan cotton swindle. Nevertheless, it served their interests to remain in these positions, and therefore they were able to make decisions that benefited their own situations as well as fulfilling, albeit in a limited way, the duties of their post.[4] But this was the past.

Corrupt Influences in the Post-Soviet Era

In the post-Soviet era, there has been a wholesale change in the active set of rules, norms, and behavior in the former USSR. Everything has changed and the old system is no longer in place. Two things in particular can be identified as having changed the public's view on corruption. The first has been the replacement of old institutions by new but weak institutions with little or no control over their members. At the same time, others have not been replaced at all, and a vacuum now exists where there was previously a degree of authority. In some cases old institutions persist but are simply falling apart. This scattered the *nomenklatura*, either by spreading its members into areas of operation from which they were previously absent, such as banking, finance, and entrepreneurship, or where they had operated but were hidden from view—for example, in big business, export/import ventures, and management of large structures now turned into private or semi-private enterprise. In an examination of post-Soviet elites, David Lane argues that the elites of the Soviet period have indeed not remained in the political corridors but those same individuals are now seen in the corridors of the new financial institutions and large enterprises of Russia.[5] It can be argued that the same dispersion of elites occurred in all of the former republics of the USSR.

Glasnost had the same downstream effects in Ukraine as it did in Russia. The policy of "openness" allowed greater freedom of the press and expression, providing an opportunity for people to make fortunes through newspapers and magazines. More importantly, it has allowed them to report on what they believe their readers ought to know, not just the official line as was the case in the USSR. The combined result of these changes has been that the actions of the former *nomenklatura,* now *biznismeny,* are coming into public view. In other words, as the former *nomenklatura* and the new business elite assert their power and flaunt their wealth, public awareness of their existence grows. There is however, no accurate measure by which to determine if there has been any *real* increase in corrupt activity since 1991.

The current phase of democratization in the former USSR has opened many closed doors and brought into light much information about what has been taking place for many decades. Take the example of former Acting Prime Minister Yukhim Zviahils'kiy, who was accused of taking enormous sums of money out of Ukraine in a raw materials scam. Another example is the case of another former prime minister, Pavlo Lazarenko, who allegedly built a vast personal fortune in Ukraine's oil and gas industry. Much attention has been paid to these cases in the media and in public discourse, and although the evidence has been inconclusive, public perception of corruption at high levels of leadership has also been heightened.

In 1991, V'iacheslav Chornovil was said to have purchased a two-story building in L'viv for the equivalent of $200. Much was made about the means by which the building was made available to Chornovil. The local press even followed the rumors; however, in the end no action was taken to investigate claims that anything illegal had occurred. Nevertheless, among L'viv residents there was a growing perception that those in power had somehow become wealthy and were able to use that wealth, when only months before it was perceived as unlikely to have been possible. At the national level, former Prime Minister Vitold Fokin was dismissed in September 1991 due to his allegedly improper behavior. One story in Kyiv was that he had been bribed for a meager sum. It was certainly not the first time that a high-ranking official in Ukraine or in the USSR had been offered a bribe.

Indeed, despite the high profile of these individuals and the sensation caused by the allegations, little in these examples suggests an actual increase in corrupt activity.

Inconclusive Evidence

The process of *glasnost*, in the spirit of democratization and satisfying the people's "right to know," resulted in a perception of increased crime and corruption never before experienced in the former Soviet Union. Is it a fact, however, that the level of corruption has increased dramatically in the former USSR? Information and awareness about corruption has increased, but this does not necessarily indicate a real increase in its incidence. In spite of this, many conclude that in fact it has.

These allegations have been used to justify the use of inconclusive evidence supported by a host of reasons explaining the difficulties of obtaining hard data on corrupt activity, citing lack of official co-operation, diplomatic complexities, and social science convention. Such difficulties have led other scholars to turn to different rationales to support conclusions of increased corruption. Many argue that in fact there are factors that have led to conditions that make corruption easier and therefore it is likely that corruption has increased. Three factors have been cited often and are worth exploring.

The first is the plodding modification of institutional procedure. Discussion of this has largely focused on the legal institutions and the development of post-Soviet law. Legal foundations and organizations actively help legislators write new acts that are enacted to replace or modify old Soviet laws. An example of this is the justice system. The Soviet criminal code, for example, has been maintained as the Verkhovna Rada ratifies changes toward creating a domestic criminal code. As well, the formal normative laws determining official behavior necessary to reflect a new economic and political system are only now replacing the old Soviet guidelines.

There are much slower steps being taken, however, to reform the rest of the justice system. In its first five years, Ukraine's parliament passed many laws, each going through a seemingly tortuous process of ratification despite a widely held view that these laws were urgently needed. Among these were indispensable budgetary laws and a new Ukrainian document in June 1996. Despite these changes in the legal foundation, the system of enforcing the laws has not kept pace with change. The process of taking cases through the system is marked by constant delays. Contracts are poorly understood and their application is rarely dependable. Part of the trouble lies in personnel being underpaid. For example, judges in Ukraine's court system are paid the equivalent of $100 per month.[6] However, slow institutional change can also be attributed to a generally poor understanding of what is expected from institutions, not only by the population at large but by the employees within the institutions themselves.

Most major institutions have been tied up in the slow process of transition, which will take time to complete. Local and regional administrations, as well as professional groupings including unions and overseeing agencies, are all undergoing major changes within their structures. Also included in the category of reforming institutions are financial and banking structures. For a variety of reasons, the state has been unable to regulate a multitude of banks and other financial institutions. Given the reputation of Soviet-era banks, there is little wonder that citizens seek to deposit their money in a bank as far as possible from the state-run part of the sector. The sparse regulation of these institutions permits them to operate in a vacuum of responsibility. According to one analyst, the reason for this has been continued interference from government and parliament. This has led to the establishment of unreliable banks that threaten not only the institutional stability of the financial sector but of the government, which is largely seen as responsible for causing this problem.[7] This can only lead people to conclude that they are living in a society without the framework necessary to protect them and their *mayino* (property); subsequently, their perceptions of corruption are heightened.

The second reason for the perception of increased corruption is attributable to the breakdown of enforcement systems and the lack of resources to rebuild them in short order. One need not look much further than the local police to understand that there has been a complete collapse of all aspects of these agencies. William Miller's findings indicate that the police forces are performing their functions worse than they had previously. Further, the level of trust in police services is low in Ukraine and indeed all over the former USSR.[8] Since 1993, police in Kyiv have been seen cruising the city in expensive American 4x4 vehicles, BMWs, and Mercedes-Benzes—cars that few of them would be able to afford on police salaries even in the West. The explanation from several sources was that the police were able to supplement their meager incomes by exacting tolls from traffic violators whose offenses the police were willing to ignore in exchange for bribes.[9] In cases in which the violation meant the suspension of a drivers license, such as driving while under the influence of alcohol, the bribe could be quite high.

In Novoyavoriv, L'viv *oblast,* teenagers were asked what kind of jobs they would like to have when they finished school; even the youngest children, boys and girls, often replied "*militsioner.*" When asked why, one respondent said that families with a father who worked for the police had "everything."[10] Children who want to be police officers for the wrong reasons do not give a good impression of the state of law enforcement. They are unconsciously aware of the fiscal benefits a powerful position may bring.

To elaborate upon the poor state of law enforcement, Richard Rose offers a barometer of trust that reveals that in a country such as Ukraine, the level of trust in the police is low and the level of distrust and skepticism about the institution is very high.[11] Supporting Rose's survey, a similar inquiry was conducted in conjunction with Ukraine's short-lived "Clean Hands" anti-corruption campaign, which surveyed citizens' views on the quality of various public services. Local police along with road police ranked well below average, in fact below the perennial "baddie," the tax inspector.[12] To add to the high level of dissatisfaction in the police force, the resources to train officers and enforce the law are declining primarily due to the lack of public funds and the poor finances of most ministerial administrations and their affiliate offices in the regions.[13] The enforcement agencies are also affected by the pillaging of quality candidates by private security firms. Further, the slow pace of legal reform has contributed to an environment in which corruption thrives. Changes in the legal transition are slow and complex, making the enforcement of law difficult not only for the enforcement agencies but also for the citizenry, which is baffled by constant changes and unequal treatment.

The third factor is the free-for-all market potential led primarily by the slow pace of legal reform, the lack of enforcement, and the novelty of a free market. This has led to a situation in which people try any means to make money, most through legal, but some through illegal channels. The freedom to seek out methods of making a living is new to people who have for the last seven decades been told what they can and cannot do. This is even more so in countries where free enterprise has always been in the hands of the "privileged few," not open to the masses. New entrepreneurs really are a novelty in a region whose last entrepreneurial group was dominated by small landowners selling their wares at a local market. The new *biznisman* has emerged, but not in the Western understanding of "entrepreneur." It may be argued that the neo-capitalist is a purer entrepreneur than his counterpart in the West.

The style of business of these new "free-for-all marketeers" has many in the former USSR wondering about capitalism and its merits, as it has proven to have serious flaws that point to the potential for high levels of corruption. Many companies operate outside the "formal" economy and many operations are set up within state enterprises, often taking advantage of the production capacity of the state-run firm. There are also many instances of illegal or semi-legal transfers of funds from the state enterprise to the private ones owned by managers and directors of the state firm. This describes one of many possible arrangements of the new entrepreneurs. However, details of such activities are difficult to come by, and statistics are virtually unknown and often left to guesswork.[14] These examples, however, do not indicate whether such activity is newly developed since independence. These forms of activity may simply be a method of business established under Soviet times that has now come to the forefront of business news, although it is not itself an indication of increased activity.

New Liberties Mask Reality

Each of the above three factors may lead to increased corruption, but they do not conclusively determine an increase in corrupt activity since the fall of the Soviet Union. What has been created is an environment in which corruption might grow, and therefore it is suggested that a strong possibility of increased corruption exists. These three elements have precipitated the perceptions of increased corruption levels. What is being manifested now in the former Soviet Union is not a new phenomenon.[15] The difference appears to be that despite the lack of institutional reform, the effective breakdown of law enforcement and legal reform, and unfettered market behavior noted by many observers, there is little new information concerning the behavior of the officials perpetuating these "crimes." What has changed, however, is the amount of media attention and the resulting outcry over certain officials and their actions.

It is a universal of political change, demonstrated by history, that in regions where recent political change has taken place, people who have been denied certain freedoms under an authoritarian regime seek to exercise their rights once the authoritarian regime is ousted. In China, as the leadership relaxes its grip on business and production matters, pockets of entrepreneurs have emerged in cities such as Shanghai, for example, and have begun to use their near-freedom to build enormous economic power. In Eastern Europe, after the fall of communism a sense of freedom led people to express their democratic rights and liberties, and individuals ventured into spheres they could only have dreamed about months prior to the collapse. An example of this is the explosion of the pornography industry within the former Eastern Bloc countries immediately after the collapse of communist regimes. Pornography, illegal in Soviet times, became symbolic of what was possible in the new era of "openness and freedom," and it tested the limits of public morality in the immediate post-communist period. Over a short period of time the legal and enforcement structures caught up to the human spirit and "bound" the pornographers to strict rules and guidelines. This situation is analogous to that in the markets of Central Europe and the former Soviet Union. So-called savage capitalism has led people to search for innovative and quick ways of making money. Some of them will cheat, lie, and even steal in order to accomplish this goal. This behavior is natural in people who are unfettered by laws, disinterested in morals, and, more importantly, not yet constrained by a social contract.

The social contract, which existed under Soviet times and was to a great extent enforced rather than accepted, disappeared when the old state collapsed. There has been no hurry to replace the old contract with a new one. This may be partly because the memory of the old system is still too recent, and the psychology of the society demands distance from the past. Another reason might be simply that the new order allows individuals an unfettered choice to seek what they desire. It is a matter of time before the sense of community and necessity for a contract returns to the populations of the former USSR.

It is not surprising that reports show that fledgling democracies exhibit an increasingly high level of corruption. This is a perception that is drawn from the increased number of newspaper reports, political rhetoric (in many cases to be dismissed as alarmist), and word-of-mouth relating of perceived corruption. The truth remains that social science and the popular press have been unable to track accurately and numerically an actual increase of corruption and instead have based their interpretation of the situation in the former Soviet Union through generally unreliable information. It is *not* inconceivable that the levels of corruption are high. Nor is it inconceivable that the level of corruption is no higher now than it was seven or twenty years ago; after all, according to studies of crime in the Soviet era and statistics from the last decade, there has been a significant increase in petty crime. What is certain, however, is that the conditions of society have changed as have the conditions in which corruption is being observed.

The examination of newspaper reports and the words of desperate politicians and officials is not sufficient to determine that corruption has in fact increased. Increased reporting and rhetoric mean that there is more attention focused on the problem; this attention is that of people and organizations such as newspapers, anxious to pursue stories with the same degree of zeal as those who seek money in the newly created market. It must be kept in mind that Soviet news gatherers were also restricted as to what they could and could not report, not to mention the accuracy of what was allowed to be reported under the old regime. Now editors are presented with an opportunity to print newspapers with sensational stories to sell to the public, strengthening perceptions of increased corruption. The sensational stories within Ukraine have been matched in the Western media, which have contributed to an "explosion of public information and media" bringing a giant spotlight to the issue of corruption.[16] At the same time, in Ukraine there has been a burgeoning of newspaper organizations directly affiliated with individual politicians and political organizations, all trying to boost their patron while denigrating the others.

One Ukrainian media observer went so far as to suggest that in fact these media organizations are not owned by political structures but are prepared to sell out to the highest bidder. The example he gave was of *Kievski Vedomosti,* which in the space of a week in January 1998 changed from being a supporter of the popular movement, *Rukh,* to disparage its leader, thereby showing its allegiance to a new patron.[17] *Pravda Ukrainy* was shut down in February 1998 after it reported on corruption within the Kuchma administration. In another example, the case of Zviahils'kiy was reported in several newspapers, notably in papers associated with the government. Some have suggested that this was part of a larger ploy to get rid of Zviahils'kiy. The same can be said of Lazarenko's case. Whether there is any substance to the possible newspaper ploys and the implications of "yellow journalism," there is nevertheless a message sent out to the people who read the newspapers.

The struggle to discern what is fact and what is merely perception does not diminish the reality that these societies have been corrupt for a long time and continue to be so. There is a great deal of deviant behavior, at one time tolerated by the communists while at other times seen as anti-social, anti-establishment behavior. The fact that the rise in the perception of and outcry over corruption may be impulsive nevertheless highlights a problem. It indicates that transition is a complicated process and that these societies are in the middle of a period of great change. New-found freedoms in the marketplace and in other forms of expression may well lead to an understanding of a new social contract.

Once the novelty of democracy and market freedom subsides and the laws and morals of the society catch up to the transformation, the perception of corruption is bound to reach a level like that of other nations with mature economies and established rules and institutions. This demands that a period of time pass for the development of a good citizenry, a model business tradition, and a general will to submit to a new social contract. So often heard throughout the early 1990s was the plea, "We want only to live as you do in the West." What is worrisome, however, is the effect that the current perception of corruption will have on the development of fledgling democracies.

B. Corruption, Democratization, and the Rule of Law

Corruption and State Building

An opportunistic virus may find an environment in which to thrive; that in itself is a troubling possibility. No less worrisome, however, is the perception that a virus is being newly propagated, particularly if in reality it had always existed but had gone unrecognized or was simply ignored. The problem with such a situation is that people's reaction to this virus has led to a change in the environment that has produced serious consequences.

It is assumed here that corruption has not increased in Ukraine over the last several years but that people have simply become aware of existing corruption in their government. In some respects, the consequences of the perception of increased corruption are not different from those of an actual increase, and they can be disastrous for Ukraine. The government's ability to transform the economy and to legitimize itself before the population will suffer as perception of growing official corruption solidifies in people's minds. The government therefore finds itself in an inextricable crisis, which puts it and civil society at risk. That risk is also corruption's greatest threat: it has the potential to render the government irrelevant to the people by alienating them from official economic activity. The ultimate result of this can be the collapse of government legitimacy and the threat of social and political upheaval.

The early disconnection from government is already manifested politically, economically, and socially. It is evident in people's disregarding government services, declining to vote, losing confidence in government actions and institutions, and refusing to participate in the transformation of government through processes such as lobbying. The disconnection from government has economic effects, as seen in the gradual withdrawal from a social welfare support system unable to meet the public's needs. The government is unable to pay wages, the social safety net becomes unreliable, and people seek non-government sources of support. In Ukraine the symptoms have begun to appear and the effects are already evident.

In a country with a government that enjoys a high level of legitimacy, it is expected that the level of political participation be relative to the strength of democratic institutions in that state. In other words, if the democratic tradition is strong, as it is, for example, in the United States, voter turnout may in fact be low. It is the tradition of democratic values that helps the government maintain legitimacy. In countries in which the tradition of democracy is not as well developed, the level of participation in elections is relatively high. In Hungary, since the collapse of the communist regime, the level of voter participation in elections has remained high, giving credence to increasing popular support for the institution of government and a growing level of democratization within Hungary.

In Ukraine the situation is somewhat different, leading to speculation that there is growing dissatisfaction with government and indeed most official institutions. Voter turnout since the independence referendum has fallen steadily. In 1991 there was widespread interest and high participation in elections. In the 1994 presidential and Verkhovna Rada elections, participation in some areas was so low that seats in the legislature were contested several times before enough voters turned out to meet the minimum numbers of votes required. Since the 1994 elections, the election law has changed, allowing for fewer people to turn out in order for an election to be considered valid. Lowering the number of people needed to validate a vote actually highlights the fact that fewer people are interested in voting in national elections. In the March 1998 elections, 69 percent of voters turned out. Notably low were figures for younger voters, who display growing dissatisfaction with government and politics.

In other words, since 1991, voter participation has decreased. Some would argue that this decrease is a normal process in all democracies—a level of voter participation is determined, and ensuing elections show that level to remain steady. In Ukraine, symptoms of low government support could set the scene for a continued decline in voter turnout. For a country with a short history of democracy, such a decline would be detrimental. The picture of low support for government in Ukraine is illustrated in several popular opinion surveys on integrity and confidence in government structures.

In countries that are seen to have high government legitimacy, there are people in government who are rated as unpopular. Despite its lack of mass appeal, the government as a whole may nevertheless retain its popularity and the institutions of government may continue to enjoy wide support. In Ukraine the government faces a major lack of support. This is evident in the evaluation of government performance by the intended beneficiaries of services. A 1997 survey by the Ministry of Justice of Ukraine and the World Bank Economic Development Institute showed that among a selection of government agencies, the Verkhovna Rada, along with the Cabinet of Ministers, ranked negatively in terms of service provision. None of the selected agencies was rated positively and only one, the State Savings Bank, was rated above average.[18] In the same survey, Ukrainians were asked to rate the integrity of various government agencies. The Verkhovna Rada and the Cabinet of Ministers tied for last place behind the local police and road traffic police (DAI).[19] Once again, none of the government agencies rated positively, and few were ranked even near "normal" on the scale.

In another survey, personalities in Ukrainian and world politics were rated on a positive/negative image scale. The highest ranked Ukrainian personality was the governor of the national bank, Viktor Yushchenko. He was the only Ukrainian personality who rated above the mean, and this only barely. All other Ukrainian personalities were viewed negatively. The Verkhovna Rada and the Cabinet of Ministers were also included in the survey, both ranking very low on the scale. The analysis of the survey concluded that 47 percent of Ukrainians blamed the government for the poor economic conditions. "Most governmental institutions and officials are thought of in negative terms. Ukrainians appear not to trust their political leaders . . . Four in ten Ukrainians (42 percent) say they place 'very little trust' and another 39 percent say they place 'almost no trust' in their national governmental leaders and politicians."[20] Such figures give a strong impression of discontent in government. Much of this is directly related to the perception that government officials and politicians are corrupt.

Another indication of growing disconnection between government and the population is the lack of lobby groups. Lobbying is a strong method of voicing opinion and gaining political clout for various citizen, organizational, and corporate interests. Strong lobby competition suggests that the government is prepared to listen to various interest groups, thus showing a degree of openness. If such efforts have been seen to be ineffective, it would be reasonable for them to be suspended. Little evidence of growing lobby efforts may also show a degree of frustration in government by a variety of groups. The frustration in dealing with the government is evident in the large number of political parties that were registered in the 1998 Verkhovna Rada elections. Only 8 of the 30 parties had enough support to meet the required 4 percent threshold of popular support to be able to sit in parliament. The majority of the parties were identified as single-issue groups more commonly associated with lobbies rather than broad-interest, mainstream parties.[21]

It is quite possible that these political groupings have lost faith in the governmental process and have chosen to enter the contest to become the government in an effort to pursue their respective causes. The issues represented by these smaller parties could easily be pursued in the normal workings of government and a structure for hearing pressure groups. Evidently such a process does not exist or does not work effectively, leading interest groups to seek political power in the legislature instead. In Ukraine, foreign organizations and individuals are able to mount lobbies, possibly with some success. Even foreign governments helped establish an international advisory council to the Verkhovna Rada in 1992 in an effort to aid Kyiv's lawmakers with the transition process and at the same time providing Western countries with a means of having their interests heard.[22] Without strong evidence of increased lobbying by Ukrainian organizations, it appears that the effectiveness of such a method is low, suggesting little or no interest in approaching and attempting to sway the government. This low interest is largely due to a widespread view that government officials are corrupt and that any attempt to lobby them will be met with resistance because they are out to serve their own needs first and foremost.

There are no available studies of the number of people accessing public services in Ukraine. Greater access to government service and a general increase in the effort of government to make its services more accessible are signs of a strong government with a broad support. In Ukraine, certain government agencies have seen an increase in client numbers. The agencies responsible for business registration or passport issuance, for example, have more people seeking their services. Nevertheless, those who offer services that have seen an increase in client numbers lament that usage figures often do not meet their expectations. Ukraine's economic ministers have often complained that the increase of new businesses registered is not as high as it should be when compared, for example, to the number in Poland.[23] In other sectors there have been declines in access to services. Thus, overall the number of people accessing a more "open" and "democratic" government has not risen to expectations; in many areas, it has declined.

It can be argued that a perception of increasing corruption leads many to suspect that the costs of accessing bureaucracy are high and the process bewildering. This, along with the falling fortunes of many Ukrainians, implies that there is a growing number of people who do without certain government services. The slow uptake on government services or the decline of usage damages the economy, in part by perpetuating the perception of increased corruption: due to less demand for services, government workers seek higher rents from the reduced number of people. This, in turn, increases pressure on those at the bottom of the economic scale who seek government services, eventually leading to their inability to pay and consequently benefit.

Diverging Interests: Power and the People

Politically there are signs that the Ukrainian government is having difficulty maintaining the people's confidence. Decrease in voter interest is a problem in many advanced democracies; however, in fledgling nations one would expect some level of increased enthusiasm at being able to change government at every election. When government is seen as corrupt, people lose interest because they believe their voice has little effect on those in power. Hence surveys show that there is less and less confidence in the government, as well as less desire to participate in the process of government through lobbying efforts and generally accessing services provided by Kyiv. Seven years of independence have not seen political interest increase; rather, interest has fallen, the old institutions within the government have remained, and public mistrust of those institutions is growing. As a result voter apathy is setting in. This indicates a trend toward government disconnection from the society.

Government disconnection through low popular support resulting from perceptions of increased corrupt activity is reflected economically as well. In Ukraine, this has reached dramatic proportions. Critically, people and business are withdrawing from the official economy as well as from government services and agencies. The result of this disconnection from the official economy is evident in figures showing sizable proportions of economic activity in the shadows. Foreign governments, companies, and organizations are also swayed by the perceptions of increased corruption, and as a result they shy away from investing in Ukraine.[24] Domestic investors also shy away. Money available for investment within the Ukrainian economy often leaves the country creating a hemorrhage of badly needed capital. The threat from all of this is a decrease in revenue, which, if allowed to decrease far enough, can lead to a cash crisis. This in turn leads to a legitimacy crisis for the government, the beginnings of which are already evident.

The growing involvement of citizens in the underground economy is not necessarily an indication of increased corruption; it is arguable that it is a sign of desperate measures being taken in a context of heightened entrepreneurial interest. It is conservatively estimated that in Soviet times the black market made up from 10 to 20 percent of GDP in Ukraine. Corruption does play a role in the recent increase in shadow activity because as more people try to access the official structures, they are faced with corrupt practices. Instead of pursuing the official route, new entrepreneurs have simply decided to avoid the corruption they perceive and continue their economic endeavors outside official channels. They are simply escaping the corruption and incompetence of the state.

The shadow economy is valued at somewhere between 40 to 60 percent of GDP according to various figures and estimates. In 1989, the World Bank estimated Ukraine's unofficial economy as having a 15 percent share of GDP. In 1994, that figure jumped to 45 percent. Reports from several sources agree that the shadow economy is large and that its rate of increase has largely matched the rate of decline in the official economy.[25] In several Western newspapers, it was reported that shadow economy figures in 1997 were as high as 60 percent.[26] These estimates are justified by the significant collapse of the official economy and the tripling of the absolute size of the unofficial economy.[27] Based on the higher estimates and 1996 GDP figures, the shadow economy stands at approximately $29 billion. The past eight years have shown a steady increase of shadow economic activity, and there is little to suggest that a plateau or decrease of such activity is likely in the near future.

Corrupt Officials

Withdrawal from the official economy is a sign of growing dissatisfaction with the government and the ongoing attempts at reform. This is often exacerbated by the direct relations that enterprises have with government officials in the form of time spent with officials and the cost of government services. Further, the burgeoning inter-enterprise arrears affect the business community as well as individuals across Ukraine. Individuals also are affected by the wage arrears crisis that continues to plague the country.

The amount of working time managers spend with government officials in Ukraine is said to amount to 30 percent. Much of that time is spent "securing" licenses and permits and "negotiating" taxes and penalties, while such activity may take up only 15 percent of a manager's time in Lithuania and as little as 8 percent in El Salvador.[28] Given so much time spent with officials, it is difficult to understand how Ukrainian managers are able to run their firms. According to one small businessman in Kyiv, "there are times in the year that I spend two, sometimes three out of five days a week in a government office for something."[29] The time spent with officials inevitably results in fees being "negotiated" for a variety of documents and services ranging from licenses to corporate registration and tax inspection.

Apart from the amount of time spent with officials, there is a considerable amount of money exchanged between taxpayers and officials. Every service and document has an official process associated with it. At each stage of the process there can be a delay and, inevitably, a payment. The power to advance within the process rests with the bureaucrat. There are occasions during which it is not the individual bureaucrat who determines the toll but an entire department demanding it as a matter of policy. Nevertheless, the beneficiary is either an individual or a small group of people and *not* the state.

People may choose not to make the payment. By doing so, they choose not to participate in the official economy. Without official registration, documentation, and sanction, they continue their enterprise within the shadow economy. There are, however, those who desire to remain officially legitimate and who do pay the "unofficial" prices for services and documents. Prices charged for various services and documents are not uncommon in other countries and are often justified to cover costs of printing or administration. In Ukraine, however, the prices set by the bureaucrats are rarely consistent with the "officially" determined price, nor are they part of any cost recuperation scheme. There are often charges for services or documents that are supposed to be provided by the government without cost or at a nominal amount. Many officials will demand whatever they feel they can extract from clients, basing their demand on the necessity of the service or document to the client and the type of business making the request.

The price for carrying out essential procedures is high—higher still if the process is time consuming. Provision of less critical services or documents may demand a lower fee. In like manner, higher prices are charged to companies with high profile or with well-advertised deals being brokered. Motorola, a well-known name in the telecommunications sector, was one company that pulled out of Ukraine in part due to exorbitant rents being charged by bureaucrats.

The amount of time and energy needed to acquire documents and services has given local entrepreneurs reason to hide their business activities from government agencies. Whatever the reasons for moving to the shadow economy, the rationale behind the decisions is based primarily on the experiences of the individual or what is heard in the media. There is a generally perceived view that there is more corruption now than during the Soviet era. Surviving in such an environment is becoming increasingly more difficult. The outcome, however, is the same: the government is seen as unable to prevent movement away from the official economy.

Another indication of a confidence crisis is the low foreign investment rate. Over the last five years there has also been a steady decline in the total financial help provided by international institutions to Ukraine. The reason is that financial aid by nature is supposed to be temporary and to be used to overcome a current crisis. The goal of such assistance is to implement macroeconomic stabilization and to create favorable conditions for economic reforms, which in turn are expected to draw investment. In Ukraine's case, this did not

Table 9.1 Unofficial Payments by Enterprises for Official Permits, Services, and "Favors"

License Type—Service—"Favor"	Average Fee
Enterprise registration	$176
Each visit by fire/health inspector	$42
Tax inspector (each regular visit)	$87
Phone line installation	$894
Lease in state space (square meters/month)	$7
Export license/registration	$123
Import license/registration	$278
Border crossing (lump sum)	$211
Border crossing (percent of value)	3 percent

Source: "Unofficial" Payments by Enterprises for Official Permits, Etc., in Ukraine During the Year 1996. Cited from Daniel Kaufmann, "Corruption: Myths, Biases and Realities: Empirical Evidence and Implications for Strategy" (Washington, D.C.: The World Bank, 1998), p. 23.

happen. Among the reasons is the high level of capital transfer out of Ukraine, which by 1995 had already reached more than $12 billion.[30] This movement of huge sums of money out of an economy in crisis has given observers a reason to draw conclusions that corruption in Ukraine may be widespread.

Kyiv has been seen as unable to control the flow of money and as unable to create a favorable environment for investment in the country itself. In June 1997, Ukraine had attracted cumulative foreign direct investment of only $1.7 billion, much of it into joint ventures. In 1996, just $459 million in foreign direct investment or the equivalent of $10 per person was brought into the country.[31] This inability to draw more resources to the country creates an image of ineffective government and to a great extent strengthens the perception of increasing corruption as well. This is not only politically dangerous; it also exacerbates internal problems such as the wage crisis, which further alienates the population.

Many industries and enterprises in Ukraine remain under the jurisdiction of the central government. The slow pace of privatization is partly responsible for this. Some institutions cannot or will not be privatized and without government support would be unable to survive. Many of those that are privatized, however, still receive transfer payments from the government and depend on them. Thus the government is directly or indirectly responsible for paying the wages of millions of Ukrainian workers. August 1997 figures show that levels of inter-enterprise arrears were at 93 billion *hryvni*.[32] Wage arrears on the government budget side show an increase to 4.7 billion *hryvni* in 1997, up from 3.7 the previous year.[33]

The financial difficulties already faced by the country and the growing difficulty in collecting taxes are the prime reasons making it difficult for the government to pay workers. Although there are some regions in Ukraine that are able to fill pay packets for workers in the region, for most of the country it is a severe problem.[34] Reports of factories paying their workers in often obsolete and useless products rather than money have been plentiful. An often-repeated example is of workers in one factory who were paid in brassieres. In worse cases, workers are not paid at all and are left for months without any income. In November 1997, state sugar production facilities in Poltava had not paid their workers wages since the previous beet harvest. At harvest time in 1997, wages were paid in sacks of raw sugar that people had to sell themselves. Workers lined highways in the region trying to hock their sugar to passing travelers. Wage arrears of seven months involved nuclear power-station workers in the period from 1993 to 1994.[35] Incidents such as these compound the erosion of popular confidence in government, not to mention the potentially dangerous working and living conditions created in the case of the nuclear industry workers. Such examples are replicated across the country and in almost every industry.

The wage payments crisis directly affects the population's attitude toward the government. When wages are not forthcoming, people unable to depend on the government seek other ways of making ends meet. The wage payments crisis is only one problem that leads to the disconnection between people and state. The government needs to provide a range of services and functions; without them, disconnection is furthered. These services and functions are many. The nonprovision of each can be attributed to the larger problem of people moving away from the official economy and leaving the government without a source of revenue.

Conclusion

During the period of transition from socialism to a market-driven democracy, good government and a working market economy can be created only if there is strong public support of the institutions and workings of the state. In Ukraine, the period of transition has been characterized by perceived corruption and poor economic performance. While the performance of the economy is being tracked, the level of corruption is not. Since the break-up of the USSR, many have claimed that there has been a dramatic increase in corruption, which has led to serious political and economic problems. While it is true that economic and political difficulties have increased, there has not been a *proven* dramatic increase in corruption. It is possible that the level of corrupt activity had simply been ignored until recently. Evidence has shown little definitive proof that corruption has increased. Ukrainians may simply have become more aware of the corruption that surrounds them.

The increased *perception* of increased corruption in many ways is responsible for collapsing confidence in the government. Thus, consideration of the consequences of the perception of increased corruption becomes important. The symptoms that lead to low confidence or disconnection include: low voter turnout, the political alienation of the population, low support for politicians, and disconnection from government institutions. Economically the consequences are difficult to measure; however, perceptions of high corruption are proven to harm investment, leading to an increase in participation in the shadow economy and high levels of capital flight. These in turn all lead to a decrease in available revenue for the government. With the inability to provide services and functions for the population, the legitimacy of the government is eroded. This has placed Ukraine into a vicious circle in which increased problems such as inter-enterprise debt and wage arrears lead more people into the shadow economy, taking with them a tax revenue source for the government leading to greater wage arrears. Corruption, or the perception of corruption, has played a major role in setting this circle in motion. Confidence in the Ukrainian government must be returned in order for the circle to be broken.

Notes

1. *Biznismeny* is the term often used by locals to describe organized crime as well as unseen forces, to which they attribute a variety of malfeasance from petty crime and murder to sophisticated forms of money laundering and fraud.

2. Among the leading studies in this area, Transparency International provides a perception index—that gives an indication of business perceptions of corruption but no gauge of incidence. Daniel Kaufman of the World Bank also provides invaluable information about effects of corruption on foreign business but has difficulty providing an overall picture of the increase of corruption.

3. Louis Allen, Kate Deveraux et al., *Political Scandals and Causes Célèbres Since 1945* (Harlow: Longman, n.d.), pp. 198–200. The Soviet Union overextended the usage of already poor soil in Central Asia, making it impossible to fill quotas set by ministries. The Uzbekistani leadership continued to report high yields of cotton while bureaucrats in Moscow received a share in the profits for keeping quiet.

4. For a detailed examination of the *nomenklatura* and their activities see Michael Voslensky, *Nomenklatura: Anatomy of a Ruling Class* (London: Bodely Head,

1984); and Arkady Vaksberg, *The Soviet Mafia* (London: Weidenfeld and Nicholson, 1991).

5. Dr. David Lane, seminar, London School of Economics, December 2, 1997.

6. Geoffrey York, "Ukrainian officials accused of derailing clean-up," *The Globe and Mail*, November 29, 1997.

7. Yuri Nechayev, "Ukraine: Banks Must Finance Investment," available online at: <http://www.cipe.org/e15/UKRAIN.HTML>.

8. See William L. Miller, Tatyana Koshechkina, and Grodeland Ase, "How Citizens Cope with Postcommunist Officials: Evidence from Focus Group Discussions in Ukraine and the Czech Republic," *Political Studies*, vol. 45, no. 3 (Special Issue, 1997), pp. 597–625.

9. These observations, from several sources, were noted by the author during a stay in Kyiv in 1993.

10. Interviews with children in Novoyavoriv, L'viv *oblast*, Ukraine, 1993. Among the items that made up "everything" were a car, several video cameras, several video players, televisions, large refrigerators, new clothes, and *Amerykanski krosovky* (American running shoes).

11. Richard Rose and William Miller, "Trust, Distrust and Skepticism about Institutions of Civil Society," *Studies in Public Policy* (Glasgow: Centre for the Study of Public Policy, 1995), pp. 9, 14.

12. *Ukraine National Integrity Survey: Citizen's Experiences of Public Service Quality, Integrity, and Corruption* (Government of Ukraine [Ministry of Justice], World Bank [Economic Development Institute], 1997), p. 7.

13. Ukraine's militia and road police fall under the jurisdiction of the Ministry of the Interior and its budget. The ministry has regional offices in major centers across the country that function as local police but under the authority of the Minister of the Interior. Some large cities have special police forces although their powers are limited.

14. Allan Gibb, "Entrepreneurship in Transition Economies: Back to the Future," available online at: <http://www.cpie.org/e17/gibb3_95.html>.

15. For a detailed historical treatment of the subject, see op cit., A. Vaksberg, *The Soviet Mafia*. See also Leslie Holmes, *The End of Communist Power* (Cambridge: Polity Press, 1993).

16. John Stackhouse, "Aid Donors vow war on graft," *The Globe and Mail*, September 20, 1997.

17. Vadim Dolganov, First Vice-President, National Television Company of Ukraine, responding to Alexei Solohoubenko of the BBC Ukrainian Service, who said that Ukraine's media services were owned by political parties. British East-West Centre, London, January 28, 1998.

18. Op. cit., *Ukraine National Integrity Survey*, p. 7.

19. DAI, or traffic police, differ from local or national police in that they are responsible solely for road traffic throughout Ukraine.

20. Petter Langseth and Geoff Dubrow (eds.), *Integrity Systems: Awareness Raising and Planning Workshops 1 & 2* (Kyiv: The Government of Ukraine, The Economic Development Institute of the World Bank, The US Agency for International Development, and Transparency International, May 23 and June 24, 1997), pp. 64–65.

21. The Ukrainian electoral law used in the 1998 parliamentary elections stipulated that any party unable to garner 4 percent of popular vote did not receive any of the proportionally elected 250 seats to the Verkhovna Rada. These were automatically distributed proportionally amongst the other parties having reached more than the 4 percent threshold. Most of the 30 parties registered to run in the 1998 elections polled below the required 4 percent. Many are single-issue parties or regional interest organizations.

22. The Council of Advisors to the Verkhovna Rada was closed down in late 1996.

23. Geoffrey York, "Embarrassment looms for Ukraine," *The Globe and Mail*, December 6, 1997.

24. The United States, it can be argued, "invests" more money in Ukraine than in any other country save Israel and Egypt. This money, however, is more likely based on security than on financial interest.

25. Gerhard Gnauck and Steffen Sachs (eds.), "Ukraine and European Security," *Report on the Aspen Institute Berlin Conference* (Berlin: Aspen Institute, April 8–10, 1995), p. 9. See also Daniel Kaufmann, "Why is Ukraine's economy and Russia's not growing?" *Transition*, available online at: <http://www.worldbank.org/html/prddr/trans/marapr97/art2.htm> (World Bank, April 1997).

26. Geoffrey York, "Ukraine's PM Dogged by Corrupt Image," *The Globe and Mail*, June 12, 1997.

27. Op cit., Daniel Kaufmann, "Why is Ukraine's economy and Russia's not growing?" *Transition:* <http://www.worldbank.org/html/prddr/trans/marapr97/art2.htm>.

28. Op cit., Kaufmann, "Why is Ukraine's economy and Russia's not growing?" *Transition*, available online at: <http://www.worldbank. org/html/prddr/trans/. marapr97/art2.htm>.

29. Valeri Solomianiuk, Director, Argoconcern. Personal interview. Kyiv, October 1997.

30. *The Economist*, September 2, 1995.

31. *Foreign Direct Investment in Ukraine* (Paris: Organisation for Economic Co-operation and Development, 1997), p. 8.

32. It is understood that inter-enterprise arrears are a means by which enterprises finance their operations. The result of high inter-enterprise arrears is long-term unpaid wages to workers.

33. *TACIS: Ukrainian Economic Trends*, September 1997, pp. 48–49, 58–61.

34. Vladimir Laktyonov and V'yacheslav Chornovil in discussion, Ukrainian Elections Project, January 25, 1998, London: British East West Centre. Laktyonov boasted about Donets'k region's ability to pay on time and in full salaries de-

spite difficulties with Kyiv over the transfer of taxation revenue. Chornovil agreed that regions such as Donets'k, L'viv, and Kyiv paid their workers on time; however, most of the country was not so fortunate, and workers are not being paid fully or on time.

35. David R. Marples, personal interview, January 19, 1998.

CHAPTER 10

Institutional Power and Ideology in the Ukrainian Constitutional Process

Oliver Vorndran

After a struggle lasting five years, the Ukrainian parliament finally adopted its post-communist constitution on June 28, 1996. This chapter attempts to conceptualize the Ukrainian constitutional process. It purports to show that the general political structures that developed during the process of transformation—from the soviet to a quasi-democratic order—shaped the internal structures of the very process itself and hence its outcome. Taking the structural problems of transformation as a reference point, I identify four main political cleavages and four different groups of actors. From this constellation—in combination with the political regionalization of Ukraine—the main political conflicts of 1991 to 1996 can be discerned. These conflicts constitute at the same time the most difficult questions in the constitutional process: What kind of nationalism? What form of government? What kind of economy? Which relationship toward Russia? The internal structure of the Ukrainian constitutional process will be analyzed along the lines of shifting interests over time, the correspondence of cleavages and alternative plausible "solutions," the lines of conflict, forms of cooperation, and the means of pressure. The findings of this chapter indicate that institutional power was the driving force in the process, while ideological questions were the main reason that Ukraine was the last state of the former Soviet Union to adopt its constitution.

I. The Context: Groups, Cleavages, and Stages

Claus Offe has shown that the post-Soviet states had to fulfill three major tasks simultaneously after the collapse of the Soviet Union: define the borders of the new and independent state, revise the political constitution[1] and adapt the economic order according to the new challenges.[2] These tasks define the main Ukrainian political cleavages since the appearance of a uniquely Ukrainian political space. These cleavages were: firstly, was Ukraine to be independent and what was the essence of the Ukrainian nation? Second, should Ukraine become a Soviet-type parliamentary republic or semi-presidential? Third, what should be the principles guiding the reconstruction of the Ukrainian economy—socialism and planning or private ownership and a free market?

The political regionalization of Ukraine with the twin poles in Galicia and the Donbas led to a situation in which there was no consensus concerning the appropriate response to the abovementioned political questions. In summary, in western Ukraine the idea of an independent, democratic, semi-presidential state with a free market was prominent, whereas in eastern Ukraine a union with Russia, the persistence of soviets, and a state-regulated, planned economy enjoyed support. A fourth (geo-) political cleavage resulted from these different political ideas: what kind of relationship with Russia should be encouraged? Should Ukraine develop its own national interests and pursue them on the basis of equal partnership, or was there a natural union and a similarity of interest between Ukraine and Russia? This ideological regionalization implied that the tasks outlined by Offe for the successor states of the Soviet Union became political cleavages within Ukraine.

As late as 1989 and onward, these cleavages shaped the main four groups[3] of the Ukrainian political elite. I identify these as:

1. *Hardliners:*[4] These were members of a group within the old Communist Party of Ukraine ([UPU] before its ban in August 1991), who were against the dissolution of the Soviet Union and the birth of an independent Ukraine, against political and economic reforms, and against cooperation with the national-democratic movement *Rukh*. Until 1991 they were led by Stanislav Hurenko. Since the Declaration of Independence on August 24, 1991 and the overwhelming support given to Ukrainian independence in the December 1, 1991 referendum, this group lost much of its influence within the PU. During the Kravchuk presidency, and especially after the parliamentary elections

of March 1994, the number of supporters of this political grouping in the Verkhovna Rada diminished, but was still alive as late as 1997 in the form of the *soyuz* (unity) faction in parliament, and more generally within the communist faction. In fact, most of them initially refused to take the oath of loyalty to the new Ukrainian constitution.

2. *Softliners Against Reforms:* These were supporters of this political tendency united in the eleventh session of Verkhovna Rada within the "Group of 239," named according to the number of deputies in that group.[5] They recognized that an independent Ukraine gave them many political and economic opportunities, and therefore they supported the dissolution of the Soviet Union. Being in positions of political or economic power during the Kravchuk presidency, they stood successfully against reforms that threatened their positions. After the March 1994 parliamentary elections they congregated mainly in the Socialist and Peasant factions and were led by Oleksandr Moroz, the new chairman of the twelfth Verkhovna Rada. Moroz had also been the chairman of the Group of 239.

3. *Softliners for Reforms:* The ideal-typical member of this political grouping was a former member of *komsomol,* striving for reform of the political and economic structures, because this would enable him or her to personally gain within the old structures. Since these *komsomol* members did not have access to decisive posts, they sought greater liberties and opportunities to realize their aspirations. In general, they preferred free market structures to a planned economy. Though the softliners for reforms managed to establish different (regional) networks,[6] they did not unite in a coherent group during the twelfth Verkhovna Rada. This was reflected in the great number of centrist factions.[7]

4. *National-Democrats:* These were the nationalists in the former movement Rukh, which split into several parties[8] and subsequently several factions[9] in parliament. The national-democrats set the political agenda in Ukraine from 1989 to 1991, because they were the only political force that offered a new concept and basis of legitimacy for the new state. They were therefore able to organize mass support for Ukrainian independence. They never again gained such political momentum and could not win more than 25 to 30 percent of the vote in subsequent parliamentary and presidential elections. They were neither competitive in elections nor dominant in parliamentary politics. In general, nationalists favor market economic reforms but oppose comprehensive economic cooperation with Russia because they

fear that Russian firms would buy out the Ukrainian economy and that Russians again would come to dominate Ukraine.

This combination of cleavages and main political groupings can be summed up in Table 10.1. After the main cleavages and political groups have been identified, the main political conflicts also need to be outlined. For this, the voter potential for the different policy options must be taken into account. After the August 1991 putsch in Moscow, it became clear that during the presidential election campaign in autumn 1991 (at the same time as the campaign for Ukrainian independence), no politician could come into office who rejected Ukrainian independence and the democratic nature of the political regime. This was confirmed in the parliamentary elections of 1994 and 1998 and, of course, in the adoption of the Ukrainian constitution in June 1996. This means that Ukraine will—with great certainty—not elect a president belonging to the hardliners—that is, belonging to the (traditional) communists.

The national-democrats constitute a second group that cannot hope to nominate a candidate for the presidency successfully. They cannot for the simple reason that their electorate is too small, mainly comprised of citizens of western Ukraine, who account for only a fifth of the Ukrainian population. Consequently, the candidates of the West, Chornovil in 1991 and Kravchuk in 1994, could not win the presidency. This again means that only the softliners—

Table 10.1

	Cleavage			
Elite Group	Independence*	Against Soviet-Parliamentarism	Private Ownership, Market Economy	Against Cooperation with Russia
Hardliner (traditional communists)	–	–	–	–
Softliner against reforms (agrarians, socialists)	+	–	–	–
Softliner for reforms (centrists)	+	+	+	–
National-democrats	+	+	+	+

Notes: "+" means "supports"; "–" means "opposes"
*The cleavage "nationalism" is too problematic to be incorporated into a necessarily simplyfying +/– scheme.

for or against reforms—are able to gain the presidency and that the other groups have to be their "foot soldiers." A look at the table makes it clear that the main conflict will arise from the different political stances taken between the softliners for and against reforms—that is, the dominant political conflicts arise around the fight for or against Soviet-type parliamentarism and for or against economic reforms. It shows too that the softliners against reforms will build a coalition with the hardliners and the softliners for reforms will build a coalition with the national-democrats, because they share the same opinions concerning the main cleavages.

So far I have tried to make clear what the cleavages within the Ukrainian political space were, how they shaped the groupings within Ukrainian politics, and the origins of the dominant political conflicts. This is the context of the Ukrainian constitutional process. I will continue by analyzing the structure of the constitutional process, referring to the interests of the different political groups and actors and the time structure of the process. My main question will be: why did Ukraine adopt a new constitution at all? This will answer a second question: why did Ukraine adopt its post-communist constitution so late, five years after declaring independence?

The Ukrainian constitutional process had three stages: the Kravchuk presidency, the process leading to the constitutional agreement on June 8, 1995, and finally the process leading to the adoption of the constitution on June 28, 1996. Each stage was characterized by a change of interest of at least one political group participating in the constitutional process, sometimes combined with a shift of strength among the main political groupings.

Stage 1: The Kravchuk Presidency

After independence was declared and the first president was elected on December 1, 1991, the need to adopt a constitution became increasingly obvious. The three main tasks outlined by Offe could be solved permanently only by adopting a new constitution. According to Offe's first task (defining new borders), the referendum on independence showed only that the people within the borders of the Ukrainian Socialist Soviet Republic desired to live in a state separate and distinct from the Soviet Union and Russia, but the question of what kind of state this should be remained unresolved. Therefore, it seems paradoxical that Ukrainian politicians managed to live without an answer to this question and without adopting a new constitution during the Kravchuk presidency. But the answer is more or less simple: the diversity of regions within Ukraine and the interests and ideology within the political elite were too great at that time to find the necessary consensus to adopt a constitution. Therefore Kravchuk chose to deal with the development of the concept of the Ukrainian nation first rather than attempting to change existing institutions, thereby risking conflicts with vested interests that controlled the existing institutions.

Therefore, I argue that Ukrainian state building during the Kravchuk presidency was characterized by two main features: the *concept without power* and the *power without concept*. The first feature—concept without power— was the development of a concept of the Ukrainian nation by Kravchuk and, of course, the movement *Rukh*. This concept of a nation could mobilize mass support at that time, had some effect as an idea, and shaped minds and political events *without* having to rely on institutional power beside the authority of the president. This concept without power was the dynamic factor of state building, having influence mainly on the creation of the new elements—theoretical and institutional—of statehood.[10]

The second feature—power without concept—was represented by the officials elected during the local, regional, and national elections in April 1990, either belonging to the *nomenklatura* or—in the West—to the movement *Rukh*. These officials in late 1991 were unprepared to rule a country by their own initiative. They were simply not prepared for it, being intellectuals only accostomed to receiving commands. These officials represented power without concept; they could not take any initiative. They had no concept because socialism and its rules had lost their legitimacy and could no longer provide orientation. At the same time the understanding of democracy and market economy as new concepts was not advanced enough to provide consensus and orientation among the elites. Democracy and a market economy served as labels for a wide range of ideas within an overall ideological vacuum.[11]

But though they had no concept, for President Kravchuk, dealing with officials in power was still more difficult than inventing new concepts and institutions. The officials in office had concrete interests in staying there, and changing these institutions meant generating conflicts of uncertain extent and—even more—uncertain consequences. Kravchuk perceived this as a threat to the process of nation building or at least for his self-portrait as conciliator and father of the nation. Motyl therefore concludes that nation building had to be prioritized over institutional reform, strengthening the nation and at the same time enabling it to bear the brunt of conflict later.[12]

In fact, Kravchuk's efforts to delineate competences between state organs were half-hearted, though bitterly needed. The political system of Ukraine suffered from the fact that the presidency as an institution was attached to a pure parliamentary system without eliminating the resulting contradictions.

This often led to double or even triple competences in relations between parliament, government, and president. During Kravchuk's presidency it was parliament, dominated by the softliners against reforms, who experimented with institutional "reform." It created the institution of presidential representatives in 1992 and abolished the same representatives in Febrary 1994.[13] Parliament granted the then-Prime Minister Leonid Kuchma special powers in autumn 1992 and withdrew them in May 1993.[14] It drafted constitutions and led public debate about them but did not adopt any version.

This fuzzy "system" of competences and powers between the governmental institutions often produced stalemate during struggles for concrete political decisions.[15] This continued experience of stalemate meant not only that (economic) reforms were delayed but also that parliament, government, and president accepted each other as legitimate and indispensible actors in the political arena. Mutual acceptance then led to cooperation between the institutions and moderation of conflict in the decision-making fight, which again allowed the development of more complex, informal rules of the game. Thus, paradoxically, unclear competences and resulting stalemate stabilized the legitimacy of existing institutions as well as cooperation among actors and institutions:

> The left and the right, like the Rada and the president, had to agree to disagree, and, in doing so, to recognise each other as genuine partners with real roles to play in the political system.[16]

This shows that President Kravchuk did not have an interest in seriously pushing the constitutional process. The second political force in the constitutional process, besides the president, was the parliament. Although one must not think of parliament as a monolithic institution, the former Group of 239 had a clear majority among the 450 deputies. This majority was too small to constitute a constitutional majority of 300, but it was big enough to impede any political reforms, a policy that rather suited their interests. Being in office and in power, not only in parliament but often also additionally as chairmen of *rayon*—or *oblast*—soviets or heads of enterprises, they did not have any interest in changing the system. Moreover, unclear competences on all governmental levels gave them even more liberty to act deliberately, to their own will and favor. Against this powerful group, the softliners for reform and the nationalists were not numerous enough to impose their will on the former Group of 239 and the president.

The result of this balance of power was that no constitution was adopted. But a second result was that during the Kravchuk presidency, parliament and president accepted each other as legitimate players in the political game, which created the basis for the conflicts still to come after the parliamentary and presidential elections in 1994, evoked by the next president Kuchma. In this respect Motyl concludes: "Seen in this light, Kravchuk's greatest achievement may be that he made Kuchma possible."[17] This conclusion leads directly to the next stage of the constitutional process.

Stage 2: From March 1994 to the Constitutional Agreement

The most striking event that distinguishes the second stages of the constitutional process from the first was the signing of the Constitutional Agreement between the president and the parliament in summer 1995. The institutional arrangement of parliament, government, and president did not differ from the first period. Also, the relative strength of these political groups had not changed remarkably. But the change of interest of one major player, the president, made the signing of the Constitutional Agreement on June 8, 1995 possible.

In contrast to Kravchuk, the new president Kuchma had always pointed out during his election campaign that he wanted to strengthen the executive.[18] Kuchma's official impetus was to promote economic reforms. For this reason he perceived political reforms as a dire necessity. He was convinced that without political reforms the executive would not be able to carry out economic reforms. Pursuing this aim, Kuchma did not dare evoke conflicts or interfere with someone else's interests. Looking back, Kuchma took one of the most important steps one month after his election. On August 8, 1994, he subordinated by decree government and state administrations to himself, the president.[19] From this date, government was no longer subordinated to parliament but to the president. At this time, Ukraine de facto changed from a parliamentary to a presidential regime. Moreover, this step meant the elimination of the government as a possible independent force in the constitutional process. Only the president and the parliament were left over as institutional actors, and they remained the only actors of the constitutional process in general, because other institutions (like the army, regional adminstrations, foreign states, etc.) and social forces (like parties, unions, etc.) did not try or were not able to participate forcefully in the process.

Kuchma did not want a full-fledged constitution at this stage of the process. Rather, he introduced a "vertical chain of command" within the executive to enhance the efficiency of the governmental machine. This became clear in the draft of the Law on State Power and Local Government in Ukraine, or, in short, the Law on Power. Kuchma did not bother about general questions of constitution making (e.g., which kind of nation Ukraine should be, what should the state symbols and the state language be, etc.). The first draft of the Law on Power did not include a definition of human and civil rights, either. These were questions for ideologists like Communists and nationalists but not for pragmatists, as Kuchma perceived himself. The centerpiece of his draft was economic freedoms, private property, the kind of regime (parliamentary or presidential republic), and the balance of power. It was intended to constitute a framework for economic reform and provide a clear delineation of powers between president, government, and parliament.

On November 30, 1994, Kuchma introduced his draft law, elaborated by the presidential administration, into parliament for consideration.[20] This draft reduced the powers of parliament considerably in comparison with the constitution of the Ukrainian Socialist Soviet Republic, which had often been amended but in essence was still the April 1978 version. When Kuchma presented his draft to parliament in a plenary session on December 22, 1994, he offended the deputies and consequently did not get the necessary majority at the first reading.[21] On the other hand, deputies did not want to expose the president and agreed to create a conciliatory commission to redraft the proposal. Finally, 220 deputies voted for (and 109 voted against) the amended draft in the first reading on December 27, 1994 just for tactical reasons, to ensure that the draft was not rejected at this early stage. This decision did not signify consent concerning the content of the draft law.[22]

During this initial phase of debate, the negotiating positions were as such: the president promoted the draft extending his powers, and the leftists in parliament rigorously rejected any kind of reform, whereas the other factions in parliament saw the necessity of reforming the political system and streamlining the executive without necessarily agreeing with the president's proposals. The parliamentary part of the conciliatory commission submitted a new version of the Law on Power on February 6, 1995. The representatives of the different factions removed the regulations that the president could dissolve parliament if it voted no-confidence in two consecutive governments (article 25) or did not confirm the budget (article 26). Additionally, the position of the prime minister was removed so that the president had to lead the government himself, without having a culprit for "bad execution" of an economic reform program and without the possibility to distance himself from a "bad" government. Because the president had to lead the government himself, the parliament could not longer vote no-confidence in the whole government (including the directly elected president); thus the article that the president could dissolve the parliament for that reason was also eliminated. Moreover, the powers of the parliament in the legislative process and in appointing officials of other state organs were strengthened.

As expected, the president did not like this version of the Law on Power cutting down his powers. He renegotiated the draft with the conciliatory commission and obtained the office of the prime minister and the ability to dissolve parliament if it did not approve the budget or the government's program. Thus the president could reinstate the essence of his former draft, and he presented this "final" version to parliament on March 15, 1995.[23] The presidium of the Verkhovna Rada then scheduled the second reading of the revised draft law for April 12. When Parliamentary Chairman Moroz gave the word to Oleksandr Steshenko[24] on that day, Steshenko accused the whole executive of being corrupt, and separated from the people and pointed out that the adoption of the Law on Power would lead to unlimited authoritarianism.[25] After these words, perceived as planned provocation, the president and most of the cabinet left the hall under protest and the very emotional debate that followed did not achieve any serious result. During the following weeks the leftist factions and Moroz further impeded efficient debates.

To bypass these laborious debates in parliament, four factions[26] on May 15, 1995 presented a Constitutional Agreement between parliament and president. The advantage of the agreement was that it did not need a constitutional majority (301 of 450 votes) but could come into force by a simple majority (signatures of the majority of deputies and the president). The president preferred the agreement to a plebiscite in trust of the population in parliament and president, which he threatened to conduct when he introduced the draft law for consideration in December, in case parliament would not adopt the Law on Power. He preferred the Constitutional Agreement to the plebiscite, because the result of a plebiscite could not be predicted with certainty and a plebiscite would have had no juridicial consequences, though it might lead to political consequences such as the dissolution of parliament.[27]

Because parliament feared a negative result in the plebiscite, and its likely subsequent dissolution, it vetoed the presidential decree on June 2 and forbade the president to use any state funds for the plebiscite. This, again, was perceived as an unlawful step by the president, who vetoed the parliamentary veto and showed his firm intention to carry out the plebiscite in a meeting with the chairmen of the *oblast* councils and administrations. On the same day, the head of the presidential administration again offered to sign the Constitutional Agreement. The president himself met a group of deputies to discuss the situation after the mutual vetoes. Finally, the parliamentary presidium proposed that the president would introduce the Constitutional Agreement as a draft law, bringing the Law on Power, already adopted in its second reading, into force. The president followed the proposal, and parliament voted on June 7, 1995 for the Constitutional Agreement with 240 votes for and 81 against.[28] On the next day it was ceremoniously signed by the president, the parliamentary chairman, and the deputies, who wished to sign it.[29]

The Law on Power in its final version allowed the president to appoint the prime minister and the cabinet without the consent of parliament. Two months after its appointment, the government had to present its program before parliament. If parliament approved the program it was not allowed to vote no-confidence in the government within one year. If the program was not approved, the government had to resign (article 22). The government was subordinated and responsible to the president and was the president's instrument to execute his policy. The prime minister acted according to the president's directives (article 29). These regulations meant that Ukraine was a pure presidential republic.

The Law on Power gave the president the opportunity to intervene in the legislative sphere in three ways. First, he had the autonomous right to issue decrees, restricted only in those cases in which the Law on Power had foreseen the formal necessity of a law. This reserve of parliamentary legislation included civil rights, the declaration of war and peace, the principles of foreign and internal policy, social policy, tax and financial policies, the budget, and also price and credit regulations (article 18). Presidential decrees were valid until a corresponding law was adopted (article 25). Second, the president could introduce "urgent" draft laws into parliament for preferential consideration (article 15, II) and herewith could influence the parliament's agenda. Finally, the president could veto laws, which in turn could be overruled by a two-thirds majority of the actual number of deputies (article 23). The opposite case, a parliamentary veto on a presidential decree, was possible only in cases in which the decrees contradicted the constitution or law. Parliament then had to submit a petition to the constitutional court at the same time (article 17, number 27). Compared with the previous draft, the final version of the Law on Power was slightly changed in favor of the parliament but still contained all essential demands of the president and enlarged his powers considerably.

Which decisive factors led to the signing of the constitutional agreement? First of all, the political will of President Kuchma to carry out reforms brought the process to its conclusion—against the interests of the large left caucus in parliament. The process then could proceed through various stages because the centrists and nationalists saw some necessity for reform and built a coalition together with the president against the leftists and the speaker, Oleksandr Moroz. This was possible because centrists and nationalists won more seats in the by-elections in autumn 1994 and thus were strengthened in comparison to the leftists. Third, under the threat of a plebiscite and the likely consequent dissolution of parliament, the deputies agreed to sign the Constitutional Agreement though it limited their powers and the power of parliament, but the agreement saved their mandate.

This last step—turning the confrontational situation of announcing a plebiscite into a situation of cooperation by mutually agreed compromise—was smoothed by two specific features of the political culture of Ukrainian elites: first, to stay in contact and speak with each other in very tense situations and, second, the preference for compromise over confrontation. Finally, some of the leftists, the Agrarian for Reforms faction and some Socialist deputies, accepted the Constitutional Agreement because it was not meant as the final word in the fight for power between the state organs but only as a transitional agreement on the way to the adoption of the constitution. In its final articles it was agreed that the Constitutional Agreement would be valid until the adoption of a new Ukrainian constitution—which should be reached within one year.

Stage 3: Adopting a Constitution

By examining the third stage of the constitutional process, we will approach the answer to the question of why Ukraine finally obtained a constitution. At first sight it is astonishing how similar the time structure of the processes, leading to the Constitutional Agreement and to the constitution were. But it is also striking how different the results of the two processes were: the Constitutional Agreement was the result of a juridicially dubious process. It had not been adopted by a constitutional majority though the agreement had the force of changing constitutional rules. It had this force not because of the legitimacy of the process but by pure will and mutual agreement of the participants. Therefore it is all the more surprising that even those political forces (mainly the communists) who opposed the agreement accepted it as the new rules of the game and acted correspondingly. Their problem was that they could not find an authority of higher standing than parliament and president combined. Nevertheless the legitimacy of the Constitutional Agreement was weak and it was accepted as a transitional regime only for a limited period of time.

In contrast, the new Ukrainian constitution was the result of a juridicially incontestable process, adopted by a constitutional majority, valid for an unlimited time, and, as the most legitimate, political, and juridicial document in Ukrainian history since 1989, the new basis of future political and social life in the country. Also, the content of the agreements were different: the Constitutional Agreement did not regulate more than the mutual relations of state organs, whereas the constitution attempts to define not only which kind of state but also which nation Ukraine shall become. The new constitution is not only a law to be obeyed by everybody but a symbol of the self-determination of a people.

How did the changes come about even though the processes were astonishingly similar? At the beginning of the third stage of the constitutional process, the interests of the political actors again had changed, because the Law on Power had changed the balance of power between the institutions. The Law on Power gave the president a far-reaching influence on the executive (government and administrations), mainly in terms of personnel decisions. The constitutional process now presented the opportunity to consolidate his position for an unlimited time span and to extend his influence on the legislative sphere by changing the structure of parliament. The aim of the president was to strengthen his power further. Thus, the president had an interest not only in the adoption of the constitution but also in the specific outcome of the process.

The interests of parliament had changed, too. Conscious of having lost power, parliament as a whole saw the constitutional process as an opportunity to regain its old powers concerning the creation of government, in the legislative sphere, and in nominating and appointing other state officials. But it was not united with respect to the specific result of the constitutional process. The leftists still preferred a soviet-parliamentary constitution, whereas the centrists and nationalists favored some kind of a parliamentary-presidential or presidential-parliamentary republic. Factions were also divided on issues like federalism/unitarism and nationhood. In the same manner as in the second stage of the constitutional process, the government itself was no independent player in the struggle but had to play on the president's side, supporting his views and steps. All participants in the process knew about this situation, their own and their opponents' interests.

In the same manner as the year before, the president took the initiative. In September 1995, the constitutional commission, representing all branches of power, installed an "expert commission" according to a proposal of the president.[30] Ensuring that the "experts" reflected mainly the opinion of the president, Kuchma wanted to depoliticize the process in its initial stage. The core point of the resulting draft was a bicameral parliament consisting of a chamber of deputies and a senate. The electoral system was not outlined in the draft, neither for the 220 deputies of the Chamber of Deputies nor for the three senators representing each *oblast* and the cities of Kyiv and Sevastopol (articles 72–74).[31]

The competences of the Chamber of Deputies included the confirmation of the prime minister (nominated by the president), confirmation of the government's program, and legislation. The president could dissolve parliament if it did not confirm the nominated prime minister within three months *or* if it did not confirm the government's program (article 89). That meant that the chamber of deputies did not have any choice other than confirming the president's government and its program if it did not want to risk its mandate. The Chamber of Deputies could vote no-confidence in the government because it could not influence the nomination of the next prime minister. Moreover, its legislative power was restricted, because all laws had to be adopted by both chambers with the majority of their elected members. If deputies and senators did not agree on a draft law, a conciliatory commission should find a compromise. If that did not work, the Chamber of Deputies could adopt a law by a two-thirds majority (articles 90, 94). Finally, the president had to sign the law or could refer the law back for a second examination (article 95).

These regulations evoked the impression that the legislative process should be stalled to give the president the opportunity to rule by decree. The Chamber of Deputies in most cases lost its influence on the nomination and appointment of other high state officials to the senate, who had to cooperate with the president in these questions. The cabinet was responsible to the president and was to be controlled by the National Assembly (article 113). This again shows that the National Assembly was restricted to a passive role in policymaking. Therefore, the heavy criticism of the draft by all sides—even by supporters of the president among the deputies, not to mention Moroz—was not surprising. The strategy of President Kuchma to depoliticize the constitutional process had failed. The president defended the draft, saying that what should be avoided was the establishment of the legislature as the highest authority in decision-making,[32] herewith fully neglecting the justification of the existence of any parliament. In a meeting with factions he told the deputies of the Verkhovna Rada that he would carry out a referendum if parliament would not adopt a constitution with a constitutional majority.[33]

Mainly for tactical reasons, the Constitutional Commission accepted the draft as the basis for further elaboration on November 23, 1995 but created a new "working group" from among its members, together with four representatives of president and parliament and two representatives of the judiciary.[34] The next step in the process was the elaboration of a new draft by the working group. This suffered from the same basic faults as the work of the expert commission. Parliament and its factions had to be regarded as the second main political force in the process (besides the president), but its four representatives did not sufficiently mirror the divergent interests and opinions within the legislature. Acknowledging the fact that the draft constitution needed the consent of *all* factions (otherwise it would not get a constitutional majority), it was clear that factions not represented in the working group would not accept the new draft. When it was finally introduced for legislative consideration, they would aim to set up a new negiotating stucture in which they could participate. That is, in fact, what happened.

Though the working group took three months to redraft the constitution, the result did not deviate considerably from the draft of the expert commission. The most significant changes were that the Chamber of Deputies would now have 370 members (article 73) and that the president could no longer dissolve the chamber if it did not confirm his nominee as prime minister (article 90). But this did not really affect the balance of power between the institutions, taking into account all other provisions of the basic law. The core point of the president's draft, the two-chamber parliament, was maintained, though 10 of 11 factions were in favor of a unicameral body.[35] Despite wide-ranging criticism of various points, a majority of the constitutional commission agreed on March 11, 1996 to introduce this draft into the legislative process.[36]

Further considerations in parliament were dominated by the critical transitional provisions of the constitutional agreement. The constitutional agreement stated that the president could carry out a referendum on a draft constitution only if parliament previously had agreed upon the draft.[37] Consent in this context meant not only consent by a constitutional majority but also by simple majority, (i.e., in its first reading). Thus parliament, especially the leftist factions (Communists, Socialists, Peasants) led by Parliamentary Chairman Moroz, aimed at any price to prevent a plenary session in which a majority of the non-leftist deputies could demand that the draft be put to a vote. This led to the absurd situation on March 18, 1996 in which the presidium of Verkhovna Rada discussed for nine hours how the draft of the Constitutional Commission would be presented to parliament: either in a plenary session or in a common session of all committees.[38]

On March 26 nationalist and centrist factions,[39] agitated by Moroz's destructive behavior and the slackening process, met President Kuchma and

Prime Minister Marchuk to propose creation of a conciliatory committee to rework the draft constitution in order to accelerate the constitutional process.[40] The nine factions united in the conciliatory committee were a considerable threat to Moroz's position as sole mediator of political positions in parliament. He feared that he might lose control over the constitutional process in parliament, and on April 2, 1996, he initiated a decision of the presidium to create an official temporary committee of the Verkhovna Rada in place of Kuchma's unofficial conciliatory committee.[41]

The question of power and influence remained the critical concern. The rightist and centrist factions proposed that the temporary committee should consist of two representatives from each faction, giving them a majority. The leftist factions proposed instead that factional representation be apportioned according to the relative strength of factions in parliament. While the still-unofficial conciliatory committee started its work in earnest, the dispute remained unresolved. On May 5, the Verkhovna Rada decided that six representatives of the Communist faction and two representatives of each other faction would be members of the temporary committee. But with a majority of votes, the centrist and nationalist factions pushed through a provision that all decisions of the committee should be taken by simple majority, with each faction having just one vote. Since the Communists were sidelined once again, they bolted from the committee in protest.[42] As for the other leftists, the Socialists and Peasants sometimes joined the committee to inform themselves about the decisions without being able to influence the negotiations.[43]

This stage of the constitutional process generated a new phenomenon in Ukrainian politics: the "conciliatory committee." This is remarkable because it is the first institution to be born of the common will of centrist and nationalist factions to work cooperatively. The result of their work, the draft constitution of the temporary committee, mirrored their interests. They abandoned Kuchma's two-chamber parliament and restored a unicameral body.[44] The draft provided that parliament would have power to confirm the prime minister, as it had before the signing of the Constitutional Agreement. Because the Senate would no longer exist, parliament regained influence over the nomination and appointment of officials, cooperating in nearly all cases with the president. Parliament would again possess exclusive law-making powers, and the temporary committee restricted the right of the president to issue decrees according to subject matter (only in the economic sphere) and for a limited time (only until the next regular presidential election).[45] Thus the role of parliament was considerably strengthened, compared to the situation before the Constitutional Agreement. Taking this into account, it is not clear why the president would give his consent to the draft.

It is not too much to say that President Kuchma's decree of June 26, 1996 shocked the deputies. He chose not the draft of the temporary committee, which had already been adopted in its first reading by parliament, but the two-chamber draft of the Constitutional Commission.[46] Both centrists and nationalist saw that their efforts had been in vain. Leftists agreed at least that the one-chamber draft of the temporary committee saved some parliamentary influence on politics. But they still disagreed on the ideological questions. In this situation all factions agreed to adopt the constitution themselves in a closed plenary session on the morning of June 27. When they heard in the evening that Kuchma had ordered his ministers with deputies mandates not to take part in the parliamentary debate in order to avoid a constitutional majority, the deputies decided to stay in parliament until the constitution was adopted. After a long night of continuous debate, the new Ukrainian constitution was finally adopted on the morning of June 28, 1996.

I will conclude with a threefold analysis of the last stage of the constitutional process that, first asks which "solutions" were found for the most disputed ideological questions in the constitution; that second, points out the decisive factors for the adoption of the constitution; and that third, finally analyzes the differences in structure between the processes leading to the Constitutional Agreement and to the constitution.

Cleavages and "Solutions"

It has to be pointed out that in the constitution only those provisions concerning ideological questions differ considerably from the draft of the temporary committee. It is a myth that the constitution was reinvented during the final night of debate. The regulations about the relation between the executive and the legislative branches (chapters IV-VI of the constitution) remained virtually unchanged. This means that adoption of the constitution was delayed not due to differences within parliament about the structure of power in the state but because of ideological differences between leftists and national-democrats over the question of how the Ukrainian nation should be defined.

Independence and nationalism defined the first main cleavage of the Ukrainian polity, as outlined at the beginning of this chapter. By the time of the third stage of the constitutional process, independence was no longer a subject of contention as a result of the Ukrainian referendum on independence, Kravchuk's efforts to conceptualize and stabilize the nation-building processes, and the persistence of the Ukrainian state. Nevertheless, the argument about the definition of the people as a sovereign subject remained. For the nationalists and their ethnic perception of nation, the wording "Ukrainian nation" (*Ukrayins'kyi narod*) was incontestable, whereas leftists, who reflected the opinion of the Russian minority in Ukraine, demanded a definition of the people as "the people of Ukraine" (*Narod Ukrayiny*). The formula accepted reads as follows: " . . . the Ukrainian people—citizens of Ukraine of all nationalities."[47] In my opinion, this formula does not "reconcile the difference in a genuine compromise and satisfy all sides,"[48] but is rather the inclusion of both opinions. In view of this, it perfectly mirrors a paradox of Ukrainian constitutional reality and the Ukrainian nation: the main reason for the Ukrainian state to justify its existence toward Russia its distinct ethnic and cultural Ukrainian nation. But Ukraine is at the same time a multiethnic state, defining its citizenship according to the principle of *ius soli*. The chosen formula provides evidence that there cannot be a voluntaristic "solution" or definition of the Ukrainian nation, prefering one definition or the other, without endangering the existence of the Ukrainian state. The Ukrainian nation is still in the process of "coming into being."

The provisions governing the state language (article 10) were heavily disputed as well. The final version simply states that Ukrainian is the state language. The provision in the draft of the temporary commission that state organs or organizations may use another language in minority enclaves, if the majority of the population agrees, was omitted. Instead, the second paragraph prescribes that the "state guarantees the comprehensive development and use of the Ukrainian language in all spheres of society across the entire territory of Ukraine" (article 10, II). This represents a significant shift in language policy. The Language Law of 1989 also demanded the introduction of the Ukrainian language, but afterwards the law was not forcefully implemented. Now the constitution obliges the state to carry out an *active* language policy. Though article 10, section III regulates the "unfettered development, use and protection of Russian, other languages of national minorities in Ukraine is guaranteed." Russian is not supported by the state—unlike Ukrainian. Moreover, the status of Russian is not different from other languages used by much smaller minorites, such as Hungarian, Romanian, Yiddish, Polish, German, and others. Thus, article 10 clearly reflects the standpoint of the nationalists.

The same is true for the description of Ukraine's national symbols: flag, emblem, and anthem. The text of the constitution (article 20) avoids the term "trident" (*tryzub*) as a description of the emblem, but the circumscription means exactly this. Nationalists conceded that the text of the anthem "Ukraine is not dead yet" is omitted from the definition in the constitution, but Verbytsky's music would remain. Summarizing the regulations of the definition of the nation, the status of the languages, and the description of the state symbols, the nationalists, supported by the president and the centrists, finally could see their concept of nation fixed in the constitution. This was due mainly to the fact that no alternative coherent concept of the Ukrainian nation was available. Neither the president, the centrists, nor the leftists could imagine something different that promised to provide a focal point for the Ukrainian nation, which was, is, and will be desperately needed.

The second main cleavage of the Ukrainian polity, the question of which kind of economy Ukraine should have, was reflected in the constitutional debate about the different kinds of ownership and their status (article 13f). Communists and Socialists again pointed out that the treatment of land as a commodity would be "treason" to the Ukrainian nation. Nothing else than this "treason" is now allowed by article 14: "The right to land ownership is guaranteed. This right is achieved and realized by citizens, legal entities and the State in accordance with the law." This regulation had not been included in the draft of the temporary committee. Moreover, article 13 protects the equal ownership rights of different kinds of owners (citizens, legal entities, or the state). Nevertheless, article 14 also contains the clause that "land is the essential national asset and receives the special protection of the state." Because the "special protection of the state" is not specified, this sentence seems to be a symbolic tribute to the left without recognizing their socialist policies. A more general clause of socialist spirit is contained in article 13: "Ownership entails responsibility. Ownership should not be used to the detriment of the individual or society." But again, this does not mean much if the general clause is not specified by law, concretely allowing or forbidding some kind of property rights.

The constitution does not say directly that the Ukrainian economy shall be a market economy, but the right to work (article 43), the right of private ownership (article 41), the right to conduct entrepreneurial activity that is not prohibited by law, the protection of competition (article 42), the right to freely choose the place of residence (article 33), and the right of free development of one's own individuality (article 23)—all integral to free and efficient markets—are guaranteed. On the other hand, the constitution contains several far-reaching social duties of the state that would require significant redistribution of income to be fulfilled, such as the right to adequate health care, housing, and minimal living standards. Those can limit the freedom of economic activity considerably. Thus, the economic question is yet unanswered.

The third main cleavage, involving the question of which kind of government Ukrainians want to live under (soviet-parliamentarism or some kind of a semi-presidential republic), had already been decided at the first reading. Opening this point up to discussion would have made the task of adopting the constitution in one night impossible to achieve. Too many details would have been needed to be worked out. Therefore, the deputies stuck to the model of a joint parliamentary-presidential republic, with the prime minister responsible to parliament and president simultaneously and a relatively strong position of the president within the executive. The chosen model was not especially liked by the president (which may have been one reason that he chose the draft of the constitutional commission for the referendum), but the president had no means to defend a stronger position.

The fourth main cleavage, identified at the beginning of this chapter, was not to be regulated by constitutional law. The question of how and to what extent the government cooperates with its Russian counterpart is one of changing circumstances and changing Ukrainian national interests. Foreign policy is too fluid to be fixed in the constitution.[49] However, the deputies found it wise to add a specification to the draft of the temporary commission, which forbids the location of foreign military bases on the territory of Ukraine (article 17, paragraph 7), aimed at the Russian part of the Black Sea Fleet located in Sevastopol. In connection with point 14 of the transitional provisions, which allows the use of existing military bases by foreign troops (on the basis of leasing agreements ratified by Verkhovna Rada), this gave the Ukrainian government a better stance in negotiations with Russia because it placed Russia in an unlawful position from the beginning without unduly limiting the negotiating freedom of the Ukrainian side.[50]

Though the main cleavages of Ukrainian politics were recognized in the constitutional debate and to a different extent regulated in the constitution itself, only one cleavage, the form of government, can be said to be "resolved." No party in the constitutional process, neither parliament nor president, could re-open the constitutional debate on this point without losing the support of the population. As I stressed earlier, the question of Ukraine's "independence" is resolved by the very fact of the adoption of the constitution, but the development of the Ukrainian nation is still an open process, which presumably will endure for decades. The ethnic content of Ukrainian nationalism is to some degree strengthened in the provisions about the definition of the nation, the status of languages, and the description of the state symbols, but only time will tell if Ukrainians are able to create a coherent "body politic." Finally, the constitution laid the basis for some kind of a market economy, but it remains undetermined which kind and which part the state can and wants to have working within it. The economic debate could shape Ukrainian politics in the future even more than the nationalism debate because it concerns the population more directly.

Decisive Factors

Having discussed the main cleavages of Ukrainian politics and their "solutions" in the constitution, I will now describe the decisive factors of the adoption of the constitution, along the institutional and the ideological lines of conflict that shaped the process. The institutional line of conflict was drawn between president and parliament and concerned first and foremost the governmental structure, the question of power.

The ideological line of conflict ran through parliament itself, concerning not only different views about the governmental structure—which here was of minor importance—but most of all questions of direct interest to nationalists: private ownership (of land); and the (market/planned) economy. The centrists mainly sided with the nationalists on these questions; consequently, the leftists found themselves in the minority. This prompted Parliamentary Chairman Moroz to play for time, accounting for his crucial role as chairman and his tactical skills in parliamentary debates. He hoped to push through the leftist cause as time ran out in the end. Moroz's attempt failed. His tactics apparently angered centrist and nationalist factions. Emerging as their common enemy, he unified the diffuse coalition of centrists and nationalists against him.[51] Kuchma supported the combined centrists and nationalists, and creation of the conciliatory and the temporary committee. Thus parliament was split, strengthening the president's negotiating position. Neither Moroz nor Kuchma could foresee that the nine centrist and nationalist factions would develop a close working rlationship, united by their common efforts. These factions (partly supported by the Agrarians for reform) possessed enough votes to threaten the adoption of the draft constitution credibly in its first reading (which was the juridicial condition for a referendum). Kuchma helped matters by ordering his minister deputies to be present at the decisive vote. At the same time neither the centrist and nationalist factions were individually strong enough to ensure passage of the draft; nonetheless, the president needed their support.

The nine factions, in the form of the temporary committee, succeeded in both lines of conflict until the first reading. After that, they were dependent on the help of the leftists to obtain a constitutional majority for their draft, or on President Kuchma, who had no legal alternative but to submit the adopted draft for referendum. Finally, both parties provided assistance: Moroz tried to save what little was left to the leftists after June 21. Facing a referendum, he pushed the debates in parliament under conditions of intense time pressure. Kuchma had provoked parliament, uniting it against him by chosing the "wrong" draft. Besides this structural situation it was the influence and ability of specific individuals that led to the adoption of the constitution.

In the end, it was the political will of President Kuchma to obtain a juridicial basis in the form of a constitution for political and economic reforms, which was the basic reason for the adoption of the constitution.[52] Kuchma had pushed through the Law on Power a year earlier, which provoked the interest of parliament in adopting a constitution.[53] He encouraged and supported the factions to create the conciliatory committee and the working of a new and different draft constitution. And finally it was President Kuchma who had provoked parliament to adopt the constitution itself by choosing the "wrong" draft constitution for referendum. Taking this into account, one may doubt the president's sincerity and good intentions. Most commentators share the opinion that Kuchma did not only stimulate the work of the parliament, he also desired greater power to sideline parliament.[54] This interpretation is supported by the fact that Kuchma ordered his minister deputies to keep away from the parliamentary session during the night of June 27, 1996. His hunger for power was demonstrated when he chose the constitutional commission's draft to be submitted for popular referendum. Kuchma did not presume that parliament could adopt the constitution. In a nutshell, Kuchma gambled and lost.

Likewise, the leftists did not entirely achieve their aims. They were successful in improving the status of Crimea as an autonomous republic and in incorporating many social rights into the constitution. But they did not at all succeed in the more important questions of nationhood, economic order, and governmental relations. The most successful actors were centrists and nationalists, who were able to realize a wider range of their aims. Having been the weakest party in the fight from the beginning (when they lacked coherent aims, did not effectively cooperate, and could not mobilize popular support), they were fortunate that the president supported them during the reworking of the draft, and that the leftists involuntarily supported them during the final night.

Lines of Conflict, Cooperation, and Means of Pressure

Having said that, I want to analyze the differences between the processes leading to the Constitutional Agreement and to the constitution, explaining the different results of these processes. The most important difference was the change in interests of the institutional players that I already mentioned above.

A second main difference concerned the lines of conflict. Only one line of conflict existed during the process leading to the Constitutional Agreement. The centrist and nationalists agreed that the president needed a "vertical chain of command" in order to control government and administration in the pursuit of his economic reform program. At no point were they principally opposed to this idea, instead they supported the president throughout the whole process. The main line of conflict did not run between the institutions but *within one* of the institutions and between the different political camps in parliament. During the constitutional process, two lines of conflict existed: between president and parliament and between groups of factions within parliament.

If we understand the relationship between the nine centrist and nationalist factions vis-à-vis the president as the central relationship, this was strained at the beginning as the president proposed his two-chamber parliament draft. Later these parties coordinated their actions to some degree, and in the final two days, conflict dominated again. The president's referendum announcement led to a kind of "forced" cooperation between the leftists and other factions. These changing coalitions at each step led to working agreements on some provisions. The first step (president versus parliamentary factions) resulted in abandonment of the two-chamber parliament. The second step (president and nine factions versus leftists) led to agreement on nearly all regulations besides the ideological questions. Finally, the third step (president versus parliament as a whole) led to the concordance of remaining ideological questions and the adoption of the constitution.

A third structural difference in the two processes concerned the forms of cooperation between the different groups of actors. In the first year after the election of parliament, during the process leading to the Constitutional Agreement (roughly the period from March 1994 to June 1995), the centrist and nationalist factions were not able to work together efficiently and thus could not effectively exert power in unison. This stood in contrast to the president and the leftists as coherent players. Because the constitutional process was perceived by the deputies themselves as very similar to the process of the year before, there is no doubt that a "learning by doing" process had taken place, enabling nationalist and centrist factions to pursue different strategies. From 1994 to 1995, the centrist and nationalist factions were pushed by the president in their actions; from 1995 to 1996 they could act autonomously.

292 • Oliver Vorndran

Finally, the means of pressure the president could apply to parliament structurally was also different in these two periods. In June 1995, he announced a plebiscite on public trust in parliament and president. The result of this plebiscite—or, in other words, a general survey—would not have had any juridicial consequences. It might have led to the illegal dissolution of parliament by the president, but this consequence could not be taken for granted. On the contrary, in June 1996 the president announced a juridicially binding referendum on the draft constitution: the political document of highest authority and legitimacy, once ratified by the people. To change or contest a freshly confirmed constitution would have been nearly impossible and thus would have constituted a very solid limitation to all political actors. This was the main problem to be avoided in 1996. Deputies liked to set their frame of reference themselves, freely performing the sovereign will on behalf of the people.

Conclusions

This chapter has focused on the institutional players in the Ukrainian constitutional process and their changing interests. The underlying assumption throughout is that the pursuit of institutional power and influence is the best way to push through other (i.e., more ideological) concerns. This focus is justified by the fact that ideological concerns were more important for the political groupings that I have called "foot soldiers" in the introduction to this chapter, and less so for the main players —"softliners for" and "softliners against reforms." It was the *institutional* interest of the president, Kuchma's quest for legitimate governmental power, that instigated the constitutional process in the second and third stages, overcoming the focus on nation—as opposed to state building—of the Kravchuk presidency.

Institutional interests were the dominating concerns of the centrists as well, who had the greatest influence on the shape of the draft in the temporary committee, adopted at the first reading, which then became the blueprint for the new constitution. It therefore seems logical that the allies of the centrists in the temporary committee, the nationalists, were more successful in pressing their ideological interests than their counterparts, the leftists. One may argue against this reasoning that the ideological questions were not successfully addressed in the temporary committee but still disputed until the early morning of June 28, 1996. On the other hand, the centrists would not have had great incentives to concede these questions to the left, which impeded the constitutional process and was not willing to cooperate for most of the process. Thus only minor, mostly symbolic concessions were made to the leftists.

Regarding the fact that the ideological questions were the most difficult to answer and were "solved" at the latest possible stage, the institutional interest may be seen as the driving force of the constitutional process, whereas ideological interests inhibited an earlier adoption of the constitution. That is not only true for the last but for all three stages of the constitutional process. Therefore I agree that "institutional interests took precedence over longstanding passions."[55]

If one were to contemplate the cleavages and main conflicts after the adoption of the constitution between softliners for and against reforms—which are still the dominating political groupings—one is tempted to predict that the question, "What kind of market economy?" will be the dominant one on the future Ukrainian political agenda. The question of whether the Ukrainian state will continue to exist was decided by the new constitution, which signaled no going back. The question "Which form of government" is also addressed by the constitution and is likely to disappear from the political agenda. However, semi-presidential systems like the Ukrainian one are open to inherent transformation, mainly depending on the ability of parliament to act coherently and to influence the appointment of government. Under present conditions, the president should be regarded as the heavyweight. Besides the economic conflict, questions of "nationhood" and "cooperation with Russia" will for a long time remain priorities of the political agenda. They are the reesult of the regional diversity of Ukraine, which might be tempered over time but which is not at all likely ever to vanish.

Notes

1. Here the term "political constitution" does not mean a written constitution only, but also changing political customs (e.g., the introduction of political competition for offices) and structures (e.g., the formation of parties, changing electoral laws, etc.).
2. Claus Offe, "Das Dilemma der Gleichzeitigkeit: Demokratisierung, Marktwirtschaft und Territorialpolitik in Osteuropa," in Claus Offe, *Der Tunnel am Ende des Lichts* (Frankfurt: Campus, 1994), pp. 57–80.
3. "Group" in this case does not necessarily mean a well-organized and coherent group of people with specified common aims but politicians of roughly the same political tendency.
4. For a definition of hard- and softliners, see Guillermo O'Donnell and Philippe C. Schmitter, *Transitions from Authoritarian Rule: Tentative Conclusions about*

Uncertain Democracies (Baltimore and London: Johns Hopkins University Press, 1991), p. 16.

5. The hardliners did not build their own faction during the eleventh Verkhovna Rada and constituted a subgroup of the larger Group of 239. The Group of 239 was officially dissolved after the putsch in Moscow in August 1991 (Joachim Preuss, "Der Fuchs hat sich gefärbt," *Der Spiegel,* no. 37, 1991).

6. For example, the Dnipropetrovs'k "Clan," the Kharkivites, or people around the former Donets'k governor Volodymyr Shcherban'.

7. These were: Agrarians for Reforms (as long as they existed from June 1995 to June 1996), the Interregional Deputy Group, Social-Market Choice, Center, Unity, Independents, Constitutional Center (after September 1997) and Reforms (which also often cooperated with the nationalist factions).

8. The party *Rukh,* Ukrainian Republican Party, Democratic Party of Ukraine, Congress of Ukrainian Nationalists, and others.

9. The faction of the party *Rukh* and the faction Statehood (which in September 1996 merged with the Center faction to found the Constitutional Center faction).

10. For example: the army, the border guards, the presidential administration and the foreign office.

11. Alexander J. Motyl, *Dilemmas of Independence: Ukraine after Totalitarianism* (New York: Council on Foreign Relations, 1993), p. 77.

12. Ibid., pp. 68–70.

13. Iryna Pohorelova, "Sic Transit Kravchuk," *Eastern Economist,* vol. 1, no. 25, p. 11.

14. Kirk Mildner, "Die Ukraine im Umbruch. Transformation und Sicherheit einer zu spit gekommenen Nation," *Beitrige aus dem Fachbereich Sozialwissenschaften,* Heft 3, 1994, Humboldt-Universitat zu Berlin.

15. Michael Zienchuk, *Ukraine: Striving for Stabilization* (Warsaw: Center for Social & Economic Research, 1995), p. 26.

16. Alexander J. Motyl, *Creeping Institutionalisation or Creeping Zareization?* Paper prepared for the conference, "Soviet to Independent Ukraine: A Troubled Transformation," University of Birmingham, June 13–14, 1996, p. 13.

17. Alexander J. Motyl, "The Conceptual President: Leonid Kravchuk and the Politics of Surrealism," in Timothy J. Colton and Robert F. Tucker (eds.), *Patterns in Post-Soviet Leadership* (Boulder, Co. and Oxford: Westview Press, 1995), p. 120.

18. FBIS-SOV-94–120, June 22, 1994, p. 44.

19. *Interfax,* August 9, 1994.

20. Oleksandr Yurchuk, "Hrushevsky Street News," *Eastern Economist,* vol. 1, no. 45 (December 5, 1994) p. 22.

21. *Interfax-Ukraine,* November 23, 1994.

22. *IntelNews,* December 29, 1994.

23. *Interfax-Ukraine,* February 13, March 1 and 15, 1995.

24. Steshenko was the chairman of the Committee for State Building, Activity of the Soviets and Self-Government, and a member of the Communist faction.
25. Yuliya Mostovaya, "Khronika sobytii," *Zerkalo Nedeli,* April 15–21, 1995.
26. Unity, Reforms, *Rukh,* and Statehood. The factions Centre and the Interregional Deputy Group took part in the further elaboration of the Constitutional Agreement.
27. Surveys showed that the public was more confident in the president than in parliament (Iryna Pohorelova, "Plebiscite: 'A Moot Point?,'" *Eastern Economist,* vol. 2, no. 19, 1995, p. 17).
28. *IntelNews,* June 8, 1995.
29. It was an agreement *de jure* between the president and parliament as institutions.
30. *IntelNews,* vol. 5, no. 288 (October 22, 1995).
31. Sevastopol should have only two representatives in the senate. Ex-presidents should be members of the senate for life, as well.
32. Oleksandr Martynenko, "It is impossible to supervise everything from Kiev. There is a need to set the rules of the game." Interview with Leonid Kuchma, *Zerkalo Nedeli,* November 18–24, 1995.
33. Ibid.
34. *Interfax-Ukraine,* November 23, 1995, and *IntelNews,* vol. 5, no. 319 (November 24, 1995).
35. *Interfax,* Decembner 22, 1995, Ol'ha Chernaya, "V iyune v kalendare mozhet poyavit'sya 'krasnyi' den." Esli parlament primet Konstituciyuí, *Kievskiye Vedomosti,* January 16, 1996.
36. Ol'ha Chernaya, "Proekt konstitucii odobren. Chto dal'she?" *Kievskiye Vedomosti,* March 13, 1996.
37. Constitutional Agreement, Part IV, para. 2.
38. Oleksandr Yurchuk, "The Constitutional Follies. VR resorts to procedural shenanigans," *Eastern Economist,* vol. 3, no. 9 (March 25, 1996) p. 7; "Konstituciya 'stuchala' v dveri parlamenta. Deputaty reshali, c kakogo vxoda ee vpustit," *Kievskie Vedomosti,* March 20, 1996.
39. These were: *Rukh,* Statehood, Reforms, Center, Unity, Interregional Deputy Group, Independents, Social-Market Choice, and Agrarians for Reform.
40. Oleksandr Yurchuk, "Hrushevsky Street News," *Eastern Economist,* vol. 3, no. 10 (April 1, 1996).
41. *Interfax-Ukraine,* April 2, 1996.
42. *IntelNews,* May 13, 1996.
43. Ol'ha Chernaya, "Levye i pravye—poka nich'ya. No u kommunistov chislennoe preimushestvo," *Kievskie Vedomosti,* May 7, 1996; *Interfax-Ukraine,* May 13, 1996 and *IntelNews,* May 13, 1996.
44. The draft is reprinted in *Holos Ukrayiny,* June 28, 1996.
45. This interpretation follows the logic and structure of the constitution. Contrary to this opinion is the text of article 106, III, which states that the president may issue decrees "on the basis and in execution of the Constitution of

Ukraine and the laws of Ukraine." This regulation reopens the opportunity to issue decrees on nearly any subject, because the wording "on the basis and in execution of the Constitution of Ukraine" does not set any limit. Additionally, the article is not limited by time. In my opinion, this regulation is one of the weakest points of the constitution.

46. *Holos Ukrayiny,* June 28, 1996.
47. Constitution of Ukraine, Preamble.
48. Kataryna Wolczuk, "In Pursuit of a Compromise: The New Ukrainian Constitution." Paper prepared for the workshop, "State Building in Ukraine," Centre for Russian and East European Studies, University of Birmingham, March 3, 1997, p. 10.
49. Since 1991, Ukraine's foreign policy has been guided by the principle of reducing dependency upon Russia, but this does not necessarily mean leaning toward the West. Whether it is in the interest of Ukraine to choose the West or Russia for partnership in a future regional or global conflict cannot be decided during the (unlimited) lifetime of the constitution.
50. Almost one year after the adoption of the constitution, on May 31, 1997, the Ukrainian and the Russian presidents signed a treaty on friendship and cooperation, which also contained a leasing agreement for the use of the naval bases at Sevastopol by the Russian part of the Black Sea Fleet.
51. Interview with Bohdan Radeiko, Parliamentary Development Project, Kyiv, August 23, 1996.
52. Compare Kataryna Wolczuk, "The Politics of Constitution Making in Ukraine" (unpublished manuscript, 1996), p. 15: "Undoubtedly, the President's determination to clarify power relations and to strengthen the Presidency was a catalyst in pushing the whole process forward."
53. "Kuchma Addresses Supreme Council," FBIS-SOV-96–057, March 22, 1996, pp. 52–56.
54. "The decision of the President to call a constitutional referendum only took place when the Verkhovna Rada had already proved that it was capable of passing the constitution" (Iryna Pohorelova, "A Constitution Is Born," *Eastern Economist,* vol. 3, no. 23 (July 1, 1996), p. 1); "The justification for the referendum was the 'incapability of Parliament,' which shows Kuchma was not interested in the Constitution's adoption by the Rada." (Olga Ansimova, *IntelNews,* July 8, 1996); Interview with Bohdan Radejko, Parliamentary Development Project, Kyiv, August 23, 1996.
55. Op cit., K. Wolczuk, "In Pursuit of a Compromise," p. 7.

CHAPTER 11

The Donbas and Crimea: An Institutional and Demographic Approach to Ethnic Mobilization in Two Ukrainian Regions

Taras Kuzio and David J. Meyer

A large proportion of the analysis and commentary of contemporary Ukrainian affairs has focused upon the division between "Ukrainian-speaking," "nationalist," and "pro-European" west Ukraine, and a "Russian-speaking," "communist," and "pro-Eurasian" east Ukraine. This highly exaggerated and rather simplistic division of Ukraine usually argues that "Russian-speakers" will naturally gravitate toward Russia, up to and including demanding the separation of their regions from Ukraine. Such a flawed analysis led to fears that Ukraine in 1993 and early 1994 was on the verge of civil war between west and east Ukraine.[1]

This chapter takes a different approach to the question of state building, regionalism, and separatism in Ukraine by focusing on two of the most problematical regions in terms of their integration into the independent Ukrainian state. The Donbas encompasses two *oblasti* (Donets'k and Luhans'k), which account for nine percent of Ukrainian territory, 17 percent of its population, and a fifth of its industrial output. Crimea has a smaller population and its contribution to the Ukrainian economy is less significant than the Donbas. Nevertheless, the historical myths associated with such "hero cities" as Sevastopol, its geopolitical and strategic location, large ethnic Russian majority, ethnic diversity, and the location of large oil and gas reserves located off shore all ensure Crimea's strategic role.

This chapter argues that ethnopolitical mobilization and separatist sentiment in Ukraine was always only confined to Crimea. We analyze the reasons why ethnopolitical mobilization has been unsuccessful in the Donbas (and, by implication, in eastern and southern Ukraine as a whole). This chapter also argues that the provision of institutions through federal territorial arrangements (either as union republics within the former USSR or as autonomous republics within the Soviet successor states) contributes to ethnopolitical mobilization.[2] We also reach a different conclusion than Arel and Wilson,[3] who both emphasized ethnic and linguistic factors as likely to lead to ethnic mobilization in the Donbas and eastern-southern Ukraine. This chapter does not investigate the links between national identity, civil society, and ethnopolitical mobilization that have already been investigated by other authors.[4]

After laying out a theoretical framework, this chapter will examine six hypotheses concerning the presence of—or the lack of—Russian ethnopolitical mobilization in Crimea and the Donbas. These include three rival hypotheses of ethnic schism, recent settlement and/or incorporation as well as economic structure and the socioeconomic crisis. We then argue in favor of three hypotheses, which, in our view, explain the existence of Russian ethnopolitical mobilization in Crimea and its absence in the Donbas. These three include institutions, ethnic capital (which includes demographics, ethnic concentration, urbanization, etc.), and political parties.

Theoretical Framework

What is ethnic mobilization? This chapter defines ethnopolitical mobilization as the construction and activation of political organizations and/or institutions that are under (or are desired to be under) the exclusive control of an ethnic group. Though the demands of these ethnic groups may be closely linked to class interests, it is the activation of ethnic identity that causes such political, cultural, and economic demands to constitute ethnopolitical mobilization. Thus, this definition includes a much broader phenomenon than secessionist, irredentist, or autonomy campaigns.

The operational definition of ethnopolitical mobilization, then, is that both masses and elites elevate ethnic identity as the most important political identity, making and answering appeals to ethnic group solidarity for the sake of the greater good of the members of that ethnic group. This chapter assumes that the primordialist approach to ethnopolitical mobilization is wrong, because if it was true that significant primordial differences (which, in the Ukrainian-Russian case, arguably do not exist) are the most salient issues between Russians and Ukrainians, then the Russians of Crimea and the Russians of the Donbas should be in a state of equally advanced ethnopolitical mobilization. Therefore, an instrumentalist and elitist type of ethnopolitical mobilization is assumed to be a better instrument for explaining the different levels of political mobilization in Crimea and the Donbas.

This chapter will argue that the Russian population of the Donbas region of the Ukraine is less ethnopolitically mobilized than the Russian population of the Crimean Autonomous Republic because the Donbas (Donets'k and Luhans'k *oblasti*) Russian elites have fewer demographic and institutional resources to carry out ethnopolitical mobilization.[5] For the purposes of this chapter, institutions will be defined as bureaucratic and political party organizations. Resources will be defined and typologized in two ways. Demographic resources include such factors as the level of income and education of the ethnic community, as well as its level of urbanization and industrialization.[6] Institutional resources include the prestige of office, the functional differentiation and role specialization of an institution as an organization, and the money and coercive organs that a bureaucracy may possess, including press and media organs. In addition, they include the ease and reduction of operational transaction costs inherent in having standard operating procedures, set rules, defined roles, and a system of rewards and punishments for the execution of these roles.

As a result of the fact that the Donbas Russian elites have fewer of these resources than the Crimean Russian elites or the Donbas Ukrainian elites, the Donbas Russian elites have chosen to allow themselves to be co-opted into the multiethnic leftist movements of the Donbas. These movements, which also contain Ukrainians and Jews as well as Russians, represent virtually all of the Donbas Russians' demands, including the reestablishment of the former Soviet Union. Only an explicitly Russian ethnic appeal is lacking. Therefore, we conclude that the Donbas Russian elites have found it more easy, efficient, and effective to mobilize their constituencies along the lines of economic and social policy issues, as opposed to mobilizing an exclusivist ethnic identity.

Furthermore, we wish to state explicitly that we do not argue that Donbas Russians are not at all politically mobilized, (because they are indeed mobilized, but *not* ethnopolitically). Nor do we argue that among them there is no Russian ethnopolitical mobilization at all, but rather that their ethnopolitical mobilization is minor and peripheral, especially in comparison to Russian ethnopolitical mobilization in Crimea.

Although Crimean Russian ethnopolitical mobilization began in the period from 1989 to 1990, the acquisition of the institutions and the bureaucracy first of the Crimean ASSR and then of the Crimean Autonomous Republic served as a catalyst that even further strengthened ethnopolitical mobilization. The result of this institutional acceleration of mobilization was a quasi-federal Ukraine containing a region so autonomous and so mobilized that it declared independence in May 1992 and threatened to follow this course again in 1995 and 1998. Therefore, we do not posit a direct causal relationship with bureaucratic institutions as the independent variable and ethnopolitical mobilization as the dependent variable. Rather, elite ethnic entrepreneurs as the independent variable, institutions and demographic factors as intervening variables, and ethnopolitical mobilization as the dependent variable. Thus, the political institutions, namely the parties and *oblast*-level administrative structures, compelled and constrained the Russian elites in certain ways and empowered them to act in other ways.

The presence of an extensive bureaucracy and a directly elected presidency in the Crimean Autonomous Republic gave Crimean elites, such as Iurii Meshkov, even more resources (prestige, legitimacy, press coverage, and even international stature) with which to mobilize the Crimean Russians. Although Meshkov had already been organizing Crimean Russian ethnopolitical mobilization before the establishment of the Crimean Autonomous Republic and even before the independent Ukrainian state, his assumption of the presidency in January 1994 turned his social movement, the Republican Movement of Crimea (RDK), into a ruling political party. The fact that an ethno-nationalist organization such as the RDK and its separate but closely allied offshoot, the Russian Party of Crimea, assumed the presidential post meant that from then on Crimean businessmen, managers, *Mafiosi,* and other economic, political, and cultural elites could gain more influence or favor with the organization if they supported the RDK's secessionist agenda. Moreover, Meshkov's position as president of the peninsula established him as the clear leader of local Russian ethnopolitics, nationalism, and secessionism.

The Donbas Russians, in contrast, have had no one overarching leader, explicitly ethnic Russian party, or movement of size, although there were smaller "Russianist" parties and several sizable parties seeking re-establishment of the Soviet Union. Donbas Russians also have no comparable position of power and prominence for a secessionist leader because the executives of the Donbas administrations (like in all other *oblasti* except Crimea) are appointees of the Ukrainian president, and the Donbas *oblast* councils are dominated by ethnic Ukrainians, who are also a majority in these *oblasti.*

Thus, given their poverty of demographic and institutional resources, the Donbas Russian elites have not been able to mobilize their constituents on a purely ethnic basis but have found it expedient to join multiethnic leftist parties in order to pursue their goals. These goals included the establishment of closer relations with Russia and the CIS; the institution of Russian as a second state language; the freedom of choice of the language of instruction in schools; and the acquisition of regional economic and local self-government. We found no evidence, contrary to what Wilson argues,[7] that the 1994 elections showed widespread support *throughout* eastern and southern Ukraine for these demands which we argue were and remain mainly restricted to the Donbas and Crimea.

We also found no evidence of support by local elites or political parties in the Donbas for political autonomy as developed in the Crimea, let alone separatism. Local reformist elites in the Donbas support the vaguely coined "economic (not political) sovereignty" and "regional self government" in the manner of "free economic zones" from which they presumably hope to benefit.[8] Such zones are being established in the southern region of Donets'k *oblast*. The Communist Party of Ukraine (KPU), as we show later, is also not a supporter of political autonomy or separatism but is in favor of the entire Ukrainian state joining the Belarusian-Russian union as the first step toward reviving the former USSR.

Similarities between the Donbas and Crimea

The large differential in the levels of Russian ethnopolitical mobilization in Crimea and the Donbas are large. Yet eight variables are relatively constant between both regions:

1. Both regions are subject to the same national minorities policy set down by Kyiv, with the exception of the fact that Crimea is an autonomous republic while the Donbas is composed of two standard *oblasti*. We hypothesize that this difference is of major importance, and we will examine it later.

2. Both regions have Russian-speaking majorities of native speakers of Russian, with 66 percent of the Donbas population claiming Russian as its "native language" in the 1989 Soviet census (a figure that probably underestimated the true extent of the number of Russian-language speakers). Crimea, though, is alone among Ukraine's regions in possessing an ethnic Russian majority. This fact is hypothesized to be of major importance and will be examined later.

3. Both regions voted for independence in 1991 (Crimea by 54 percent and the Donbas by 83.88 percent).[9]
4. Both regions are experiencing Ukraine's socioeconomic crisis.
5. Both regions were subordinated first to Moscow and now to Kyiv.
6. Both regions were the sites of major Russian military defeats and victories, both in World War II and in earlier centuries.
7. Both regions have had very close and sizable economic, political, and cultural ties with both Ukraine and Russia.
8. Both regions are located adjacent to Russia.

The two regions differ mostly in their economic, ethnodemographic and institutional structures, and historical factors, such as when they were added to the Russian Empire and under what conditions. For example, the Donbas has even more native Russian speakers than Crimea, and these native Russians or Russian speakers and their ancestors have lived in Donbas for even longer than the Russians of Crimea. Nevertheless, the Donbas Russians are, counterintuitively, more quiescent than Crimean Russians.

Why, then, is there now a difference in the level of ethnopolitical mobilization of both regions?

Rival Hypotheses

Ethnic Schism

Ian Bremmer applied Albert Hirshman's paradigm of "exit, voice, and loyalty" to the case of the Russian populations in Ukraine. This paradigm includes "ethnic attachment," which he defines as "the sense of ethnic identification with the territory in question or . . . the extent to which members of an ethnic group consider the land upon which they are living to be "theirs," and "ethnic schism," which he defines as "the differentiation between ethnic groups."[10] The theory predicts that ethnic groups with high attachment to the land will opt for voice as opposed to exit or integration.

Ethnic schism includes racial, linguistic, religious, and cultural differences. Large differences between groups tend to inhibit integration, and so the greater the ethnic schism, the more difficult the possibilities of integration. Bremmer concludes that Russians and Ukrainians exhibit a low sense of ethnic schism, while both Crimea and the Donbas rate high for Russian ethnic attachment.

Ethnopolitical cleavages are lacking in the Donbas (because there the majority of Russians and Ukrainians are of one mind, as shall be argued later).

It is precisely this factor that helps to explain the relative absence of Russian ethnopolitical mobilization in the Donbas. It is simply not necessary to mobilize on an ethnic basis if the other ethnic group agrees with you. Therefore, the presence of ethnic schism, defined as major cultural differences and hate legends, is not useful for explaining the differential between the mobilization level of Donbas and Crimean Russians because both groups are very close culturally and even emotionally to their Ukrainian neighbors. This is true despite the fact that in Crimea the two ethnic groups show rather different political orientations, unlike in the Donbas, where the two ethnic groups have similar voting patterns:

| Donbas: | No Schism | No Mobilization |
| Crimea: | No Schism | Mobilization |

Therefore, we believe:

1. Ethnic schism is not a necessary condition for ethnopolitical mobilization.
2. Crimean ethnopolitical mobilization is not caused by fear or hate of the local Ukrainian population at the grass-roots level. Therefore, ethnopolitical mobilization is probably caused by elites who seek to increase their power and prestige. In addition, these elites are less hostile to the East Ukrainian and formerly Russophone President Leonid Kuchma than to his predecessor, who may have been *perceived* as both anti-Russian and as a "nationalist."

Recency of Settlement (and/or Incorporation Hypothesis)

Scholars often hypothesize that the Russians of Crimea feel that they should have the right to be independent and are therefore more receptive to ethnopolitical appeals because of the following three assertions. First, it has been noted by many observers that Crimea is the only region of Ukraine where ethnic Russians are an absolute majority. Second, Crimea's relatively recent incorporation into Ukraine in 1954 is seen as an illegitimate and arbitrary act of the Soviet authorities, whereas the Donbas is perceived as part of the ancient and primordial Ukrainian homeland. Third, most Crimean

Russians feel that they should be independent or, at least, should behave politically with ethnic cohesion because they or their parents were born in Russia. Donbas Russians, however, are more reconciled to Ukrainian rule because they and their recent ancestors lived in the Ukrainian SSR.

While these three hypotheses may be true concerning Crimea, there are a number of reasons to believe that the demographic situation and the historical-psychological perceptions in the Donbas are not very much different than those of Crimea. For example, most of the Russians in *both* the Donbas and Crimea settled there only after World War II.[11] Therefore, if recency of settlement or having parents or grandparents who were born in Russia tends to make Russians more amenable to ethnopolitical mobilization, then the Donbas, where a great part of the Russian population has lived only since the postwar era,[12] should have a similar level of Russian ethnopolitical mobilization as Crimea. Yet it clearly does not.

It may be the case that the hypothesis that Donbas Russians are less ethnopolitically mobilized than their Crimean brothers and sisters because they view the incorporation of the Donbas into Ukraine as more legitimate than the incorporation of Crimea into Ukraine in 1954. Unfortunately, there is no way to test the hypothesis other than to conduct a large survey on the issue, which no one has yet seen fit to undertake.

Does the fact that Crimea was colonized or resettled by Russians in the last fifty years have any influence on the fact that Crimean Russians mobilized? We will argue that this fact is not relevant to the mobilization question.

First of all, how would one hold all other variables equal except recency of settlement so as to prove that recent settlement increases the level of ethnopolitical mobilization? Although one could point to ethnopolitically mobilized recent settlers in Crimea, the West Bank, and Algeria in the 1950s, one could also point to very docile recent settlers in the United States, Canada, Australia, New Zealand, and the European Union, as well as in much poorer countries in Africa and Southeast Asia. On the other hand, there are many peoples of ancient and indigenous habitation, such as Karabakh Armenians, Hutus, Tutsi, and Bosnian and Krayina Serbs, who are very ethnopolitically mobilized indeed. Moreover, it is clear that both Russian communities feel a high attachment to the land. According to a study undertaken by the Moscow Center for the Study of Public Opinion in 1991, 90 percent of the Russians in Crimea and 89 per cent in eastern Ukraine (including the Donbas) agreed with the statement, "I do not feel myself to be a stranger in this Republic."[13] Therefore, the recency-of-settlement hypotheses have no hard evidence to support them as the main reason why Crimean Russians are more ethnopolitically mobilized than the Donbas Russians.

Another argument that is often utilized is that because ethnic Russians are in the majority in Crimea, they are therefore more likely to be ethnopolitically mobilized. At the same time, Russians are only a few percentage points from being a majority in the Donbas *oblasti*. Although it cannot be definitely proven, it is likely that these few percentage points may be of very little significance in the receptivity of the Russian population to mobilization. Furthermore, it is significant that throughout history many areas of the world have a local majority of an ethnic group that is a national minority, but these local majorities are not ethnopolitically mobilized. Even on a national level, being in the majority does not necessarily cause ethnopolitical mobilization, or as least not under many conditions. The examples of the black South Africans under apartheid, the Indians under the Raj, and numerous examples of other colonized peoples prove the point.

This leads one directly to the question, "Where does one draw the boundaries in defining where a national minority becomes a local majority?" The importance of this question is behind such familiar issues as racial gerrymandering in the United States. The question leads directly into another question with which this chapter will deal at length; namely, "Is it not the institution or the very existence of this arbitrary boundary demarcating where one is a majority or a minority within the constituency area of a democratic institution that determines, or at least strongly influences, the ease with which an ethnic group may be politically mobilized?" The suggested answer to this question will be found in the section concerning the resource-centered hypotheses about the infrastructural power of institutions and of the structure of ethnic capital. But first, another rival hypothesis will be examined.

Socioeconomic Crisis Hypothesis

If a bad economy is the cause of ethnopolitical mobilization, we should expect to find that Russians in the Donbas, which, like Crimea, is experiencing Ukraine's sharp economic downturn, should be just as ethnopolitically mobilized as Crimean Russians. It is frequently supposed that the reason for the difference in the levels of Russian minority ethnopolitical mobilization is that Crimean Russians may conclude that their peninsula will benefit from Russian annexation and Russian tourism. Meanwhile, Donbas Russians may fear that if they are annexed by the Russian Federation, they will not obtain subsidies from Moscow and they will become simply another money-losing region of Russia. Indeed, the cost of production of coal in the Donbas is high and is even increasing.[14] However, a more in-depth look at the economics of dependency in both regions shows that there is not as much basis for the above assertions as one might expect, and that, in fact, there is much evidence to support opposite conclusions.

The following evidence shows that the Donbas relies on Russia even more than Crimea does and that the Donbas is actually more economically independent from Ukraine than Crimea is. Yet Donbas Russians are not as ethnopolitically mobilized as are Crimean Russians, which one might expect to find if a region relied economically more on a country to which it wanted to be annexed.[15]

The problem is further compounded by the fact that the Donbas formerly enjoyed a privileged status within the former Soviet Union, owing to its crucially important coal-mining industry. Furthermore, the Donbas region was closely managed from Moscow, resulting in a high dependency on its economic links with the former USSR and Soviet center. The local Communist Party leader Georgii Biko holds that the Donbas industry used to depend up to 70 percent on supplies from Russia's economy and up to 85 percent on supplies from the economy of the former USSR as a whole.[16]

Moreover, in 1985 the Donets-Dnipro region accounted for 36.4 percent of Soviet ferrous metallurgical production. "This reflected the all-Union importance of the iron and steel industry of the latter region, based upon Donbas coal . . . Donets-Dnipro is also a major producer of heavy machinery."[17] Data available suggest that Donets-Dnipro also produced significant amounts of the Soviet Union's primary industries, fuels, machine building and metal working, and even food production. This evidence is cited to underline the fact that the Donbas was closely tied to the remainder of the Soviet economy, probably more so even than Crimea. Therefore, if economic ties to the former Soviet Union were the determining factor causing Russian ethnopolitical mobilization, Donbas should be more mobilized than Crimea. Since they are not, all-Union economic ties should be excluded as the primary cause of Russian ethnopolitical mobilization in Ukraine, although they may serve as a catalyst.

Some observers have theorized that the Donbas may be less ethnopolitically mobilized because Donbas Russian elites know, or at the very least have strong reason to believe, that if they were part of Russia they would not receive subsidies from the Russian government. This is true, particularly since the former Russian Viktor Chernomyrdin government tightened up on the extension of soft credits in an attempt to cut inflation in the Russian Federation. On the other hand, the Donbas (if not already in the present, then in the future) may be able to play the ethnicity card to blackmail Kyiv into subsidizing its failing industries. This fact makes it all the more surprising that the Donbas Russians have not yet mobilized ethnopoliti-cally. But the other side of this argument is that the Donbas was also heavily reliant on Russia and the remainder of the Soviet Union, and that this could equally serve as an incentive to engage in ethnopolitical mobilization with the goal of secession.

The Donbas working class "is in fact less well qualified than that in other industrial areas of the Ukraine, more dependent on the collective provision of welfare, and more anxious about its prospects in a genuinely marketised economy."[18] Therefore, it is logical to conclude that the ethnic Russians, be-cause they do not have the institutional and/or demographic resources nec-essary to mobilize ethnopolitically, must ally with ethnic Ukrainian workers who are in the same position of facing layoffs and closures of their factories and mines. Hence the support of Russophones for left-wing political forces.

Meanwhile, other observers argue that Crimea is more secessionist be-cause it relied heavily on all-Union, but especially Russian, tourism. How-ever, it should be pointed out that it was not only the Donbas economy that was heavily reliant on the remainder of the Soviet Union, especially Russia. Crimea, in fact, is also heavily dependent on Ukraine both for trade and for basic material and energy inputs, such as water and electricity.[19] Crimea re-ceives 85, 75, and 85 percent, respectively, of its fresh water, industrial pro-duction, and electricity from Ukraine. Former President Kravchuk therefore was fond of pointing out to the Crimeans that "The economic consequences of Crimea's separation from Ukraine would be catastrophic."[20]

Moreover, in Crimea, Ukrainian capital investment per person was higher than the republican average by about 15 to 20 percent, unlike in the Donbas, which actually lost investment to Kyiv.[21] Therefore, *both* Crimea and the Donbas were and remain heavily dependent on both Ukraine and Russia. Since the variables of economic and resource dependency are held constant, they cannot explain the differential in the dependent variable—namely, why the Russians of the Donbas are not as ethnopolitically mobi-lized as Russians in Crimea.

Explaining Different Levels of Ethnopolitical Mobilization

Institutionalist Hypothesis

Why is there no regional association of Donbas Russian elites? The most likely answer is that there are no uniquely ethnic Russian power structures or even ethnic Russian-dominated institutions of an ostensibly interethnic nature in the Donbas region. Without any institutions dominated by their own elites, the Donbas Russians did not have elites with enough resources and power to mobilize their communities.

Brubaker predicts that Russian minorities in the new republics of the former Soviet Union will demand communal rights and privileges and will mobilize if these are not granted, fearing that any government that does not recognize communal rights will de facto or *de jure* discriminate against them.[22] But Brubaker's hypothesis does not explain why some Russians in some regions will be more resistant to the formally liberal model of rule, while others will be quiescent.

Brubaker sets forth the presence of the institutions of the national republics as the key reason why some nationalities successfully mobilized while others did not.[23] Thus, Brubaker's proposition can be logically extrapolated to form the hypothesis that Crimean Russians are mobilizing because they dominated pre-existing political institutions that were left over from the Soviet era and have further transformed them in the era of Ukrainian independence. This section of the chapter will attempt to show that this institutionalist hypothesis, in conjunction with demographic patterns that will be explored later, does indeed form a powerful explanation of why Crimean Russians are mobilized while the Donbas Russians are not.

An institutionalist explanation for Crimea's higher level of mobilization is that Crimean Russian elites, because of their elevated status as the heads of an autonomous republic, were able to use the infrastructural power and resources of their positions to mobilize the ethnic Russians of Crimea behind a campaign for greater autonomy and even independence. Roeder notes that expanded autonomy is one way for ethnic cadres to enlarge the resources within their control. Autonomy increases their discretion in the allocation of positions for power within the republic and in the administration of educational and employment policies.[24] Therefore, the elites of Crimea and the Donbas would be expected to equally want such autonomy. Indeed, both Donbas Ukrainians and Donbas Russians primarily demand greater regional autonomy, usually including the federalization of Ukraine. They also demand social guarantees from the state, the institution of Russian as a second state language, dual citizenship, closer relations with Russia, and greater integration into the Commonwealth of Independent states (CIS).[25] Nevertheless, Crimean Russian elites in the local parliament have been able to organize more effectively for the attainment of the above-mentioned goals because of their dominant position at the head of formerly powerful institutions.

When demands in the Donbas have been prioritized they show little public concern for linguistic, ethnic, or separatist issues (such as political autonomy, state support for national minorities, dual citizenship, etc.). We hypothesize that demands for the revival of the former USSR are linked to nostalgia for the socioeconomic stability of the Soviet era and a protest against declining living standards in the post-Soviet era. These more overtly ethnic and political demands tend to be prioritized only by elites in Crimea where they find a receptive public audience. See Table 11.1.

Roeder holds to an elite-centered theory of ethnopolitical mobilization in which neither primordial nor instrumentalist motives are sufficient, but are necessary.[26] It was this kind of institutional change—namely, the establishment of Ukrainian independence and the elevation of Crimea from an *oblast* to an autonomous republic (in effect, a virtual state within a state)—that enabled and motivated Crimean Russian elites to mobilize their community ethnopolitically. Their initial success gave them new resources that allowed them to acquire still further resources and demand even more. The Donbas Russian elites, however, did not even dominate their *oblast* councils and thus were not able to start the accumulative process of ethnomobilization to acquire institutions that facilitated further mobilization. The ability of Crimean Russian elites to enact such a successful strategy was rooted in the Soviet federal system.[27]

Roeder's institutional approach asserts that the institutions that allowed the Soviets to rule and to maintain order then became hijacked by ethnic entrepreneurs and were used as a means of ethnopolitical mobilization.[28] In the same way, this chapter argues that Crimean Russians are more mobilized

Table 11.1   Attitudes of the Population of Southern and Eastern Ukraine

Priority	Percent
Employment and social guarantees	41
Revival of the USSR	32
Law and order	26
Support for business	22
Return to socialism	21
Privatization	21
Russian as a second state language	20
Consolidation of Ukrainian statehood	15
Greater autonomy	13
Dual citizenship	11
Support to national minorities (including Russians)	8

Source: Iryna Bekeskina, "The Social and Economic Attitudes of the Population of Southern and Eastern Ukraine," *Political Portrait of Ukraine,* no. 3 (October 28, 1994).

than the Donbas Russians because the Crimean ASSR, and later the Crimean Autonomous Republic, possessed institutions that the Russian local majority could use in the process of ethnopolitical mobilization by marshaling resources and channeling ethnic grievances into formal interest articulation and policy formation.

Roeder predicts that the ethnic groups that are relatively advantaged will be the most ethnopolitically assertive.[29] Indeed, on the eve of the disintegration of the former USSR, ethnic Russians in Ukraine were more urbanized, more highly educated, and more highly paid than Ukrainians (346 to 314 rubles respectively).[30] But if income alone were the most important criteria, then the Donbas should be just as ethnopolitically mobilized as Crimea.

The fact that ethnic Russians dominated the Supreme Soviet of the Crimean *oblast* was the first level of institutionalization that gave them the ability to mobilize further for more autonomy and for the increase in resources that such autonomy provided. These resources were then used to mobilize Crimean Russian masses. The beginning of the acceleration of the institutionalization of the power of the Crimean Russian elites was the September 1990 petition of the Crimean Supreme Soviet to its USSR and Russian SFSR counterparts to re-establish the Crimean ASSR.[31] On January 20, 1991, a referendum was held in which 82 percent of the electorate participated, yielding a 93.2 percent vote in favor of the restoration of "the Crimean ASSR as a subject of the USSR and as a party to the Union Treaty."[32] On February 12, 1990, the Ukrainian Supreme Soviet restored the Crimean ASSR. A few months later, on the same day that Ukraine declared independence, August 24, 1991, Meshkov founded the RDK, aiming for the eventual secession of Crimea. On September 4, 1991, the Crimean parliament declared state sovereignty as a constituent part of Ukraine, and on February 26, 1992, the Crimean parliament voted to change the name of the Crimean ASSR to the Crimean Republic.[33] Just a little more than two months later, on May 5, 1992, the Crimean Russian elites felt that they had enough resources and institutional infrastructure to declare independence from Ukraine. Such action may have partially been in reaction to the impending July 1992 presidential decree on appointing presidential prefects.[34]

The above survey provides some crucial evidence concerning this chapter's main hypothesis that ethnic entrepreneur control of institutions is the independent variable causing ethnic mobilization of Russians in Ukraine. The Donbas Russians are ruled by an executive appointed by the Ukrainian president. Not only does this deprive the Donbas Russian ethnic entrepreneurs of crucial resources, but these prefects also greatly strengthened Kyiv's local power. Most importantly, the institution of such prefects gave Kyiv the ability to keep ethnopolitical mobilization, particularly the secessionist variety, to a minimum.

In contrast, at the time of the May 1992 Crimean declaration of independence, despite the fact that Kravchuk had already issued the decree on presidential prefects, Crimea had no presidential representative to rein in the secessionists. In fact, it was not until December 17, 1992 that the Ukrainian parliament passed the "Law on the Representation of the President of Ukraine in the Republic of Crimea."[35] The institution of Crimean presidential prefect was seriously implemented only by Kravchuk's successor, Kuchma, which greatly strengthened Kyiv's ability to deal with Crimean separatism. In the words of Vasily Kiselev, presidential prefect in Crimea, "I immediately said that Crimeans who did not care to live in Ukraine could pack their bags and leave."[36]

Instead of using a prefect to suppress Crimean Russian elites, Kyiv tried to placate the Crimean parliament by giving them even more power on June 30, 1992. Indeed, the Crimean Autonomous Republic had acquired so much autonomy that a few months later the parliamentary newspaper *Holos Ukraiiny* carried an article entitled, "The Republic of Crimea is a legal democratic and civic state inside Ukraine."[37] The justification for such a masthead will now be examined.

On June 30, 1992, the Ukrainian parliament passed a law "On the Delineation of Power Between the Organs of State Rule of Ukraine and the Republic of Crimea." The law established dual citizenship of both Crimea and Ukraine for inhabitants of the peninsula and granted Crimea property rights to all the land and natural resources on its territory.[38] The powers and resources thus made available to the Russian elites controlling this institution were truly impressive. In addition to this, on May 28, 1992, the Ukrainian parliament voted to allocate six billion rubles to Crimea to invest in social programs and to solve credit and monetary problems. Such large amounts of aid to the Crimean Autonomous Republic could only have strengthened the power of Crimean Russian elites like Meshkov, as these new funds could be used for patronage in building up his secessionist RDK party and in carrying out other means of ethnopolitical mobilization of the Crimean Russian population. Freedom to do this was further enhanced by the fact that Crimea was granted special economic status on June 1, 1992.

In economic matters, the ethno-politically mobilizing Crimean government was strengthened by being given the right to nationalize property and to tax.[39] More financial power was ceded to it on October 19, 1993, when then-Crimean Parliamentary Speaker Nikolai Bagrov signed a new protocol with President Kravchuk that re-created a Crimean Republican Bank, a Crimean Bank for Hard Currency Exchange, and a one-channel taxation system, so that taxes collected would remain on the peninsula. Crimea also gained the right to register representatives of foreign firms that conducted business in the Crimean Autonomous Republic.[40]

The fact that Kyiv ceded the power to appoint the chief executive of the Crimean Autonomous Republic and agreed merely to have a representative that was in many ways like a foreign embassy probably did much to cement the control of the Crimean Russian ethnic entrepreneurs. Within one year they succeeded in electing one of their own, Meshkov, the foremost secessionist on the peninsula, as their president.

Armed with such formidable capabilities and resources, it is little wonder that the Crimean Russian elite were able to mobilize their community to the extent that they felt free to do.[41] It is significant that such a radical action came after the institutional grip of the Crimean Russian elites was even further strengthened by the decision of the Crimean parliament on September 17, 1993 to pass a law establishing a presidency. Elections were held on January 30, 1994.[42] By this time the Russian community was so mobilized that only one of the six candidates in the Crimean presidential election supported the peninsula remaining a part of Ukraine, and that one candidate was Bagrov, the Russified Ukrainian who authored Crimea's first declaration of independence.[43]

The effects of instituting the presidency were immediate and powerful. "As it turned out, by propelling Meshkov to centre stage the presidential election set the preconditions for a renewed conflict between Kyiv and Simferopol and, by all accounts, has strengthened Moscow's position vis-à-vis Kyiv," Solchanyk argued.[44] An example of the use of the institutional strength of the presidency is the following: " . . . President Meshkov put three questions to the Crimean electorate that were designed to strengthen his negotiating position with Kyiv."[45] This is a classic example of Crimean Russian ethnic entrepreneurs using their institutional infrastructural power to attempt to mobilize their ethnic Russians.

The Crimean Russian political elites, especially those in the Communist Party and the ex-*nomenklatura* in the secessionist movement (like Meshkov), utilized ethnic mobilization as a way of trying to maintain their special status and to preserve their power. But in the Donbas the Russians are a minority in both *oblasti,* and the Russified Ukrainians consider themselves to be Ukrainians or are largely indifferent to bald appeals to Russian nationalism. The existence of the Crimean ASSR and then the Crimean Autonomous Republic explains why Crimean Russian elites would be in a much better position to mobilize their community, while the Donbas Russians had no distinct corps of native cadres of their own. Because the self-consciously Donbas Russians are too few in number and have no institutional levers of their own to use, ethnopolitical mobilization has not taken place.

The election of Meshkov, leader of the RDK, as Crimean president in January 1994 proved to be the highlight of the separatist movement. With the abolition of the institution of Crimean presidency and the placing of the Crimean government under Kyiv's direct control in March of the following year, the range of institutions available for ethnopolitical mobilization narrowed. Since 1995 the Supreme Soviet and Cabinet of Ministers in Crimea have been dominated by pro-Kyiv loyalists drawn from the Tatar, centrist (for example, the Party of Economic Revival and the Agrarians), and left-wing political spectrum (communists), which is opposed to separatism and Russian ethnopolitical mobilization. By 1997 the majority of the former "pro-Russian" political forces had "forgotten about their slogans calling for the annexation of Crimea to Russia." Instead they had moved toward a less radical and more broadly focused agenda similar to "pro-Russian" groups in the Donbas that advocate defense of Russian-language speakers and Ukraine's membership of the Russian-Belarusian Union (but no longer separatism).[46] This decline in ethnic separatism in Crimea was also facilitated by the signing of the Russian-Ukrainian interstate legislation in May 1997, which recognized Ukrainian sovereignty over Crimea.

Ethnic Capital Hypothesis

Demographic hegemony or parity alone is not sufficient to cause ethnopolitical mobilization. However, the question ignores the crucial issue of institutional power, which serves as a strong catalyst or vehicle for transforming demographic resources into actual political, economic, and ethnopolitical mobilizational power. Nevertheless, in order to create or to capture the institutions necessary for carrying out ethnopolitical mobilization, a certain amount of demographic resources are necessary.

In 1979, Russians constituted 47 percent of the urban population in Luhans'k, 46 percent of the urban population of Donetsk, and 74 percent of the urban population of Crimea. The Russian percentage of the rural population was 27 percent in Luhans'k, 19 percent in Donets'k, and 58 percent in Crimea.[47] The strong Russian presence in the cities of the Donbas is even further magnified by the presence of the Russified Ukrainian population, and together they form a majority that is Russian in language and culture. The city of Donets'k is 44 percent Russian and 68 percent Russian-speaking. The city of Luhans'k is 45 percent Russian and 64 percent Russian-speaking, while Crimea is 67 percent Russian and 83 percent Russian speaking.[48] The Russian population of the Donbas is 3.6 million, and 66 percent of the Donbas population claimed Russian as its native tongue in the 1989 Soviet census.[49]

The fact that only 32 percent of the Donbas claimed Ukrainian as its "native language" in the 1989 census should not be taken to mean that the Ukrainian language is "foreign" to the inhabitants of the Donbas. Only 15 percent of Russians, Belarusians, and Jews professed no understanding of Ukrainian. Meanwhile, 42.5 and 37.2 percent respectively either knew the Ukrainian language or understood it.[50] But there was little optimism among those polled that their knowledge of Ukrainian would improve because of the low level of language adaptation among those used to utilizing the previous Soviet state language (Russian). Volodymyr Bilets'kyi, head of the Ukrainian Culturological Centre in Donets'k and editor of the magazine *Skhid*, believed that at the current level of "Ukrainianization" it would take between 80 and 100 years before the number of Ukrainian language schools reflected the ethnic balance in the *oblast*.[51] Similarly, in Crimea, ethnic Ukrainians, who account for a quarter of the population, possessed only two Ukrainian-language schools.[52] In contrast, 586 Russian-language schools and fifteen Crimean Tatar schools catered to the ethnic Russian and Tatar populations of the peninsula.[53]

According to the 1989 Soviet census, eastern Ukraine is 15.9 percent rural. Thus, one can deduce that the region's population is 84.1 percent urban. The Donbas is both highly urbanized and highly industrialized. Therefore, its Russians and Ukrainians should be among the most highly mobilized (certainly to the same degree as Crimea), according to such theorists as Joseph Rothschild. Thus, urbanization and industrialization alone are not sufficient to cause ethnopolitical mobilization.

That the Donbas Russians are politically mobilized, but not by ethnicity, is demonstrated by the fact that they participated in presidential elections and voted for a Russified Ukrainian, Kuchma, by 54.3 percent in both Donets'k and Luhans'k *oblasti*. Oleksandr Moroz, head of the Socialist Party of the Ukraine and candidate of the left in the 1994 presidential elections, received only 25.4 percent and 16.3 percent respectively in both *oblasti*. Nevertheless, this mobilization in the Donbas is socioeconomic—not ethnic or linguistic—in nature. A total of 80 percent of Donets'k voters supported the idea of a federal Ukraine, 87 percent approved the proposition that Russian should be used as a second state language in Ukraine (90.4 percent in Luhans'k), and 88.7 percent believed that Russian should be "the language of education, science, and administration" (90.9 percent in Luhans'k). Meanwhile, 88.7 percent were in favor of Ukraine becoming a full member of a treaty of economic union with the remainder of the CIS (90.7 percent in Luhans'k).

Most (though not all) Russified Ukrainians (and even Donbas Russians) have shown no disloyalty to Ukrainian statehood.[54] They have merely elected politicians like Kuchma who claimed he would be amenable to closer ties with Russia. These Russified Ukrainians often seem to be just as afraid of having the Ukrainian language and culture forced upon them as Russians are; hence, they vote for many of the same candidates that the Russians do. Indeed, Arel and Wilson hypothesize that the fact that Russophone Ukrainians exist and often side with Russians on political issues is one of the main reasons why Ukraine has avoided ethnic conflict.[55]

Another dimension of Russian ethnic capital (demographic structure) and how it affects Russian political behavior is the element of class structure in the various regions of Ukraine. One might assume that Russians, as the majority in Crimea, are at least moderately well distributed across classes. In the Donbas, however, the situation is otherwise.

If it is true that the Donbas Russians are mostly working class, then one might assume that they have found class ties and class interests to be more important than ethnic ties, especially since they share a Russian cultural framework with many, if not most, of their Ukrainian fellow workers. Rothschild asserts that the mutual cultural rejection by a dominant and a subordinate ethnic group can succeed in facilitating political integration provided that the dominant group allows "life chances" (socioeconomic opportunities) to equalize and that the subordinates are not secessionist.[56]

In the Ukrainian case, Russians and Ukrainians are not mutually rejecting each other's cultures, as millions of Ukrainians either speak fluent Russian or are actually Russified, and most Russians can at least understand Ukrainian, while 33 percent speak it fluently. Although "life chances" are just about equal at this moment, with no significant discrimination, fear of future discrimination and reduction in "life chances" seems to exist in both regions. This would explain why both regions voted for the more moderate and more conciliatory Kuchma over Leonid Kravchuk.

But why would such fears be even greater in Crimea than in the Donbas? Precisely because in Crimea the Russian elites have the institutional resources and infrastructure to engage in panic-mongering and rabble-rousing and the trappings of officialdom to legitimize such activity. Rothschild does not explain why a group might be secessionist in the first place, other than that the ethnic elites see it in their personal best interests to secede, and they use their power and resources to convince their ethnic group of this. Nor does Rothschild explain why one group of ethnopolitical entrepreneurs would be more successful at mobilizing than another group of ethnopolitical entrepreneurs.

Moreover, in the Donbas the Russian elites can and must compete with Ukrainian politicians, who may attract Russian votes. Likewise, the Russian politicians must try to attract Ukrainian votes. Because the two populations are so culturally similar, the Donbas political elites must try to adopt centrist positions that will attract the mainstream majority. In contrast, Crimea has an overwhelming majority of ethnic Russians, and therefore more extreme and particularistic appeals can be made because the politicians need not make much effort to attract Ukrainian and Tartar voters. Also, since many Crimean Ukrainians are Russified, there is even less of a need to adopt positions conciliatory to Ukrainian nationalism, whereas opposing Kyiv in the name of the *Ruskiy narod*[57] may be rewarded. With an ethnic power base intact, Crimean Russian elites feel free to engage in more radical politics against the center in Kyiv. In fact, the Russian elites seem to feel themselves to be so secure that they can afford to take part in extensive infighting. An example of this was the bitter feud between then-Crimean President Meshkov and then-Crimean Parliamentary Speaker Sergei Tsekov in late 1994.

Since the Russians of the Donbas are accustomed to living with a huge like-minded, Russified Ukrainian community that comprises a large local majority when in coalition with the Russians, Donbas Russians feel no need to mobilize ethnically against the Ukrainian ethnic group. Instead, they feel a need to mobilize as a general political movement or as a region against another general political movement and region, the least Russified and more nationally conscious western and central Ukraine. Moreover, the Donbas elites have political allies in the regions of south Ukraine and the Black Sea Littoral *oblasti*, including, of course, Crimea. The Crimean Russian elites, on the other hand, possess enormous demographic hegemony magnified by institutional domination. Therefore, they face very little electoral threat, and they even obtain electoral support from the highly Russified local Ukrainians (47 percent of whom claim Russian as their mother tongue). Fearing "Ukrainianization" or at least manipulating such a fear to ensure that they are themselves re-elected, Crimean Russian elites used the state institutions that they dominated in order to mobilize and politicize Russian ethnicity as a means of whipping up support both locally and internationally.

Ethnic and Nonethnic Political Parties Hypothesis

The nature of the political parties in which the Russian minority of Ukraine participate is a salient point that bears out the thesis that the leftist parties of the Donbas have co-opted Russian cultural and socioeconomic demands and voiced them in universalist terms, thus avoiding parochial ethnonationalist mobilization. The Crimean Russian elites, in sharp contrast, have engaged in overt ethnopolitical mobilization right from the start of Ukraine's *perestroika*-era independence drive.

Thus, even movements for greater regional autonomy have not taken on an ethnic coloration, and they have adopted such non-ethnic names as "The Movement for a Democratic Donbas," "The Movement for the Revival of the Donbas," and "The Civic Congress of Ukraine." This behavior is quite different from that of such organizations as the RDK, which are blatantly ethnic and chauvinistic in their appeal and constitution. The RDK was renamed the Republican Congress of the Crimea-Party of the Republican Movement of Crimea at its October 1992 congress.[58] The Russian Party of Crimea was formed in February 1993 as a radical offshoot of the RDK.[59]

The pro-Russian and separatist movements of Crimea have undertaken a number of metamorphizations since then. The collapse of the Russia Bloc grouped around the RDK between 1994 and 1995 due to in-fighting and a tougher Ukrainian response, led to a decline in ethnomobilization on the Crimean peninsula. The Russia Bloc had always been opposed by a powerful anti-Russian nationalist Crimean branch of the Communist Party of Ukraine (KPU), which is hostile, like its parent body, to separatism. The Crimean branch of the KPU opposed an independent Crimean state and, again like the KPU, backed Ukraine's membership of a revived USSR.[60] Since 1995 the Crimean Russian ethnonationalist movement is only a pale shadow of its former self, with anti-separatist and anti-Russian nationalist forces within the Tatar, centrist, and left camps representing the majority within the only two Crimean institutions still existing (the Supreme Soviet and the Cabinet of Ministers). The government was led by a close relative of Kuchma's, Anatoly Franchuk, while the parliamentary presidium was divided between Tatars and the Party of Economic Revival (the Crimean "Party of Power").

Within the Supreme Soviet, the "pro-Russian" deputies were grouped within the *Soyuz* (Union) faction, which commanded only 40 out of 96 seats. *Soyuz* is composed mainly of former members of the Russia Bloc. In contrast to the separatist agenda of the former Russia Bloc, though, *Soyuz,* like its Donets'k-based Civic Congress ally in the 1998 parliamentary elections, backs Ukraine's membership of the Russian-Belarusian Union—not separatism and

Russian ethnopolitical mobilization. Outside the Crimean Supreme Soviet and government, ethnic Russian nationalists are grouped in the Congress of Russian Communities of Crimea.[61]

Significantly, it was regional and economic autonomy, not political autonomy or separation, that the Donbas miners demanded in the strike movement of 1993. Again, in the March 1994 parliamentary elections, "The [Donbas] candidates who represent[ed] political parties are mainly adherents of strong pro-Russian and left-wing parties demanding regional autonomy within Ukraine."[62] Among the political parties and their politicians in the Donbas who were seeking closer ties to Russia (but not secessionism or exclusive Russian nationalism), we had the Inter-Regional Bloc for Reforms (MRBR), Civic Congress, the Slavic, Labor, Socialist, and Communist parties. The Liberal Party supported the "nationalist" and pro-European Kravchuk candidate in the 1994 presidential elections. Many of these political parties were established between 1992 and 1993 in Donets'k to defend regional and economic interests.[63] But the proliferation of these political parties since 1992 in the Donbas should not be confused with a vibrant civil society. Not a single political party has developed an infrastructure in Donets'k, one of Ukraine's largest cities.[64]

Since the 1994 elections, Kuchma has distanced himself from the "pro-Russian" MRBR, and its leader, Vladimir Grynev, his adviser on regional questions, was released. The Constitutional Democratic Party and the MRBR created the *SLON* election bloc for the March 1998 parliamentary elections; it was one of the few blocs to unsuccessfully campaign on a linguistic and ethnic platform in defense of "Russian speakers." Since becoming president in July 1994 Kuchma has expressed little interest in following the prescriptions of Grynev and the MRBR on language questions and federalism. Instead, the pro-European People's Democratic Party and the New Ukraine bloc have become Kuchma's "Party of Power" and election bloc respectively in the 1998 and 1999 elections. Meanwhile, the Labor Party, a party originally established by enterprise directors lukewarm toward reform, has moved away from its earlier flirtation with "pro-Russianism." During the 1998 parliamentary elections it formed the "together" bloc with the pro-European Liberal Party, a party established by "New Ukrainians" (that is, private entrepreneurs). The Socialist Party and its allies in the 1998 elections, the Peasant Party, whose membership are composed mainly of ethnic Ukrainians, have also moved away from their earlier "pro-Russian" stance toward a more "national communist" line. The KPU, with its more ethnically mixed membership, has maintained its distance from both a "national communist" and overtly ethnic Russian platforms in favor of a Soviet restorationist program.[65]

Another example of a pro-autonomy but non-ethnic party is the Donbas Inter-Front (Internationalist Front). A Donbas political scientist and journalist at the newspaper *Donetskii Kriazh,* Dmitrii Kornilov, established the Ukrainian Inter-Front in December 1990 in order to oppose the implementation of the 1989 "Law on Languages," which declared Ukrainian to be the sole state language of Ukraine. The Inter-Front gave rise to the Democratic Movement of the Donbas, which was founded in October 1991 in Luhans'k and is led by Oleksandr Makhmudov, a former head of the Donets'k City Council, and Yurii Boldyrev of the former coal miners' movement. The Inter-movement's program called for "regional autonomy for the Donbas within a federal Ukraine," local state status for the Russian language, and dual citizenship between Russia and Ukraine. It promised to "struggle against ethnic prejudice," and to uphold "the right of the individual to free choice: in language use."[66] Thus the presence of such multiethnic left-wing parties that have co-opted Russians by voicing their demands has made it unnecessary for Donbas Russians to mobilize ethnopolitically, thereby facilitating political mobilization around regional, social, and economic issues instead. The Inter-Front of the Donbas, unlike in the three Baltic states or Moldova, was never controlled by the Communist Party and never supported a separatist agenda. By the period 1993 to 1994 it wound down, because the local population had lost interest.[67]

It may be argued by some that the KPU is ethnonationalist because it favors the reconstruction of the Soviet Union. However, such a demand is not necessarily ethnonationalist, since the KPU would doubtlessly like to see all regions of Ukraine, regardless of their ethnic makeup, join a neo-Soviet state.[68] Moreover, communist ideology, with its focus on internationalism, is generally anti-national in theory if not always in practice. Thus, despite the fact that ethnic Russians would certainly dominate any neo-Soviet state, the appeal to reconstruct such a state for ideological or philosophical reasons is a multiethnic appeal, and in the economically depressed Donbas where there is no hope of maintaining most jobs if Ukraine carries out reforms, re-creating the integrated Soviet economic space is strongly appealing to all of the Donbas ethnic groups. Therefore, communist mobilization with a goal of re-creating the Soviet Union is not actually an ethnic mobilization. Even the revived KPU seems to have Soviet restoration only as a long-range goal, with regional autonomy as a more immediate one.

Conclusions

Donbas Russians need not mobilize ethnically when they can mobilize more easily, efficiently, and effectively as a purely political and regional force, operating in cooperation with Russified Ukrainians and other regions. In contrast, Crimean Russians find it easier and more profitable in terms of gaining local and international support to mobilize as a Russian ethnic group instead of as a broader socioeconomic movement. This statement does not contradict our previous institutionalist arguments, because demographic factors influence the ability to utilize institutions as mobilizing tools. Therefore, the differences in ethnodemographics and cultural identities between the two regions are magnified by their different kinds of institutions and the presence or absence of Russian ethnic hegemony over them. These institutions and demographic situations cause the Russian elites in both regions to have a different structure of payoffs and incentives. Hence, they choose different mobilizational strategies: in the Donbas, socioeconomic mobilization; in Crimea, ethnopolitical mobilization.

Notes

1. See T. Kuzio, "Borders, Symbolism and Nation-State Building: Ukraine and Russia," *Geopolitics and International Boundaries,* vol. 2, no. 2 (Autumn 1997), pp. 35–55.
2. See T. Kuzio, *Ukraine: State and Nation Building: Studies of Societies in Transition* (London: Routledge, 1998), pp. 67–99 and "The Perils of Multiculturalism: A Theoretical and Area Studies Approach to the Former USSR," *Contemporary Political Studies,* vol. 3, (1998)., pp. 108–123.
3. Dominique Arel, "Ukraine: The Temptation of the Nationalising State" in Vladimir Tismaneanu (ed.), *Political Culture and Civil Society in the New States of Eurasia* (Armonk, NY: M. E. Sharpe, 1995), pp. 157–188, and Andrew Wilson, *Ukrainian Nationalism in the 1990s: A minority faith* (Cambridge: Cambridge University Press, 1997). In a later article co-authored with Graham Smith, A. Wilson adopts a more sanguine view about the possibilities of ethnic mobilization in the Donbas and eastern Ukraine. See note 4.
4. See T. Kuzio, "National Identity in Independent Ukraine: An Identity in Transition," *Nationalism and Ethnic Politics,* vol. 2, no. 4 (Winter 1996), pp. 582–608; op cit., T. Kuzio, *Ukraine: State and Nation Building,* pp. 144–166; Paul S. Pirie, "National Identity and Politics in Southern and Eastern Ukraine," *Europe-Asia Studies,* vol. 48, no. 7 (November 1996), pp. 1076–1104; Stephen Rapawy, *Ethnic Identification in Ukraine,* IPC Staff Paper No. 90 (Washington, DC: U.S. Bureau of the Census, August 1997); and Graham Smith and A. Wilson, "Rethinking Russia's Post-Soviet Diaspora: The

Potential for Political Mobilisation in Eastern Ukraine and North-east Estonia," *Europe-Asia Studies,* vol. 49, no. 5 (July 1997), pp. 845–864.

5. We are thankful to Ian Bremmer for the insight that demographic factors and the infrastructural power of institutions are forms of resources, and that such demographic and institutionalist arguments are theories about resource-based power.

6. Alexander J. Motyl, *Sovietology, Rationality, Nationality: Coming to Grips with Nationalism in the USSR* (New York: Columbia University Press, 1990), pp. 36–52.

7. Op cit., A. Wilson, *Ukrainian Nationalism in the 1990s,* p. 167.

8. The June 1993 coal miners' strike was organized by local Donbas elites and came suspiciously close after the June 23 presidential decree granting "economic sovereignty" to Crimea. The Donbas elites were patently jealous and wanted similar privileges to be granted to their region. See *Moscow News,* no. 30, 1993. The head of one of the largest Donbas mines, Yukhym Zviahils'kyi, and Valentyn Landyk, a local entrepreneur and then-head of the Labor Party, were brought to Kyiv to become acting prime minister and deputy prime minister, respectively. This proposal was made by then-Prime Minister Leonid Kuchma to then-President Kravchuk in a successful attempt at appeasing the Donbas.

9. In the December 1, 1991 referendum, 83.90 and 83.96 percent in Donetsk and Luhansk *oblasts,* respectively, voted in favor of Ukrainian independence.

10. Ian Bremmer, "The Politics of Ethnicity: Russians in the New Ukraine," *Europe-Asia Studies,* vol. 46, no. 2 (March-April 1994), p. 264.

11. In a poll in the possession of the authors conducted by the Center for Political Studies, University of Donetsk, in June 1997 in Donetsk *oblast,* two-thirds of those polled were born in Ukraine and a third migrated there; 75 percent of the Crimean population arrived on the peninsula after 1945. This was also confirmed during an interview with Elena Kurilo, Institute of World Economy and International Relations, Ukrainian National Academy of Sciences: London, November 16, 1994.

12. Orest Subtelny, *Ukraine: A History* (Toronto: University of Toronto Press, 1988), p. 525.

13. Evgenii Golovakha, Natalia Panina, and Nikolai Churilov, "Russians in Ukraine" in Vladimir Shlapentokh, Munir Sendich, and Emil Payin (eds.), *The Russian Diaspora: Russian Minorities in the Former Soviet Republics* (Armonk, NY: M. E. Sharpe, 1994), p. 65.

14. Denis J. B. Shaw and Michael J. Bradshaw, "Problems of Ukrainian Independence," *Post-Soviet Geography,* vol. 33, no. 1 (January 1992), p. 18.

15. Monika Jung, "The Donbas Factor in the Ukrainian Elections," *RFE/RL Research Report,* vol. 3, no. 2 (March 1994), p. 52.

16. Ibid., M. Jung, p. 52 and A. Wilson, "The Growing Challenge to Kyiv from the Donbas," *RFE/RL Research Report,* vol. 2, no. 33 (August 20, 1993), p. 9.

17. Op cit., D. J. B. Shaw and M. J. Bradshaw, p. 16.
18. D. Arel and A. Wilson, "The Ukrainian Parliamentary Elections," *RFE/RL Research Report*, vol. 3, no. 26 (July 1, 1994), p. 14.
19. T. Kuzio, *Russia-Crimea-Ukraine: Triangle of Conflict. Conflict Studies* no.267 (London: Research Institute for the Study of Conflict and Terrorism, 1994), p. 29. See also T. Kuzio, "The Crimea and European Security," *European Security*, vol. 3, no. 4 (Winter 1994), pp. 734–774.
20. Mykola Shpakovatyi (ed.), *Leonid Kravchuk, Our Goal—A Free Ukraine* (Kyiv: Globus, 1994), p. 45.
21. David R. Marples and David F. Duke, "Ukraine, Russia and the Question of Crimea," *Nationalities Papers*, vol. 23, no. 2 (June 1995), p. 273.
22. Rogers Brubaker, "Nationhood and the national question in the Soviet Union and post-Soviet Eurasia: An institutionalist account," *Theory and Society*, vol. 23, no. 1 (1994), pp. 68–69.
23. Ibid., p. 62.
24. Philip G. Roeder, "Soviet Federalism and Ethnic Mobilization," *World Politics*, vol. 43, no. 2 (January 1991), p. 219.
25. Op cit., M. Jung, pp. 51–52.
26. Op cit., P. G. Roeder, p. 231.
27. Ibid., p. 199.
28. Ibid., p. 202.
29. Ibid., pp. 197 and 202.
30. Op cit., E. Golovakha, N. Panina, and N. Churilov, pp. 62–63.
31. Ukraine's leaders at the time knew they had little choice but to elevate the Crimea from an *oblast* to an autonomous republic because Crimea's leaders threatened to petition the USSR Supreme Soviet to annul the 1954 transfer of Crimea from the Russian SFSR to Ukraine. If this had happened, Ukraine would have become an independent state in 1992 without Crimea. Interview with L. Kravchuk, Kyiv, November 28, 1995. See also Edward Ozhiganov, "The Crimean Republic: Rivalries for Control" in Alexei Arbatov et al. (eds.), *Managing Conflict in the Former Soviet Union: Russian and American Perspectives* (Cambridge, MA: The MIT Press, 1997), pp. 98–100 and T. Kuzio, *Ukraine Under Kuchma: Political Reform, Economic Transformation and Security Policy in Independent Ukraine* (London: Macmillan, 1997), pp. 67–89.
32. Svetlana Svetova and Roman Solchanyk, "Chronology of Events in Crimea," *RFE/RL Report*, vol. 3, no. 19 (May 13, 1994), p. 27.
33. Ibid.
34. A presidential decree of April 14, 1992 (with the amendments of July 24, 1992) established a nation-wide system of local state administration. Under the terms of these decrees, the president nominated heads of the executive power at every level of local government, thus providing a parallel structure to the existing hierarchy of *oblast* (provincial) and *rayon* (county), city and town councils. The former Soviet system was amended and divided into two levels—

provincial self-government whose functions included representation of the interests of the local population and clearly defined responsibilities in the economic and social spheres, and local government under the general control of the state administration. This measure seriously limited the capacity of regional councils to express demands for autonomy and evoked the resistance of certain influential provincial circles (*Holos Ukrayiny,* August 8, 1992).

35. Ibid., p. 28.
36. *Vseukrainskiye Vedomosti,* April 11, 1997.
37. *Holos Ukrayiny,* September 29, 1992.
38. R. Solchanyk, "The Crimean Imbroglio: Kyiv and Simferopol," *RFE/RL Research Report,* vol. 1, no. 33 (August 21, 1992), p. 15.
39. D. J. Shaw, "Nationalization of Resort Complexes by Crimea," *Post-Soviet Geography,* vol. 34, no. 1 (January 1993), p. 72.
40. Op cit., D. Marples and D. F. Duke, p. 282, Martin Klatt, "Russians in the 'Near Abroad,'" *RFE/RL Research Report,* vol. 3, no. 32 (August 19, 1994), p. 39 and op cit., T. Kuzio, *Russia-Crimea-Ukraine,* p. 22. On the development of Crimean autonomous institutions, see *Robitnycha hazeta,* June 23, and *Holos Ukrayiny,* June 25, and September 18 and 25, 1993. The Law "On the Presidential Representation in the Crimean Republic" is published in *Holos Ukrayiny,* January 27, 1993. Sevastopol does not fall under Crimean jurisdiction, and therefore its presidential prefect was already in place.
41. Op cit., A. Wilson, "The Elections in the Crimea," *RFE/RL Research Report,* vol. 3, no. 25 (June 24, 1994), p. 7.
42. Op cit., S. Svetova and R. Solchanyk, pp. 31–32.
43. Op cit., D. Marples and D. F. Duke, p. 283.
44. R. Solchanyk, "Crimea's Presidential Election," *RFE/RL Research Report,* vol. 3, no. 11 (March 18, 1994), p. 3.
45. Op cit., A. Wilson, "The Elections in the Crimea," p. 14.
46. *Holos Ukrayiny,* May 29, 1997.
47. Chauncy D. Harris, "The New Russian Minorities: A Statistical Overview," *Post-Soviet Geography,* vol. 34, no. 1 (January 1993), p. 15.
48. Op cit., D. J. B. Shaw and M. J. Bradshaw, p. 11.
49. Op cit., M. Jung, pp. 51–52, and A. Wilson, "The Donbas between Ukraine and Russia: The Use of History in Political Disputes," *Journal of Contemporary History,* vol. 30, no. 2 (April 1995), p. 267.
50. Cited from a poll in the possession of the authors conducted by the Center for Political Studies, University of Donetsk, in June 1997 in Donetsk *oblast.*
51. Interview with V. Bilets'kyi, Donetsk, August 29, 1996.
52. *Kryms'ka Svitlytsia,* February 24, 1996. This sorry state of affairs was admitted to even by Sergei Shuvaynikov, head of the Congress of Russian Peoples of the Crimea, in an interview in *Holos Ukrayiny,* November 1, 1997.
53. Office of the United Nations High Commissioner for Refugees, *CIS Digest,* no. 159 (February 19, 1998).

54. D. Arel and A. Wilson, "Ukraine under Kuchma: Back to 'Eurasia'?" *RFE/RL Research Report,* vol. 3, no. 32 (August 19, 1994), p. 9.

55. Ibid., p. 12.

56. J. Rothschild, *Ethnopolitics: A Conceptual Framework* (New York: Columbia University Press, 1981), p. 112.

57. *Rus'kiy narod* can refer in a narrow sense to only ethnic Russians as the "Russian people" or to eastern Slavs as joint descendants of the medieval state of Kyiv Rus'. In the Tsarist era the three eastern Slavs were therefore all designated as "Russians." The majority of ethnic Russians consequently still find it difficult to accept Ukrainians or Belarusians as separate ethnic groups.

58. *Holos Ukrayiny,* October 31, 1992.

59. Op cit., T. Kuzio, "Russia-Crimea-Ukraine," p. 33.

60. When asked if separatist forces in Crimea exist, Leonid Grach, leader of the Crimean Communist Party and parliamentary speaker replied "They are quite powerful, but we do not support them, although we do advocate a rapprochement of the Russian and Ukrainian peoples" (*Nezavisimost,* June 25, 1997).

61. See the report of the founding meeting of the Congress of Russian Communities of the Crimea in *Vseukrainskiye Vedomosti* (April 12, 1997) which described it as a "traditional, hysterical anti-Ukrainian show."

62. Op cit., M. Jung, p. 53.

63. Grigorii Nemirya, "A Qualitative Analysis of the Situation in the Donbas," in Klaus Segbers and Stephen De Spiegeleire (eds.), *Post-Soviet Puzzles. Mapping the Political Economy of the Former Soviet Union,* vol. 2 (Ebenhausen: Stiftung Wisenschaft und Politik, 1995), pp. 56–57.

64. Interview with Valentyn A. Laktionov, deputy chairman of Donetsk city council, London, January 26, 1998.

65. A. Wilson, "The Ukrainian Left: In Transition to Social Democracy or Still in Thrall to the USSR?" *Europe-Asia Studies,* vol. 49, no. 7 (November 1997), p. 1311.

66. Op cit., A. Wilson, "The Growing Challenge to Kyiv from the Donbas," p. 9.

67. Interview with D. Kornilov, London, January 26, 1998.

68. Op cit., T. Kuzio, *Ukraine: State and Nation Building,* pp. 69–118.

CHAPTER 12

Conclusion: Institutionalizing Democracy in a Divided State

Paul D'Anieri

An effective state, in Robert Putnam's definition, is one that is able first to make decisions and then to implement them.[1] As the chapters in this volume show, the Ukrainian state has fallen woefully short on both counts. The chapters by Vorndran, D'Anieri, Wise and Pigenko, Garnett, and Zyla highlight the first shortcoming—the internal divisions in the government and rampant corruption; those by Kravchuk, Krawchenko, and Kuzio focus on the second—the inefficacy of the state in its relations with society. Given the authors' nearly uniform assessment of institutional weakness, as well as the divisions in Ukrainian society and newness of its democracy, it is reasonable to inquire whether liberal democracy can take root in Ukraine, and if so, how much it will resemble the liberal democracy practiced in the rest of Europe.

In this conclusion I initially address what might be called the "Huntington problem"; that is, the susceptibility of new democracies to violence and authoritarianism due to the inability of their weak states to cope with the demands of a mobilizing society.[2] However, I assert that the threat to Ukraine is not as severe as one might imagine, because of a second characteristic of Ukrainian politics, which receives attention in the chapter by Paul Kubicek: the weakness of Ukrainian *society*. The ineffective Ukrainian state is unlikely to collapse under the burden of societal demands, because in fact society has been largely quiescent, and therefore does not provide the second half of Huntington's recipe for collapse. Indeed if the problem for many developing countries and new democracies is that they have "strong societies and weak states," Ukraine is in the unusual position of having a weak society *and* a weak state.[3]

This conclusion will therefore move beyond discussion of the state as a self-contained entity to explore the societal context of state behavior and the relationship between state and society. Joel Migdal asks, "if we are to understand the inherent limitations of states we must develop a focus on *process*, one that starts with the web of relationships between them and their societies."[4] After presenting in more detail the characterization of Ukraine as a weak state in a weak society, I address first the political implications of the system. In what ways does it ease pressure on the state and in what ways does it make the state's job more difficult? Second, I ask how this situation might change. If a strong democracy depends on a strong civil society, but civil society depends on a strong state,[5] how can either be created in a society that possesses neither?

Weak Society, Weak State

The significance of Huntington's argument in the political science literature—and of collapsed democracies in the real world—prompts us to look hard at Ukraine's weak state and to look for political threats that might bring it down. Given Ukraine's deep ethnic and linguistic diversity, the chances for societal conflict to overcome state capacity might appear great, as some have predicted. But there is little evidence, either scholarly or impressionistic, that the Ukrainian state is in any great danger at all. The most substantial challenge to state integrity has been the periodic agitation for secession in Crimea and the Donbas, problems that seem to be resolving themselves rather than escalating.[6] At the same time, however, we cannot take the seemingly logical next step by concluding that the state has any meaningful influence over society. Rather than one being dominant, or the two locked in battle, what appears in Ukraine are a state and society that are impervious to one another, each being relatively autonomous and immune from pressure by the other but unable (or unwilling) to press its demands on the other.

Their mutual insularity is demonstrated in the preceding chapters. Robert Kravchuk's analysis of subnational revenues is perhaps the clearest demonstration of the state's weakness respecting the larger society. The ability to raise and collect taxes is the *sine qua non* of state power and the source of most other state powers, but Ukrainian society has been largely successful in avoiding payment of taxes (and many other laws) through a variety of means, some of which are highlighted in Roman Zyla's chapter on corruption. Tax collection rates are an especially telling indicator of state capacity, because taxation is one state goal that is not disputed among the various elite factions. Ukraine's fragmentation (especially in parliament between communists, nationalists, and reformers) cannot be the primary cause of non-collection of taxes; the various factions agree on that goal. No one wants to lead a moneyless—and hence powerless—state.

The essay by Kubicek tells the other side of the story in vivid terms, focusing on interest groups, which in the standard view are means for specific interests in society to make themselves heard in the halls of government. By providing means of aggregating and transmitting popular sentiment to government, interest associations are a primary means (along with periodic elections) for society to make demands on the state. But unlike elections, interest groups permit societal demands to be articulated clearly, specifically, and continuously over time. In the case of Ukraine, however, in Paul Kubicek's words, "their freedom to maneuver and their role in the policymaking process have both been highly circumscribed." Moreover, there remain very few interest groups in Ukraine, and the major ones that do exist are largely controlled by the state. There is little indication that this situation is changing. It may be that the sparseness of interest groups and other civic organizations represents the hangover from the Soviet past, and will improve with time, but so far there has been little change on this score. One is prompted to ask whether something continues to hinder the formation of societal interest organizations.[7]

In characterizing the relationship of interest groups to the state, Kubicek uses the concept of "state corporatism," meaning that the major interest groups, and especially trade unions, are de facto creatures of the state and largely serve the interests of the "party of power." However, there is a substantial difference between state corporatism in Ukraine and that in other societies in which it exists. In the standard models, corporatism allows state, business, and labor elites to broker compromises, with the understanding that the labor elites can "deliver" their groups' support.[8] Or in an alternate model, Lijphart shows that in some ethnically divided societies, corporatism involves compromise between the elites of each ethnic group and the state, with the ethnic elites securing the agreement of their respective groups.[9] As Kubicek observes, these groups are not mechanisms for state goals to be implemented in society any more than they are means for society to make demands on the state. Rather, in Ukraine they seem to play the role of insulating state and society from each other. They represent workers but refrain from confronting either state or industry. They are allied with the state, but only to the extent of protecting existing privileges. Thus

Ukrainian interest groups so far have served to insulate state from society rather than to integrate the two.

While the sources of state weakness have been discussed in some detail in the preceding chapters, the sources of passivity in Ukrainian society merit further study. Here we can only sketch the outlines of the problem. Much of this passivity has to be ascribed to the legacy of totalitarianism. While the term "totalitarianism" was in some academic disrepute in the declining years of the Soviet Union, it highlights an important legacy of the system that goes beyond authoritarianism.[10] In authoritarian systems, public dissent is largely repressed, but the ability of citizens to form associations is not, as long as the activities of those associations remained within boundaries drawn by the state. In the Soviet system however, there was practically no scope at all to form societal groups—even for cultural purposes—beyond the reach of the state and party.

The state and party injected themselves so thoroughly into associational life that independent social and political activity—except on a very small scale, and usually underground—was impossible until Mikhail Gorbachev's reforms. Thus, in the case of interest groups, there was little to build on when democracy and independence emerged suddenly in 1991. Nor was there any tradition of social organizing. On the contrary, the firmly established tradition was that organizing could be highly dangerous and was unlikely to be effective. In sum, society was thoroughly atomized during the Soviet era (not to mention the Tsarist era that preceded it in most of Ukraine).

There is no clear reason to expect a rapid emergence of interest groups in post-Soviet societies. In any society, interest group formation, and emergence of other means by which society makes demands on the state, are plagued by problems in the logic of collective action. In his influential *Making Democracy Work,* Robert Putnam shows the importance of "social capital" in overcoming these dilemmas, but he finds this to be something of a vicious circle—one builds social capital through successful organizing, but successful organizing is built on social capital.[11] Thus in explaining the lack of civic traditions—and of effective state institutions—in parts of Italy, Putnam finds that the root of the problem reaches back nearly a thousand years to a time when society was atomized by an effective authoritarian state.

By extension, the lack of social capital in Ukraine has prevented formation of strong societal groups, in turn preventing effective government, in a cycle that has recurred for several centuries. Putnam's analysis does not mean that the same must be true for Ukraine, but it does warn that a stronger society in Ukraine, one that organizes itself and makes demands on the state, will not necessarily emerge organically by itself.

The legacy of totalitarianism is likely to be particularly strong in post-Soviet Ukraine, because the Soviet system was not decisively overthrown. As Jon Elster, Claus Offe, and Ulrich Preuss, argue, the absence of a revolution that overthrew the old elite and destroyed the former state sets the post-Soviet transitions apart from those in Latin America and Southern Europe that are often used as models.[12] Building new interest groups from scratch would be a daunting task in Ukraine, but building them in an arena where some remnant of the Soviet system claiming to be an interest group already exists would be nearly impossible. A full treatment of the potential for society to self-organize, and make demands on the state—to form spontaneously and organically a "civil society"—is beyond the scope of this conclusion and this book. But understanding the development of institutions and the state will require a fuller understanding of that issue than we currently possess.

Implications for State and Institution Building

If this argument is correct, that Ukraine combines a weak state with a weak society, what are the implications for state and institution building in Ukraine? Here we enter a debate concerning the interdependence of state building and the development of civil societies. While it is largely agreed that democracy requires the presence of a civil society, it is widely argued as well that civil society can exist only in the space created for it by an effective state. Civil society and the state seem to be in some sort of chicken-and-egg relationship. Hence there is debate over whether the transition must proceed in a preconceived logical sequence, with some steps waiting until prerequisite stages have been completed, or whether all steps must be taken simultaneously because they are all interdependent. Rather than attempting to resolve this debate here, I simply hope to review it briefly and speculate on its implications for the Ukrainian case.

Alexander Motyl forcefully asserts the "the logical necessity of sequencing."[13] In particular, he contends that an effective state is a prerequisite to civil society:

> . . . [P]olitical authority is the point of reference of the autonomy of social institutions. In the absence of the state, therefore, social patterns of behavior obviously can and do exist, but in being territorially unbounded and defined exclusively in terms of the individuals comprising them, such behavior is more akin to the black-marketeering and kitchen debates found in totalitarian states and less akin to a genuine civil society. In sum, no state, most probably no civil society.[14]

Thus Motyl concludes that "sequencing is necessary and . . . the correct sequencing is, most probably, the state first, rule of law second, civil society third, the market fourth, and democracy fifth."[15] He points out that without a functioning state, which provides both an arena in which civil society can operate and an object of its efforts, there is no room for civil society to emerge, clearly an important problem in Ukraine. After all, many Ukrainians would ask, what is the point of organizing an interest group when the state is both unwilling and unable to take society's problems seriously? Elster, Offe, and Preuss, however, argue strongly against the "sequencing" view, not on theoretical grounds but on the matter of practical considerations. While they agree that in theory an effective state is needed to tackle the other objects of the transition, they point out that in order to proceed sequentially, the state must be able to defer other goals that are important to society. New post-communist states defer societal demands to begin working toward these goals. Granting Motyl the theoretical point, they argue that sequencing is practically impossible. Kuzio's chapter in this volume tends to support Elster et al., arguing that theory aside, Ukraine has embarked on all of its critical goals simultaneously. Moreover, he argues, civic nationalism may be necessary for this simultaneous transition to succeed, and it is therefore not as destructive a force as some analysts have maintained.

However, the weakness of Ukraine's society has a potentially important impact on the feasibility of sequencing (leaving aside the question of whether it is desirable). If it is the case that Ukrainian society has not been placing harsh demands on the new state, then it may indeed be possible for the state to resist tackling certain problems while focusing on others. Indeed, the slow pace of economic reform, especially in the agricultural sector, indicates that certain tasks could be put off. Most notably during the presidency of Leonid M. Kravchuk, from 1991 to 1994, the Ukrainian state pursued in large part what Motyl advocated, focusing on state and nation building, placing construction of the market economy and development of democratic institutions on the back burner. Leonid D. Kuchma, president since 1994, has adopted a different set of priorities, de-emphasizing nation building while embarking (slowly) on economic reform and more decisively on institutional reform in presidential-parliamentary relations. One might argue that he was able to de-emphasize nation building precisely because Kravchuk had already achieved some success in this area. In that sense, Ukraine's experience might provide at least partial evidence that sequencing is possible in countries with quiescent societies. More broadly speaking, the ability to sequence reforms is likely to vary, both across states and across time within states.

The converse of this question of the state's ability to create the conditions for development of civil society is the effect of society's passivity on the development of the state. This question has received much less attention; most scholars have been preoccupied with the problems of strong societies, neglecting the problems of weak ones. The problem in Ukraine is not that the society is liable to support an anti-democratic change in the system or the repression of minority elements. On the contrary, there is considerable evidence that despite widespread disagreement on the specifics of particular policies, Ukrainians of all regions and political orientations support democracy and are quite tolerant of those with whom they disagree. The problem in terms of institutional development is that if the society is largely passive, content to resist the demands of the state but not to make demands of its own, state leaders may have little incentive to improve the state's performance. Can an effective democratic state develop in the absence of societal pressure?

On the rare occasions that large-scale demonstrations have been mounted in Ukraine, they have generally achieved their purpose, sometimes with important consequences. The first instance pre-dated independence, when hunger-striking students forced the resignation of Prime Minister Vitaly Masol in October 1990. The most significant instance of grass-roots agitation came in June 1993, when striking Donbas coal miners forced a decision to hold elections for parliament and president in 1994, squeezing out the parliament that had been held over from the Soviet era. It is especially significant that in both cases, protesters were not seeking only *private* gains for themselves (as has occurred more recently in the case of strikes by workers demanding back wages), but rather *universal* gains for the whole society. In other words, Ukrainian social actors have found it possible to overcome certain collective action problems that obstruct self-organization, finding that when they did, they could achieve impressive results. Why have they not asserted themselves in this way more often? That is a question not addressed in this book, but it is one that will have a strong bearing on the prospects for development of an effective democratic state in Ukraine.

Thus in considering state-society relations and the process of state building, the passivity of Ukrainian society may be seen as both a positive and negative factor. The good news is that the society, despite its considerable cleavages, is not making such heavy demands that the state is in danger of collapsing under those demands. Moreover, the society's passivity may allow the state to avoid some of the difficulties inherent in trying to form a state, civic nation, civil society, free market, and democracy simultaneously, precisely by permitting the state to delay work on some of these projects while pursuing the fundamentals. The bad news is that one of the primary forces for reforming the state may be absent. Moreover, not only is society passive in its demands on the state, it is passive in responding to the state's demands and can resist some of the means by which the state might seek to strengthen and develop itself (e.g., in the collection of taxes).

Can the Ukrainian State Reform Itself?

If the society cannot or will not force the state to become more effective, can the state do so by itself? This question, in turn, raises three more: (1) Will elite conflict promote or inhibit institutional development? (2) Will the current constitutional arrangements facilitate more effective governance? (3) Will the state somehow find a way to overcome societal resistance to state efforts?

It appears axiomatic that elite conflict undermines state efficacy, and hence that the severe divisions in the Ukrainian elite (which reflect those in society) impede institutional development. A major theme of chapters by D'Anieri and Wise and Pigenko is that divisions within the parliament and between the parliament and president led to stalemate, rendering reform impossible. However, while elite conflict impedes policymaking in the short term, it may create the impetus to institutional reform in the longer term. It is important to recall that in most of the western democracies, which Ukraine hopes to emulate, institutional efficacy preceded democracy, and resulted instead from efforts to regulate elite rivalry. The British case is most notable, in which institutional conflict between the parliament and the crown drove the two over time to develop clear norms of institutional prerogatives.

The several attempts made thus far in Ukraine to clarify and rationalize intra-governmental relations have resulted from intra-elite tensions. Most notably, the constitution was revised in several steps to repair an institutional set-up that was not working. Clashes between parliament and the executive over the relative prerogatives of the two branches did not prevent the adoption of the 1995 Law on Power, nor the 1996 Constitution, as Wise and Pigenko show. By subordinating the prime minister to the president, the newer arrangements significantly ameliorate the dilution of executive power that hampered Ukraine until that time. This dealt with only one problem, but the point here is that the Ukrainian state does possess some internal ability to reform itself effectively.

We must be cautious in evaluating the modifications made in the 1996 Constitution. It seems clear that subordinating the prime minister to the president was an improvement. It is much more difficult to say, however, whether the balance struck between presidential and parliamentary power will increase or decrease the ability of those two organs together to make and execute laws. The question of whether presidential, or semi-presidential, or parliamentary systems are most effective in transition societies (and in stable democracies) has partisans on all sides. It appears that for the problems Ukraine faces, strengthening the president at the expense of the parliament, which was the effect of the 1995 Law on Power and 1996 Constitution, ameliorates one set of problems but aggravates another.

The problem resolved by subordinating the prime minister to the president rather than to the parliament is the lack of decisive reform policies, especially in the economic sphere. For that reason western advisers to both Ukraine and Russia have advocated strengthening executive decree powers as a route to overcome divided or anti-reform parliaments. However, while solving one institutional problem, it might exacerbate another one. Increasing the executive's powers will likely increase the decisiveness of state policy, it might at the same time undermine the likelihood of executive-legislative compromise on a single reform plan and hence the ability to make effective policy.

As presidents acquire more power to rule by decree, or generally more leverage to impose their will over the objections of parliaments, there is less reason for the president to compromise with parliament. In one sense, that is exactly what is intended—a president who will not "water down" initiatives to deal with a divided or conservative parliament. Here the decisiveness of governmental decision-making is enhanced. However, ability to bypass parliament is likely to undermine the success of any plan. As Barnett Rubin asserts, implementing a far-reaching reform plan in society, and especially an economic reform plan that requires short-term sacrifice, requires the legitimacy created by a democratic policy process.[16] Shifting power away from legislatures, which through their representative function are the main fount of democratic legitimacy, will tend to undermine the legitimacy of the reforms in question. Achieving such legitimacy is essential in a state in which many are skeptical of the merits of economic reform, and almost everyone in society is skeptical of the designs of the government. If one of the major problems for the Ukrainian state is its inability to compel society to cooperate in fulfilling its plans, one of the reasons may be that these plans themselves have never been fully vetted in parliament. In sum, increased executive authority may increase the likelihood of a coherent reform plan, but only at the expense of the ability actually to implement a plan.

At this point the political dimension of the reform plan is inescapable. In Ukraine as well as in Russia, a primary motivation for augmenting executive power has not been overcoming an *institutional* deficiency per se but rather overcoming *political* opposition in the parliament to the plans of the executive. In both states, the presence of a large bloc of communist and other anti-reform deputies with the ability to block reforms has produced a perceived need to cut parliament out of the process. This makes perfect sense in the eyes of the executive, but to repeat, it hardly lays the groundwork for securing broad social cooperation. The more difficult task is to first get a working majority in parliament, which Ukraine has never had, and second, to achieve a situation in which that majority is of the same party as the head of government. For this reason some have argued, against conventional wisdom, that a straight parliamentary system is ideal, because it provides the best chance of a unified government in pursuit of a coherent plan of reform.[17] Obviously, for Ukraine the choice of a form of government has been made, and it is pointless to second-guess it. This discussion does highlight, however, that efforts at institutional reform must consider not only the goal of reaching a decisive policy, but also the goal of generating the political unity of will that will permit a weak state to implement it in a resistant or, at best, unenthusiastic society.

In mid-1998, it appears that Ukraine may be on the verge of having the first working majority in its parliament since 1991. The bad news is that this majority is of the left and appears lukewarm to any kind of reform. Nonetheless, by bargaining with the president over policies and delivering parliamentary support for any compromise reached, a leftist majority may be more conducive to state effectiveness and to economic reform than a parliament with no majority at all.

For this reason, in Ukraine as in any democratic state, the question of state efficacy cannot be separated from the divisions in the society. The main law-making organ in a democracy is a legislature that inevitably will reflect society's divisions, even if it helps to narrow them. On this score, the recent alteration of Ukraine's election law has the potential to improve substantially the efficacy of the legislature in passing legislation and hence of the state overall. The 1998 parliamentary elections produced a much more consolidated party structure in parliament. At the same time, however, at least in its first few months, that parliament has been every bit as divided as the previous one. Institutional reform can only do so much in a society that is badly divided. Nonetheless, it does not seem out of the question that at some time over the next few election cycles, a majority could be constructed out of center and right-wing forces.

Such a majority would likely be a very narrow one, which raises another institutional question that has received almost no attention: the rules of procedure in the parliament. In some systems, parliamentary rule can proceed with a majority of one vote, because there are no procedures that permit a minority the ability to block legislation. In others, rules allow minorities a range of blocking tactics that in fact mean that in many situations not just a majority but a supermajority may be necessary to rule. Differences between the rules in the U.S. House and Senate are instructive here. In the standoff over selection of a speaker of parliament in 1998, minority forces on both sides were able to block election of candidates they opposed not by denying them the 226 votes needed to win, but by absenting themselves from the proceedings and denying the vote the quorum (300 deputies present) required by the rules for a valid vote. In practice, electing a speaker required not just 226 votes but the acquiescence of at least 300 deputies (two-thirds) of the parliament. As Ukraine's new electoral law has the effect over time of consolidating parliament, the rules of parliamentary procedure will be an increasingly important factor in determining that body's ability to legislate effectively.

The question remains: what if the society remains so badly divided that the parliament remains ineffective? Can democracy take root without a functioning legislature? In particular, can an augmented executive offset the dysfunction of a legislature? It is difficult to imagine how this would work, which is why in most parliamentary systems, the absence of a majority in parliament is automatically grounds for new elections. Ultimately, for the Ukrainian state to be effective, there has to be at least some consolidation of political opinion in society. It is for this reason that Taras Kuzio focuses on the importance of forging a civic nation—only by somehow narrowing the differences across the country will the societal basis for effective democracy exist. There is no need for consensus, for the whole point of democracy is to allow divergent interests to arrive at acceptable compromises. But there needs to be sufficient agreement that a majority of society can find some compromise position that they will prefer to inaction. Ukraine has not yet reached that point.

Summary

In summary, the essays in this volume have explored many facets of a single problem: the lack of decisive and effective institutions in post-communist Ukraine. This concluding essay has sought to link the problems of the state to the problems of society, and to consider the relationship between them and prospects for improvement in the situation. The problem most fundamentally is that a functioning democratic state seems to rely on a civil society, while a civil society seems to rest upon a functioning democracy. In his analysis of democratic development in Italy, Putnam argues that once the combination of ineffective state and lack of civil society is established, it tends to be self-reinforcing, as does the combination of effective democracy and strong civil society.

If the Ukrainian state will not be reshaped by society, and society will not (in the short term) be reshaped by the state, the hope must be that they will reshape themselves. This is not as unlikely as it may seem. Between 1995 and 1998, the Ukrainian state completely reshaped itself, redefining executive-parliamentary relations and revamping the system of electing the parliament. There is also change afoot in society as increasing numbers of Ukrainians are socialized in post-Soviet rather than in Soviet conditions, though this may go slowly. The most important change in society is the increasing acceptance by all citizens of Ukraine that Ukraine will indeed remain separate from Russia and that it is their country.

One cannot be too optimistic, for this book has elucidated many reasons to believe that Ukrainian state and society indeed are not capable of significantly reshaping themselves. The grounds for believing that the Ukrainian state can become effective and democratic lie not in the chances for a rapid reordering of affairs but rather in the view that what we have witnessed since 1991 is the beginning of a very long story.[18] The rest of the story remains to be written, but the significant point for policymakers and for political scientists to keep in mind is that the outcome has most likely not yet been determined.

Notes

1. Robert D. Putnam, *Making Democracy Work: Civic Traditions in Modern Italy* (Princeton: Princeton University Press, 1993), p. 9.
2. Samuel P. Huntington, *Political Order in Changing Societies* (New Haven: Yale University Press, 1968). See also Jack Snyder, "Averting Anarchy in the New Europe," *International Security*, vol. 14, no. 4 (Spring 1990), pp. 5–37; and Edward D. Mansfield and Jack Snyder, "Democratization and the Danger of War," *International Security*, vol. 20, no. 1 (Summer 1995), pp. 5–38.
3. See Joel S. Migdal, *Strong Societies and Weak States* (Princeton: Princeton University Press, 1988).
4. Joel S. Migdal, "Studying the State," in Mark Irving Lichbach and Alan S. Zuckerman (eds.), *Comparative Politics: Rationality, Culture, and Structure* (New York: Cambridge University Press, 1997), p. 211.
5. On the interdependence of civil society and effective states, see Alexander Motyl, *Dilemmas of Independence: Ukraine after Totalitarianism* (New York:

Council on Foreign Relations, 1993), p. 69; and Barnett R. Rubin, "Conclusion: Managing Normal Instability," in Barnett R. Rubin and Jack Snyder (eds.), *Post-Soviet Political Order: Conflict and State Building* (London: Routledge, 1998), p. 177.

6. José Casanova, "Ethno-linguistic and religious pluralism and democratic construction in Ukraine," in Rubin and Snyder, *Post-Soviet Political Order,* pp. 81–104; Paul D'Anieri, "Ethnic Tensions and State Strategies: Understanding the Survival of the Ukrainian State," paper presented at the annual meeting of the Association for the Study of Nationalities, Columbia University, New York, April 1998.

7. Of course, starting from "ground zero," Ukraine may suffer from "logic of collective action" problems. See Mancur Olson, *The Logic of Collective Action* (Cambridge, MA: Harvard University Press, 1965).

8. See Peter J. Katzenstein, *Corporatism and Change: Austria, Switzerland, and the Politics of Industry* (Ithaca: Cornell University Press, 1984); Philippe Schmitter, "Still the Century of Corporatism?" *Review of Politics,* vol. 36, no. 1 (January 1974), pp. 85–131; and Philippe Schmitter and Gerhard Lehmbruch (eds.), *Patterns of Corporatist Policymaking* (Beverly Hills: Sage, 1982).

9. Arend Lijphart, *Democracy in Plural Societies: A Comparative Exploration* (New Haven: Yale University Press, 1977), pp. 99–103.

10. Alexander Motyl, "Building Bridges," in Motyl (ed.), *Thinking Theoretically About Soviet Nationalities: History and Comparison in the Study of the USSR* (New York: Columbia University Press, 1992).

11. Putnam, *Making Democracy Work,* chapter 6.

12. Jon Elster, Claus Offe, and Ulrich Preuss, *Institutional Design in Post-communist Societies* (New York: Cambridge University Press, 1998), chapter 1.

13. Motyl, *Dilemmas of Independence,* p. 67.

14. Motyl, *Dilemmas of Independence,* p. 69.

15. Motyl, *Dilemmas of Independence,* p. 70.

16. Rubin, p. 177.

17. See Juan J. Linz, "Presidential or Parliamentary Democracy: Does It Make a Difference?" in Linz and Artururo Valenzuela (eds.), *The Failure of Presidential Democracy* (Baltimore: Johns Hopkins University Press, 1984), pp. 3–87.

18. Taras Kuzio, *Ukraine: State and Nation Building* (London: Routledge, 1998), chapter 1.

Bibliography

Books and Monographs

Administrative and Territorial Reconstitution of Ukraine: Ways and Prospects, Analytical Report no. 1 (Kyiv: Ukrainian Center for Peace, Conversion and Conflict Resolution and the Friedrich Ebert Stiftung, January 1994).

Allworth, Edward (ed.), *Tatars of the Crimea: Their Struggle for Survival* (Durham, NC: Duke University Press, 1988).

D'Anieri, Paul, *Economic Interdependence in Ukrainian-Russian Relations* (New York: State University of New York Press), D'Anieri, Paul, Kravchuk, Robert, Kuzio, Taras, *Politics and Society in Ukraine* (Boulder: Westview, 1999).

Dawson, Jane I., *Eco-Nationalism: Anti-Nuclear Activism and National Identity in Russia, Lithuania and Ukraine* (Durham: Duke University Press, 1996).

Development's in Crimea: Challenges for Ukraine and Implications for Regional Security. Proceedings from an International Conference, October 23–25, 1994, Kyiv, Ukraine (Washington, D.C.: The American Association for the Advancement of Science, the Ukrainian Center for Independent Political Research, Kyiv, and The Harriman Institute, Columbia University).

Drohobycky, Maria (ed.), *Crimea: Dynamics, Challenges, and Prospects* (Lanham, Maryland, and London: Rowman and Littlefield and the American Association for the Advancement of Science, 1995).

Drum, Bernard, *Mass Privatization in Ukraine* (Washington D.C.: World Bank, May 1994).

Garnett, Sherman W., *Keystone in the Arch: Ukraine in the Emerging Security Environment of Central and Eastern Europe* (Washington, D.C.: Carnegie Endowment for International Peace, 1997).

Goncharenko, Alexander, *Ukrainian-Russian Relations: An Unequal Partnership.* RUSI Whitehall Paper 32 (London: Royal United Services Institute, 1995).

Ham, Peter van, *Ukraine, Russia and European Security: Implications for Western Policy,* Chaillot Papers no. 13 (Paris: Institute for Security Studies, West European Union, February 1994).

Hare, P. G. (ed.), *Structure and Financing of Higher Education in Russia, Ukraine and the European Union* (London: Jessica Kingsley Publishers, 1997).

Jaworsky, J., *Ukraine: Stability and Instability.* McNair Paper 42 (Washington, D.C.: Institute for National Strategic Studies, National Defense University, August 1995).

Kis, Theofil I., *Nationhood, Statehood and the International Status of the Ukrainian SSR / Ukraine.* University of Ottawa Ukrainian Studies, Occasional Papers No. 1 (Ottawa: University of Ottawa Press, 1989).

Kravchuk, Robert S., *Ukrainian Political Economy, 1991–1996* (New York: St. Martin's Press, forthcoming 2000).

Kuzio, Taras, *Ukraine: The Unfinished Revolution. European Security Studies 16* (London: Institute for European Defence & Strategic Studies, 1992).

Kuzio, Taras, and Wilson, Andrew, *Ukraine: Perestroika to Independence* (London and New York: Macmillan/St. Martin's Press and Edmonton: Canadian Institute for Ukrainian Studies, 1994).

Kuzio, Taras, *Ukraine-Crimea-Russia: Triangle of Conflict. Conflict Studies 267* (London: Research Institute for the Study of Conflict and Terrorism, 1994).

Kuzio, Taras, *Ukrainian Security Policy.* Washington Paper 167 (Washington, D.C.: The Center for Strategic & International Studies and Praeger, 1995).

Kuzio, Taras, *Ukraine: Back from the Brink. European Security Studies 23* (London: Institute for European Defence & Strategic Studies, 1995).

Kuzio, Taras, *Ukraine Under Kuchma: Political Reform, Economic Transformation and Security Policy in Independent Ukraine* (London and New York: Macmillan, St. Martin's Press, 1997).

Kuzio, Taras (ed.), *Contemporary Ukraine: Dynamics of Post-Soviet Transformation* (Armonk, NY: M. E. Sharpe, 1998).

Kuzio, Taras, *Ukraine: State and Nation Building.* Routledge Studies of Societies in Transition 9 (London and New York: Routledge, 1998).

Motyl, Alexander J., *Dilemmas of Independence: Ukraine After Totalitarianism* (New York: Council on Foreign Relations, 1993).

"Peoples, Nations, Identities: The Russian-Ukrainian Encounter," *The Harriman Review,* vol. 9, nos. 1–2 (Spring 1996).

Rapawy, Stephen, *Ukraine and the Border Issues* (Washington, D.C.: Center for International Research, U.S. Bureau of the Census, May 1993).

Rapawy, Stephen, *Ethnic Reidentification in Ukraine,* IPC Staff Paper No. 90 (Washington, D.C.: U.S. Bureau of the Census, August 1997).

Seytmuratova, Ayshe, *Mustafa Dhemilev and the Crimean Tatars: Story of a Man and His People. Facts, Documents, How to Help* (New York: Center for Democracy, 1986).

Sheehy, Ann, *The Crimean Tatars, Volga Germans and Meshketians: Soviet treatment of some national minorities.* Report No. 6 (London: Minority Rights Group, n.d.).

Siegelbaum, Stephen and Daniel Walkowitz (eds.), *Workers of the Donbas Speak: Survival and Identity in the New Ukraine* (New York: State University of New York Press, 1995).

Strekal, Oleg, *The Crimean Conflict and Its Implications for Ukraine's National Security.* Information Paper No. 2864 (Ebenhausen: Stiftung Wissenschaft und Politik, September 1994).

Ukrainian Experience in Human Minority Rights. Analytical Report no. 2 (Kyiv: Ukrainian Center for Peace, Conversion and Conflict Resolution and the Friedrich Ebert Stiftung, January 1994).

Ukraine: The Situation of Ethnic Minorities (Ottawa: Research Directorate, Immigration and Refugee Board, September 1993).

Velychenko, Stephen, *National History as Cultural Process: A Survey of the Interpretations of Ukraine's Past in Polish, Russian and Ukrainian Historical Writing from the Earliest Times to 1914* (Edmonton: Canadian Institute of Ukrainian Studies, University of Alberta, 1992).

Velychenko, S., *Shaping Identity in Eastern Europe and Russia: Soviet-Russian and Polish Accounts of Ukrainian History, 1914–1991* (New York: St. Martin's Press, 1993).

Vydrin, Dmytro and Dmytro Tabachnyk, *Ukraine on the Threshold of the XXI Century: Political Aspects* (Kyiv: Lybid, 1995).

Wanner, Cathy, *Burden of Dreams: History and Identity in Post-Soviet Ukraine.* Post-Communist Cultural Studies (Pennsylvania: Pennsylvania State University Press, 1998).

Wilson, Andrew, *The Crimean Tatars.* A Situation Report on the Crimean Tatars for International Alert (London: International Alert, 1994).

Wilson, Andrew, *Ukrainian nationalism in the 1990s: A minority faith* (New York: Cambridge University Press, 1997).

Articles

State and Nation Building

Arel, Dominique, "Ukraine—The Temptation of the Nationalising State," in Vladimir Tismaneanu (ed.), *Political Culture and Civil Society in Russia and the New States of Eurasia: The International Politics of Eurasia,* vol. 7 (Armonk, NY and London: M. E. Sharpe, 1995), pp. 157–188.

Arel, Dominique, "A Lurking Cascade of Assimilation in Kiev?" *Post-Soviet Affairs,* vol. 12, no. 1 (January-March 1996), pp. 73–90.

Barrington, Lowell, "The Domestic and International Consequences of Citizenship in the Soviet Successor States," *Europe-Asia Studies,* vol. 47, no. 5 (July 1995), pp. 731–763.

Bilinsky, J., "Ukraine: The Multiple Challenges to Independence," *Forum* (The Harriman Institute), vol. 7, nos. 1–2 (1993–1994).

Bilinsky, Yaroslaw, "Are the Ukrainians a State Nation?," *Problems of Communism,* vol. 61, nos. 1–2 (January-April 1992), pp. 134–135.

Birch, Julian, "Ukraine—A Nation-State or a State of Nations?" *Journal of Ukrainian Studies,* vol. 21, nos. 1–2 (Summer-Winter 1996), pp. 109–124.

Boukhalov, Oleksandr and Serguei Ivannikov, "Ukraine" in Betty M. Jacob, Krzystof Ostrowski, and H. Jeune (eds.), *Democratic and Local Governance* (Honolulu: Matsunaga Institute of Peace, 1993), pp. 225–242.

Boukhalov, O., and S. Ivannikov, "Ukrainian Local Politics After Independence," *The Annals of The American Academy of Political and Social Science,* vol. 540 (July 1995), pp. 126–136.

Burant, S. R., "Foreign Policy and National Identity: A Comparison of Ukraine and Belarus," *Europe-Asia Studies*, vol. 47, no. 7 (November 1995), pp. 1125–1144.

Casanova, José, "Ethno-linguistic and religious pluralism and democratic construction in Ukraine," in Barnett R. Rubin and Jack Snyder (eds.), *Post-Soviet Political Order: Conflict and State Building* (London and New York: Routledge, 1998), pp. 81–103.

D'Anieri, Paul, "Nationlism and International Politics: Identity and Sovereignty in the Russian-Ukrainian Conflict," *Nationalism and Ethnic Politics*, vol. 3, no. 2 (Summer 1997), pp. 1–28.

Furtado, Charles F. and Michael Hechter, "The Emergence of Nationalist Politics in the USSR: A Comparison of Estonia and the Ukraine," in Alexander J. Motyl (ed.), *Thinking Theoretically About Soviet Nationalities: History and Comparison in the Study of the USSR* (New York: Columbia University Press, 1992), pp. 169–204.

Furtado, C. F., "Nationalism and Foreign Policy in Ukraine," *Political Science Quarterly*, vol. 109, no. 1 (Spring 1994), pp. 81–104.

Futey, Bohdan, "Comments on the Law on the Constitutional Court of Ukraine," *East European Constitutional Review*, vol. 6, nos. 2 and 3 (Spring and Summer 1997), pp. 56–63.

Golovakha, Evgenii, "Elites in Ukraine: Evaluation of the Project's Elite Survey" in S. Klaus and S. De Spiegeleire (eds.), *Post-Soviet Puzzles: Mapping the Political Economy of the Former Soviet Union, Emerging Societal Actors—Economic, Social and Political Interests: Theories, Methods and Case Studies*, vol. 111 (Baden-Baden: Nomos Verlagsgesellschaft and Stiftung Wissenschaft und Politik, 1995), pp. 167–242.

Golovakha, E. I., and N. V. Panina, "The Development of a Democratic Political Identity in Contemporary Ukrainian Political Culture" in R. F. Farnen (ed.), *Nationalism, Ethnicity, and Identity: Cross National and Comparative Perspectives* (New Brunswick, N.J.: Transaction Books, 1994), pp. 403–425.

Grabowicz, George, "The Wages of Colonialism and the Pitfalls of Post-Colonialism," in M. Pavlyshyn and J. E. M. Clarke (eds.), *Ukraine in the 1990s:* Proceedings of the First Conference of the Ukrainian Studies Association of Australia (Melbourne: Monash University, 1992), pp. 27–37.

Grabowicz, Oksana, "Soviet Collapse and Ukrainian Independence: The Cultural and Psychological Factors," in M. Pavlyshyn and J. E. M. Clarke (eds.), *Ukraine in the 1990s:* Proceedings of the First Conference of the Ukrainian Studies Association of Australia (Melbourne: Monash University, 1992), pp. 135–145.

Hagen, Mark Von, "Does Ukraine Have a History?" *Slavic Review*, vol. 54, no. 3 (Fall 1995), pp. 658–673.

Hague, Judy, Rose Aidan, and Bojcun Marko, "Rebuilding Ukraine's Hollow State: Developing a Democratic Public Service in Ukraine," *Public Administration and Development*, vol. 15, no.4 (October 1995), pp. 417–433.

Holowisky Ivan Z., "Linguistic Policy as a Political Weapon," *Ukrainian Quarterly*, vol. 2, no. 1 (Spring 1994), pp. 13–20.

Isaievych, Iaroslav, "Ukraine and Russia: The Burden of Historical Tradition and Contemporary Realities," *Journal of Ukrainian Studies*, vol. 20, nos. 1–2 (Summer-Winter 1995), pp. 5–14.

Kohut, Zenon E, "History as a Battleground: Russian-Ukrainian Relations and Historical Consciousness in Contemporary Ukraine," in Frederick S. Starr (ed.), *The Legacy of History in Russia and the New States of Eurasia. The International Politics of Eurasia,* vol. 1 (Armonk, NY and London: M. E. Sharpe, 1994), pp. 123–146.

Kuzio, Taras, "National Identity in Independent Ukraine: An Identity in Transition," *Nationalism and Ethnic Politics,* vol. 2, no. 4 (Winter 1996), pp. 582–608.

Kuzio, Taras, "Borders, Symbolism and Nation-State Building: Ukraine and Russia," *Geopolitics and International Boundaries,* vol. 2, no. 2 (Autumn 1997), pp. 36–56.

Kuzio, Taras, "The East Slavic Conundrum: History and National Identity," Paper presented to the conference, "National Identities, History, Geography, Image," Institute of Contemporary British History, University of London, April 20–22, 1998.

Kuzio, Taras, "The Perils of Multiculturalism: A Theoretical and Area Studies Approach to the Former USSR," *Contemporary Political Studies,* vol. 1, 1998, pp. 108–123.

Kuzio, Taras, "Ukraine: Coming to Terms with the Soviet Legacy," *The Journal of Communist Studies and Transition Politics,* vol. 14, no. 4 (December 1998), pp. 1–27.

Kuzio, Taras, "National Identity and Foreign Policy: The East Slavic Conundrum," in Taras Kuzio (ed.), *Contemporary Ukraine: Dynamics of Post-Soviet Transformation* (Armonk, NY: M. E. Sharpe, 1998), pp. 221–244.

Kuzio, Taras (with Marc Nordberg), "Nation and State Building, Historical Legacies and National Identities in Belarus and Ukraine: A Comparative Analysis," *Canadian Review of Studies in Nationalism,* vol. 26, nos. 1–2 (1999).

Kuzio, Taras, "The Sultan and the Hetman: Democracy Building in Belarus and Ukraine in a Grey Security Zone," in Jan Zielonka and Alex Pravda (eds.), *Democratic Consolidation in Eastern Europe: International and Transnational Factors* (forthcoming).

Laba, Roman, "The Russian-Ukrainian Conflict: State Nation and Identity," *European Security,* vol. 4, no. 3 (Autumn 1995), pp. 457–487.

Lapychak, Chrystyna, "The Quest for a Common Destiny," *Transition,* vol. 2, no. 18 (September 1996).

Markus, Ustina, "The Bilingualism Question in Belarus and Ukraine," *Transition,* vol. 2, no. 24 (November 1996).

Marples, David, "New Interpretations of Ukrainian History," *RFE/RL Research Report,* vol. 2, no. 11 (March 1993).

Maryniak, Iryna, "Belarus and Ukraine: Nation Building in Babel," *Index on Censorship,* vol. 22, no. 2 (March 1993), pp. 20–33.

Molchanov, Mikhail A., "Borders of Identity: Ukraine's Political and Cultural Significance for Russia," *Canadian Slavonic Papers,* vol. 38, nos. 1–2 (March-June 1996), pp. 177–193.

Motyl, Alexander J., "Structural Constraints and Starting Points: The Logic of Systematic Change in Ukraine and Russia," *Comparative Politics,* vol. 29, no. 4 (July 1997), pp. 433–447.

Nivat, Anne, "No More Russian Television in Ukraine," *Transition,* vol. 2, no. 24 (November 1996).

Panina, Natalia, "Interethnic Relations and Ethnic Tolerance in Ukraine: An In-Depth Analytical Report," in K. Segbers and S. De Spiegeleire (eds.), *Post-Soviet Puzzles: Mapping the Political Economy of the Former Soviet Union, The Emancipation of Society as a Reaction to Systematic Change: Survival, Adaptation to New Rules and Ethnopolitical Conflicts,* vol. 4 (Baden-Baden: Nomos Verlagsgesellschaft and Stiftung Wissenschaft und Politik, 1995), pp. 101–122.

Pirie, Paul S., "National Identity and Politics in Southern and Eastern Ukraine," *Europe-Asia Studies,* vol. 48, no. 7 (November 1996), pp. 1076–1104.

Plokhy, Serhii M, "Historical Debates and Territorial Claims: Cossack Mythology in the Russian-Ukrainian Border Dispute," in F. S. Starr (ed.), *The Legacy of History in Russia and the New States of Eurasia. The International Politics of Eurasia,* vol. 1 (Armonk, NY, and London: M. E. Sharpe, 1994), pp. 147–170.

Plokhy, S. M., "The History of a 'Non-Historical' Nation: Notes on the Nature and Current Problems of Ukrainian Historiography," *Slavic Review,* vol. 54, no. 3 (Fall 1995), pp. 709–716.

Prizel, Ilya, "The Influence of Ethnicity on Foreign Policy: The Case of Ukraine," in R. Szporluk (ed.), *National Identity and Ethnicity in Russia and the New States of Eurasia, The International Politics of Eurasia,* vol. 2 (Armonk, NY, and London: M. E. Sharpe, 1994), pp. 103–128,

Prizel, I., "Ukraine's Foreign Policy as an Instrument of Nation Building" in John W. Blaney (ed.), *The Successor States to the USSR* (Washington, D.C.: Congressional Quarterly Inc, 1995), pp. 196–207.

Prymak, Thomas, "Hrushevsky and the Ukraine's 'Lost' History," *History Today,* vol. 39, no. 1 (January 1989).

Rubchak, Marian J., "Christian virgin or pagan goddess: feminism versus the eternally feminine in Ukraine" in Rosalind Marsh (ed.), *Women in Russia and Ukraine* (Cambridge: Cambridge University Press, 1996), pp. 315–330.

Saunders, D., "Russia and Ukraine under Alexander II: The Value Edict of 1863," *The International History Review,* vol. 17, no. 1 (February 1995), pp. 23–50.

Saunders, David, "What Makes a Nation a Nation? Ukrainians since 1600," *Ethnic Groups,* vol. 10 (1993), pp. 101–124.

Saunders, David, "Russia's Ukrainian Policy (1847–1903): A Demographic Approach," *European History Quarterly,* vol. 25, no. 2 (April 1995), pp. 181–208.

Shaw, D. J. B., and M. J. Bradshaw, "Problems of Ukrainian Independence," *Post-Soviet Geography,* vol. 33, no. 1 (January 1992), pp. 10–16.

Shevchuk, I. Yuri, "Citizenship in Ukraine: A Western Perspective" in S. J. Micgiel (ed.), *State and Nation Building in East Central Europe: Contemporary Perspectives* (New York: Institute on East Central Europe, Columbia University, 1996), pp. 351–369.

Shumbatiuk, Karina, "Public Administration in Ukraine: Organization and Development," in Jak Jabes and Mirko Vintar (eds.), *Public Administration in Transition* (Bratislava: 1995).

Shved, V'iacheslav, "The Conceptual Approaches of Ukrainian Political Parties to Ethno-Political Problems in Independent Ukraine," *Journal of Ukrainian Studies,* vol. 19, no. 2 (Winter 1994), pp. 69–84.

Simon, Gerhard, "The Ukraine and the End of the Soviet Union," *Aussenpolitik,* vol. 43, no. 1 (1992), pp. 62–71.

Simon, G., "Problems Facing the Formation of the Ukrainian State," *Aussenpolitik,* vol. 45, no. 1 (1994), pp. 61–67.

Slezkine, Yuri, "Can We Have Our Nation State and Eat It Too?" *Slavic Review,* vol. 54, no. 3 (Fall 1995), pp. 717–719.

Solchanyk, Roman, "Ukraine, Belorussia, and Moldova: Imperial Integration, Russification and the Struggle for National Survival" in Lubomyr Hajda and Mark Beissinger (eds.), *The Nationalities Factor in Soviet Politics and Society:* The John M. Olin Critical Series (Boulder, CO, and Oxford: Westview Press, 1990), pp. 175–203.

Solchanyk, Roman, "The Uncertain Road to Independence," RL 10/91, *Report on the USSR,* vol. 3, no. 1 (January 1991).

Solchanyk, Roman, "Ukraine: Kravchuk's Role," RL 322/91, *Report on the USSR,* vol. 3, no. 36 (September 1991).

Solchanyk, Roman, "Ukraine: A Year of Transition," *RFE/RL Research Report,* vol. 2, no. 1 (January 1993).

Solchanyk, Roman, "Ukraine: A Year of Crisis," *RFE/RL Research Report,* vol. 3, no. 1 (January 1994).

Strekal, O., "Conflict Potential in Modern Ukraine: Sources and Developments" in Reimund Seidelmann (ed.), *Crises Policies in Eastern Europe* (Baden-Baden: NOMOS, 1996).

Subtelny, Orest, "The Current State of Ukrainian Historiography: An Overview," in H. Koshcarsky (ed.), *Ukraine Today: Perspectives for the Future.* Proceedings of the Conference "Ukraine Today-Perspectives for the Future," June 19–21, 1992 (Commack, NY: Nova Science Publishers, 1995), pp. 3–26.

Subtelny Orest, "The Current State of Ukrainian Historiography," *Journal of Ukrainian Studies,* vol. 18, nos. 1–2 (Summer-Winter 1993), pp. 33–54.

Subtelny, Orest, "Imperial Disintegration and Nation-State Formation: The Case of Ukraine," in J. W. Blaney (ed.), *The Successor States to the USSR* (Washington, D.C.: Congressional Quarterly Inc, 1995), pp. 184–195.

Sysyn, Frank, "The Reemergence of the Ukrainian Nation and Cossack Mythology," *Social Research,* vol. 58, no. 4 (Winter 1991), pp. 845–864.

Szporluk, Roman, "Nation-Building in Ukraine: Problems and Prospects," in J. W. Blaney (ed.), *The Successor States to the USSR* (Washington, D.C.: Congressional Quarterly Inc, 1995), pp. 173–183.

Szporluk, Roman, "Ukraine: From an Imperial Periphery to a Sovereign State," *Daedalus,* vol. 126, no. 3 (Summer 1997), pp. 85–120.

Torbakov, Igor, "Historiography and Modern Nation-Building," *Transition,* vol. 2, no. 18 (September 1996).

Vishnevsky, Yuri and Dan Rosenblum, "Ukraine: The Birth of a Nation," *Forum,* vol. 9, no. 2 (Winter-Spring 1995), pp. 25–29.

Wilson, Andrew, "The Donbas between Ukraine and Russia: The Use of History in Political Disputes," *Journal of Contemporary History,* vol. 30, no. 2 (April 1995), pp. 265–289.

Wilson, Andrew, "Ukrainian Nationalism: A Minority Faith," *Slavonic and East European Review,* vol. 73, no. 2 (April 1995), pp. 282–288.

Wilson, Andrew, "Myths of National History in Belarus and Ukraine," in Geoffrey Hosking and George Schopflin (eds.), *Myths and Nationhood* (London: Hurst, 1997), pp. 182–197.

Zviglyanich, Volodymyr, "Ethnic Economics: Is a Ukrainian Economic Model Possible?" *Ukraine Business Review,* vol. 4, nos. 1–2 (December 1995-January 1996), pp. 1–4.

Regionalism, National Minorities, and Language

Aarrevaard, Timo, "Ukrainian Cities: Weak Soviets and Strong Mayors," *The Journal of Post Communist Studies and Transition Politics,* vol. 10, no. 4 (December 1994), pp. 55–70.

Arel, Dominique, "Voting Behavior in the Ukrainian Parliament-The Language Factor," in Thomas F. Remington (ed.), *Parliaments in Transition: The New Legislative Politics in the Former USSR and Eastern Europe* (Boulder, CO: Westview Press, 1994), pp. 125–158.

Arel, Dominique, "Language Politics in Independent Ukraine: Towards One or Two State Languages?" *Nationalities Papers,* vol. 23, no. 3 (September 1995), pp. 597–622.

Arel, Dominique, and Valentyn Khmelko, "The Russian Factor and Territorial Polarization in Ukraine," *The Harriman Review,* vol. 9, nos. 1–2 (March 1996), pp. 81–91.

Birch, Sarah, and Ihor Zinko, "The Dilemma of Regionalism," *Transition,* vol. 2, no. 22 (November 1996).

Bremmer, Ian, "Ethnic Issues in Crimea," *RFE/RL Research Report,* vol. 2, no. 18 (April 1993).

Bremmer, Ian, "The politics of ethnicity: Russians in the new Ukraine," *Europe-Asia Studies,* vol. 46, no. 2 (March-April 1994), pp. 261–283.

Brumberg, Abraham, "Not So Free At Last," *The New York Review of Books,* October 22, 1992.

Bukkvoll, Tor, "A Fall From Grace for Crimean Separatists," *Transition,* vol. 1, no. 21 (November 1995).

Buromensky, M. V., "Is it Possible to Implement the Law 'On National Minorities' in Ukraine?" *Human Rights in Ukraine,* no. 2, 1993.

Chiper, Ioan, "Bessarabia and Northern Bukovina" in Tuomas Forsberg (ed.), *Contested Territory: Border Disputes at the Edge of the Former Soviet Empire* (Aldershot: Edward Elgar, 1995), pp. 107–127.

Churilov, Nikolay, and Tatyana Koshechkina, "Public Attitudes in Ukraine," in Richard Smoke (ed.), *Perceptions of Security. Public opinion and expert assessments in Europe's new democracies* (Manchester and New York: Manchester University Press, 1996), pp. 189–208.

Deychakiwsky, Orest, "National Minorities in Ukraine," *The Ukrainian Quarterly,* vol. 50, no. 4 (Winter 1994), pp. 371–389.

Fisher, Alan, *The Crimean Tatars* (Stanford: Hoover Institution Press, 1978).

Friedgut, Ted, "Pluralism and Politics in an Urban Soviet: Donets'k" in Carol Saivetz and Anthony Jones (eds.), *In Search of Pluralism: Society and Post-Soviet Politics* (Boulder, CO: Westview Press, 1994), pp. 45–61.

Friedgut, Ted, "Perestroika in the Provinces: The Politics of Transition in Donets'k," in T. H. Friedgut and Jeffrey W. Hahn (eds.), *Local Power and Post-Soviet Policies* (Armonk, NY: M. E. Sharpe, 1994).

Golovakha, Evgenii, Natalia Panina, and Nikolai Churilov, "Russians in Ukraine," in Vladimir Shlapentokh, Munir Sendich, and Emil Payin (eds.), *The New Russian Diaspora: Russian Minorities in the Former Soviet Republics* (Armonk, NY: M. E. Sharpe, 1994), pp. 59–71.

Hesli, Vicki L., Arthur H. Miller, William M. Reisinger, and Kevin L. Morgan, "Social Distance from Jews in Russia and Ukraine," *Slavic Review,* vol. 53, no. 3 (Fall 1994), pp. 807–828.

Hesli, Vicki, "Public Support for the Devolution of Power in Ukraine: Regional Patterns," *Europe-Asia Studies,* vol. 47, no. 1 (January-February 1995), pp. 91–121.

Holdar, Sven, "Torn Between East and West: The Regional Factor in Ukrainian Politics," *Post-Soviet Geography,* vol. 36, no. 2 (February 1996), pp. 112–132.

Holowinsky, Ivan Z., "Linguistic Policy as a Political Weapon," *The Ukrainian Quarterly,* vol. 50, no. 1 (Spring 1994), pp. 13–20.

Jung, Monika, "The Donbas Factor in the Ukrainian Elections," *RFE/RL Research Report,* vol. 3, no. 12 (March 1994).

Kistersky, L. and Serhii Pirozhkov, "Ukraine: policy analysis and options" in R. Smoke (ed.), *Perceptions of Security: Public opinion and expert assessments in Europe's new democracies* (Manchester and New York: Manchester University Press, 1996), pp. 209–227.

Klatt, Martin, "Russians in the 'Near Abroad,'" *RFE/RL Research Report,* vol. 3, no. 32 (August 19, 1994).

Kolstoe, Paul, *Russians in the Former Soviet Republics* (London: Hurst & Company, 1995), chap. 7, "The Eye of the Whirlwind: Belarus and Ukraine," pp. 166–199.

Kushnirsky, F. I., "Free Economic Zones in Ukraine: The Case of Odessa," *Ukrainian Economic Review,* vol. 11, no. 3 (1996), pp. 117–124.

Kuzio, Taras, "Murder in Crimea," *The Economist* January 13, 1994.

Kuzio, Taras, "Crimea Seeks Independence from Ukraine," *Jane's Intelligence Review Pointer,* no. 4 (February 1994).

Kuzio, Taras, "Crimea—Europe's Next Bosnia?" *Conflict International,* vol. 9, no. 3 (March 1994).

Kuzio, Taras, "Ukrainian Election Results Point to Growing Regionalism," *Jane's Intelligence Review Pointer,* no. 6 (April 1994).

Kuzio, Taras, "Will Crimea Be Europe's Next Flashpoint?" *European Security Analyst,* no. 30 (April 1994).

Kuzio, Taras, "Crimean Crisis Deepens," *Jane's Intelligence Review Pointer,* no. 8 (June 1994).

Kuzio, Taras, "The Crimea and European Security," *European Security,* vol. 3, no. 4 (Winter 1994), pp. 734–774.

Lakiza-Sachuk, Natalija and Natalie Melnyczuk, "Ukraine After Empire" in Leokadia Drobizheva, Rose Gottemoeller, Catherine McArdle Kelleher, and Lee Walker (eds.), *Ethnic Conflict in the Post-Soviet World: Case Studies and Analysis* (Armonk, NY: M. E. Sharpe, 1998), pp. 109–128.

Lazzerini, Edward J, "Crimean Tatars: The Fate of a Severed Tongue" in Isabelle Kreindler (ed.), *Sociolinguistic Perspectives on Soviet National Languages* (Berlin: Mouton de Gruyter, 1985), pp. 109–124.

Lazzerini, Edward J., "Crimean Tatars," in G. Smith (ed.), *The nationalities question in the post-Soviet states* (London and New York: Longman, 1996), pp. 412–435.

Lees, Andrew, "The Potential of Dniepropetrovsk," *Ukraine Business Review,* vol. 2, no. 3 (Autumn 1994), pp. 42–44.

Madi, Istvan, "Carpatho-Ukraine" in T. Forsberg (ed.), *Contested Territory: Border Disputes at the Edge of the Former Soviet Empire* (Aldershot: Edward Elgar, 1995), pp. 128–142.

Markus, Ustina, "Crimea Restores 1992 Constitution," *RFE/RL Research Report,* vol. 3, no. 23 (June 1994).

Marples, David R., and David F. Duke, "Ukraine, Russia and the Question of Crimea," *Nationalities Papers,* vol. 23, no. 2 (June 1995), pp. 261–289.

Materski, Wojciech, "Eastern Poland," in T. Forsberg (ed.), *Contested Territory: Border Disputes at the Edge of the Former Soviet Empire* (Aldershot: Edward Elgar, 1995), pp. 143–155.

Melvin, Neil, *Russians Beyond Russia: The Politics of National Identity.* Chatham House Papers (London: Royal Institute for International Affairs, 1995), chap. 5, "Russians, regionalism and ethnicity in Ukraine," p. 78–99.

Meyer, David J., "Why Have Donbas Russians Not Ethnically Mobilized Like Crimean Russians Have? An Institutional/Demographic Approach" in S. J. Micgiel (ed.), *State and Nation Building in East Central Europe: Contemporary Perspectives* (New York: Institute on East Central Europe, Columbia University, 1996), pp. 317–330.

Mihalisko, Kathleen, "The Other Side of Separatism: Crimea Votes for Autonomy," RL 60/91, *Report on the USSR,* vol. 3, no. 3 (February 1991).

Naboka, Serhiy, "Nationalities Issues in Ukraine," *Uncaptive Minds,* vol. 5, no. 1 (Spring 1992), pp. 75–80.

Nemir'ya, Grigorii, "A Qualitative Analysis of the Situation in the Donbas" in Klaus Segbers and Stephan De Spiegeleire (eds.), *Post-Soviet Puzzles: Mapping the Political Economy of the Former Soviet Union, Emerging Geopolitical and Territorial Units. Theories, Methods and Case Studies,* vol. 11 (Baden-Baden: Nomos Verlagsgesellschaft and Stiftung Wissenschaft und Politik, 1995), pp. 451–466.

Oltay, Edith, "Minorities as Stumbling Block in Relations with Neighbours," *RFE/RL Research Report,* vol. 1, no. 19 (May 1992).

Ozhiganov, Edward, "The Crimean Republic: Rivalries for Control" in Alexei Arbatov et al. (eds.), *Managing Conflict in the Former Soviet Union: Russian and American Perspectives* (Cambridge, MA: The MIT Press, 1997), pp. 83–135.

Panina, Natalia V. and Evgenii I. Golovakha, "Interethnic Relations and Ethnic Tolerance in Ukraine," *Jews and Jewish Topics in the Soviet Union and Eastern Europe*, vol. 1, no. 14 (Spring 1991).

Petersen, Philip, "Crimea-Triumph of Moderation or Eye of the Storm?" *Jane's Intelligence Review*, vol. 7, no. 4 (April 1995).

Petheridge-Hernandez, Patricia and Rosalind Latiner Raby, "Twentieth-Century Transformations in Catalonia and the Ukraine: Ethnic Implications in Education," *Comparative Education Review*, vol. 37, no. 1 (February 1993), pp. 31–49.

Pirie, Paul S., "Donets'k—In the Vanguard of Reform in Ukraine," *Ukraine Business Review*, vol. 3, nos. 10–11 (July-August 1995), pp. 21–22.

Potichnyj, Peter J., "The Struggle of the Crimean Tatars," *Canadian Slavonic Papers*, vol. 17, nos. 2–3 (Spring-Summer 1975), pp. 302–318.

Reisch, Alfred A., "Transcarpathia's Hungarian Minority and the Autonomy Issue," *RFE/RL Research Report*, vol. 1, no. 6 (February 1992).

Resler, Tamara J., "Dilemmas of Democratisation: Safeguarding Minorities in Russia, Ukraine and Lithuania," *Europe-Asia Studies*, vol. 49, no. 1 (January 1997), pp. 89–106.

Ryabchuk, Mykola, "Two Ukraines?" *East European Reporter*, vol. 5, no. 4 (July–August 1992).

Sasse, Gwendolyn, "The Crimean Issue," *The Journal of Communist Studies and Transition Politics*, vol. 12, no. 1 (March 1996), pp. 83–100.

Sheehy, Ann, RL 305/87, "Crimean Tatars Demonstrate for Restoration of Autonomous Republic in Crimea," *Radio Liberty Research Bulletin* July 27, 1987.

Shevtsova, Lilia, "Ukraine in the Context of New European Migrations," *International Migration Review*, vol. 26, no. 2 (Summer 1992), pp. 258–268.

Shul'ga, Nikolai, "Regionalisation, Federalisation and Separatism in Ukraine: Historical Roots, New Realities and Prospects" in Klaus Segbers and Stephan De Spiegeleire (eds.), *Post-Soviet Puzzles: Mapping the Political Economy of the Former Soviet Union, Emerging Geopolitical and Territorial Units. Theories, Methods and Case Studies*, vol. 11 (Baden-Baden: Nomos Verlagsgesellschaft and Stiftung Wissenschaft und Politik, 1995), pp. 467–488.

Smith, Graham and Andrew Wilson, "Rethinking Russia's Post-Soviet Diaspora: The Potential for Political Mobilisation in Eastern Ukraine and North-east Estonia," *Europe-Asia Studies*, vol. 49, no. 5 (July 1997), pp. 845–864.

Socor, Vladimir, "Five Countries Look at Ethnic Problems in Southern Moldova," *RFE/RL Research Report*, vol. 3, no. 32 (August 1994).

Solchanyk, Roman, "Ukrainian-Russian Confrontation Over the Crimea," *RFE/RL Research Report*, vol. 1, no. 7 (February 1992).

Solchanyk, Roman, "The Crimean Imbroglio: Kiev and Simferopol," *RFE/RL Research Report*, vol. 1, no. 33 (August 1992).

Solchanyk, Roman, "Centrifugal Movements in Ukraine on the Eve of the Independence Referendum," RL 408/91, *Report on the USSR,* vol. 3, no. 48 (November 29, 1991).

Solchanyk, Roman, "The Politics of Language in Ukraine," *RFE/RL Research Report,* vol. 2, no. 10 (March 5, 1993).

Solchanyk, Roman, "The politics of state building: centre-periphery relations in post-Soviet Ukraine," *Europe-Asia Studies,* vol. 46, no. 1 (January-February 1994), pp. 47–68.

Solchanyk, Roman and Svetlana Svetova, "Chronology of Events in Crimea," *RFE/RL Research Report,* vol. 3, no. 19 (May 13, 1994).

Stewart, Susan, "Ukraine's Policy toward Its Ethnic Minorities," *RFE/RL Research Report,* vol. 2, no. 36 (September 1993).

Stewart, Susan, "The Tatar Dimension," *RFE/RL Research Report,* vol. 3, no. 19 (May 1994).

Subtelny, Orest, "Russocentrism, Regionalism, and the Political Culture of Ukraine," in Vladimir Tismaneanu (ed.), *Political Culture and Civil Society in Russia and the New States of Eurasia: The International Politics of Eurasia,* vol. 7 (Armonk, NY and London: M. E. Sharpe, 1995), pp. 189–207.

Szporluk, Roman, "The Strange Politics of L'viv: An Essay in Search of An Explanation," in Zvi Gitelman (ed.), *The Politics of Nationality and the Erosion of the USSR* (London: Macmillan, 1992), pp. 215–31.

Takach, Arthur, "In Search of Ukrainian National Identity: 1840–1921," *Ethnic and Racial Studies,* vol. 19, no. 3 (July 1996), pp. 640–659.

Teague, Elizabeth, "Russians Outside Russia and Russian Security Policy" in Leon Aron and Kenneth M. Jensen (eds.), *The Emergence of Russian Foreign Policy* (Washington, D.C.: United States Institute of Peace Press, 1994), pp. 81–105.

Tulko, Alex, "Conflicting Reports Fuel Crimean Tension," *Transition,* vol. 1, no. 6 (April 28, 1995).

Umbach, Frank, "The Crimean Question," *Jane's Intelligence Review,* vol. 6, no. 5 (May 1994).

Vardys, Stanley V., "The Case of the Crimean Tatars," *Russian Review,* vol. 30, no. 2 (April 1971), pp. 101–110.

Wilson, Andrew, "The Growing Challenge to Kiev from the Donbas," *RFE/RL Research Report,* vol. 2, no. 33 (August 1993).

Wilson, Andrew, "Crimea's Political Cauldron," *RFE/RL Research Report,* vol. 2, no. 45 (November 1993).

Zaionchkovskaia, Zhanna, "Interethnic Tensions and Demographic Movement in Russia, Ukraine and Estonia" in Leokadia Drobizheva, Rose Gottemoeller, Catherine McArdle Kelleher, and Lee Walker (eds.), *Ethnic Conflict in the Post-Soviet World: Case Studies and Analysis* (Armonk, NY: M. E. Sharpe, 1998), pp. 327–336.

About the Authors

PAUL D'ANIERI is Associate Professor of Political Science at the University of Kansas and a faculty associate of the Center for Russian and East European Studies. He is the author of *Economic Interdependence in Ukrainian-Russian Relations* (Albany: State University of New York Press, 1999) and (with Robert S. Kravchuk and Taras Kuzio) *Ukrainian Politics and Society* (Boulder: Westview Press, 1999). In 1993–1994 he was Fulbright Visiting Lecturer at the University of L'viv, and in 1998 was Visiting Professor at Harvard University.

SHERMAN W. GARNETT is a Senior Associate at The Carnegie Endowment for International Peace in Washington, D.C. He has written *Keystone in the Arch: Ukraine in the Emerging Security Environment of Central and Eastern Europe* (Washington, D.C.: Carnegie Endowment, 1997) as well as a number of articles on Russia, Ukraine, and the security problems of the post-Soviet space. He previously served for ten years in the Office of the Secretary of Defense, working primarily on global and regional arms control issues and policy toward the states of the former USSR.

ROBERT S. KRAVCHUK is Associate Professor in the School of Public and Environmental Affairs at Indiana University. He is the author of numerous books and articles about Ukraine, including (with Paul D'Anieri and Taras Kuzio) *Ukrainian Politics and Society* (Boulder: Westview Press, 1999), and *Ukrainian Political Economy* (New York: St. Martin's Press, forthcoming 2000). From 1993 to 1994, he served as the U. S. Treasury Resident Budget Advisor to the Ministry of Finance of Ukraine. From 1995 to 1996, he was Financial Advisor to the president of the Federation of Bosnia-Hercegovina, in Sarajevo. Kravchuk has also taught at University of Connecticut and in the Ukrainian Academy of Public Administration in Kyiv.

BOHDAN KRAWCHENKO is vice rector, Academy of Public Administration, Office of the President of Ukraine, and chair of the steering committee, Local Government and Public Sector Reform Initiative, Open Society Institute, Budapest. Educated at Bishop's, Toronto, Glasgow and Oxford Universities, he taught at the University of Alberta, Canada prior to moving to Ukraine in 1991. In 1995 he received an honorary doctorate from the University of North London. He is the author of *Social Change and National Consciousness in Twentieth Century Ukraine* (Canadian Institute of Ukrainian Studies and Macmillan, 1985) and editor of *Ukrainian Past, Ukrainian Present* (Macmillan, 1993).

PAUL KUBICEK is the Kenneth Boulding Post-Doctoral Fellow in the Institute of Behavioral Sciences at University of Colorado. He taught at L'viv State University in 1992–1993, and also taught at the University of Koç, Istanbul, Turkey. He is the author of *Broken Ties: The State, Interest Associations, and Corporatism in Post-Soviet Ukraine* (Ann Arbor: University of Michigan, 1999).

TARAS KUZIO is Honorary Research Fellow in the Department of Politics at the University of North London. Between 1995 and 1998, he was a Senior Research Fellow in the Centre for Russian and East European Studies in the University of Birmingham. He is the author of numerous books and articles about Ukraine, including: (with Andrew Wilson) *Ukraine: Perestroika to Independence* 2nd ed. (New York and London: St. Martin's Press and Macmillan, 1999); (with Robert S. Kravchuk and Paul D'Anieri) *Politics and Society in Ukraine* (Boulder: Westview Press, 1999); *Ukraine: State and Nation Building* (London: Routledge, 1998); *Ukraine Under Kuchma* (New York and London: St. Martin's Press and Macmillan, 1997); and *Ukrainian Security Policy* (Washington, D.C.: Center for Strategic and International Studies, 1995).

DAVID J. MEYER is a doctoral student in the Political Science Department at Columbia University in New York. He has taught at Touro College in New York, and as a Docent at Saratov State University in Russia. He is currently completing his doctoral dissertation on the role of institutions and demographics in choosing the mobilization strategies of post-Soviet elites.

VOLODYMYR PIGENKO is a doctoral candidate in the joint Ph.D. Program in Public Policy and Political Science at Indiana University. His research concerns the voting behavior of Ukrainian parliamentarians. He is also a staff member of the Indiana University Ukrainian Parliamentary Development Project.

OLIVER VORNDRAN completed the M.A. Program in Political Science, Public Law and Political Economy at the University of Freiburg, Germany, where he was also Research Fellow in the Seminar for Political Science. In 1996 to 1997, he conducted doctoral research on the Ukrainian constitutional process at the University of Birmingham. Since July 1998, Vorndran has been with the Bertelsmann Foundation, Guetersloh, Germany.

CHARLES R. WISE is Professor of Public and Environmental Affairs at Indiana University, where he serves as Director of Indiana University's Ukrainian Parliamentary Development Project, and is also Research Director in the Center on Congress. His published work on parliamentary development and public law may be found in many journals, including: *Democratization; Communist and Post-communist Studies; Journal of Legislative Studies; Public Administration Review;* and *Public Administration and Development.*

ROMAN P. ZYLA is a doctoral student in the School of Slavonic and East European Studies at the University of London. His current work centers on the effects of corruption in Eastern European business development and the emergence of the private business sector in Ukraine.

Index